ACTION

PERCEPTION

RGER

AFFECTION

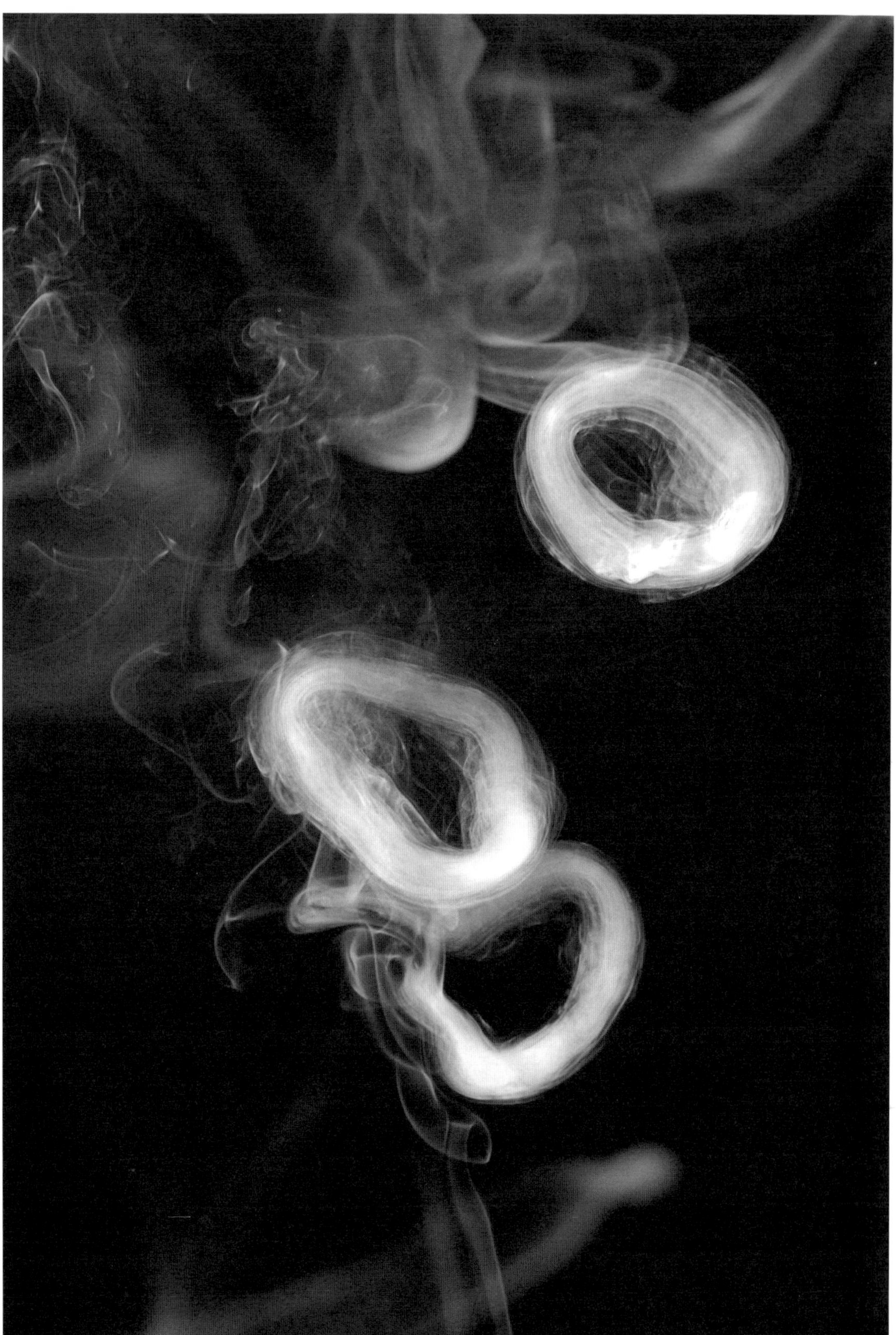

The 3 Rs: Repetition, Repetition, Repetition

ON BIOGRAPHY (MASCULIN)

OR

PUBLIC IMAGE LIMITED

by Stuart Bailey

Photograph by Anu Vahtra

No matter. Try again. Fail again. Fail better.

I have always considered this classic Beckettian aphorism a single-bullet autobiography; the essence of a lifework effectively distilled to 34 letters, 7 gaps and 4 dots which convey all the usual morbidity, lucidity, brutality, brevity, humour, humanity, focus and death more efficiently than any of those words together or apart ever could. In short, its form is wholly appropriate for both subject and subject matter, but it also manages to describe the condition of biography itself: fundamentally flawed. The grotesque processes of condensation and distortion involved in the selection and combination of a life's details condemn any attempt to fall way short, and the best we can do is to fall again, fall longer. Despite this less than optimistic premise, biography as a genre seems only ever to increase in popularity and—by implication—relevance, as if taking on a life of its own. This text you are reading has something of the attitude of a low rent private eye chasing a biography of that life. It stalks a number of maverick writers and their maverick subjects, following leads, taking notes and intermittently transcribing fragments of dialogue.

--

The British novelist, poet, critic and film-maker B.S. Johnson christened the protagonist of his first novel Travelling People (1963) Henry Henry to emphasize those obtuse abstract qualities a name suggests prior to any further description: to emphasize his Henryness. Johnson was also exercising his tendency to expose the mechanics of fiction according to his lifelong dictum 'telling stories is telling lies', which involved regularly tripping the reader up to avoid any comfortable slip into passivity. In short, the cartoon improbabilty of the double-barreled name was designed to maintain a non-suspension of disbelief. Johnson also intended to name the anti-hero of his subsequent novel Henry to suggest the continuity of both Henrys representing the same character: himself. Later he changed Henry to Samuel in direct homage to Beckett, one of a trilogy of mentors after Sterne and Joyce, but in a last-minute loss of nerve decided the reference was too direct, particularly as he was also opening the novel with a Beckett quote and his technique was noticeably derivative anyway. Instead, both character and novel became Albert Angelo (1964), surnamed after The Angel, the area of north London which provides the backdrop.

The logical conclusion of Johnson's quest against what he saw as the dormant, redundant fiction of the traditional English novel was to base his own writing on real-life events rather than imagination whilst avoiding straight autobiography. His early work was based on, for example, experiences during summer holiday work in Ireland; as a supply teacher in north London; or channeled through a memoir of a friend who had recently died from cancer. Johnson's critics were quick to point out that by insisting on autobiography as source material the author was essentially writing himself into a corner: he would soon run out of stimulating experiences, then what? Johnson's responses were imaginative and varied: a trip as a supernumerary aboard a north sea fishing boat to 'trawl' his memory in forced isolation; a projected interior monologue account of eight people in an old people's home; and an excavation beyond his own life resulting in a biography of his mother, The Matrix Trilogy, of which he managed to complete only the first of an intended three volumes, called See The Old Lady Decently. The two subsequent books were to be titled Buried Although and Amongst Those Left Are You.

Running horizontally across thick spines, the three individual titles would form a single composite sentence.

Johnson's biographer Jonathan Coe hints that the task of this novel was ultimately too painful for Johnson to follow through. He took his own life in 1973 aged 40, and the first volume was published posthumously in 1975. Two weeks before the suicide, however, he had also completed work on what turned out to be a swansong documentary for the BBC, candidly titled Fat Man On A Beach. This 40-minute detour through a very English brand of surrealism involved Johnson recounting various autobiographical anecdotes, telling bad jokes and reading his own poetry in windswept North Wales. It effectively abbreviates most of Johnson's philosophical and professional beliefs, including the exposition of the filming process—visible crew, nonsensical editing, emphasized mistakes—years before it became a staple of postmodern TV, in the same manner that his novels reflexively exposed the mechanics of rhetoric and embraced chaos. This was most effectively demonstrated in the last book published during his lifetime, Xtie Malry's Own Double-Entry (1973), though his editor considered this particular character name a typographical conceit too far and forced him to rechristen the protagonist 'Christie'. A certain schizophrenia is played out through Johnson's body of work. On one hand he sets out to expose the lies of his form, on the other he insists on the truth of his content, and somewhere in this blind spot of paradox lies the essence of his character; true stories.

--

In 1970 B.S. Johnson had also made a short biographical TV documentary about his eighteenth-century namesake Samuel Johnson, and this year, 35 years on, Jonathan Coe's account of B.S. Johnson's life Like A Fiery Elephant won the Samuel Johnson prize for biography. A similar sense of elliptical destiny begins Coe's account of Johnson's life, as he recalls sitting down with his parents one evening at the age of thirteen in 1974 to watch a documentary about their family seaside holiday town: Fat Man On A Beach. Thirty years on he writes:

> Like B.S. Johnson, I have a strong puritanical streak, and it remains one of my core beliefs that a work of literature should speak for itself, without the need for glossing, interpreting or contextualizing by reference to its writer's life. But how naive that sounds, even as I write it down! We live in a culture of radio and television interviews, newspaper profiles, public readings with question-and-answer sessions, which has ensured that novels themselves—far from being self-contained statements, as having anything remotely final about them—have merely become one (early) stage in a larger process: a process devoted, essentially, to the scrutiny and interrogation of writers' lives in the name of that insatiable curiosity which feeds on anyone reckless enough to set themselves up as a public figure ... which means, in effect, that we no longer READ literature: we cross-examine it, forensically, in the light of its writers' lives, assuming that it's in the gaps, the interstices, the shortfalls between theory and practice that the real truths about human nature will emerge.

Coe's preface is titled 'The industrious biographer (an exposition without which you might have felt unhappy)', in which he discusses the whole problem of literary biography with a kind of simultaneous love/hate I encountered repeatedly during the research for this piece. Love for the potential of biography to enlighten the nature of a life/work relationship. Hate for the particular monster combination of stereotype, cliché and speculation that literary biography in particular has evolved into. Crucially, Coe begins by defining the importance of Johnson's novels—for himself as much as anyone else—as being 'literary heresies' ('at odds with convention or received wisdom'), then adopts this as a guiding principle for his own book, consistently challenging his own conceptions of what a biography should and shouldn't be. Coe is admirably rigorous but never pedantic with this self-questioning, tapping into Johnson's working spirit of being doggedly committed to some notion of The Truth, however flawed, and ending up with what feels like a plausibly intimate and accurate portrait.

This is a highly designed biography. The main section is built on the premise that as Johnson's writings were, by his own admission, more or less autobiography already, they should form the bedrock. So Coe selects 160 fragments of Johnson's writing from the whole spectrum of his output, including letters, notes, diary entries, and a transcribed conversation as well as sports journalism, poetry, film treatments and excerpts from the novels, arranges them chronologically in terms of biographical content, then acts as a guide, leading the reader from fragment to fragment, fleshing out information and carefully speculating on events and meanings.

> ... the result will be fragmentary, unpolished. There will be gaps, where through misfortune or obstruction or sometimes sheer inertia I will not have been able to find out as much as I would have liked. And where I lapse into speculation, I shall try to be upfront about it. I shall try to be honest. That much at least Johnson himself would have appreciated.

By the end, the faint figure of Coe has emerged alongside Johnson the elephant, along with a delicate but clear subplot concerning the nature of the changing relationship between the biographer and his subject over seven years of work. The magic of this feat is how it alters as incrementally, subtly and devastatingly as most human relationships. The final fragment is, naturally, Johnson's own suicide note, by which point Coe has appropriated his subject's brutal economy effectively enough to describe it as 'a kind of concrete poem':

> This is my last
> Word

--

Coe describes Johnson's taste as being markedly British and homogenic, so it is unlikely he was aware that the Russian exile Vladimir Nabokov had already double-named the main character of his 1955 novel Lolita, Humbert Humbert. In a Playboy interview Nabokov explained: 'The double rumble is, I think, very nasty, very suggestive. It is a hateful name for a hateful person.' As with Johnson's characters,
the implausibility of Humbert's double name is merely the most immediate and visible tip of the book's constant reference to its own artifice and involution. Nabokov had already written an autobiographical memoir, Conclusive Evidence, in 1951, later updated into a 'definitive version' called Speak, Memory in 1966. Nabokov's 'other masterpiece', Pale Fire, written seven years after Lolita in 1962 is something else altogether, a Russian doll of fictional biography. In a foreword by one Charles Kinbote we are introduced to the structure of the book, consisting of an epic poem by his recently deceased neighbour, friend and colleague John Shade, followed by Kinbote's own line-by-line annotations of each stanza, from which a heady, tragic narrative of misunderstanding unravels for the remainder and main body of the book. It concludes with Shade's death in the final line of the poem, a full-circle repetition of the first: 'I was the shadow of the waxwing slain'.

The degree to which Nabokov exalts in his virtuosity for embedded references, allusions and in-jokes is matched only by The Annotated Lolita, compiled in 1970 and updated in 1991 by Nabokov scholar Alfred Appel, Jr. with the author's coy authorisation and assistance. Appel rigorously applies the construct of Pale Fire to Lolita, compiling some 900 notes (almost half as long as the novel itself) which results in a kind of 'reality' version of Pale Fire, or, rather, a more shadowy and convoluted blurring of the borders between fact, fiction, biography and autobiography. (Nabokov himself observed that 'reality' is one of the few words which mean nothing without quotes.) Appel refers to correspondences with Pale Fire throughout his introduction and notes, stating, 'This edition ... is analogous to what Pale Fire might have been like if poor John Shade had been given the opportunity to comment on Charles Kinbote's Commentary.' Appel also feels it necessary to state his own 'reality' credentials in the third person: '... he is a veteran and a grandfather, a teacher and taxpayer, and has not been invented by Vladimir Nabokov.' Finally, consummately summing up the doppelganger effect of Pale Fire and The Annotated Lolita, 'in place of a note on the text', Appel reuses Kinbote's (fictional) preface to Pale Fire to introduce his own new (factual) annotations to Lolita, as if playing out Borges' story 'Pierre Menard, Author of the Quixote', where an identical text is 'infinitely richer' in a later context.

Among the myriad other examples of biographical play that pepper Appel's notes are Nabokov's various anagrams and near-anagrams of his own name—Vivian Darkbloom in Lolita, some close relation to his previous novels' Vivians, Bloodmark, Badlook and Calmbrood (the 'k' replaced by 'c' in Nabokov's native Russian). And in one of the most extraordinary sections towards the end of Lolita, Humbert describes how his rival character Clare Quilty (famously portrayed by Peter Sellers in Stanley Kubrick's adaptation) left traces of his stalking drive across the United States by signing himself under a variety of cryptic names and locations in the guestbooks of the motels where they stayed. After Quilty has abducted Lolita. Humbert traces their route backwards across the country, desperately collecting these flashes of identity which depict the sinister intelligence of his counterpart and alter-ego. In the original novel, the reader is left to work these out, like an embedded crossword puzzle. Some are relatively easy to decode—'Donald Quix, Sierra, Nev.', for instance—but most require Appel's annotations:

> Dr. Kitzler, Eryx, Miss.
> For Kitzler—H.H.'s tag for Eryx, the cult of Aphrodite, where 'religious prostitution' was indeed practiced. The abbreviated form of Mississippi adds to the pun cluster an incongruous note of formality; 'translated' it reads 'Dr Clitoris, Venus, Miss'—and 'miss venus' is the archetypal if not the ultimate beauty contest winner.

Ultimately, The Annotated Lolita is a biographical vignette of Nabokov himself; a peculiarly intimate angle on the particular vertiginous mechanics of his mind. Or as B.S. Johnson's authorial voice, entering at the close of his novel Mother House Normal puts it: 'a diagram of certain aspects on the inside of his skull!'

--

Then again:

> If you really want to hear about it, the first thing you'll probably want to know is where I was born, and what my lousy childhood was like, and how my parents were occupied and all before they had me, and all that David Copperfield kind of crap, but I don't feel like going into it, if you want to know the truth.

So drawls the opening of J.D. Salinger's Holden Caulfield in Catcher In The Rye which, perhaps more than any other modern novel, has been adopted by generations of disaffected youth as a surrogate autobiography. This was demonstrated most infamously when found in the pocket of Mark Chapman as he shot and killed John Lennon on the steps of New York's Dakota building in 1980, and claimed by Chapman to be his testimony. In the front of the book he had inscribed 'This is my statement', supposedly referring to Lennon's embodiment of the phonyism Holden vituperatively denounces throughout. That opening sentence also doubles as a pretty faithful summary of Salinger's own opinion of biography (and particularly literary biography). A notorious recluse, Salinger withdrew from the public domain in the mid-1950s, having maintained an impressive wall of silence around both his life and work which endures today, well into his eighties.

The biographical details of a recluse are, of course, hunted and collected more avidly than anyone else, and this paradox of being famous for not wanting to be famous was one of a number of thoughts which informed Ian Hamilton's curious 1988 book In search of J.D. Salinger. Hamilton intended to use Salinger as a trigger to write about the elusive nature of biography, or more particularly, the relationship between the biographer and biographee, not really expecting to get anywhere by pursuing the writer himself.

> According to my outline, the rebuffs I experienced would be as much part of the action as the triumphs—indeed it would not matter much if there were no triumphs. The idea—or one of the ideas—was to see what would happen if orthodox biographical procedures were to be applied to a subject who actively set himself to resist, and even to forestall, them ... It would be a biography, yes, but it would also be a semispoof in which the biographer would play a leading, sometimes comic, role.

Hamilton proceeds by splitting himself into two —the rational, responsible biographer, and the emotional, excitable detective—whose constant alter-ego monologues trace the story to its ultimate dead-end, when Salinger's lawyers succeed in paraphrasing the book to a shadow of its former self.

--

Salinger's book jacket biographical notes were always minimal, and most recently completely removed altogether, along with any publicity photograph. In the jacket blurb for the original edition of Franny And Zooey he wrote simply 'I live in Westport with my dog'—both of which were untrue. Another author with outspoken views on this matter, Milan Kundera, has consistently whittled his own blurb down to the current: 'Milan Kundera was born in 1929 in Czechoslovakia and since 1975 has been living in France'. The covers of the books which were still published in Czech before he was banned by the communist regime contained a fairly detailed biography, but since he stopped writing in Czech in the early 1990s, Kundera has supervised the details on all new original French editions, and their subsequent translations.

In fact, the stubbornness with which Kundera resists any form of autobiography is so extreme that since 1985 he has refused all interviews. This can not merely be dismissed as some idiosyncratic trait. It is essential for Kundera's understanding of the autonomy of a text, consistent with his whole body of work. In the essay 'The Art of the Novel', Kundera wrote his own dictionary, clarifying crucial words in relation to his novels. One of them clearly expresses his position regarding biographies:

> NOVELIST (and his life)
> 'The Artist must make posterity believe he never lived', Flaubert said. Maupassant kept his portrait from appearing in a series of famous writers: 'A man's private life and his face do not belong to the public.' Hermann Broch said about himself, Musil, Kafka: 'The three of use have no real biographies.' Which does not mean that their lives were meager in event, but they were not destined to be noteworthy, to be public, to become bio-graphy. Someone asks Karel Capek why he doesn't write poetry. His answer: 'Because I loathe talking about myself.' The distinctive feature of the true novelist: he does not like to talk about himself. 'I hate tampering with the precious lives of great writers, and no biographer will ever catch a glimpse of my private life,' said Nabokov. Italo Calvino warned: no one should expect a single true word from him about his own life. And Faulkner wished 'to be, as a private individual, abolished and voided from history, leaving it markless, no refuse save the printed books.' (Underline: BOOKS and PRINTED, meaning no unfinished manuscripts, no letters, no diaries.) ...

In The Unbearable Lightness Of Being, Kundera is emphatic about similarities between his characters and his personal life:

> Characters from my novels are my own possibilities which were never realized. That's why I like them all equally, yet, they all frighten me: all of them crossed a border which I was circumnavigating. It is this crossed border (border, after which ends my own I) that attracts me. Only there begins a mystery which novels investigate. A novel is not a confession of the author, it is the interrogation of the nature of human life in the trap which became the world.

Kundera was born in the provincial Czech city of Brno. His father was a pianist and pupil of the the composer Leos Janáček. Since moving to France, Kundera (an avid musician himself) has consistently promoted the work of Janáček, which was largely unknown outside the Czech Republic, writing texts for opera programmes, taking part in radio discussions, and most recently publishing a modest book about him, My Janáček. He argues that Janáček is not just an interesting composer from some exotic part of Europe but nothing less than 'a creator of modern opera. Born in 1854, Janáček is older than the great Romantic composers such Puccini or Straus, 20 years older than the 'father of modern music' Schönberg, and some 30 years older than Bartók and Stravinsky. Unlike many other modern artist who were affiliated to groups or movements, Janáček worked alone in Brno. His groundbreaking opera Jenufa had to wait 17 years before first being performed in Prague, the center of Czech culture. Unpublished and unheard, this work has has effectively been derailed from the railtrack of history. Kundera compares it with a premier of Stravinsky's The Rite Of Spring, which was first performed in Paris in 1913 where it created an unforgettable scandal, ending with a fist fight in the audience. 'Now imagine that the world only gets to hear The Rite Of Spring after 20 years of gestation, in 1933. It would be still lovely music, audience would clap, but it wouldn't be a music to open up new horizons, new possibilities, inspires its contemporaries, and makes history'.

In fact, Janáček was still forced to to accept a compromise and allow the opera's chief conductor to modify the style and orchestration before he could see Jenufa performed in Prague's National theatre 17 years late. Though obliged to be grateful to be played in Prague, since he was turning 60, it was humiliating to see his distinctive unsentimental realism 'improved' in a style which he detested. Janáček objected the 'romantic lie' of the opera tradition, yet it was only in this conventionalized form that the Czech nation could accept his work, and it took another 69 years before Jenufa was performed for the first time as he intended it. That was outside Czechoslovakia, in 1982, thanks to the American conductor Charles Mackerras.

Max Brod, a German jewish author, composer, and journalist living in Prague, was Janáček's strongest supporter during his lifetime. An incurable romantic, Brod had difficulty understanding Janáček's work, yet translated his largely unknown operas to German to make them more accessible to a wider public. Brod was also the guardian angel and closest friend of another underrated Czech artist, Franz Kafka. Following Kafka's death in a sanatorium, Brod was the executor of his will. In a personal letter to him, Kafka asked him to destroy all his unpublished writings, diaries, and letters. Instead, Brod edited and published the unfinished papers in six volumes, and promptly wrote Kafka's biography. To complete Kundera's dictionary entry:

> ... According to a well-known metaphor, the novelist demolishes the house of his life and uses its bricks to construct another house: that of his novel. From which it follows that a novelist's biographers unmake what the novelist made, and remake what he unmade. Their labour, from the standpoint of art utterly negative, can illuminate neither the value not the meaning of a novel. The moment Kafka draws more attention than Joseph K., the process of Kafka's posthumous dying begins.

--

George Perec built his own autobiography W, Or The Memory Of Childhood (1975) from two discrete materials. He explains the structure in his introduction:

> In this book there are two texts which simply alternate; you might almost believe they had nothing in common, but they are in fact
>
> inextricably bound up with each other, as though neither could exist on its own, as though it was only their coming together, the distant light they cast on each other, that could make apparent what is never quite said in one, never quite said in the other, but only in their fragile overlapping.
>
> One of these texts is entirely imaginary: it's an adventure story, an arbitrary but careful reconstruction of a childhood fantasy about a land in thrall to the Olympic ideal. The other text is an autobiography: a fragmentary tale of a wartime childhood, a tale lacking in exploits and memories made up of scattered oddments, gaps, lapses, doubts, guesses and meagre anecdotes. Next to it, the adventure story is rather grandiose, or maybe dubious. For it begins to tell one tale, and then, all of a sudden, launches into another. In this break, in this split suspending the story on an unidentifiable expectation can be found the point of departure for the whole book: the points of suspension on which the broken threads of childhood and the web of writing are caught.

The letter 'W', ('double-U', but 'double-Vé' in French), already embodies this idea and is the name of the island 'in thrall to the Olympic ideal' which takes up one half of the book. The other is 'The Memory of Childhood', even though the opening sentence of this half reads: 'I have no childhood memories'. It is also interesting to note that the main character of the 'W' story is named Gaspard Winckler. This is not his original name; he has in fact been given a passport that used to belong to a child, a sickly boy named Gaspard Winckler, who has now disappeared off the coast of W. So the actual autobiography is represented by the 'or' point of the book's whole title, or more concisely, the intersection in the letter W where the two V's meet.

The name Gaspard Winckler reappears in Perec's Life: A User's Manual, written over nine years and published in 1978, three years after W, Or The Memory Of Childhood, which comprises 99 chapters about the inhabitants of a ten-storied building in Paris. The structure of this book is dictated by a famous chess problem: how to visit every square on the board using only the knight's move. The system alludes to the jigsaw puzzle or patchwork of the building and accords a structure whereby the everyday and arbitrary can find their place within the series of L-shaped steps from room to room. It is essentially a biographical study of the life of a fictional house, told through the stories of several generations over a hundred years. Perec was a member of OuLiPo (Ouvroir de Littérature Potentielle), the French collective that explored the crossover of writing and mathematics. Puzzles were always a key inspiration for Perec, and a second recurring motif in the book is the jigsaw puzzle, played out through the relationship between the jigsaw maker and the jigsaw doer. As the reader repeatedly re-enters rooms and lives, he traces one underlying story of the life of the building's multimillionaire owner, Bartlebooth. Born into unspeakable wealth and indifferent to the temptations of women, power, art or money itself, at the age of twenty he decides to devise an arbitrary project to keep him occupied for the rest of his life. For the first ten years he will learn to paint watercolours; for the following twenty he will travel the world painting seaports at the rate of one a fortnight, then ship each one back to Paris where a hired craftsman will turn them into jigsaw puzzles; and for the final twenty years he will return to Paris and reassemble the 500 paintings, recreating the images of his life memories, after which they will be turned back into solid pictures, returned to the location they depict, and dipped into detergent to remove the image, leaving a blank sheet of paper. In short, a half-century recursive exercise of moral, logical and aesthetic substance, beginning and ending with zero.

Gaspard Winckler is the craftsman who creates puzzles from Bartlebooth's watercolours and who ultimately exacts an obscure revenge on the rich Englishman. Towards the end of the book Bartlebooth's eyesight diminishes to the point of blindness, and as the pace winds down agonizingly to his fitting pieces by touch alone, then with the aid of description from an assistant, it becomes clear that he will never succeed in reaching his goal and the predetermined autobiographical project will remain incomplete, or: the jigsaw-maker will have won. The entire novel, in fact, takes place the second before Bartlebooth dies, in front of an incomplete puzzle, as Winckler's masterstroke is revealed:

> On the tablecloth, somewhere in the crepuscular sky of the four hundred and thirty-ninth puzzle, the black hole of the sole piece not yet filled has the almost perfect shape of an X. but the ironical thing, which could have been foretold long ago, is that the piece the dead man holds between his fingers is shaped like a W.

When Perec died, his friend and fellow writer Harry Mathews wrote The Orchard: a remembrance of Georges Perec, a collection of memories each beginning with the words 'I remember'. He did this daily, adopting a mode of writing used by Perec in his 'Je me souviens' ('I remember', 1978), until he, quite simply, forgot to. The first reads: 'I remember sometimes arranging to meet Georges Perec on the bus or the metro. He always sat by a window, and I recognized him from far away—his afro hair and his goatee gave his face the projective power of a primitive mask.'

--

Peter Sellers famously attributed his prodigious character acting as being a fortunate consequence of lacking any personality of his own. He was a self-proclaimed vessel to contain others' fiction, and Stanley Kubrick would later describe his acting as a kind of instinctive hysteria. In TV interviews, Sellers generally responds to all questions in character—or a variety of characters, bending accents, dialects and even posture to suit his answer. Sellers' enigma is the subject of three very different films, which together reveal as much about the nature of biography than their spectre of a subject. In reverse order, the recent Hollywood biopic The Life And Death Of Peter Sellers (2004) offers a one-dimensional portrait, construced on base Freudian cause-and-effect: a suggestive closeness with his mother, the behaviour of a spoilt-child, an inability to maintain relationships with women, and an increasing solitude, melancholy and appetite for self-destruction.

A few years earlier the BBC had also produced a film of Sellers' life, Peter Sellers As He Filmed It (2001), which tells much the same story through a remarkable trove of home movie footage which Sellers obsessively compiled throughout his life. The film is montaged almost entirely from this footage, with archive clips from various TV and film appearances, all judiciously annotated by formal voiceover. Where the Hollywood version drives home the clichés, the BBC version is rich in charm and subtlety, the intricacies of character bleeding through the clips, whether happily forcing his son to pose for his own backyard comic vignettes, or miserable and detached on an Indian spiritual trail. The stories remain the same in both films, but in this version they are plausible; this is less to do with the fact that the material is visually authentic, and more to do with the inclusion of irrational mood swings, chance happenings and overall chaos. Where Hollywood filters out humanity, the BBC distills it.

In 1971, Jerzy Kosinski published his second novel Being There. Soon afterwards he received a bizarre telegram from its lead character, Chance the Gardener: 'Available in my garden or outside of it.' A telephone number followed, and when Kosinski dialled it Peter Sellers answered. After convincing Kosinski, for years afterwards, Sellers attempted to interest Hollywood in an adaptation, and finally, in 1979, with the clout he had gained from the Pink Panther series, the film was made together with director Hal Ashby. Sellers as Chance is shut away from the world, working in the enclosed garden of an elderly couple, his only knowledge of the world from TV, and lacking any social character of his own. When the couple die, the gardener is suddenly released into a world where the innocence of his non-personality and regurgitated TV-speak is consistently misinterpreted, and the result is a double-edged satire on politics, television and social mores. In the wake of the biographical detail supplied by The Life And Death Of ... and ... As He Filmed It, Being There might be regarded as the true unofficial Sellers biography; the unauthorised authorised version. Next to Hollywood 'fiction', and self-directed 'fact', this hybrid of the two feels closest of the three.

The screenplay of Being There was adapted from the novel by Kosinski himself, a Polish Jew exiled to the USA, whose first novel, The Painted Bird, quickly became a bestseller, and whose central metaphor—if a captured crow is beautifully painted and released to go back to its flock, the other crows will attack and kill it because it is different—was a blueprint for his own life. Born Jerzy Nitodem Lewintopf, under Nazi threat his family was rechristened Kosinski, the Polish equivalent of Smith, and though Jerzy could tolerate this disguise, he could not maintain his anonymity. Instead, he cultivated a certain infamy as a socialite and minor actor as well as a writer, along with a reputation as a plagiarist, liar and conman. A damning Village Voice article in 1982 revealed his books were largely ghostwritten by various editors, or more or less directly translated from Polish sources unknown to English speakers, which explains the striking stylistic differences from one supposedly autobiographical novel to the next.

--

In 1999 German academic Klaus Stadtmüller delivered a biographical lecture on Kurt Schwitters. He had compiled extracts from Schwitters' poems, letters and notes, arranged chronologically to tell the story of Schwitters' life and work—an aural equivalent of the Sellers home movie footage. After the performance, British writer David Lillington went up to ask Stadtmüller for a copy of his script, which he now saw consisted of sheets onto which Stadtmüller had pasted typewritten fragments and cut-up photocopies from books, along with his own handwritten annotations, collaging his material in the same manner and spirit as Schwitters' own work. Lillington noted the ad hoc formal beauty of this essentially functional script by someone steeped in the art and writing of Schwitters, and argues that Stadtmüller had created, in this way, the best short biography of Schwitters to date.

But a few other contenders were produced by the Polish film-maker, writer and designer Stefan Themerson, who knew Schwitters for the last five years of his life. The first was a particularly tactile monograph, Kurt Schwitters In England, published in 1958 by his own Gaberbocchus press, the second was a lecture delivered to a group of Cambridge students three years later, and the third a graphic translation of this lecture, 'Kurt Schwitters on a Time Chart', compiled around the time of the lecture but not published until the end of the 1960s (in the design journal Typographica), by which time Themerson had written this unpublished 'postface' to editor Herbert Spencer:

> Here it is. And I am horrified. I have read it again, and I hate every word of it. This book is a monstrosity. What I would really have liked—well, I would have liked to be able to enjoy K.S.'s work lightly, for the "pleasure it gives to the eye". And yet I couldn't write it in that key. It's wrong, possibly, nevertheless it irritates me when I see people handling a collage by K.S. as if it were a bunch of lovely flowers. Perhaps because I know that they grew not in a glasshouse but in that bloody stinking bit of European history nobody wants to remember.
>
> Let me quote a philosopher who ended his book with words that have become almost a cliché. He says: ... he who understands me finally recognizes my propositions as senseless, when he has climbed out through them, on them, over them. (He must so

> to speak throw away the ladder, after he has climbed up on it.) Perhaps the reader must endure this book, (together with its time-chart and other nonsense), and then throw it away. Perhaps that is what he must do in order to enjoy K.S's work rightly.

Themerson's friend and colleague Anthony Froshaug also found himself on the receiving end of similar concerns. Busy preparing a small monograph about Themerson's background and diverse activities, Froshaug sent his subject an incomplete draft for comment, and received this typically forthright reply:

> Mixture of biographic data & personal reminisces—I have my doubts about it. 1st you were not present at the birth of the subject. 2nd factual information (... born in ... &c) creates an aura of objectivity and this overflows onto personal reminisces making them appear less personal than they really are or were [...] I do not like that kind of literary research which consists in finding bits of author's life and ad hoc connecting them with some bits of work. It seems to me essentially non-scientific, prejudicial, irrelevant, misleading, & altogether too easy ...

Froshaug's interests were as maverick and diverse as Themerson's—a complex compound of typography, writing, science and mathematics—and he became similarly outspoken about the dangers of glossing over, of interpreting without scientific method, of romance. In an early book review of Herbert Spencer's Pioneers Of Modern Typography he wrote:

> Why celebrate people in books if you cannot say what they did, and why, for what (and for how much)? I should not like to celebrate my death, laid out on a coffee-table.

These two sentences hung over Robin Kinross—literally, on the wall over the laser printer—as he prepared a monograph on Froshaug during the 1990s. After much deliberation, Kinross chose to dissect the book into life (Documents Of A Life) and work (Typography & Texts), as two separate volumes published together in 2000 and housed in a single slipcase—despite 'his life and work being more intertwined than most'. The reasons were foremost practical, in terms of both sorting and arranging material clearly for the reader, as well as allowing it to be presented in a form light and small enough for the hand, true to Froshaug's practical, human-sized principles. But ultimately, what initially appears a brutal and even paradoxical division serves only to bring the life and work closer together; the books effectively mirror each other, and the clarity of organisation allows the reader to reconcile them himself.

In many respects the result resembles Jonathan Coe's account of B.S. Johnson. Both biographers were working under the implicit pressure of writing about writers who had strict ideas about how things should and shouldn't be done, both were tackling literary biography with serious reservations about the genre bordering on disgust, and both were dealing with marginal subjects rooted in the same era of postwar austerity, working out a kind of painfully human wing of high modernism in isolation. Both Kinross and Coe were working through the late 1990s and early 2000s, in an era of unsurpassed public interest in lowest-common-denominator celebrity. And significantly, both respond with humility, by taking what is already there and framing it appropriately.

> Early on I decided that I would not attempt to write a biography of Anthony Froshaug. I do not believe this is an appropriate form for him. Indeed, perhaps the conventional biographical narrative that pretends intimate, even superior knowledge of another person is not an appropriate or reasonable form for the life of any human being.

While the Typography & Texts volume is a fairly standard work survey of annotated graphic work and texts, the Documents Of A Life half is less conventional. Again comparable to Coe's excerpts of Johnson's texts, Kinross compiles a chronological scrapbook, drawn from the disarray of Froshaug's papers, including photographs, excerpts from unfinished fiction, teaching projects, correspondence, postcards and notes. The book does not claim to be exhaustive, but edited on the basis of an intimate understanding of the subject's ideas, showing items only where appropriate. Finally, the books demonstrate Froshaug's key legacy as a teacher through the role of Kinross as conscientious student (in the least official but widest reaching sense), richly manifest in the depth of rigour and love throughout.

Johnson once described the ability to laugh at himself louder than others as the only thing that kept him going. A similar frowning humour is exercised in the following, slightly hysterical autobiographical note Froshaug wrote about himself for the notes at the back of Art Without Boundaries (1972), an early survey of modernist art and design from a British perspective:

> Born in london, 1920. Trained in drawing and wood-engraving at Central School of Arts and Crafts, 1937–39 (five terms). Never allowed into typography room. Freelance designer and typographer from 1941, believing that mechanical composition could do as well as hand. Work regarded as 'backwash of the continental movement of the 1920s', therefore unacceptable or minimally paid. Fell in love with printing: from love and economic stress and difficulties in having accurate layouts carried out at second-hand, bought 25 worth of minimal equipment (type, l.c. only, spaces, strip leads, tweezers, galley, Adana H/S No. 2. Found old rusty stick and some survival type and cases in Cornwall; had screwdriver, cotton-wool, spanners, paper, ingenuity). Customers prepared to leave typographer alone, if end-product printed. Immense interest in emotional and structural meaning of text. Desire to find visual form matching verbal. Never thought could teach, but approached by Jesse Collins (1947) to do a day a week at Central, 'because you have authority'. Flabbergasted, but the teaching seemed to work. Driven back to minimal living, moved to Cornwall (5s. per week rent), doing 130 jobs a year. Earned £4 per week. Returned to London on appointment as senior lecturer in typography at Central (1952–53). Appointment not confirmed, since place needed for trade appointee, in order to help extension of school being built to house apprentices. (Apprentices not forthcoming.) First understood that teaching not a matter of educating potentially superb students, but rat-race. Disgusted, resolved never to teach again. Re-established press, Cornwall (6s. per week rent). Tempted by anarchist dream of Hochschule für Gestaltung, Ulm, to learn German and take up professorship in graphic design and visual communication (1957–61); also established typography workshop in the college. Appointed to royal college of art as first-year tutor in graphic design (1961–64), teaching 'stars', trying to help them to become human. Huge disagreement with organization, behaved most disagreeably. (As R. Sandford said, some years later, here comes Anthony, pretending to be a human being.') Senior lecturer and first director of visual communication course, Watford college of technology. Had one good student, helped a few others. Used-up by teaching left to study architecture at architectural association school (1967–69). Part-time tutor, Coventry college of art and design (1969–70), at present visiting lecturer, central school of art and design (1970–). With great encouragement from friends (=ex-students), printing workshop re-established, London, 1971.

What might easily by dismissed as being throwaway or flippant here is actually sublime. Froshaug's self-portrait not only itemises his work, it EMBODIES it. The isolation, melancholy and bitterness which fed the intensity of his work are embedded in its rhetoric, which manages to laugh at itself as well as criticise others. By parodying biography's ridiculous abbreviation of life it carries the modest but convincing weight of jocuseriousness, and like Beckett's opening one-liner, contrary to first impressions, the text is generous and expansive.

--

All the examples followed here are plausible precisely because they are human, pushing for uncharted territory and guided by the particular idiosyncracies of their subjects while never quite knowing where they will end up. Propelled by this momentum—what Paul Elliman has referred to as 'the breath of life'—each of these biographies has assumed its own personality. They are character-building, but the characters always seem to materialize, spectre-like, in the gap between two poles:

Between the truth and fiction of B.S. Johnson.
Between the annotated truth and fiction of Vladimir Nabokov.
Between the fame and infamy of J.D. Salinger.
Between the novelist and protagonist of Milan Kundera.
Between the 2 V's of Georges Perec's W.
Between Hollywood and the home movies of Peter Sellers.
Between the pastiche and spirit of Kurt Schwitters.
Between the trial and error of Stefan Themerson.
Between Anthony Froshaug's love and hate.

Any resemblance to persons fictional or living in this work is purely coincidental.

Thanks to Peter Bilak, David Lillington, and Louis Lüthi, who provided entire blocks of this text.

PHASE IV

Screenplay by Gerry Beegan
(after Saul Bass)

SOUND: OMINOUS SYNTHESISERS, WHICH CONTINUE FOR MUCH OF THE FILM.

SPECIAL EFFECTS. WE ARE DRIFTING THROUGH A MESH OF STARS. THERE ARE SO MANY THAT THERE IS NO FORM OR PATTERN. WE MOVE FORWARD.

THE WORDS 'PHASE I' APPEAR, LETTER BY LETTER IN THE TOP RIGHT HAND CORNER OF THE SCREEN IN A MOONBASE TYPEFACE, TINY AND GREEN, AS IF THEY WERE BEING TYPED ON AN EARLY COMPUTER SCREEN DISPLAY.[1]

A BLACK CIRCLE APPEARS IN THE MIDDLE OF THE SCREEN. PLANETS CIRCLE IT. WHEN THE PLANETS ALIGN TRIPPY LIGHTSHOW PATTERNS EXPOLODE FROM THE EDGES OF THE CIRCLE LIKE SUN SPOTS.[2]

JAMES LESKO (voice-over) That spring we were all watching the events in space and wondering what the final effect would be. Mystics predicted earthquakes and the end of life as we knew it.

EXTERIOR. CLOSE UP OF CONICAL DEPRESSION.

JAMES LESKO (voice-over) When the effect came, it was almost unnoticed because it happened to such a small insignificant form of life.

AN ANT APPEARS FROM THE HOLE AND STANDS SILLOUTTED AGAINST THE NIGHT SKY.

LESKO (voice-over) One biologist, an Englishman named Ernest Hubbs, saw something, got nervous, and started investigating.

SHOTS OF ANTS UNDERGROUND IN A CIRCLE, ANENNAE TWITCHING. EXTREME CLOSE UP OF INDIVIDUAL ANTS SHOWING VARIOUS GEOMETRIC MARKINGS ON THEIR HEADS.

LESKO (voice-over) While I was messing around with number theory at the university, Hubbs was already onto something. Ordinary ants of different species were doing things that ants don't do: meeting, communicating, apparently making decisions. Hubbs kept making notes. Only fragments of what he knew got out, he kept most of it to himself, so when I got into it I didn't know a damn thing.

ONE ANT CRAWLS ALONG UNDERGROUND PASSAGES PAST GEOMETRIC MARKINGS ON THE WALL, PAST VARIOUS ANT ACTIVITIES, TO THE QUEEN WHO IS LAYING EGGS. THEY COMMUNICATE VIA ANTANNAE-WRIGGLING. EXTREME CLOSE UP OF NETWORK OF LINES IN THE QUEEN'S EYE.

CUT TO THOUSANDS OF ANTS SWARMING OVER A SPIDER.

ERNEST HUBBS (voice-over) Memorandum to R. Flanders Smith. Secretary National Science Foundation. Proposal an immediate full-scale attack on the threat to other life forms in the subject area. An experimental station to be manned by one senior scientist, myself, and an associate, J.R. Lasko, a qualified information specialist with cryptological background. Speed is of the essence.

EXTERIOR. THE DESERT. BRIGHT SUNLIGHT. A TRUCK IN CENTRE OF SCREEN DRIVES TOWARDS US. THE TRUCK DRIVES THROUGH AN ABANDONED TOWN PAST A BILLBOARD WHICH SAYS, 'PARADISE CITY HOME OF THE GOOD LIFE'. CLOSE UPS OF RUINED BUILDINGS, AN EMPTY BIRD CAGE. THROUGH THE WINDSCREEN OF THE TRUCK WE SEE TALL THIN TOWERS MADE OF MUD. THE CAR STOPS AND THE SCIENTISTS GET OUT. TUBBS IS OLDER AND BEARDED, LESKO, YOUNGER AND MORE CASUAL IN BASEBALL CAP, DENIM SHIRT AND JEANS.

LESKO This is the place.

HUBBS This is it.

THE SCIENTISTS STAND IN FRONT OF THE TOWERS. FROM SLITS AT THE TOP THE ANTS OBSERVE THEM.

THE TRUCK DRIVES TO A FIELD OF CORN WHERE THE ANTS HAVE CUT A CIRCLE THROUGH THE CROP.

EXTERIOR. A VERDANT FARM, A YOUNG GIRL, KENDRA, RIDES A HORSE THROUGH THE FIELDS. THE SCIENTISTS VISIT THE REMAINING LOCALS IN ORDER TO GET THEM TO EVACUATE THE AREA. HUBBS GIVES THE FAMILY (KENDRA, HER GRANDPARENTS) AND A HIRED HAND AN OFFICIAL ORDER TO QUIT. HE LIES TO THEM ABOUT THE REASONS FOR THEIR HAVING TO LEAVE, BUT THEY IGNORE HIS ULTIMATUM, DETERMINED TO STAY WHERE THEY ARE.

EXTERIOR. A HAWK HOVERS IN THE SKY. THE WORDS 'PHASE II' APPEAR, LETTER BY LETTER IN THE TOP RIGHT HAND CORNER OF THE SCREEN.

HUBBS (voice-over) Friday, 8 o'clock. The zone should now be clear of population. We can now proceed with the next step.

EXTERIOR. THE RESEARCH STATION A SILVER GEODISIC DOME NEAR THE TOWERS.

HUBBS (voice-over) The experiment has begun.

INTERIOR OF DOME. LESKO BOOTS UP HIS HUGE MAINFRAME COMPUTER AND TURNS ON HIS PLOTTER. LOTS OF SWITCHES ARE SWITCHED, BUTTONS PRESSED. HE TYPES, TWIRLS KNOBS. HIS SCREENS ARE SILENT.

EXTERIOR. TWO DAYS LATER. THE TOWERS. HUBBS SHOOTS AT THE DOMES WITH A SHOTGUN. ONE FALLS. HE METHODICALLY DEMOLISHES ALL OF THE REMAINING ANTS' TOWERS TO PROVOKE A RESPONSE.

HUBBS Let's see some action.

INTERIOR. THE DOME. LESKO IMMEDIATELY PICKS UP THE ANT LANGUAGE ON HIS MONITORS.

LESKO Hi there.

EXTERIOR. THE FARM. NIGHT. THE ANTS INVADE KENDRA'S FARM, SWARMING OVER THE FARMHOUSE AND FORCING THE FAMILY TO FLEE IN THEIR TRUCK.

INTERIOR. THE DOME. LESKO SHOWS HUBBS HOW HE IS ANALYSING THE ANT ACTIVITY. THEY LOOK AT A MONITOR.

LESKO I take my ant signals and I run them through the digitizer. I record them on tape, I write them down and I look for a correlation between what they say and what they do.

EXTERIOR. THE TRUCK DRIVING SPEEDILY THROUGH THE DESERT. ANTS SWARM INTO THE CAB CAUSING IT TO CRASH NEAR THE DOME. KENDRA'S GRANDPARENTS HEAD FOR ITS SHELTER.

INTERIOR. THE DOME. THE SCIENTISTS ARE LOOKING AT LESKO'S PRINT-OUTS.

LESKO This shows that these little mothers talk to each other.

THE GENERATOR OUTSIDE THE DOME EXPLODES. HUBBS IS SURE THAT THE ANTS ARE RESPONSIBLE AND SETS OFF A POISONOUS SPRAY.

HUBBS I'm going to counter with 100% yellow.[3]

EXTERIOR. SPRAY HEADS SURROUNDING THE DOME SHOOT OUT YELLOW LIQUID WHICH COAT THE HUMANS LURCHING TOWARDS THE DOME. THEY FALL TO THE GROUND. THE SPRAY CONTINUES.

EXTERIOR. SUNRISE. OUTSIDE THE DOME. THE AREA SURROUNDING THE DOME IS COVERED WITH YELLOW POISONOUS DUST. HUBBS AND LESKO EMERGE IN THEIR PROTECTIVE GEAR, LOOKING LIKE SPACE-MEN OR ROBOTS, TO FIND SOME DEAD ANTS AND THE DEAD HUMANS. HUBBS GOES STRAIGHT TO THE BURNT OUT GENERATOR AND STARTS EXAMINING IT TO DETERMINE THE CAUSE OF THE EXPLOSION.

LESKO People are dead back there, don't you understand?

HUBBS (coldly) Yes, very sad. People get killed sometimes. I think this yellow should hold its potency for three or four days. We can start collecting ants now.

HUBBS GATHERS THE ANTS WHICH CRAWL OUT OF HOLES IN THE HAND OF ONE OF THE BODIES.[4]

KENDRA WHO, BY A STROKE OF LUCK, WASN'T CAUGHT IN THE SPRAY EMERGES FROM A NEARBY HOUSE AND COLLAPSES. THE SCIENTISTS CARRY HER BACK TO THE DOME.

INTERIOR. THE LAB IN THE DOME. WHILE KENDRA IS RECOVERING THE SCIENTISTS ARE IN THE LAB EXAMINING THE NEWLY-COLLECTED ANTS IN A GLASS MAZE.

LESKO Little sons of bitches.

HUBBS Ha ha ha. No, no, they are not individuals, they are individual cells, tiny parts of the whole. Think of their society, James, perfect harmony, perfect division of labour. Think of them building elaborate structures, according to plans which they know nothing of, but which they execute perfectly. So defenseless in the individual, so powerful in the mass.

KENDRA ENTERS, SEES THE ANTS AND SMASHES THE CONTAINER. THEY LEAVE THE LAB, TURNING ON A SPRAY, BUT HUBBS HAS BEEN BITTEN.

INTERIOR THE COMPUTER AREA. CLOSE-UPS OF DIALS, SCREENS, PRINTOUTS.

HUBBS (voice-over) Monday 2am. Lesko continues to make progress deciphering the ant language from the tapes recorded during the first skirmish.

EXTERIOR. THE AREA AROUND THE DOME. A FULL MOON. OTHER CREATURES (SNAKES, LIZARDS, SCORPIONS) LEAVE THE AREA.

EXTERIOR. THE AREA AROUND THE DOME. DAYBREAK. THE DOME IS SURROUNDED BY SMALL STRUCTURES WHICH REFLECT SUNLIGHT ONTO THE DOME.

INTERIOR. INSIDE THE DOME. KENDRA IS WAKING ON HER BED. LESKO ARRIVES AND ATTEMPTS TO CHAT HER UP.

KENDRA I'm sorry about what happened yesterday.

LESKO If I were you I'd have bopped those ants pretty good myself.

KENDRA My grandparents are dead aren't they?

LESKO Yeah, they are. But don't you have parents?

KENDRA LOOKS DOWN AT THE FLOOR AND SHAKES HER HEAD.

LESKO Well, you must be hungry. Come on, I'll get you some breakfast.

THEY WALK THROUGH THE COMPUTER AREA. KENDRA PICKS UP A MEMORY BOARD.

KENDRA Can I ask a question? What do you do here?

LESKO (with purposeful vagueness) Just a little research into statistical probabilities.

KENDRA Must be interesting.

THEY ARRIVE IN THE MAIN AREA OF THE DOME WHERE HUBBS IS LOOKING AT THE MONITORS. ON THE SCREENS ARE NEW REFLECTIVE STRUCTURES.

HUBBS As you can see, James, we are under siege. The temperature is already up five degrees and of course the sun is not yet at full strength.

LESKO We're going to fry in here.

HUBBS Human beings can exist in temperatures in excess of 120 degrees. Our computer shuts down at 90.

INTERIOR. THE COMPUTER AREA. LATER THAT DAY. LESKO ADJUSTS HIS DIALS. KENDRA APPROACHES.

LESKO Kendra, Do you want to see what

we're doing? (He nods towards the surveillance monitors which show the ants' reflectors)
We want to knock them down before they burn us out.

HE TURNS A DIAL AND AN INTENSE NOISE STARTS.

LESKO White sound. That's every sound in the world jammed together to make one terrific noise which we're going to broadcast to those mounds out there. When we do interesting things are going to happen.

EXTERIOR. THE REFLECTIVE STRUCTURES. THE DISORDERED, INARTICULATE NOISE SENDS THE TOWERS TUMBLING, KILLING MANY OF THE ANTS.

INTERIOR. THE COMPUTER AREA. THE ANTS HAVE EATEN THROUGH THE WIRES OF THE AIR CONDITIONER IN THE DOME AND THE COMPUTER SHUTS DOWN.

INTERIOR. UNDERGROUND. THE ANTS ARRANGE THE BODIES OF THEIR FALLEN COMRADES IN NEAT ROWS. THEY REVERENTLY GATHER AROUND TO PAY THEIR RESPECTS TO THEIR DEAD.
THE CAMERA PANS GENTLY OVER THE CEREMONY. SOUND: SYNTHESIZERS PLAY A MOURNFUL FUNERAL MARCH.

INTERIOR. THE COMPUTER AREA. NIGHT.
AS TEMPERATURES DROP THE COMPUTERS START UP AGAIN. LESKO IS TYPING INSTRUCTIONS ON HIS KEYBOARD.

HUBBS What are you doing?

LESKO I'm sending a message to the ants.

HUBBS Where is your message?

LESKO On the plotter.

HUBBS STAGGERS OVER TO THE PLOTTER, NURSING HIS SWOLLEN ARM. HE PULLS OUT THE PAPER. ON IT IS A SQUARE

HUBBS (scornfully) This is no message.

LESKO Mathematics is the universal language among intelligent creatures. If there is an intelligence there I want it to know that there is an intelligence here.

EXTERIOR. CLOUDS DRIFT ACROSS THE MOON. THE WORDS 'PHASE III' APPEAR, LETTER BY LETTER IN THE TOP RIGHT HAND CORNER OF THE SCREEN.

INTERIOR THE DOME. NIGHT. HUBBS LIES ON HIS BUNK. LESKO IS ON THE TOP BUNK.

LESKO Why don't they kill us? Why play these games? What do they want?

HUBBS The ants are organized by the queen. She is at the centre of the colony. It is she who speaks. If she dies discipline and organization would crumble.

LESKO The war is over, Hubbs. They have the power. The only hope is that they answer our message and we convince them that we are worth keeping alive.

HUBBS I think I could locate the queen and kill her. Lock the tracker onto her voice when she speaks.

LESKO What makes you think she would speak to you?

INTERIOR. THE COMPUTER AREA.
THE PLOTTER STARTS UP. THE SCIENTISTS AND KENDRA GATHER AROUND. THIS IS THE ANTS' REPLY.

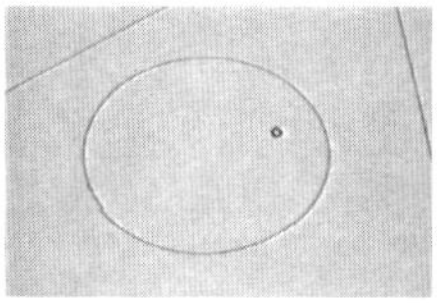

LESKO What does it mean, what the hell does it mean, a circle with a dot ... An intelligence test. Could the circle be this place, the dot a person, someone they want?

KENDRA (nervously) They want somebody. Why would they want somebody?

LESKO (enigmatically) To talk to them.

KENDRA You mean they might be angry at someone who did them some harm? What would they do to that person? Would they let the others go free?

HUBBS James, come here.

HUBBS POINTS AT ONE OF THE MONITORS WHICH SHOWS A LOW STRUCTURE IN THE DESERT AT SOME DISTANCE FROM THE DOME.

HUBBS I believe I have located the queen. She's there.

EXTERIOR. OUTSIDE THE DOME.
THE DOOR OPENS AND KENDRA STEPS OUT BAREFOOT. SHE IS CONVINCED THAT SHE IS THE 'SOMEONE' THE ANTS WANT AND HOPES TO DEFLECT THE ANTS' WRATH. NERVOUSLY SHE HEADS AWAY FROM THE DOME TOWARDS THE QUEEN'S STRUCTURE. A SMALL NUMBER OF ANTS SWARM OVER HER FEET. SHE STARTS TO SING.

KENDRA Oh sweet to walk in pilgrims way, leaning on the everlasting arms.[5]

SHE STUMBLES BUT KEEPS GOING INTO THE DISTANCE.

INTERIOR. THE DOME. HUBBS AND LESKO, VERY HOT AND TIRED. LESKO IS DRAWING ON A GRAPH PAD. HUBBS IS UNSUCCESSFULLY TRYING TO GET HIS BOOTS ON HIS SWOLLEN FEET.

HUBBS You must go. We must show them man will not give in.

LESKO Did I tell you I have figured out their first message? The dot is you, they want you.

HUBBS They shall soon have me.

LESKO I'm sorry Hubbs, it's not going to happen your way.

LESKO GOES TO THE COMPUTER TO SEND HIS MESSAGE. HE SEES KENDRA'S NOTE TO THE SCIENTISTS, 'YOU'RE FREE NOW' SCRAWLED ON A COMPUTER PRINT OUT.

LESKO Kendra!

EXTERIOR. OUTSIDE THE DOME. HUBBS, BAREFOOT, STAGGERS AWAY FROM THE DOME, ONE ARM HANGING LIMPLY BY HIS SIDE. LESKO FOLLOWS HIM AND ATTEMPTS TO HOLD HIM BACK. BLINDED BY THE REFLECTORS HUBBS FALLS INTO A MAN TRAP. MILLIONS OF ANTS EMERGE FROM A GRID OF HOLES ON THE WALLS AND SMOTHER HIM.

LESKO LOOKS INTO THE HOLE HELPLESSLY. HE BEATS HIS FIST ON THE GROUND.

LESKO Hubbs, Hubbs, Hubbs! Goddamn you, Hubbs!

EXTERIOR. DESERT. MIDDAY. LESKO IN A PROTECTIVE SUIT STRUGGLES ACROSS ROUGH GROUND, SPRAYING THE ANTS FROM A BACKPACK. HE FALLS, HIS VISOR CRACKS, HE GRADUALLY TAKES OFF THE SUIT.

LESKO (voice-over) I would still like to believe that, given time, we could have come to an understanding, some rational accommodation of interests, some agreement. But that's not the way it's going to be. We have only one chance, a direct assault on their queen.

EXTERIOR. DESERT. LESKO IN JEANS AND T-SHIRT LOOKS DOWN ON THE TYPE OF CONICAL STRUCTURE WE SAW AT THE START OF THE FILM.

LESKO There you are.

INTERIOR. THE QUEEN'S LAIR. LESKO SLIDES DOWN THE SLOPE AND LANDS IN A CLEAN, SANDY GEOMETRIC SPACE. THINGS SLOWLY EMERGE THROUGH THE SAND. AT FIRST THEY SEEM TO BE FEELERS, BUT THEY ARE KENDRA'S FINGERS. SHE RISES UP FROM THE SAND AND MOVES SLOWLY AND CONFIDENTLY TOWARDS LESKO.

LESKO They wanted us.

INTERIOR/EXTERIOR/SPECIAL EFFECTS. KENDRA EMBRACES LESKO AS THEY ARE SWEPT UP IN A TRIPPY SEQUENCE OF SUPERIMPOSED SUNS, INSECT EYES,

YOGA POSITIONS AND HANDS. THEY ARE A NEW ADAM AND EVE. HAND IN HAND THEY STAND LOOKING AT THE SUNRISE WITH THE ANTS.

LESKO (voice-over) We knew then we were being changed and made part of their world. We didn't know for what purpose. But we knew we would be told.

AS THE SUN COMES UP THE WORDS 'PHASE IV' APPEAR AT THE BOTTOM OF THE SCREEN.

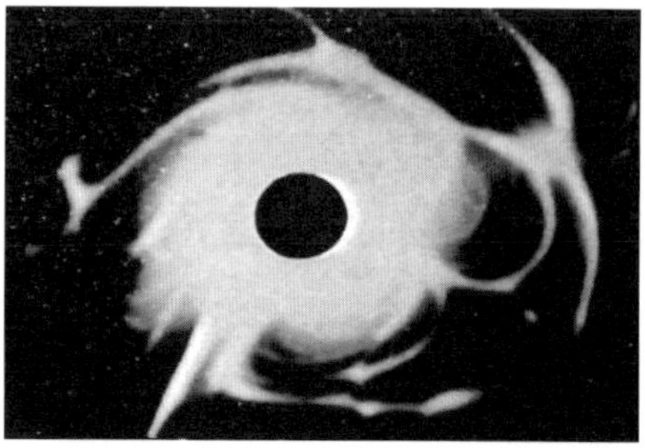

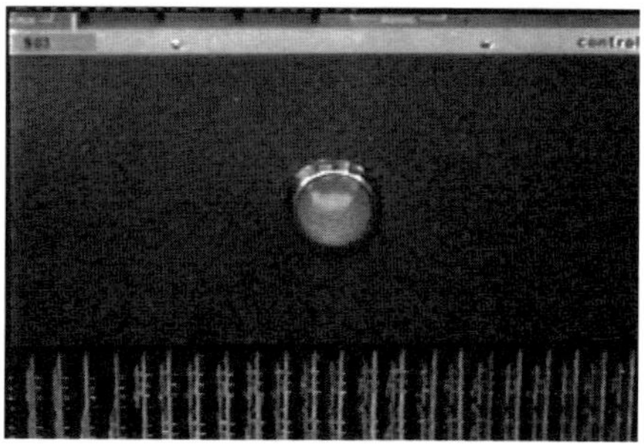

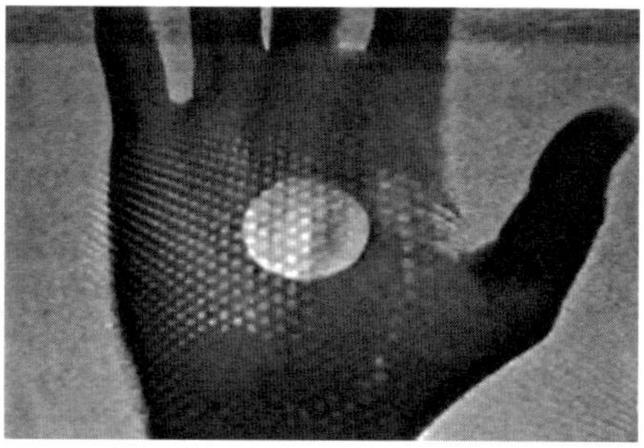

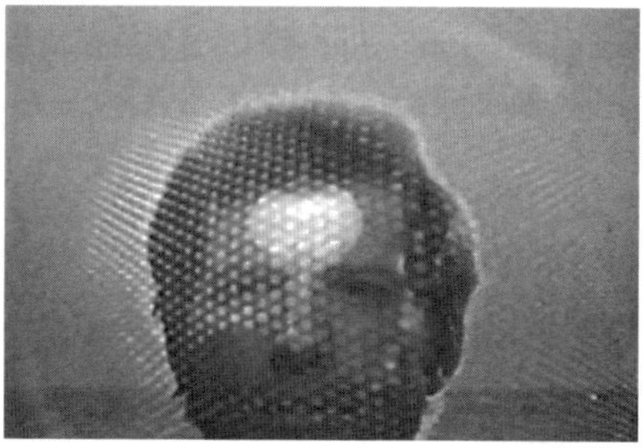

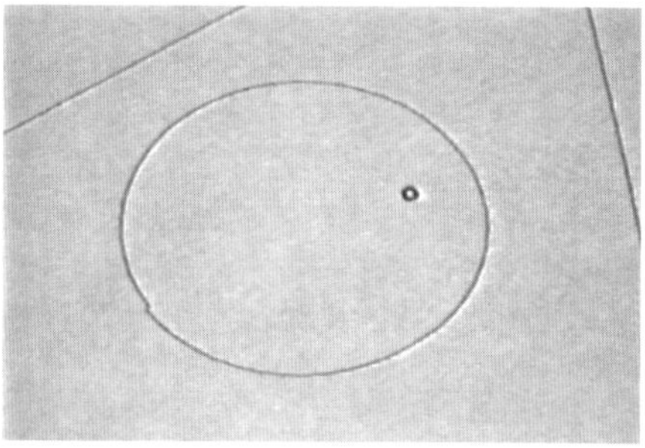

NOTES
1. The titles for the film are so minimal they barely exist. At various points in the movie the same type appears, telling us that we are entering Phases II and III. The actual title of the film appears only in the closing credits: we do not enter Phase IV until the movie is over. Apparently Bass was contractually obliged to use an LA firm for the titles, though presumably he had editorial control. This may be why there aren't any titles as such. See Arnold Swartzman, 'Saul Bass—Anatomy of a Mentor', in Baseline 22, 1996, pp. 17–24.
2. Like Bass's other films the movie does have a logo, but a much more subtle one than, say, The Man With The Golden Arm. The circle which opens the movie as a globe in space permeates the film, reappearing in the centre of the screen again and again, variously as the moon, a gun barrel, the sun, a red warning light, and most importantly as the ants' final message to the humans. The circle is at once all-encompassing and yet so minimal as to be almost absent.
3. This may well be a graphic design in-joke.
4. A nod to Luis Buñuel's Un Chien Andalou. Life magazine's review of the film noted: 'There are sequences in Phase IV that seem to have been lifted intact from a surrealist's fever dream.'
5. 'Leaning, leaning, leaning on the everlasting arms', sung with unforgettable menace by Robert Mitchum as a murderous preacher in Charles Laughton's Night Of The Hunter (1955).

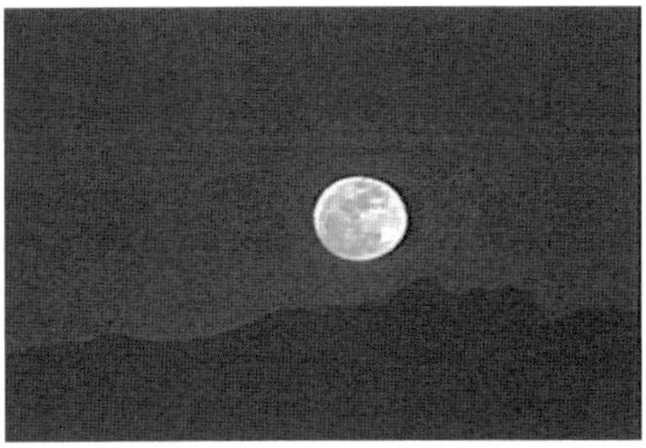

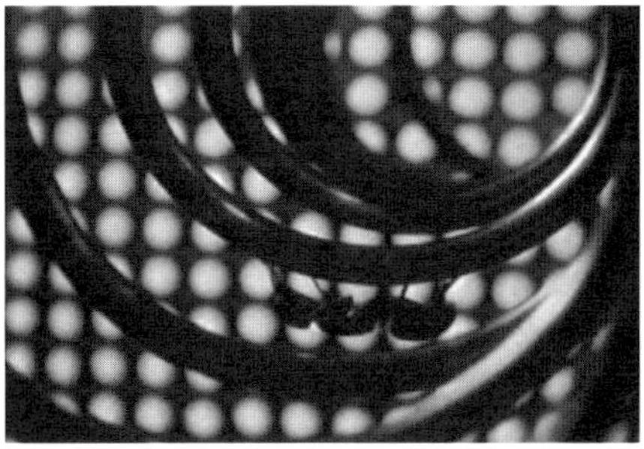

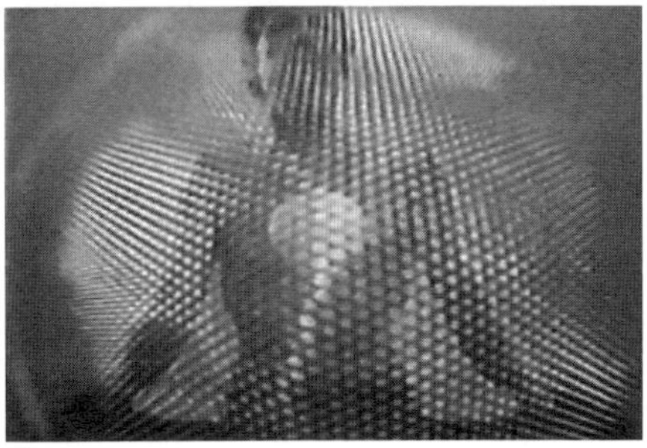

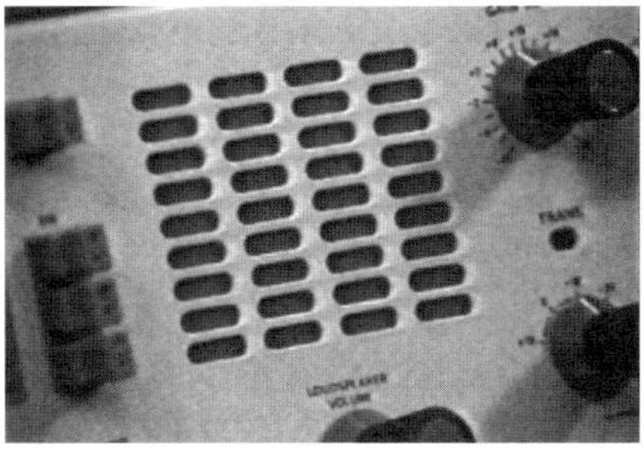

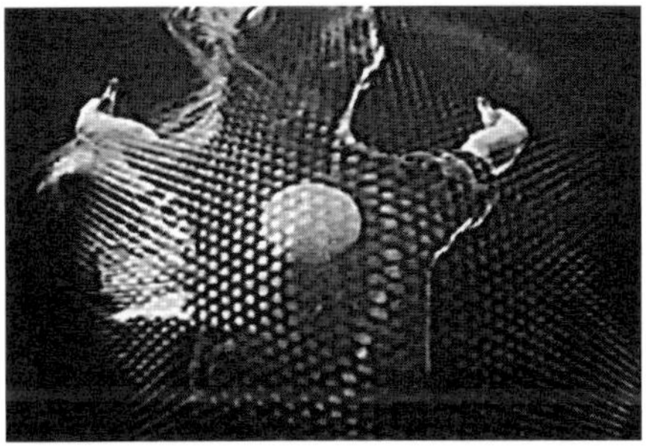

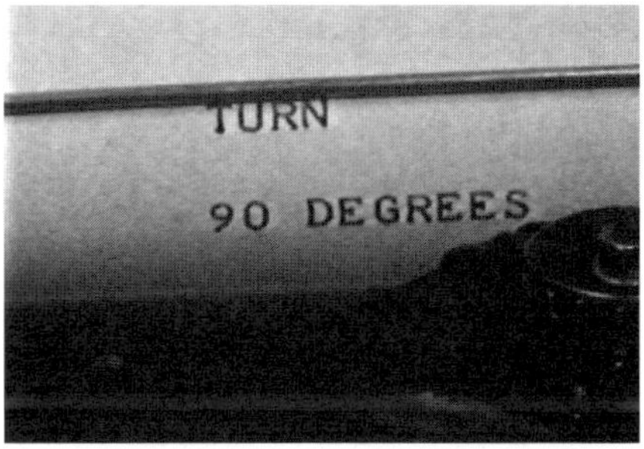

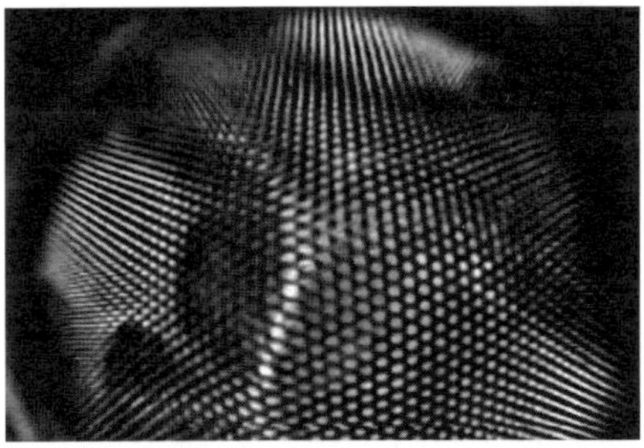

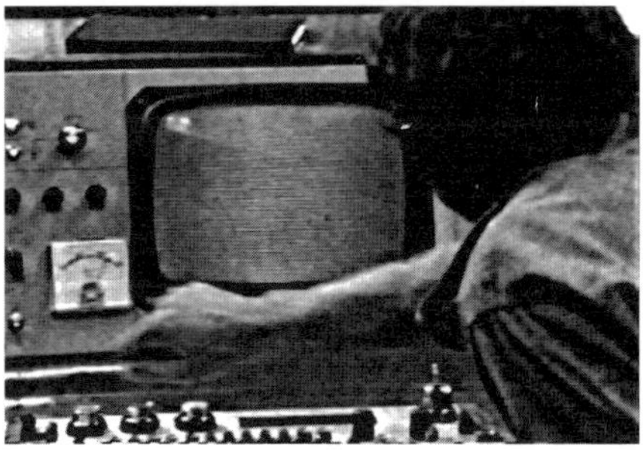

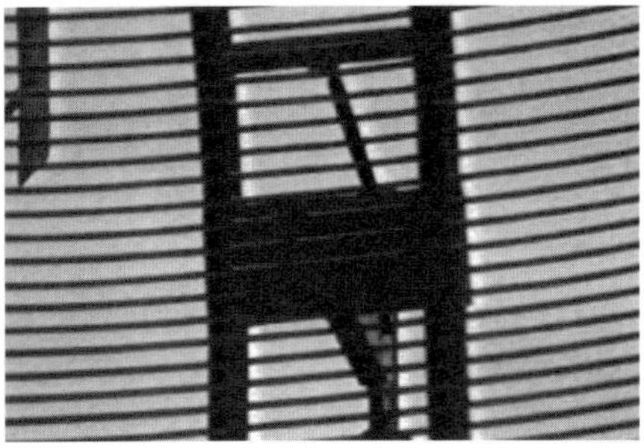

All stills from Phase IV

DIRECTED BY SAUL BASS

Notes on PHASE IV by Gerry Beegan

Saul Bass is best known for his great film title sequences. His career stretched from the fifties, with Carmen Jones (1954) and The Man With The Golden Arm (1955) to his work for Scorsese in the nineties, Goodfellas (1990) Cape Fear (1991) The Age Of Innocence (1993) and Casino (1995). He had a long-term collaboration with Hitchcock, producing titles for Vertigo, Anatomy Of A Murder, and North By Northwest. But Bass also managed to infiltrate the movies themselves. The shower scene in Psycho—perhaps the most celebrated scene in Hitchcock's entire oeuvre—was directed by Bass, not Hitchcock. The battle scenes in Spartacus were also his. Of course, what made his title sequences so innovative in the first place was the fact that they were miniature movies in themselves. They have typically been described as prologues to the main film. Scorsese speaks of them as 'setting the tone, providing the mood and foreshadowing the action of the picture',[1] and that was Bass's own stated intention as well, but you could take this a little further and see these mini-movies as parasites on the host film. They have a self contained dramatic life of their own and are often more visually exciting than the full movie that followed them.

I knew that Bass had directed a number of worthy-sounding short documentaries in the 1960s, such as Why Man Creates (1968). With his second wife Elaine he also made The Solar Film, a ten minute short commissioned by Robert Redford in 1981 to promote solar energy. Then there was Quest, a half-hour film based on a Ray Bradbury story. But I had no idea he had ever made a full-length movie until late one night I set the video to record a schlocky-sounding Channel 4 sci-fi movie about ants, and only realised on playing it back that it was Bass's one and only feature film, Phase IV.

Released in 1973, Phase IV is a low-budget movie that wasn't particularly successful in movie theatres. The posters, which I imagine were not by Bass, give the impression of a horrific shocker with rampant ants and lots of blood. But audiences who were expecting a conventional sci-fi horror film must have been disappointed. There aren't any spectacular special effects; the ants don't grow to gigantic size and terrorize Manhattan. Like most of his work the film is extremely minimal, but rather than giving us the fast pace that we might expect from his title sequences, Bass lets the action develop very slowly. There are six actors in the film, but only two have more than a couple of lines of dialogue. There are only three locations. In fact, most of action takes place either in and around a geodesic dome in the desert, or underground in the ants' colony. Crucially, the ants probably have equal screen time as the humans, and they are often more sympathetic than the human characters. Audiences may have been disappointed that there aren't clear good guys and bad guys, and there isn't an obvious message to the movie, nor a tidy resolution. The whole thing is mysterious and open ended; we don't know precisely what got the ants started on their mission, and by the end of the movie we still don't know what that mission is. Phase IV is the unknown.

--

It may not have been a hit at the box office but there is a lot to love in this film, especially its simplicity. The performances, the narrative structure, the dialogue, the way it is filmed, the art direction—all are stripped to their minimalist core. The movie is intensely visual but within a very controlled field. Single objects, ants, hands, trucks, planets, are starkly and simply placed in the centre of the screen. Several of the most dramatic sequences are simply close-ups of ants moving around computer circuits and through machinery. The art director, John Barry, who also shaped the look of A Clockwork Orange and many Bond movies, combines this tense spare quality with distinctly 1970s futuristic elements. He creates some wonderful early computers, huge mainframes with great Spirograph-like screen displays and lots of buttons. There is a fine stately synth soundtrack by David Vorhaus, whose 1969 album White Noise was a pioneering moment in English electronica, and the movie also features 'montage music' by Stomu Yamashta who went on to become a Prog-rock luminary.

The drama and dialogue are safely stripped down: the ants don't have to do much acting and no actual speaking; the humans speak in short, clipped statements, or in scientific jargon. Despite this lack of dialogue this is a film about communication. In fact, the main character James Lesko (Michael Murphy) is a professional communicator. He is an information scientist, a specialist in cryptology who has applied game theory to the language of killer whales. He is a moderay Dr Doolittle, and in Phase IV he and his partner Ernest Hubbs are trying to figure out why these ants are communicating in a new way. Lesko's name calls to mind the caves of Lascaux in France which contain the oldest know visual images, and which, for modernists such as Paul Rand or Philip B. Meggs, mark the beginning of visual communication.

Mainly through Lesko, Bass gives us a compendium of visual and aural languages. At various points in the film Lesko draws a square in the dust with his finger, draws with a pencil and ruler, writes, types on a golfball typewriter, programs his computers, prints on his plotter, reads his punch tape, and analyzes geometric displays. The movie's voice-overs by Lesko and Hubbs consist of taped scientific memos. Most of the film's action takes place in a geodesic dome which is crammed with communication and surveillance devices such as radar, TV monitors, phones and computers. The driving force of the film is the ability, or inability, of characters and species to communicate. Its message is that successful communication is crucial to survival.

Caring and co-operative, brave and even sensitive, Bass made the talkative ants the heroes of the movie. What worries the scientists and what drives the narrative is that the ants are communicating, passing messages from one to the other, organizing and sharing information across traditional tribal divisions. They are always gathering in groups and waving their antennae at each other. The ants use this shared information to undertake grand building schemes. As Hubbs says: 'Think of them building elaborate structures, according to plans which they know nothing of, but which they execute perfectly. So defenseless in the individual, so powerful in the mass'. The first thing they do to announce their presence is to build some towers which look a bit like Artimede light fittings. They then design and build some crop circles. They love geometry, grids, repetition and order. Yet they don't take it too far: the ant structures lack the starkness of high modernism and instead possess a crafty warmth and an vernacular roughness.

Unlike the ants, the humans play their cards very close to their chests. Hubbs, the chief scientist, and the film's bad guy is a bully and a loner intent on deceiving everyone—not only the ants, but also Lesko, the locals, and his superiors back at base. Rather than sharing information like the ants, Hubbs attempts to hoard it in order to safeguard his power. Hubbs is therefore unable to connect and empathize with others. He cannot, for instance, understand Lesko's jokes. In his memoranda to his superiors Hubbs speaks in stilted, clinical, scientific jargon. As Lesko says at the beginning of the movie, 'Only fragments of what he knew got out, he kept most of it to himself, so when I got into it I didn't know a damn thing.' Indeed, the scientists, whose whole business is to know things, remain in the dark for the rest of the movie. Even at the end of the film the humans, including the audience, don't know what's going to happen next. Once Lesko's obscure mission is underway the two scientists rarely communicate honestly or directly with each other. Even though they are supposedly collaborators they prevaricate, avoid answering questions, and repeatedly withhold information. Their longest and frankest conversation occurs when they lie on bunk beds, neither able to see the other.

--

Lesko's final words—'We knew then we were being changed and made part of their world. We didn't know for what purpose. But we knew we would be told'—reinforce the message that it is the communicators and co-operators who will triumph. The human attempt at creating the good life in Paradise City had failed. The tribalism, individualism and class divisions of the old way just don't work. The old self-centred society in which scientists hoard their knowledge will be swept away by a true utopia in which everyone works for the common goal. So the film can be read as a call for a rational, collective future. The ants aren't just communicators and designers: they are workers and comrades.

Working in Hollywood in the 1950s Bass was very aware of the left, and was affected by the blacklisting of alleged communist sympathisers. His first wife was, in fact, involved with members of the American Communist movement. Could Phase IV and its themes of the individual and the group be Bass's response to this?[2] Indeed what does the film's title mean? In Marxist terms the fourth and final phase of human social organization was 'True Communism'. Social organization developed from absolutism to bourgeois democracy; and from bourgeois democracy to proletarian revolution. At some point in the future society would develop from this dictatorship of the proletariat. In 'The Critique of the Gotha Programme' Marx theorized that after the revolution and the dictatorship of the proletariat a pure form of communist organization would develop. In this final phase distinctions of class and of profession would no longer be relevant; instead, all would labour for the good of the collective. In his words:

> In the higher phase of communist society, after the tyrannical subordination of individuals, according to the division of labour, and thereby also the distinction between mental and physical labour, has disappeared, after labour has become not merely a means to live but is in itself the first necessity of living, after the forces of production have also increased and all the springs of co-operative wealth are flowing more freely together with the all-round development of the individual, then and then only can the narrow bourgeois horizon of rights be left far behind and society will inscribe on its banner—'From each according to his ability, to each according to his needs.'

This does sound rather like the ant world which Hubbs grudgingly admires, a society in which each individual works selflessly for the common good. This final perfect phase of communism has never been reached, just as we do not actually reach Phase IV in the film. Phase IV is the utopian, or dystopian, future just out of reach. Bass, who may have been pulled in both directions on this, does not give us a neat answer, but the film suggests that open communication, a communism of information, is the only rational way forward.

--

Coda:

INTERIOR. A SPOTLESS CALIFORNIA RANCH-STYLE KITCHEN. BREAKFAST TIME. THE 1950S TILED WORK SURFACE IS SPOTLESSLY CLEAN. THE OWNER, WHO IS ON VACATION, IS AN OBSESSIVE COMPULSIVE WITH A FEAR OF WATER. CLOSE UP ON SINK AREA. UNDER THE DISH DRAINER IS A SMALL PIECE OF CHICKEN WHICH A THOROUGH CLEAN UP THE PREVIOUS NIGHT HAS OVERLOOKED. SCORES OF ANTS ARE STREAMING TO AND FROM THE CHICKEN CARRYING AWAY TINY PARTICLES OF FOOD. THEIR TRAIL LEADS OVER THE TILES, DOWN THE DRAWERS AND BEHIND THE FRIDGE. A HOUSESITTER, GERRY BEEGAN, SLEEPLESS, TENSE, IN NEED OF A HAIRCUT, WEARING BLACK T-SHIRT AND BOXER SHORTS, ENTERS WITH A COPY OF THE SAN FRANCISCO CHRONICLE. HE SEES THE ANTS.

BEEGAN Little fuckers.

HE BEGINS TO CRUSH THE ANTS WITH INCREASING FRENZY, AT FIRST SWOTTING INEFFECTUALLY WITH THE NEWSPAPER, THEN USING A FINGER AND KITCHEN TOWEL. BUT MORE AND MORE ANTS KEEP COMING. FINALLY, IN DESPERATION, HE RUBS THEM OUT INDIVIDUALLY WITH HIS BARE FINGERS.

BEEGAN Fucking. Commie. Bastards.

NOTES

1. From 'Film by Elaine and Saul Bass', in Idea, 41.241, Nov 1993, pp. 66–71.

2. This would not have been Bass's first left wing film. Stanley Kubrick's Spartacus (1960), for which he designed the titles and the battle scenes was controversial at the time as the book on which it was based was thought to be a metaphor for the coming Communist revolution. The screenwriter was the blacklisted Dalton Trumbo, who was writing under his own name for the first time since his refusal to cooperate with the House of Un-American Activities Committee witch-hunt.

E AND O

Simon Critchley on Samuel Beckett's FILM

> We never know self-realization.
> We are two abysses—a well staring at the sky.
> (Fernando Pessoa, The Book of Disquiet)

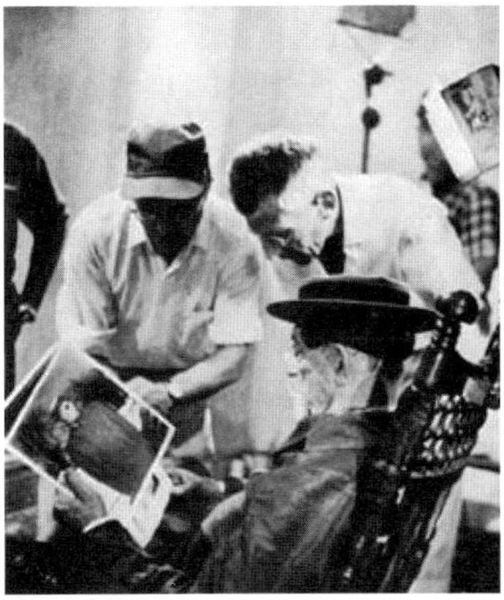

Samuel Beckett wrote just once for the cinema. Film was written in 1963 and first shown publicly in 1965, forty years ago.[1] Film was shot in New York in 1964, with the opening external shots in Lower Manhattan close to Brooklyn Bridge and the rest in Greenwich Village, and it was the occasion of Beckett's one and only trip to the United States. The film was the idea of Barney Rosset, Beckett's New York publisher and legendary editor of the Grove Press in its long heyday from the 1950s to the 1970s. Film was the movie debut of Alan Schneider, Beckett's most trusted, long-serving and long-suffering theatre director in the United States. It stars Buster Keaton in his one of his last movie appearances (he made several B-movie beach movies before his death in February 1966). Beckett said of Keaton that 'he had a poker mind as well as a poker face' and their relationship did not get off to a good start. Schneider tells a story of their first meeting in Keaton's hotel room, where Beckett awkwardly tried to engage in conversation with Keaton while the latter replied in monosyllables, drank a beer and watched the baseball game on TV. Beckett was a huge sports fan and considerable sportsman himself—the only winner of the Nobel Prize for Literature to be mentioned in Wisden's Cricketers' Almanack, playing first-class cricket for Trinity College Dublin—and even went to see the New York Mets at Shea Stadium during his trip to New York. A little sadly perhaps, Keaton was the fourth choice for the role, behind Charlie Chaplin, Jack MacGowran and Zero Mostel. That said, Keaton is excellently cast and his entire physical presence, in particular the extraordinary face with which the movie finishes, seems to carry the entire tragi-comedy of Film. What is sadder than the face of an ageing comedian? We somehow expect a comic's face to be eternally frozen in their glory days; think of the late movies of Laurel and Hardy or The Marx Brothers, where youthful elasticity and energy has given way to wrinkles and clichéd, plodding self-parody.

There is something oddly and deliberately anachronistic about the period in which Film is set. Beckett laconically and typically remarks, 'Period: about 1929. Early summer morning'. What exactly does 'about 1929' mean? This is a typical Beckettian elision. Let's not forget that 1929 was quite a year, with the first presentation of the Academy Awards (Keaton's 1929 movie, which didn't win any prizes, was Spite Marriage), and in October there was a little something down the road from the setting of Film called the Wall Street Crash. Yet, as readers of Beckett will know, many of his novels and plays are set in a comically unreal period between the wars, a world full of bicycles, bowler hats, dark suits, and whimsically anachronistic technology.
The other salient feature about the period in which Film is set is that it is silent; well, apart from a 'sssh' in the opening scene. In the original project for Film, Beckett notes, 'Climate of film comic and unreal'; and he adds that the Keaton character, 'should invite laughter throughout by his way of moving'. Is Film funny? It is certainly not VERY funny and one does not exactly fall about laughing watching it. As one of Beckett's characters in the Trilogy remarks, 'Nothing is funnier than unhappiness, I'll grant you that.' We would do well to keep those words in mind as we watch Film.

The dramatic agon of Film is about 'the agony of perceivedness'. There are a few minor characters in Film: an oddly antique couple with a man wearing a pince-nez and a woman carrying a lorgnon or eye-glass in the opening scene (the woman was originally meant to be carrying a monkey, but I guess no monkeys were available in Greenwich Village in 1964); there is also an old woman carrying flowers in the staircase scene, and some wonderful domestic animals in the scene in the room: a cat and dog, a parrot and a particularly handsome goldfish. The two main characters are E and O: Eye and Object. The Eye is the camera, so that throughout Film we are looking at the Object, or the Keaton character, through the eye of the Eye, as it were. The camera has subjectivity, indeed one might go further—and I will come back to this later—and add that the camera IS subjectivity, or is one side of an essentially divided subjectivity. The drama of Film consists in E's pursuit of O, who is in flight from E. E perceives O and therefore what O is in flight from is being perceived as such, where perceivedness is experienced as an agony.

Although the main line of cinematic perception is E's view of O, the camera's perception of Keaton, there are also crucial moments in Film where O himself perceives others and, in the final scene, perceives E itself. More exactly, O perceives E and sees that O is E itself. Eye and Object, or perceiver and perceived, are the same, or two sides of the same split subjectivity. The two lines of perception are technically distinguished with a filter, which gives a slightly blurry effect, like a muslin cloth.

(WATCH FILM)*

What is Film about? Well, firstly, obviously and stupidly it is about film. That is, it is concerned with the genre of film itself, the nature of the cinematic medium. To this extent, there is not just a laconic economy or simplicity to Beckett's title, but also an arrogance, even a hybris: his one experiment with film is a definition of the nature of the cinematic medium itself. Otherwise said, as Alain Badiou would put it, Beckett is concerned with the GENERIC character of film, or film as a way of giving character to the generic. This concern with the generic is not unique to Film, and one might say that Beckett's work attempts definitions of each of the aesthetic genres with which it engages: the short story, the novel, radio, television and, of course, the play. Indeed, the piece of writing that precedes Film from 1963 is a play called Play, which has many similarities with Film, particularly on the theme of perceivedness. It ends with the line, 'Am I as much as ... being seen'.

This concern with the generic character of film as such—that is, with the nature of moving image—is something that Gilles Deleuze brings out in his writings on Beckett's Film. As far as I know, Deleuze discusses Film in two places: in a short and brilliant text from 1986, 'Le plus grand film Irlandais ("Film" de Beckett)', and a discussion in the first volume of his work on cinema, L'image-mouvement, where it occupies an important transitional moment in the argument of the book.[2] Without going into too much detail, Deleuze sees Film as exploring the three sorts of images that make up the movement-image and which define what he calls the 'general tendency of experimental cinema'. These are the action-image, the perception-image and the affection-image and they can be seen sequentially in each of the three scenes of Beckett's Film. With the action-image, Deleuze refers to the figure of O running along a wall, an image which is, Deleuze writes, '... the first cinematographic act'; with the perception-image we see the character in the interior of the room being perceived from the back on both sides but never face-to-face; and finally, with the affection-image the camera turns around the room to face O and we witness the perception of the self by the self, pure affection or cinematic auto-affection, which culminates in the seeming death and immobility that we see at the end of Film. However, as every reader of Beckett knows, his protagonists rarely die, and it is in this inability to die, this endless living on, that Beckett's entire comedy consists, witness Vladimir and Estragon trying, but failing, to hang themselves in Waiting For Godot. In tragedy, people die; in comedy people live; in Beckett's tragic-comedy people who want to die are condemned to live on. Funny isn't it?

Deleuze sees Beckett's work, both in Film and in the television pieces like Quad, to which he devotes a wonderful interpretation in 'L'épuisé' ('The Exhausted'), as culminating in 'the luminous plane of immanence, the plane of matter and its cosmic eddying of movement-images'.[3] For Deleuze, what is glimpsed in Film and, for him, this defines the essential trajectory of Beckett's work from the early novels to the late

* www.ubuweb.com

drama and prose pieces and which culminates in a cultivation of the soundless, voiceless image, is 'the world before man, before our own dawn ...'. It is here that I would like to mark a disagreement with Deleuze and in what follows I will offer a strongly divergent interpretation. Far from seeing Beckett's work as announcing 'the world before man', I see Beckett as constantly struggling with the irreducibility of the human world. There is no reduction of experience to a time before our dawn, but rather a deathless groping in our all-too-human twilight. I've always found this deathless groping as the source of Beckett's humour noir, yet Deleuze seems peculiarly deaf to both Beckett's sense of humour, his sense of the human, and his sense of humanity's humorousness. Let me explain myself by going back to the beginning and back to the original project for Film, the text that Beckett wrote in 1963.

--

Beckett's Film—and let's say film as such in its generic character—is concerned with a clearly stated and compelling philosophical problem that derives from Berkeley's famous proposition ESSE EST PERCIPI, to be is to be perceived.[4] One might ruminate much on the relation of Beckett to his 17th Century idealist compatriot. But in my view one can easily go awry by reading too much into the apparent philosophical sources of Beckett's work, many of which have their source in the 17th Century, in particular the occasionalism of Geulincx and Malebranche, which exerted a powerful influence over the young Beckett and whom he studied carefully. There is a common fallacy that is oddly and sadly even more widespread amongst non-philosophers than philosophers, that art is somehow EXPLAINED by philosophy. It is not. To be clear, I am not suggesting the cultivation of philosophical ignorance, as I might be seen as arguing myself out of a job. Yet, to interpret an artwork in terms of a pre-existing philosophical or conceptual grid is not to encounter an artwork, it is simply to confirm that pre-existing grid. It is to see through the artwork and not to see it. This problem is particularly acute in the case of Beckett, where his text is nicely littered, cluttered even, with philosophical allusions and passing references. In my view, one should treat these philosophical allusions as red herrings and one must tread carefully to avoid slipping on them. In a particularly irritable and slightly insouciant exchange in a 1961 interview with Gabriel D'Aubarède, Beckett notes,

> 'Have contemporary philosophers had any influence in your thought?'
> 'I never read philosophers.'
> 'Why not?'
> 'I never understand anything they write.'
> 'All the same, people have wondered if the existentialists' problem of being may afford a key to your works.'
> 'There's no key or problem. I wouldn't have had any reason to write my novels if I could have expressed their subject in philosophic terms.'

With those cautionary words ringing in our ears, I'd like to stay with Beckett's words and images as much as I can. If the meaning of Beckett's work were somehow translatable into philosophical terms, then there would be no reason to write a play, a novel or a screenplay. Beckett begins the original project for Film with some general remarks, which are extremely intriguing and very gnomic. He writes,

Esse est percipi

All extraneous perception suppressed, animal, human, divine, self-perception maintains in being.

Search of non-being in flight from extraneous perception breaking down in inescapability of self-perception.

This is Beckett's cinematic variation on the Berkeleyan thesis: if to be is to be perceived, then both the things perceived and the perceiver are maintained in being through perception. Such is the philosophical position that is normally called empirical idealism, which Samuel Johnson famously sought to refute by kicking a stone. We are aware of things, of things perceived, and we are also aware of ourselves, we have self-awareness through self-perception. Now, what Beckett adds to this thesis is revealed in the last sentence of the above quotation: if self-perception is inescapable, then what we are searching for is an escape from self-perception. Beckett's thesis—if we may call it that, knowing that it is not the right word—is that human existence is defined by a search for non-being. Let's note in passing the curious inversion of Spinoza here: the human being is not defined by a CONATUS ESSENDI, by a persistence or striving to maintain itself in being, but rather by a desire for non-being. This desire is displayed in a movement of flight from extraneous perception and from self-perception, a flight from both perceived objects and the self-perceived subject. Yet—and this is the crucial complement to Beckett's thesis—this search for non-being breaks down in the inescapability of self-perception. Despite Beckett's protestations, this amounts to a clear, indeed startling, ontological claim, a claim about what there is: self-perception is what maintains us in being, but what we desire, what we crave, what we yearn for, is non-being, that is to say, the escape from being. Human existence, we might say, is defined by a movement of flight against that existence. That is, the movement or very KINESIS of human existence is defined by a desire to escape the condition that defines our existence. Otherwise said, we are divided against ourselves by a desire that attempts to deny that which makes ourselves the selves that they are. In other simpler words, we are a paradox.

Let's go back to Beckett's words: if existence is defined by a search for non-being and a movement of flight from extraneous perception, then this is impossible and the search breaks down in the inescapability of self-perception. Existence is irremissible and irresistible. Although we are defined by a flight against the agony of perceivedness, the melancholy conclusion is that we are stuck ineluctably with ourselves, that is, with self-perception. We are riveted to the fact of a subjectivity that is divided between Eye and Object, a division at the heart of the self that makes the self what it is and which maintains it in being for as long as self-perception persists. For Beckett, unlike Hamlet, to be or not to be is not the question. It is to be while wanting not to be, and this constitutes a fact to which we are answerable prior to any questioning.[5]

It is this entire existential drama that is being filmed as Film itself. We might say that this is the ontological condition of cinema, of moving images that we perceive and of self-perception. We watch the Object, Keaton, who only IS insofar as he is perceived by the Eye or the camera, and we watch him try to escape perceivedness. Each scene shows him being drawn tighter and tighter into the net of perceivedness, from the street, to the staircase, to the room, to the rocking chair with its gentle to and fro. If there were world enough and time, then it would be interesting to talk about Beckett's spiritual furniture and his obsession with rocking chairs, which is something that can be seen from an early novel like Murphy to a wonderful late dramaticule called Rockaby, where the action—if that is not an exaggeration— consists in a woman rocking in a chair listening to her recorded voice,

> till in the end
> the day came
> in the end came
> close of a long day
> when she said
> to herself
> whom else
> time she stopped
> time she stopped
> going to and fro

The piece ends with the words,

> so in the end
> close of a long day
> went down
> let down the blind and down
> right down
> into the old rocker
> and rocked
> rocked
> saying to herself
> no
> done with that
> the rocker
> those arms at last
> saying to the rocker
> rock her off
> stop her eyes
> fuck life
> stop her eyes
> rock her off
> rock her off.

There is much in Beckett about the movement to and fro, between being and non-being, of being as being rocked, being lolled back and forth or up and down. In Krapp's Last Tape, the wizened, older character listens, as in Rockaby, to the recorded voice of a younger version of himself, who is both more hopeful and more idiotic. The portion of tape to which he listens repeatedly is an epiphanal moment with a lover while punting on a lake,

> I lay down across her with my face in her breasts and my hand on her. We lay there without moving. But under us all moved, and moved us, gently, up and down, and from side to side.

At the core of Beckett's work is this movement to and fro, of a gentle rocking up and down; or, in the words of a slightly later dramaticule, of coming and going.

But I digress. In Film existence is stripped down to its minimum condition, its basic elements: me myself perceiving myself in a rocking chair. Here, when all the animals in the room have stopped perceiving the Object, when they have been covered up, when the picture of God the father has been ripped to pieces, along with the photographs of the Object's life, when all that remains is the gentle to and fro of the rocking chair, here at the end of the film we are confronted with the inescapability of self-perception. The self confronts itself: E perceives O with an expression that Beckett nicely describes as 'impossible to describe, neither severity nor benignity, but rather acute INTENTNESS'. Intentness is an interesting word, which connotes attentiveness, heedfulness, or even care, but without intimacy. At the other end of the line of perception, O becomes aware of E perceiving it and freezes, semi-stands up, appears to scream silently, sits down, covers its face, uncovers its face, covers its face again, and then rocks more slowly until the rocking dies down, to and fro, to and fro, 'rock her off, rock her off.'

Is the Keaton character dead at the end of Film? Au contraire (as Beckett once said when he was asked 'Est-ce que vous êtes anglais?' by an American journalist in Paris). If O were dead, then there would be an escape from perceivedness and self-perception, which there isn't. Life goes on, not on a plane of pure immanence, as Deleuze claims, but on a plane of paradox, movement to and fro, and self-division; the physical human plane rather than some metaphysical airplane. The essential thing is that we go on. As Beckett famously writes at the end of the Trilogy, 'you must go on, I can't go on, I'll go on'; or again, at the end of Worstwood Ho, 'Try again, fail again, fail better'. One goes on in failure. It's not much, but it's human—'a lobster couldn't do it', as Beckett quips. One goes on and that's how it is, Comment C'est, in the title of Beckett's extraordinary 1961 novel. Existence is shaped by a movement of flight that tries to escape that existence, a movement that fails and one begins again, ON COMMENCE, ON RECOMMENCE. How is it? It is to begin, COMMENCER. For me, this is the core of the ethic of courage that defines Beckett's work.

--

What I have said so far amounts to no more than an attempted commentary on two sentences at the beginning of the original project for Film, listed as 'General'. Arguably, this is not stunning progress. But there is a third sentence, which appears to be rather bad news for my interpretation. It reads,

> No truth value attaches to the above, regarded as of merely structural and dramatic significance.

So, after having laid out his ontological thesis, Beckett very casually withdraws it. Now, there is much to be said about Beckett's withdrawals and qualifications. Indeed, I think one can see an entire logic of denial in Beckett. He will say something and then immediately unsay it, letting the affirmation and denial spin together in an antithesis that it would be philosophical bad manners to name dialectics. This is what Beckett calls, and I call in following him, 'the syntax of weakness'. For example,

Live and invent. I have tried. Invent is not the word. Neither is live. No matter. I have tried.

And again,

I resume, so long as, so long as, let me see, so long as one, so long as he, ah fuck all that, so long as this, then that, agreed, that's good enough, I nearly got stuck.

And again,

There I am back at my old aporetics. Is that the word? I don't know.

Throughout Beckett's work, one is presented with a series of self-undoing, self-denying sentences, where the affirmation and its negation unharmoniously chime together to produce the effect of aporia. An aporia is a perplexity, a path that appears to be blocked or criss-crosses into a cul-de-sac, in which we run back and forth like the cat and dog in Film. I have tried to show elsewhere that this syntax of weakness is a comic syntax or the syntax of Beckett's dark comedy. For example, Clov to Hamm in Endgame:

Do you believe in the life to come?

Hamm to Clov:

Mine was always that.

And again, Mahood to himself,

The tumefaction of the penis! The penis, well now that's a nice surprise, I'd forgotten I had one. What a pity I have no arm.

So, it is perfectly characteristic and inconsistently consistent of Beckett to take back in the third sentence what he appeared to advance in the first two sentences. Both the proposition and its negation are to be taken seriously, in a seriously comic sense. If we take another look at that third sentence, we might ask ourselves: what might Beckett mean by saying that his propositions are of 'merely structural and dramatic convenience'? As if what Beckett was writing was MERELY a film, or MERELY a play, or MERELY a novel. As if Beckett were MERELY using his variation on the Berkeleyan thesis in order to produce an amusing cinematic diversion. Unless one might hypothesize that the whole being of Beckett's art is mere: it is the articulation of things, persons and existence itself in their mere being.

--

At a particularly troubled moment in Beckett's life after the death of his real father and separation from his symbolic father, Joyce, Beckett went into psychoanalysis in London with Wilfrid Bion. The analysis lasted for nearly two years, throughout 1934–35, when Beckett was in his late 20s and Bion was a training analyst at the Tavistock Clinic. Not much is known of the detail of the analysis, although James Knowlson produces some extraordinary testimony from Beckett, where he confesses that he found his analysis with Bion utterly engrossing and helped him with the chronic range of psycho-somatic symptoms with which Beckett was suffering: panic attacks, cardiac arrhythmia, night sweats and general feelings of morbidity.[6] There is also no doubt that analysis with Bion helped Beckett to overcome his pathological self-immersion and isolation and begin to connect with other people. However, let me tell an anecdote in this connection. After giving a talk in London to a group of psychoanalysts many years ago, possibly on Beckett, an elderly psychoanalyst said to me afterwards in the pub that Bion once said of Beckett, 'There was nothing I could do with the boy. He was too happy'. Although this is almost certainly apocryphal, it is one of the deepest remarks anyone has ever made about Beckett. Beckett's work is an anti-depressant that works by returning us to what Freud called 'normal human misery' and giving us the courage to endure, to go on, and to go on with a wry and deeply human humour. It is the very antidote to nihilism. But Bion's alleged remark also opens up a can of psychoanalytic red herrings to accompany our aforementioned philosophical ruddy fish. Indeed, one may well want to interpret Beckett's syntax of weakness in psychoanalytic terms, as the pattern of affirmation and negation that is at the core of analytic experience, or rather the pattern of negation that the analyst seeks to interpret. However, I want to look at another wonderful denial slightly later in the original project for Film under the illuminating heading 'Suggestion for room'. It reads,

Suggestion for room. This obviously cannot be O's room. It may be supposed it is his mother's room, which he has not visited for many years and is now to occupy momentarily, to look after the pets, until she comes out of hospital. This has no bearing on the film and need not be elucidated.

This is a very peculiar speech act, wonderful for its banal detail and characteristic because of the denial with which it ends. If the nature of the room has no bearing on the film and need not be elucidated, then why elucidate it, particularly when it bears so directly and obviously in the drama of Film itself and indeed more widely on Beckett's life and work. Recall the aporetic opening words of Beckett's Molloy and indeed the entire Trilogy:

I am in my mother's room. It's I who live there now.

I don't know how I got there. Perhaps in an ambulance, certainly a vehicle of some kind.

It was Beckett's mother who paid for his psychoanalysis in London (psychoanalysis was illegal at the time in Ireland) and whose 'savage loving', as Beckett called it, was at the core of his troubles. It is often only when one's father has died that the full extent of the chronic relationship of dependence on one's mother is revealed.

Mention of mother opens up another dimension of perceivedness, perceivedness by the past. This takes place through the use of the photographs in the closing scene of Film, those anachronistically comic and unreal images that O scans in careful succession. Let me recall the dramatic action here: O is going to his mother's room in order to avoid being perceived.

Question: why would you go to your mother's room if you don't want to be perceived? There would seem to be an abundance of perception and self-perception in one's mother's room. Answer: in order to look after the pets as Beckett suggests in the above note

Question: so, why does he kick out or cover up all the animals? Answer: to avoid the agony of perception by animals.

Question: so, why is O going to his mother's room? Answer: perhaps O lives there now.

Question: is this of merely structural and dramatic convenience that has no bearing on the film and need not be elucidated? Answer: doubtless.

O then examines and destroys the photographs of his life, photographs that he has brought with him in a folder that also begins to perceive him with its two eyelets, which echo the two eye-like holes in the back of the rocking chair. O seeks to eliminate the past and escape into non-being. But, as we have already seen, this is impossible and we are glued ineluctably to ourselves in a way that we can seek to evade, but we cannot escape. To be riveted to the fact of a divided subjectivity is also to be riveted to the past. The inescapability of self-perception is also that of a past that cannot be excised or extirpated.

Note the nature of the photographs in the closing scene of Film: 6 months, 4 years, 5 years, 20 years, 21 years, 25 years and then the aged monster of the antique face of Keaton. In the original project for Film, Beckett suggests 30 years old for this last image, whereas Keaton was more than twice that age at the time of the filming of Film. With the 6th photograph, O pauses and touches his daughter's face with his forefinger. It is hardly a huge movement, just a slight caress of the hand, yet it communicates both tenderness and transience in a way that is more powerful than any grand pathetic gesture. It also reminds us of a crucial aspect of Beckett's work with which I would like to close, namely what Badiou calls its nostalgia for the past, a feeling of tender loss, of lost intimacy and lost time. Far from being some sort of abstract and cold modernist, Beckett's work is marked by an intensity of feeling, at times a sentimentality, for a past whose presence is gone, but which flickers and burns in a way that cannot be torn up in little pieces and thrown on the floor. What might we call this? In a word, SAUDADE, which is a fascinating Portuguese word meaning longing, melancholy and nostalgia. At its core is the experience of an indolent, dreaming wistfulness, an existential lassitude or langour. One can experience saudade for someone, for something, or for somewhere that is dear to one. As such, saudade is a yearning for an impossible object, usually an object from the past, as in the above-quoted passage from Krapp's Late Tape. But Fernando Pessoa, whom Beckett read approvingly in 1969 while convalescing on the Canary Islands, fascinatingly speaks of saudade for the future, which has both an existential and a political significance in his writings. My point is that there is something of this saudade in Beckett's writing, turned towards past and future, a yearning for a lost past and a courageous hope for the future.

NOTES

1. Beckett, The Complete Dramatic Works (Faber, London, 1986), pp. 321–34. Subsequent page references given in text.
2. See Deleuze, Essays Critical And Clinical, trans. D. Smith & M. Greco (Verso, London, 1998), pp. 23–26; and Deleuze, Cinema 1, The Movement-Image, trans. H. Tomlinson & B. Habberjam (University of Minnesota Press, Minneapolis, 1986), pp. 66–70.
3. Although published as a small book in French, together with pieces by Beckett, in English it is included as the final essay in Essays Critical and Clinical, op.cit. pp. 152–74.
4. See Berkeley, 'A Treatise Concerning the Principles of Human Knowledge', part 1, paragraph 3, in Berkeley, Philosophical Works, ed. M.R. Ayers (Dent, London, 1975), p.77–78.
5. Permit me another note of caution about philosophical interpretations of Beckett. Beckett was invited to Frankfurt by Siegfried Unseld, head of Suhrkamp publishers, in 1961. He was obliged to listen to Adorno's interpretation of Endgame, during which the philosopher insisted that the character Hamm was derived from Hamlet. Things did not go well and Unseld describes the exchange: 'Beckett said, "Sorry, Professor, but I never thought of Hamlet when I invented this name". But Adorno insisted. And Beckett became a little angry ... In the evening Adorno started his speech and, of course, pointed out the derivation of "Hamm" from "Hamlet" ... Beckett listened very impatiently. But then he whispered in my ear —he said this in German but I will translate it into English—"This is the progress of science that professors can proceed with their errors".'
6. James Knowlson, Damned To Fame. The Life Of Samuel Beckett (Bloomsbury, London, 1996), pp. 171–82.

Patrick Heron

The colour of genius

PATRICK HERON, who has died at the age of 79, was one of the half dozen important British painters of the twentieth century. Many things contributed to this country's late awakening to the power and importance of modern art after the second world war, but among them Heron's work as painter, critic and polemicist was a key factor.

When Heron began his professional life, the great modern French masters were relatively unregarded here. His painting and writing were seminal in ending an English tradition of narrative, inward-looking figurative painting. He regarded Matisse as the greatest master of the century and would dearly have loved to elevate Bonnard to second place: these were the two painters from whom he drew most.

It was sometimes remarked that Heron got by on his colour; that he was no draughtsman. This was untrue. His drawing was as incisively accurate as that of Ben Nicholson, the friend from whom he inherited the studio overlooking Porthmeor beach at St Ives. But his portraits of the late 1940s and early 1950s, such as the one of Herbert Read, were not successful, and the big compositions, like *Christmas Eve* and *Harbour Window With Two Figures*, were only doubtfully so, though it is unlikely that Heron himself, a great protagonist for his own achievements as well as those of the other painters he admired (Matthew Smith, William Scott, Peter Lanyon and Roger Hilton foremost amongst the British) ever thought so.

These linear paintings were attempts to combine the rigour of Braque's shallow space with Bonnard's tapestry-like "all-overness", to use Heron's inelegant but accurate phrase. But the over-complicated line on the flattened picture plane worked against them, reducing them to an illustrative mode of Cubism. Still, the 1998 Tate retrospective of his work ("20 years too late," Heron remarked), arranged so that the last gallery with the late paintings adjoined the first gallery with pre-war and early post-war work, showed that the elements on which his career would be founded were already in place.

When the mesh of lines dropped away, he was free to concentrate on his abiding commitment, the non-figurative exploration of colour and the effect on the retina of the juxtaposition of pure colours (he insisted on the term "non-figurative": all art, he would say, was abstract).

Patrick Heron was born in Headingley, the son of Tom Heron, an entrepreneur, who moved to Cornwall when Patrick was five to set up a garment factory in three converted fishermen's cottages overlooking Newlyn harbour. This was to blossom into Cresta Silks at Welwyn Garden City, with McKnight Kauffer designing the stationery and packaging and Wells Coates the exemplary modernist shops. Patrick, still a schoolboy, made some remarkably successful designs for the fabrics. If not a prodigy, he certainly had a high talent that dated back to the age of three, as an extant drawing of *Cuistow Old Man* testifies. Before the war, he had a year at the Slade School of Art, but never felt it gave him very much.

Tom Heron was a pacifist; Patrick likewise. His chronic asthma would have excluded him from military service, but he insisted on registering as a conscientious objector and worked as an agricultural labourer for three years until doctors ordered him to desist. He returned to Cornwall and worked for Bernard Leach for the final 14 months of the war. One of his friends was the Guardian journalist Mark Arnold-Forster, who, a few years later, sold him Eagle's Nest, a house with a famous garden high above the Atlantic at Zennor, near St Ives, where Heron had spent childhood holidays.

Heron's move to Eagle's Nest coincided with his move into non-figurative painting, and among his first works of the period were the garden paintings, opalescent meshes of colour streaked and dribbled vertically on to the canvases.

Painting, as he found it in the late 1940s, was sunk in insularity. The Tate Gallery's modern collection, from Impressionism to Fauvism and Cubism, was thin and inferior. It was during this time that Heron was also an art critic for *Arts* magazine of New York, for the New English Weekly and then the New Statesman. He deplored the criticism of John Berger, not because it was Marxist but because it was prescriptive, and he coined the phrase "Art Is Autonomous" for an article he wrote in rebuttal of Berger's arguments.

He stuck to this phrase throughout his life, meaning not that art is uninfluenced by society, but that it cannot be used as a tool within society; that once an artist begins to play to the gallery his work descends to propaganda or pot-boiling. His best criticism was collected in *The Changing Forms of Art*, long out of print when the Tate published another collection, *Painter As Critic*, to make available again some of the most perceptive and trenchant English criticisms of 20th-century modernism.

Heron saved his own propaganda for his later writing, sometimes in ferocious defences of the landscape of the Penwith peninsula against would-be developers or the Ministry of Defence. His most notable piece was the almost 14,000-word article spread over three days in the Guardian in 1974 in which he attacked the marketing of the New York school of painters by galleries and critics, principally the critic Clement Greenberg, who at this stage was actually dictating to painters and sculptors their disposition of forms and colours.

Partly because he had been the first champion in England of the Abstract Expressionists, Heron's word now carried great weight and checked a tendency even, or especially in English art circles to discount the achievement of the St Ives group of painters. But it also confused the issue. In spelling out in dates and paintings how he personally had by several years got in ahead of, say, Morris Louis, with his vertical stripe paintings, Heron seemed to suggest that St Ives and New York were doing the same kind of thing. Certainly there were cross-influences between the two, and the Americans looked at the work of the St Ives group as well as vice versa, but the roots of the Americans lay in European Symbolism and Expressionism, whereas the St Ives group were closer to the English landscape tradition, or, in Heron's case, to the school of Paris.

For a colourist of Heron's generation, the great challenge and exemplar was the Matisse of the *papier decoupés*, the abstracts cut and pasted out of sheets of gouache-soaked paper, like the wonderful *L'Escargot* that Heron saw many times during his visits as a trustee of the Tate. Heron himself made hundreds of small gouaches, deploying a range of colours brushed on with tiny Chinese watercolour brushes — even on the 10ft canvases — originally in adjacent colour areas pushing up to a fuzzy separating edge, though later the edge became a clean break (Heron called himself at this period a "wobbly hard-edge painter").

THE aim, as it had been since Gauguin, Cézanne, and, of course, Heron's beloved Bonnard, was to make all areas of the painting of equal importance; there was to be no such thing as an image laid on a ground — the sum of several images made up the totality of the main image, the finished painting. The variations seemed infinite; but then in 1979 Heron's wife Delia, his childhood sweetheart, died quite unexpectedly. For a time he did not paint at all, then he began afresh a series of paintings which retained the images of his later work but returned to the misty effect of the garden paintings of the early 1950s. Delia had been mainly responsible for restoring and giving new life to the Eagle's Nest garden. Maybe this new approach to painting was the only way left for Patrick to commune with her.

A few years ago, Heron asked me my age. Fifty-six, I told him. "Lucky bugger," he said. He himself had turned 70, but he still had productive years ahead, including the late garden paintings carried right through until his Tate retrospective, the window at the St Ives Tate and Big Painting Sculpture, the project at Stag Place, Victoria, carried through with the help of his son-in-law Julian Feary.

Heron accepted a CBE but rejected a knighthood, for what Downing Street apparently took to be the utterly frivolous reason that it would make him look silly to other serious artists. There has been talk in the family of turning Eagle's Nest into a permanent gallery for Heron's art, something about which he was untypically diffident. But a Heron museum above the Atlantic would certainly be a beacon shining from a great period of British painting.

Patrick Heron is survived by his daughters, Katharine, an architect, and Susanna, also an artist.

Michael McNay

Patrick Heron, artist, born January 30, 1920; died March 20, 1999

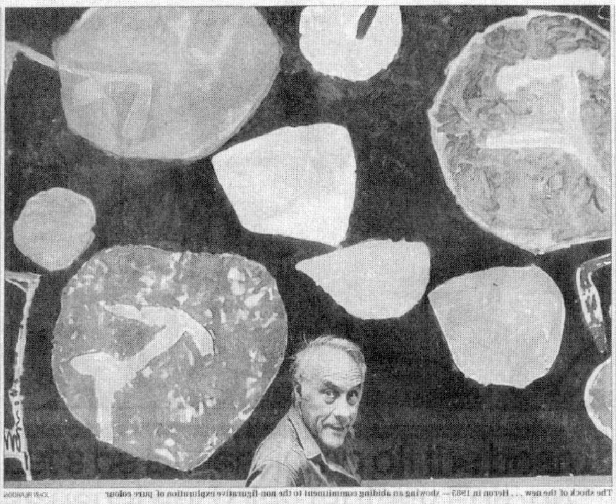

The shock of the new . . . Heron in 1983 — showing an abiding commitment to the non-figurative exploration of pure colour JOHN REARDON

Ravishing beauty born out of chaos

PATRICK HERON, dressed in clashing shades of acrylic knitwear, a lurid purple scarf slung rakishly about his neck, stood on a chair in my art school studio and berated me about colour. I never asked why he stood on the chair. His voice was a bit wheezy, reedy and almost camp. "As I wrote in 1954," he said, "colour is the only direction for painting."

This was 1973, the chair was his soapbox, and I, a cowering student, was his only audience. He reminded me then of a psychedelic Lord Soper. Heron really believed in colour; he was evangelical about colour; he was a walking advertisement for colour and painting.

He was, I thought then, a bit bonkers. He believed, for instance, that cars were nowadays brightly coloured on account of paintings like his, which had attuned the public consciousness to the pleasures of colour, and that the influence of painters — like Bonnard and Matisse — had dragged British culture out of its grey and umber post-war dinge.

Walking with him around his Tate Gallery retrospective last year, he gave me a running commentary on his recent work, punctuated with hilarious impersonations (he was a great mimic) and gossip. But he was most at home amongst the painted stripes, the fuzzy singing lozenges and blobs and his huge "wobbly hard-edge" canvases.

His last paintings were full-on, risky, filled with bright squiggles, painterly flurries and cartoon doodles. They should have been chaotic and absurd, but they were instead open and vital, eye-rocking and beautiful. Heron's retrospective was ravishing, and had the vitality of a much younger artist.

As a painter, Heron got younger as he got older, and couldn't care less for distinctions between abstraction and figuration. The paintings were, instead, filled with life. He briefly returned to portraiture in 1997, with a portrait of A S Byatt, now in the National Portrait Gallery. It looked as if it took just a moment to paint. His last paintings were, I think, very much about capturing the vitality of the moment, and were a celebration of it. He was a passionate and civilising influence on the culture of the past 50 years.

Adrian Searle

Ernie Wise

The one with the short, fat, hairy legs

ERNIE WISE, who has died aged 73 following a triple heart bypass operation, was, with Eric Morecambe, one of the two best-loved comedians Britain has ever produced. They were friends for 44 years, partners for most of that time, and seemed inseparable, like two halves of a whole. When Morecambe was pole-axed for several months by a series of heart attacks in the early 1980s, Ernie, in the words of one observer, "wore the bravely puzzled air of a man trying to scratch a newly-amputated leg". The bespectacled, gangling comic genius died in 1984. After that Ernie soldiered on like the old show-business trouper he was, but, inevitably, nothing he touched could recapture the lustre of his years with Morecambe.

Yet Ernie was much more than Eric's straight man. He was a wonderful comedian in his own right, often winning just as many laughs as his partner. Comparison with Oliver Hardy is not misplaced: Hardy summed up his own appeal as "a very stupid guy who thinks he's a cut above another stupid guy".

Ernie refined this stance and created a brilliantly funny, unique persona for Eric to bounce off: vain, snobbish, puritanical, mean, sexually naive, magnificently smug and given to delusions of artistic grandeur — Ernie: "My mother's got a Whistler." Eric: "Now there's a novelty" — and almost all the humour came from Eric debunking Ernie's pretensions.

The comic and his "feed" were thus equals — a rarity in traditional double-acts. Rooted in the ping-pong cross-talk of variety, Morecambe and Wise were also knowing and sophisticated, with Eric far more laid-back, sexually experienced and streetwise than the pompous, bustling little Ernie. "Don't say that — you make us sound like a cheap music-hall act," Ernie would snap irritably from time to time. "But we are a cheap music-hall act," Eric would respond before looking out at the audience and confiding, *sotto voce*: "This boy's a fool."

In most of their shows they played somewhat less successful versions of themselves — two comedians sharing a flat and all the dull chores involved. Sometimes they shared a bed as well, with Eric sitting bolt upright in his pyjamas, smoking a pipe, while Ernie boasted about the latest "play what I have wrote". The suggestion that they might be gay never arose.

Nevertheless, this air of comfy domesticity brought another subtlety — Eric's basic insecurity — to the act, the impression that if the high-flying "Mr Showbiz" Ernie ever left the nest, Eric would feel very alone. This was reinforced at the end of some of their later television shows, when Ernie would smirkingly accept the congratulations of sycophants while, in the background, a completely deflated Eric, with flat cap, shabby raincoat and carrier bag, would wander out of the studio.

In real life they lived miles from each other — Morecambe with his wife and family in Harpenden, and Wise with his wife, Doreen, a former dancer, in Peterborough. They stayed in different hotels when touring. The deep affection that radiated from the stage or screen could not be faked, however, and the public responded warmly to their obviously close friendship. All good comedians make you laugh, of course, but Morecambe and Wise added something rarer; they made you happy.

Ernest Wiseman was born in Leeds, the son of a railwayman. In the evenings his father sang at local working men's clubs, and Ernie was introduced into the act when he was seven. They were billed as Carson and Kid, and Ernie was required to sit on his father's knee, snivelling audibly while Mr Wiseman sang tear-jerkers such as *Little Pal* and *When Daddy Goes Away*.

Eric Bartholomew (Morecambe's real name) and Ernie Wise first met at an audition for Youth Takes A Bow, a child talent show, when Eric was 13 and Ernie already a member of the troupe. The second world war caused a temporary hiccup in their burgeoning professional relationship: Wise served in the Navy and Morecambe was a Bevin Boy.

They resumed their friendship in 1947 when Morecambe auditioned for the role of "feed" to a comic in Lord Sanger's variety circus at Godalming in Surrey. The comic, ironically, was Ernie Wise, and so the partnership began. At first, their act was a ragbag of styles and thefts: routines borrowed from Abbott and Costello, Ernie doing a bit of clog-dancing, Eric "blacking-up" to sing G H Elliott numbers.

Over the years, however, as they became increasingly useful additions to variety bills up and down the country, the act evolved. Eric was funny, pure and simple. Ernie was funny, too, but had other skills: he was a fine dancer and a good singer. But he thought he was Fred Astaire and Frank Sinatra rolled into one, and it was Eric's job to disabuse him of these notions.

In the 1950s, they were theatre bill-toppers and moved, unsuccessfully at first, into television. It was not until they joined forces with the writers Sid Green and Dick Hills (and, much later, Eddie Braben) in the early 1960s that they were able to re-create their variety success in the more intimate medium. Daringly they abandoned jokes as such, building all their humour from the relationship. "Some comedians reel off jokes as if they've just come out of a book," said Ernie. "There's no future in that. You bring yourself into the public eye, but where do you go from there?"

When they were firmly established as Britain's top double-act, the generous Morecambe was delighted with the laughs Ernie was getting. "It's taken him longer because he's never had the lines before. Now he's becoming a character, a personality." Did Ernie resent all the years he spent without getting good lines? "No. I've always really been a song-and-dance man. I call myself the thin end of sanity. You've got to have some sanity somewhere." Eric: "He might have resented it on a Monday, but when he got paid on a Friday..."

THEIR shows for the BBC and later ITV — still regularly re-broadcast — were comfortingly familiar: some front-of-curtain banter (usually the funniest part of the show), followed by a sketch or two, and then one of Ernie's deliberately atrocious plays, based on classics such as *Wuthering Heights* or *Mutiny On The Bounty*, with guest stars like Glenda Jackson, Peter Cushing and André Previn. Even Harold Wilson appeared in a *Morecambe And Wise Show*.

In the mid-1960s they starred in a number of films that failed to recapture their small-screen personalities, although they were commercially successful because the team was so well-loved. From time to time they returned to their roots, topping variety bills. Live at Southport in the 1970s, their first entrance brought them the kind of reception normally associated with rock stars.

Their popularity had not even begun to wane when Eric Morecambe died. Ernie was devastated, personally and professionally. Years earlier, when Oliver Hardy died, a French newspaper headlined the story "Laurel et Hardy est mort", and Stan, realising the truth of this, never again appeared in public as an entertainer.

Ernie Wise found himself faced with a similar decision, but, poignantly, he was still a comparatively young man and tried to fall back on his old song-and-dance skills. He was in a West End musical and did some television work, but his every appearance as a solo turn only served to remind the public of what had been lost.

This was no reflection on Ernie — he was still regarded with huge affection — but there seemed no real place for him until he became a chronicler of a lost showbiz age, drawing on his vast experience, always ready with a quote or an anecdote about days gone by, a familiar figure at comedy awards ceremonies and the like. Ruddy-faced and white-haired, he spent the 1990s as a father-figure of British comedy, immensely respected.

In their heyday, Morecambe and Wise often finished their stage and television shows by singing their theme song, *Bring Me Sunshine*. Ernie Wise and his dear friend brought sunshine into all our lives.

Stephen Dixon

Ernest Wiseman (Ernie Wise), comedian, born November 27, 1925; died March 21, 1999

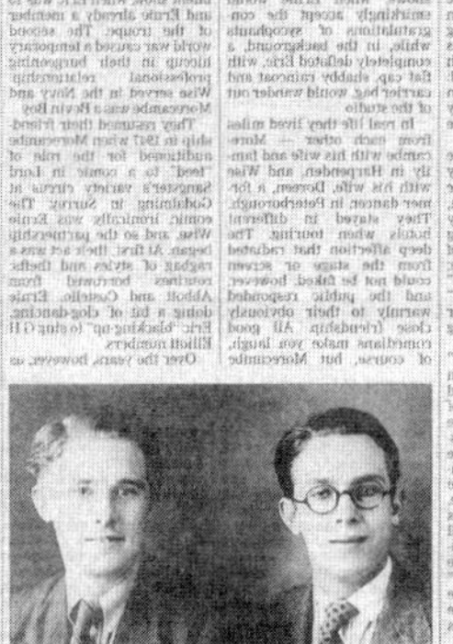

In the beginning . . . two young comics starting out in 1947

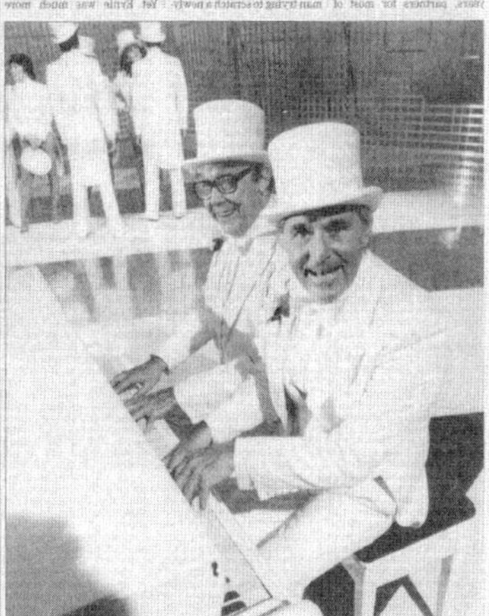

Bring me sunshine . . . Eric and Ernie make merry in a classic Christmas show routine

Corrections and Clarifications, today's birthdays and the Country Diary have been held over

Death Notices

GIBSON, Joan Parker, [illegible]

SHIEL, Louisa (Weeza), [illegible]

In Memoriam

[illegible]

Dame Iris Murdoch

A witness to good and evil

IRIS MURDOCH, the novelist and philosopher who has died aged 79, was one of the best and most influential writers of the 20th century. Above all, she kept the traditional novel alive, and in so doing changed what it is capable of. She was not the heir — as she early and wrongly imagined — to George Eliot, but to Dostoevsky, with his fantastic realism, his hectically compressed time-schemes, his obsessions with sado-masochism and with incipient moral anarchy. Her best novels combine Dostoevsky with Shakespearian romance and love-comedy.

When asked by whom she had been influenced, she was wont to reply she would like to have been influenced by Homer, Shakespeare, Tolstoy, Dostoevsky and Proust. This is not a modest list, and nor is her achievement a modest one.

Iris Murdoch was born in Blessington Street, Dublin, an only child. Her father, Hughes Murdoch, was a minor civil servant — a "gentle, bookish man" she later called him — who came from County Down Presbyterian stock. He had served in King Edward's Horse in the first world war, and, being a cavalryman, had escaped the holocaust of the trenches. Iris described him as a really good man, something whose rarity she only later came to be impressed by, not a religious man in any ordinary sense, a "great inspiration to me and certainly the greatest influence in my life".

The influence was literary as well as moral. "He was a very literary man, he loved books and tales. I could read at an early age. He wanted to discuss books with me, so I was reading Treasure Island, Kim and the Alice stories. These were the first books I remember enjoying, and I discussed them with my father."

One day on the way to church he had met a pretty 18-year old girl, Irene Richardson wanted to train as a singer, and had a wonderful voice. They married, and the singing career languished. Iris inherited a somewhat more uncertain version of her mother's "shebeen soprano", loved a sing-song, and on a small number of public occasions in later life was capable of breaking into song.

Though they all moved to London in her first year, her Irish origins mattered to her. Her only relatives lived in Dublin and Belfast, there were summer holidays in Ireland, and she would claim to feel Irish, even Anglo-Irish, all her life. Her mother could make some claim to be Anglo-Irish in the Ascendancy sense. An early Richardson is recorded in O'Hart's *Irish Pedigrees* as possessing Graybhallock in 1619 — the large property now known as Drum Manor Forest Park. Iris put echoes from her own family history into a few novels. Murdoch lovers will, for example, recall the name Graybhallock, with its County Tyrone connections, from *An Unofficial Rose*.

The first name of Effingham Cooper in *The Unicorn* — which is set in a mythicised County Clare — was that of her maternal grandfather. Nolan, in the same novel, was the grandmother's maiden name. Iris wished to identify with both Protestant and Catholic elements in her family background — one cousin had purportedly become Catholic. The family included another very distinguished woman writer, who wrote under the name of Henry Handel Richardson. In *The Red And The Green*, set in Dublin around the time of the Easter Rising, partly in Blessington Street, and involving a good deal of original research on her part, she invented a mythologised Whig Ascendancy past for herself.

After the Troubles began again in the late 1960s, Iris would say that "one's heart is broken over Ireland". She saw the activity of the IRA, like that of the Communist Party — with which she was briefly involved — as an example of how a few ruthless, opinionated and evil people can maim a whole society. She felt passionately that Irish Protestants had an incontestable right to call themselves Irish. She tried to write about Ireland later, for example while composing *The Book And The Brotherhood* (1987), but found she could do so only partially. Perhaps the twin veins of fantasy and puritanism in her owed something to her Irishness.

Family life at home was a "happy trinity". Iris ascribed to her lack of siblings both a happiness that she only later came to understand to have been exceptional, and also an inspiration to write, as a way of inventing imaginary brothers and sisters: twins abound in the early books. She later said she would not have tolerated a sibling; by then she was cooking up the plot of *The Green Knight* (1993), which depends upon a murderous sibling rivalry, a theme at which she excelled.

She was happy at Badminton, the progressive girls' boarding school which she described as left-wing and high-minded. One contemporary recalled her there as an adolescent, pretty and serious, pricking out seedlings. She learnt Latin and Greek and acquired a love of languages. In later life she would read poetry in French, German, Italian, Spanish and Russian. Indira Nehru (Gandhi) was among her friends; there were scholarships for Jewish girls, so she knew about refugees before the war.

Between 1938 and 1942 she was up at Oxford reading Greats. Kingsley Amis and Roy Jenkins were contemporaries. She went to Eduard Fraenkel's lectures, the great Agamemnon class which went on for years. "She was absolutely captivating," another contemporary, M R D Foot, recorded. "She had personality and that wonderful Irish voice. Practically everyone who was up with Iris fell for her." She briefly flirted with the Communist Party — enough to have her entry to the US on a Rhodes scholarship refused.

Ten days after she had finished her exams she was conscripted as an assistant principal at the Treasury. It was the second part of the Blitz, and Iris, on occasion, took refuge during the bombing in her bath — and listened to the sound and the fury outside. Like William Golding, and perhaps Muriel Spark, the second world war made her think anew about human wickedness and irrationality.

From 1944-6 she worked for the United Nations Rehabilitation and Relief Association in camps in Belgium — she met Sartre briefly in Brussels, and not long after published the first study of his work. She was also in Austria, helping displaced persons. Work meant finding food and blankets, and sometimes a new nationality, for people who were lost and destitute. Some feeling about homelessness and exile, and "an utter breakdown of society", came out of that experience.

THEN she was in love with two victims of Hitler. The first was Frank Thompson — E P Thompson's older brother — whom it was assumed Iris would marry. He was parachuted into Macedonia during the war, and marched with the partisans towards Sofia, Bulgaria. He was captured and executed by the Nazis. A volume of poems by Catullus, and a Byzantine coin found in his pocket, were later presented to Iris by the Bulgarians. The second, the poet and anthropologist Franz Steiner, a scholarly Czech-Jewish refugee, lost both his parents through death in a concentration camp, and suffered a coronary in 1949 from which he never fully recovered. He died in November 1952. "I loved him greatly," Iris later said. "I was with him on the evening before his death. We parted happily in the expectation of meeting again soon. I still miss him." The gentle Peter Saward in *The Flight From The Enchanter* (1956), would seem to owe something to Steiner. That book was completed before the publication of *Under The Net* (1954) and has as much claim to be her Ur-novel. It is full of refugees, and meditates on displacement and uprooting. What are good and evil, what is courage? How is it that a few fanatics — Nazis in Weimar Germany, communists in post-war Europe, the IRA — can drive their cultures mad?

This is an obsession which connects the very earliest of Iris's novels to those novels that were written 30 years later, for example *The Good Apprentice* (1985) and *The Message To The Planet* (1989), with their own Holocaust meditations. The enchanters and magusses of her fiction belong on an international stage, and have always a political dimension.

Had the war not supervened, Iris might have continued her studies as a Renaissance art historian. With her first degree she got a post in Cambridge for a year and then in Oxford, where she taught philosophy from 1948 to 1963. She is remembered as a generous and brilliant teacher — very beautiful, with great big eyes and striking dresses. There was a brief period teaching philosophy at the Royal College of Art in the 1963-67. She found the wildness of the students picturesque, and this gets into the novels of that decade.

In 1952 John Bayley, a humble junior instructor, saw Iris from his Oxford window pedalling past on her bicycle, and fell in love with her at first sight. Even from a distance, he insists, he could tell that she was "mature, sensible, mysterious and humorous". Two weeks later they met at a party, found they both lived in the same street, and bicycled home together. They married in 1956. She cooked for the first fortnight, not well, then he took over.

It was a famous literary partnership. He rose to become Warton Professor of English, published *Romantic Survival*, *The Characters Of Love* and books on Tolstoy and Pushkin. He is also a novelist and an energetic reviewer. Marriage made it easier for Iris to write, because all the events of her imagination were dire and tumultuous, whereas her ordinary daily life could now be calmer. They toured the world, often for the British Council, giving joint lectures. There was a big rambling house in Steeple Aston, succeeded from 1989 by a Betjeman villa in north Oxford, but in a car-free area, quiet and easy for shopping. She sewed like mad, and wore plimsolls to ease the pressure of arthritis, not least when she went to the Palace to collect her DBE.

Under The Net, her first published fiction, was her fourth written one. T S Eliot at Faber had refused a predecessor on grounds of paper-shortage, in terms just sufficiently cold to make her decide not to send him any of the successors. This must count as one of Eliot's less far-sighted critical — and financial — judgments.

The rhythm of around eight months's gestation — "a time of awful torment, when you're dealing with a lot of dead pieces and you have to wait for some kind of animation", followed by about six months writing, once established, did not often vary — unless there was some big piece of philosophy or a play on the way. "No more novels, no more philosophy", she would despairingly cry to friends during the composition. This was a ritual cry, which only turned true towards the end, when her memory started seriously to let her down with the onset of Alzheimer's disease. She seemed proud that she could not type or use a word-processor. She used a fountain pen for two drafts — "One should love one's handwriting", she used to say — and took the second draft in a plastic bag in order personally to deliver it to her publisher.

SHE was loyal to Chatto, with whose redoubtable Norah Smallwood she worked for many years. Carmen Callil called her the queen of Chatto. Once Callil cut one of her books. "Please restore everything", said Iris. She would rather be read by fewer readers who were more intelligent. Callil obliged.

What was she like? There are myths here, as well as truths. She created, in Rozanov in *The Philosopher's Pupil* (1983), one character who feared that after his death he would be wrongly praised as a saint, and seems to have meant this as a whimsical warning about being turned into the Abbess of north Oxford herself. Yet she would answer all fan-mail by hand, with no help from a secretary who — this was her fear — would eat up further time. As a result she was plagued by bores who returned for more. "Pals for life" she once despairingly complained. There were often 12 letters per day and then 300 at Christmas. She helped her mother's window cleaner publish a detective novel. When A S Byatt's son was killed, Iris listened to her and wept, and let her say the things that no-one else would.

It may have been a myth that Bayley was wholly uninvolved in her work during composition. He certainly proposed at least some of Charles Arrowby's whimsical and disgusting recipes in *The Sea, The Sea*. She claimed never to paint from life and would not accept sub-editing. Dogs at least were certainly lifted from life — our blue-eyed collie is immortalised as Anax in *The Green Knight*. She wished to keep herself out of the novel. Yet in Bradley in *The Black Prince* she created one ironic and very un-self-flattering self-portrait. It was said that she would never talk to journalists about her love-life or her kitchen: she did both.

She is read in Japanese and Russian and French, and belongs to her worldwide readership as much as she does to us. The British notoriously underestimate their great artists. We see them as smaller than they are, needing them explained to us by those from outside, and this is one true measure of our provincialism.

A train story: travelling between Paddington and Oxford, she once sat out the hour watching a hungry reader of one of her own novels turn the pages with obvious fascination, oblivious to its author sitting opposite. "Say what you like", she reflected: "I can at least tell a story."

Iris could do more than that. We can now see that, in *A Severed Head* (1961), she prophesied the dionysiac 1960s before they happened: the 1960s seem to have been as colourful and experimental a decade for her as for any of us.

But she had something important to say about desire in human life, generally, and its relationship with goodness. She wrote well about the rivalry between men and about the Oedipal conflict between strong-willed mothers and their Nietzschean offspring. She could capture those moments of startled vision when we see our world without preconception. She could describe the ordinary and make it magical.

A Fairly Honourable Defeat (1970) marvellously retells the story of *Much Ado About Nothing* with a modern-day Christ and Satan added, in South Kensington. *The Black Prince* (1973) is by far the most self-revelatory and yet also the most artificial of all her dark comedies, with its meditation on Hamlet and on the black Eros. *The Sea, The Sea*, which won the Booker prize in 1978, is enabled by *The Tempest*, just as *The Good Apprentice* (1985) is by the parable of the Prodigal Son and *The Green Knight* (1993) by Sir Gawain. All these combine myth with realism, and are built to last.

IRIS wrote Gothic 20 years before Angela Carter, and romance years before David Lodge. It is striking to read the latter's strictures, in a review of *A Fairly Honourable Defeat* as a romance, 15 years before he turned to explore the same sub-genre himself. She helped pioneer writing about homosexuality as merely one part of human life. It is typical of her quiet subversiveness that it is only the gay partnership that survives in *A Fairly Honourable Defeat* — the heterosexual relationships all fall apart under the strain of a typical Murdoch plot. Apart from Mary Renault, few women novelists write with as much conviction from the point of view of male homosexuals, and no other woman writer so well impersonates men.

Indeed she kept a debate about human difference alive, through the bad years when the fools of both extreme right and left had sheepishly pretended that it did not matter, or even did not exist anyway. Human difference also meant moral difference. How is it that some human beings are morally better than others? What is it that might make a man good, even in a concentration camp? Consider Korczak, who gave his life in Treblinka, or Kolbe in Auschwitz, or, indeed, Frank Thompson. How did it come about that in the epoch of greatest political evil, the century of Stalin and Hitler, moral terms had simultaneously been evacuated of any absolute significance by philosophers?

The Sovereignty Of Good (1970), *The Fire And The Sun: Why Plato Banished The Artists* (1976) and *Metaphysics As A Guide To Morals* (1992) have been important to theologians, to aestheticians, and moral philosophers and seem likely to remain so. She could not believe in a personal god demonic enough to have created the world whose sufferings are so clear to us, yet wanted religion to survive, too. She took confession once, and alarmed the priest concerned with her moral passion and her vehemence. She was taught a form of Buddhist meditation also, and wanted Buddhism to educate Christianity, to create a non-supernatural religion. God and the after-life were essentially anti-religious bribes to her. Her vision of the world as sacred looks forward to ecology and the Green movement.

VISITING a cottage I share in mid-Wales in 1995, a cottage which abuts a graveyard, Iris Murdoch asked happily and with much interest: Do you know many of the dead people in your cemetery? Dying was, for her, not simply the intensely significant Wagnerian last moment that Christianity can make of it, but rather an undramatic part of everyday moral life. Redemption meant for her the Buddhist hope that one might gradually, moment-by-moment and day-by-day, learn to perceive less selfishly.

Such a process of learning is necessarily a calling-into-question of what is normally meant by "identity". Indeed, she would often speak of herself as having no strong identity. And yet the capacity so to forget herself depended equally on an unusually strong sense of who she was. In the bar of a train in 1981, an enthusiastic lady greeted Iris Murdoch as Margaret Drabble. "How can you tell," Iris quizzically and patiently enquired "that I'm not Doris Lessing, Iris Murdoch, or Muriel Spark?" "I'd know you anywhere Margaret," cried the enthusiast.

She connected goodness against the temper of the times, not with the quest for an authentic identity so much as with the happiness that can come about when that quest can be relaxed. We are fortunate to have shared our appalling century with her. I count myself among the many who hope to have been taught by her, and who will miss her terribly.

Peter Conradi

Iris Murdoch (Dame Jean Iris Bayley), novelist and philosopher, born July 15, 1919; died February 8, 1999.

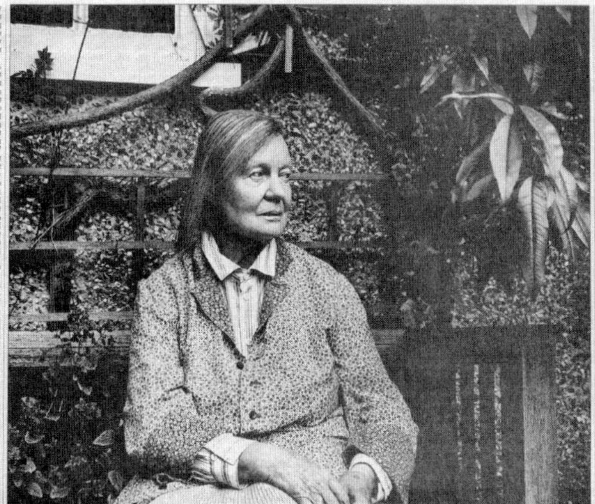

PHOTOGRAPH: EAMONN McCABE

Dame Iris Murdoch ... she connected goodness against the temper of the times

Death Notices

CORRECTIONS AND CLARIFICATIONS

Birthdays

Joe Williams

Nothing but the blues

THE image-making industry might now be a respiratory system supporting every celebrity, but it never meant much to Joe Williams, one of the best-loved, least-hyped, and least affected of all jazz singers. Williams, who has died at the age of 80, after walking out of the Las Vegas hospital where he was being treated for a respiratory ailment, was one of the Count Basie Orchestra's most celebrated vocalists. A singer of immense sophistication and range, he consistently proved throughout a long career that the direct and unvarnished art of the blues continued to have immense potential for every generation.

As a singer, Williams could display the majestic forthrightness of the early blues shouters yet have a thoughtful, elegant and subtle jazz tone on standard songs and ballads. It made him an ideal front man for the bluesy jazz of the Basie band and ideally equipped for the solo career that followed his tenure with it. Like Billy Eckstine, the first black pop star in the 1940s, Williams coupled the earthiness and vigour of the blues with an instrument-like facility on more complex materials.

He had an acting life too, playing Bill Cosby's father-in-law, Grandpa Al, on The Cosby Show in the 1980s. Williams and Cosby (a lifelong jazz fan) were close, and the reminiscences Williams told as Grandpa Al were often true accounts of his former life after his move to Chicago.

But the blues were Williams's roots. Like the finest exponents of the idiom, he constantly sounded as if he were laying bare the most intimate joys and frustrations of his own life to each listener individually, opening to each night's new audience a window on his soul.

The singer was born Joseph Goreed in Cordele, Georgia and raised by his mother and grandmother. As a child he amused himself listening to jazz and opera on the radio, learning the piano and singing the spirituals he heard at the Methodist church where his mother was organist. Early in his life, his mother took him to Chicago in an attempt to start a new life away from the privations of black life in the Southlands. While she worked as a servant, the teenage Joe sold newspapers, carried ice and perfume and just about any task that would bring in a nickel.

Though Chicago was beginning to lose its sheen as the dominant jazz city by the beginning of the 1930s, it was still a town boiling with music, and the teenage Williams was able to persuade some of the South Side bandleaders to try him out. In the 1930s, at 14, he led the singing group The Jubilee Boys in church performances.

HE made his professional debut in 1937 with the clarinettist Jimmy Noone and also joined tenorsax giant Coleman Hawkins for a while. But his big break came in 1943, when he was working as a security guard at the Regal Theater, meeting the leading jazz luminaries. The Regal's manager spotted Williams's talent and sent him to the Tick Tock in Boston to audition for Lionel Hampton's band, which also had its own powerhouse blues singer, Dinah Washington.

It was while he was singing with Hampton that Count Basie's musicians heard him, and advised the boss to hire him. "I can't give you what you're worth," Basie told him. "But, things get better for me, they get better for you." Basie had been impressed by Williams' big, reverberating sound and a range that extended beyond the traditional limits of the blues, long before he finally hired him.

Yet it was with blues, and particularly the 1955 hit of Memphis Slim's Every Day I Have The Blues, that the Williams-Basie chemistry made its biggest impact on the public. They played together 1954-1961, and Williams often performed with Basie until the bandleader's death in 1984 — the year Williams won a Grammy for best jazz vocalist with his Nothin' But The Blues album. The singer always dedicated his You Are So Beautiful to Basie's memory.

From 1961, Williams went on the road as a soloist, which he continued to do into his seventies. Though in his later years the spine-tingling edge went from his high range and the lustrous smoothness of his delivery began to show a ripple, he retained his old revealing power and gravity and added a contemplative stillness on slower pieces that was almost as affecting as his more tumultuous earlier work. Williams appeared with every kind of band from jazz small groups to full orchestras (he memorably recorded under the classical conductor Robert Farnon in 1993) and applied his musicality, swing and indomitable spirit to every situation.

Into the 1990s, he sang on cruise ships, at festivals and in hotels and clubs, and when he wasn't keeping up his 40-week-a-year schedule, he was on the golf course. He believed his responsibility to an audience was to help it contact "the harmony of life", and said in a 1988 interview: "I remember Edward (Duke Ellington) saying, 'I'm just a messenger boy for God.' Much of what we do comes through us. I thank God for what comes through me."

Joe Williams is survived by his fourth wife Jillean, his son, Joe, and daughter, Anne.

John Fordham

Joe Williams, blues and jazz singer, born December 12, 1918; died March 29, 1999

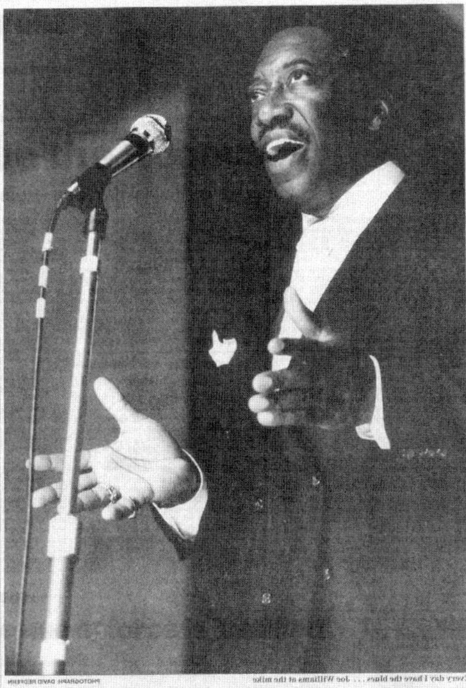

Every day I have the blues . . . Joe Williams at the mike

PHOTOGRAPH: DAVID REDFERN

A Country Diary

WOLSINGHAM, Weardale: Blue sky from horizon to horizon, but an eye-wateringly cold north-westerly tugged ash keys from twigs and sent them spinning across the pasture. Thousands had already germinated in the spring grass — a three-inch tall forest in the making, soon to be cut down by returning sheep.

Dew-covered, spiky leaf rosettes of spear thistle — armed and immune to grazers — and the bright yellow stars of celandines studded the rough grass. Barren strawberry, easily told apart from wild strawberry in spring because its petals don't overlap, was coming into bloom on the ant hills.

It's been a mild winter, but a slow spring, with the first primroses struggling into flower in cold March winds. Holly bushes still carry last year's berries, surplus to mistle thrushes' requirements, while current year's flower buds are beginning to form further along their branches. We followed the path to a muddy sunken lane, etched into the landscape by centuries of passing wheels, hooves and feet, skirting flooded tractor-wheel ruts filled with floating mats of green algae, generating rafts of oxygen bubbles in the sunshine.

Our destination was a Scots pine plantation, to look for red squirrels that still survive here in dwindling numbers. When we arrived the signs were good: piles of freshly shredded cones around pine stump feeding tables — but no squirrels. So we pushed on to the end of the track, into a sheltered oak wood where we could just sit and listen.

You can hear spring dawning: blackbird song echoing through the trees, the squeaky sounds of displaying peewits in the pastures, bubbling calls of curlew courtship from the moorland edge and the chattering of fieldfares passing overhead, buffeted by March winds and leaving just as the blackthorn in the hedges is coming into blossom.

PHIL GATES

Birthdays

Anna Coote, director of public health, the King's Fund, 52; **Prof Kay Davies**, geneticist, 48; **Chris Evans**, broadcaster, 33; **Prof Roderick Floud**, economic historian, 57; **Sir Anthony Gill**, chairman, Docklands Light Railway, 69; **David Gower**, cricketer, 42; **Sir Nicholas Henderson**, diplomat, 80; **Ali MacGraw**, actress, 61; **William Manchester**, US historian, 77; **John Morris**, cricketer, 35; **John Murdoch**, director, Courtald Institute Galleries, 54; **Jane Powell**, screen actress, 70; **Charles Price**, broadcaster and former US diplomat, 68; **Steve Race**, broadcaster, 78; **Dr Richard Repp**, historian, 65; **Debbie Reynolds**, actress, 67; **Bryan Robertson**, writer and broadcaster, 74; **Arnold Sidebottom**, cricketer, 45; **Rosemary Spencer**, ambassador to Holland, 58; **Sheila Whitaker**, director, London Film Festival, 63; **Dafydd Wigley**, MP, leader, Plaid Cymru, 56.

CORRECTIONS AND CLARIFICATIONS

IN A DIGEST of world media comment on the Kosovo crisis yesterday (What the world's media say, page 5), we wrongly gave the name of an Albanian opposition newspaper as Press Review. The organ in question is called Albania.

THE CHESS board on the cover of G2, March 29, was the wrong way round: rotate through 90 degrees to place it in the correct position, with a white square bottom right. The diagram of the game between Bloodgood and Borgar on page 4 was wrong, with both bishops on white squares.

IN A report about controversy on the Isle of Wight over the change in use of a building from a pub to a private house, page 5, March 22, we said: "Unusually, an inspector from the Department of the Environment has been called in to head the public inquiry." The DoE say it's not unusual. It is what they usually do.

It is the policy of the Guardian to correct errors as soon as possible. Please quote the date and page number. Readers may contact the office of the Readers' Editor by telephoning 0171 239 9589 between 11am and 5pm Monday to Friday. Surface mail to Readers' Editor, The Guardian, 119, Farringdon Road, London EC1R 3ER. Fax: 0171 239 9897. e-mail: reader@guardian.co.uk

Death Notices

ANSTEY, John [illegible]

[illegible]

POTT. [illegible]

[illegible]

David Manners

Frightfully good luck in Hollywood

DAVID Manners will always be associated with one of the greatest of horror films, Tod Browning's Dracula (1931), starring Béla Lugosi in the title role. Manners, who has died aged 97, played Jonathan Harker, the rather stiff fiancé of the Count's prime victim, Mina.

What one remembers most about him is a closeup of his neck as his beloved, now a vampire, stares hungrily at it. Just as she is about to strike, the hero protects Harker with a crucifix. In the finale, Harker rescues Mina from Dracula's castle crypt. "We thought he'd killed you, dear Mina," he says. "The daylight stopped him. Oh, if you could have seen the look on his face." Although it was Manners's most famous role, it was the least interesting in the film. His good looks and youth — he made his last film at the age of 35 — kept him in tailor's dummy parts.

His best role was actually in the all-male Journey's End (1930), his first film. Based on the play by R C Sherriff, set in the first world war trenches, it was also the debut feature of British-born director James Whale, who would make his reputation with Frankenstein. Manners had charm as Second Lieutenant Raleigh, an 18-year-old who thinks it's "a frightful bit of luck" to be assigned to the company of Captain Stanhope, whom he hero-worships.

Manners claimed to be a descendant of William the Conqueror, but he was Canadian, born in Halifax, Nova Scotia, and splendidly christened Rauff de Ryther Duan Acklom. He was related, on his mother's side, to Lady Diana Cooper and the Duke of Rutland, and on his father's side to Sir Arthur Conan Doyle.

After touring with Basil Sydney's theatre company in 1924, he made his Broadway debut in Dancing Mothers, starring Helen Hayes. The stage manager was George Cukor, with whom Manners became close friends, and who directed him in the film version of Clemence Dane's A Bill Of Divorcement (1932). It was Katharine Hepburn's first film, and Manners, already with a dozen pictures behind him, gave her great encouragement on the set. He played her fiancé, rejected because of madness in her family. He and Hepburn were to be reunited (although he had a minor role) in his last film, A Woman Rebels (1936).

Manners had made an impression as the caliph in the first of three versions of Kismet (1930), and as one of four injured flying aces desperately living it up in Paris in William Dieterle's The Last Flight (1931). In the same year he managed to avoid sentimentality in his performance as a blind pilot saved from suicide by Barbara Stanwyck in Frank Capra's The Miracle Woman.

Manners was fetching in a toga in the Eddie Cantor musical Roman Scandals, and in The Warrior's Husband (both 1933), and played the title role in The Mystery Of Edwin Drood (1935). But it was on Universal horror movies that his reputation rested. He again came to the rescue of the heroine in The Mummy (1932), starring Boris Karloff. In The Black Cat (1934), he is the husband of a woman about to be Karloff's sacrificial victim.

In 1936, having earned enough money, as well as having inherited a decent amount, Manners gave up acting in order to write two novels and two well-received philosophical works. He returned to the Broadway stage a couple of times in 1946: in Maxwell Anderson's problem play Truckline Cafe, and in Oscar Wilde's Lady Windermere's Fan.

Manners, who was married briefly, lived for some years with the writer William Mercer in Pacific Palisades, where the couple ran an art gallery. He had been a regular visitor to George Cukor's gay Sunday salons at the director's West Hollywood mansion. In the last few decades, he lived a reclusive life in Santa Barbara, occasionally being tracked down by fans.

Ronald Bergan

David Manners, actor, born April 30, 1901; died December 23, 1998

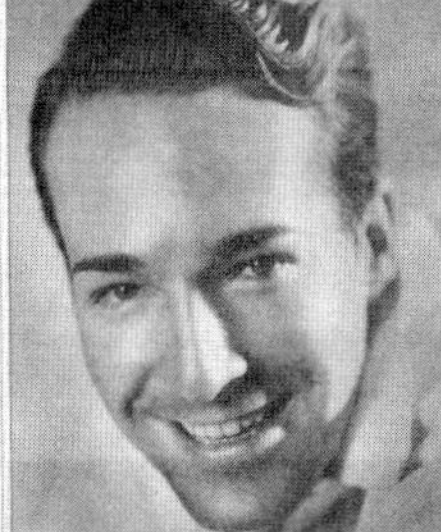

Manners . . . a short lifetime in tailor's dummy roles

Peter Hammond

Orthodox views on architecture

THE priest, writer, teacher and artist, Peter Hammond, who has died aged 78, self-effacingly concealed his learning and talent. His book about the Greek Orthodox Church, The Waters Of Marah, is a ground-breaking portrait of a church in its community and a brilliantly observed travel book about a country recovering from civil war — where a monastery kitchen has cats "lean as idyllic saints". When he observed that "Kastoria reveals its secrets only to those who are prepared to spend several days scrambling up and down the stony paths below the 19th century metropolis", the reader can be sure that author had done so.

Peter was born in Bromley. War prevented him going to the Royal College of Art. Instead he spent four years as a rating on corvettes decoding radio messages on North Atlantic convoys. In 1946 he went to Merton College, Oxford to read history and won a scholarship to research in an Orthodox Christian country, spending two years in Greece's eastern northern mountains, after which came The Waters Of Marah.

Back in Oxford, Peter was ordained and became general secretary of the Anglican and Eastern Church Association. He organised the translation from the French — and did the lion's share of the work — on Vladimir Lossky's The Mystical Theology Of The Eastern Church. The work was a revelation in the English-speaking world and remains the best introduction to the subject.

As vicar of Bagendon in Gloucestershire, Peter co-founded the interdenominational New Churches Research Group, which discussed how modern architecture could be made to work for church "congregations". The group inspired his book Liturgy And Architecture, and also Towards A Church Architecture, with him as editor, and author of its first essay.

HE WAS eloquently sceptical about Basil Spence's Coventry Cathedral, seeing it as a continuation of an exhausted tradition of grand church building. What was needed, he argued, were "functional structures designed to serve and articulate the communal activities which provide the one valid reason for building churches at all".

From 1962 to 1980, he was at Hull College of Art, teaching art, music and literature. In 1980, he returned to Greece and discovered the rocky Cycladic island of Amorgos. He studied its monastery, rich tradition of vernacular architecture and vibrant village life, with the intention of writing a book on Greek landscape, architecture and community. Throughout the wind-battered Amorgos winter, he lived in a modest room, drawing and photographing, clambering over dozens of churches, befriending monks and villagers with such success that he became one of the best-informed of the village gossips. Sadly the book remains unfinished.

He never remarried after a divorce, but retired to eyrie-like premises in Lincoln Cathedral close. A stream of people visited that haven of books, drawings and maps, thick with tobacco smoke, the aroma of sturdy soups and good conversation. He was made a canon and took an active interest in the conservation of the cathedral.

Only with his death did many people realise what a great presence he had been in their lives. He is survived by his former wife and three sons.

Thomas de Waal

Peter Hammond, priest, writer, artist, born February 24, 1921; died March 1, 1999

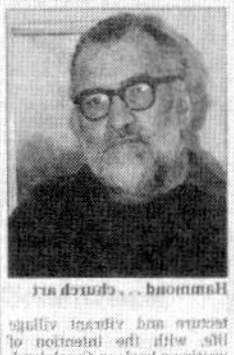

Hammond . . . church art

Group Captain Peter Johnson

No victory through air power

NOT until the mid-1960s did the name of Group Captain Peter Johnson, who has died aged 90, mean anything to me. But a senior retired RAF officer who could write as interesting and original a book as Neutrality: A Policy For Britain had to be worth a visit, since I had never heard it suggested before that a Swiss or Swedish-style neutrality might be appropriate for Britain. A lasting friendship began.

Johnson's life cut through the layers of this century. His father, a remote figure, drowned when HMS Cressy, part of what was then called mockingly "the live bait squadron", was sunk in 1914. (Little Peter, taken aboard a few months before in Portsmouth, had thought the great ship magnificent.) Born with half a silver spoon in the family mouth, Peter was sent to a preparatory school; then, as the family fortunes tumbled, he was sent to the Royal Naval College at Dartmouth where he could, as a naval officer's son, get a free education.

The experience was not happy, and he drifted about in the 1920s as an unsuccessful door-to-door salesman for an unpleasant breakfast cereal called Aviator Wheatflakes. Then, in 1929, he joined the RAF and in 1935 got married.

The League of Nations Union Peace Ballot of 1935 seems to have started his political thinking. Johnson and his wife, Joan, voted for military measures against any country which attacked another. They supported the League and understood Britain's critical role in it.

Theory turned to practice when his squadron was posted to Aden to be ready to counter Mussolini's forces should they attack Abyssinia. His idealism took a hard blow with the Hoare-Laval Pact which gave the Italian dictator a green light. Johnson said: "My country's leaders had deceived the world (and myself) into believing that we were engaged on a crusade, only to find that we were the victims of a back stairs intrigue."

Johnson took a civilian job while remaining in the RAF reserve. In 1939, he returned to full RAF life as a trainer of pilots and then commanded a Lancaster bomber squadron. The story of this is recounted in The Withered Garland (1995), a very modest book in which his personal bravery is allowed no part. Progressively his doubts about the legality and morality of what he was doing increased. "I was being ordered to lead my squadron to be the spearhead of a large force of bombers on a mission of a type which had continually been rejected by the British people and their rulers as inhuman.

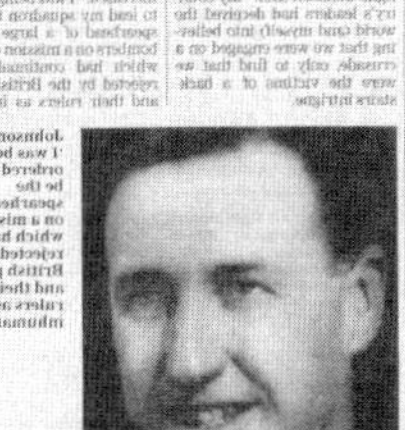

Johnson . . . 'I was being ordered to be the spearhead on a mission which had been rejected by the British people and their rulers as inhuman'

criminally infringing the rather shadowy concepts known as the laws of war."

This made it harder for Johnson, when sent by Air Chief Marshal Harris to Germany to assess the effects of such bombing. He had to conclude that, despite all the killing, the results had never been as successful in damaging military capability and civilian morale as had been claimed. He was too honest not to admit that the condemnations of the Nuremburg war crimes trials might well, in other circumstances, have been applied to him.

After the war he became director of civil aviation in Germany and then civil air attaché at the British Embassy in Bonn until he retired. Though retirement is hardly the right word. His books, and writings in the New European, were always worth reading. He travelled extensively visiting the United States at the age of 88 and was planning a visit to North Africa at the time of his death.

His increasing deafness was a source of frustration but, never lost for a sense of humour, he knew how to turn it to advantage. He had a son and daughter from his first marriage. In 1982, he married Ann Bower.

Bruce Kent

Group Captain Peter Johnson, born November 13, 1908; died February 12, 1999

Obituaries

Publican and chronicler of Irish immigrant life on the building sites of London

Jerry O'Neill

A Victorian upbringing in Limerick was the real origin of JM O'Neill's highly regarded novels of London low-life. The father of "Jerry" O'Neill had been a postmaster in a provincial city riven by class divisions. So, as a youngster, Jerry holidayed in Lahinch, the Clare resort much favoured by the professional classes, rather than in Kilkee, which was the watering place for the Limerick proletariat.

In his adult life, Jerry, who has died aged 77, was to ennoble and mythologise both English and immigrant Irish labour on London's building sites. Through his play God is Dead on the Balls Pond Road, and his first novel Open Cut, he brought to artistic life that previously unknown culture of "de buildins".

In Jerry's own words, this was "... a world of kerbside sweat and manpower, open-cut tunnels, timber shafts looking across a chaos of traffic. Gangs eat in cafes if they can, wait for the evening of warmth and drink, sleep like the dead until the alarms explode them into another day."

Death and maiming were regular. "Smashed cadavers pulled into the daylight, hardly wept over, coffined with raised glasses and whip-rounds, sent to the limbo cemeteries of Finchley and Leytonstone." Jerry O'Neill knew that world, as a hiring agent for John Murphy, one of London's biggest Irish contractors. Before that experience, he had spent 30 years as a nomadic bank clerk, kicking off from a first job in Kilrush, Co Clare, moving to Ulster, where he played football for Newry Town under an assumed name (neither the bank nor other local elements would have tolerated "in goal: JM O'Neill").

Wanderlust took him abroad, banking for Barclays giving him a passage to Nigeria and Ghana, observing "the fag-end of Empire", a milieu he exploited in the novel Commissar Connell, whose lead character was described by one reviewer as "a fugitive Irish gone native". It was a description that might have suited the itinerant O'Neill himself. He settled in London, living and loving the capital, especially the river run of history along Rotherhithe, where he was to set his novel Canon Bang-Bang.

This was a black and funny book about a bent priest who was nearer to God than his pursuing superiors, all of them intent on depriving him of a golden inheritance of development acres in Docklands. O'Neill used his insider knowledge of building, banking and even religion to create truly original characters, sliding about in a landscape washed by the permanent Thames.

In 1967, he became landlord of the Duke of Wellington pub in Islington. Before his writing was published, and during his tenure of 13 years, Jerry managed to retain and expand the local clientele with his avuncular landlordism, dispensing charity to the needy, handouts and hospitality for births, weddings and funerals and "Art for the Culchies". A defunct snooker-room became, on alternate nights, an Edwardian music hall and a folk kitchen, and at weekends turned into a real live theatre, where some gritty plays of London immigrant life were performed.

There, too, when the glasses were tidied away, Jerry repaired to work in secret on his early two books, with what a friend once described as "demonic energy that could survive the ramshackle carnival of running a London pub".

When Open Cut was published, the second novel, Duffy is Dead, was already completed. At 65 years of age, he was on his way in a longed-for new adventure, making sense of his variegated life, in those novels that some reviewers seized upon, praising him in ways that suggested he might become a minor literary cult.

He lived long enough to pen another three novels; and long enough, too, to return to that Limerick and Kilkee, so long avoided, with his devoted wife, Mary. She bore him five children, of whom four survive.

Kevin O'Connor

JM (Jerry) O'Neill, novelist, playwright and publican, born September 27, 1921; died May 21, 1999

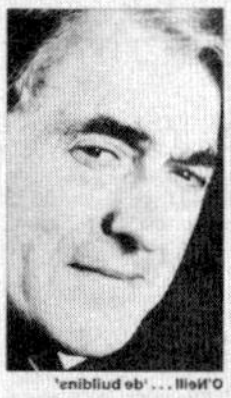

O'Neill ... 'de buildins'

Tottenham Hotspur's great push-and-run team inside-right

Les Bennett

Les Bennett, who has died aged 81, was a salient member of the exciting "push-and-run" Tottenham Hotspur football team of the early 1950s. A glory of that team was that so many of its players were Londoners who had grown up with the club, and Les was just such a local.

He was born not far from White Hart Lane in Wood Green, one of a family of 12. As a boy, he was an Arsenal fan and was a ball boy at the 1932 Cup Final, where he must have shared in the dismay of Arsenal fans, seeing their team beaten due to the so-called "over the line goal", scored when the Newcastle United inside-right, Richardson, pulled the ball back after it had run out of play, enabling the Newcastle centre-forward, Allen, to score.

Bennett's footballing talents showed early. As a schoolboy, he played for Wood Green, Middlesex and London schools. But it was Tottenham, rather than Arsenal, who spotted and signed him as a promising inside-right in August, 1935.

Until then he had been working in his family's plastering business. He joined Tottenham's "nursery" team at Northfleet, turning professional only in May, 1939, when he was already 21. In November he made his first appearance in the senior team, in a wartime League match against Watford, scoring a hat trick.

Bennett was five feet ten and a half inches tall, lean and well-built, and an inside-right of notable ball skills, though he did have the sometimes perilous habit of avoiding a tackle by turning back with the ball. He was called up into the army during the second world war and travelled widely: from Northern Ireland to Burma, India to Egypt. He was picked by the Northern Ireland League, was an England reserve, but he never won a full England cap.

After the war, he gained a regular place in the Spurs attack, and was ideally suited to the push-and-run, one touch, game introduced by Arthur Rowe, Spurs' pre-war captain and centre-half, when Rowe became manager in the summer of 1949. The attack, a team consisting of Walters, Bennett, Len Duquemin, Eddie Baily and Les Medley, was spectacularly successful. It romped through the Second Division in that 1949-50 season, scoring 81 goals, of which Bennett, in 35 appearances, got 14.

The following season saw Spurs take the Championship. By then, Bennett had a challenger for his position in Peter Murphy, but he played 25 times and scored another seven goals. Earlier, he had three times been top scorer for Tottenham in Division Two, with 15 goals in

> The team romped through the Second Division in that 1949-50 season

1946-7, the first "official" post-war season, and 19 goals in the two ensuing campaigns. Later, he moved to West Ham United where, in a year and a half, he scored another three League goals in 26 games. Bennett went on to be player-coach with Clacton Town and in 1959-60 with Romford.

West Ham used him for a time as a scout. He would turn up for a match at White Hart Lane, wearing a happy grin, and announcing, in his strong North London accent, "I'm spying!" Later he returned to Clacton to manage a caravan site, became a security guard at the University of Essex and, on retiring in 1984, came back to live in Tottenham in 1997.

Les Bennett can be glimpsed in the 1947 James Mason film Odd Man Out, directed by Carol Reed, as a pedestrian who suddenly reveals footballing skills.

He is survived by his ex-wife Kathleen (they married in 1951 and divorced in 1987), and son Colin.

Brian Glanville

Les Bennett, footballer, born January 10, 1918; died April 29, 1999

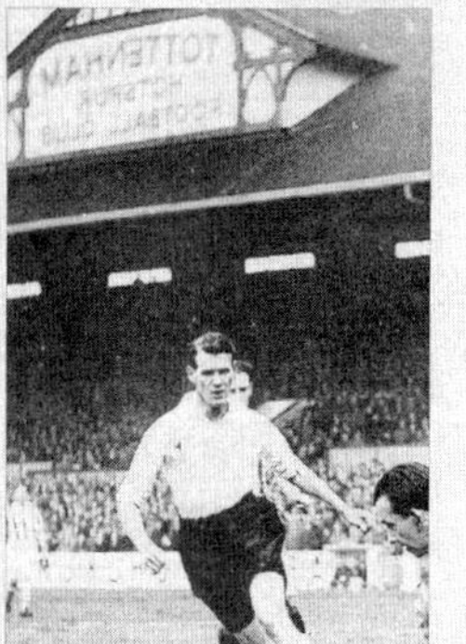

Bennett ... three times top scorer for Spurs

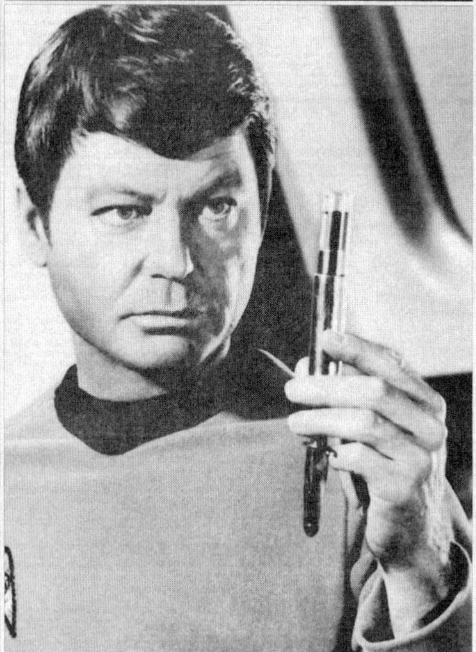

'I'm a doctor, not a ... ' insert job description of choice ... Kelley as McCoy aboard the Enterprise

DeForest Kelley

Star Trek's doc, boldly going where no medic has gone before

DeForest Kelley, alias Dr Leonard McCoy, the medic of the USS Enterprise in the original Star Trek series, has died aged 79. He is going to be missed at the fan conventions. There was something about Kelley's crusty and caustic doctor, nicknamed "Bones", that gained him a huge and affectionate following from those who adored Trek, from its very first episode on television in 1966 to the feature film Star Trek VI: The Undiscovered Country, in 1991.

The character of Dr McCoy was set up to provide the plain-spoken balance between the impulsive Captain James T Kirk (William Shatner) and the cool Vulcan logic of Mr Spock (Leonard Nimoy). Among the many catch phrases from the series that have entered the language was McCoy's line, addressed to Kirk, when asked to cope with the trials that beset the Enterprise on its mission in fairly deep space: "Damn it, Jim," he would say with exasperation, "I'm just a country doctor." There were many variations on that ("not a lawyer"; "not a bricklayer").

The Atlanta-born Kelley, son of a Baptist minister, had actually planned to become a doctor, just like the uncle who had delivered him. But his family could not afford to send him to medical school and Kelley, who sang in the church choir, began performing on local radio shows. (One of the rare examples of his singing in the movies was his rendition of Row, Row, Row Your Boat in Star Trek V: The Final Frontier, 1989). He also worked as an elevator operator and an usher and later performed on the stage. It was during the run of a play that he met Carolyn Dowling, his wife of 54 years, who survives him.

After serving in the Army Air Forces in New Mexico during the second world war, he was transferred to Los Angeles to act in a US navy training film, Time to Kill. A Paramount studio scout saw him in the film, which led to a three-year contract with the studio in 1947.

Kelley made an impressive feature debut as a man who believes he has committed murder under hypnosis in Fear In The Night, an excellent film noir based on a story by William Irish. However, his Southern drawl, sour expression and somehow mean eyes, set in a definitely lived-in face, got him cast as a heavy in the TV westerns of the time (The Lone Ranger, Gunsmoke, Bonanza) and on the big screen.

Among his most notable roles employing that scowl professionally were those in Tension At Table Rock (1956); as Morgan Earp in Gunfight At The OK Corral (1957), in The Law And Jake Wade (1958) and Gunfight At Comanche Creek (1964). He might have continued in relative obscurity had it not been for a meeting with TV producer Gene Roddenberry, which catapulted him into the 23rd century.

In 1966, Roddenberry asked Kelley to a screening of the original pilot show for Star Trek, which starred movie actor Jeffrey Hunter as the captain. Over lunch in the studio commissary, Roddenberry offered him a choice of two roles, one of which he described as "this green-painted alien". Kelley, who had no taste for science fiction, chose the other role — that of the ship's resident surgeon — not imagining that the series would ever become a cult.

Kelley appeared in almost all the episodes over the next three years, prepared "to boldly go" where no medic had gone before, helping the bridge command crew to survive alien infections and phaser shoot-outs, even if bit players and extras were famously expendable onscreen.

He didn't mind being typecast, and enthusiastically attended as many fan conventions as he could get to over the years. The only thing he seemed to dread were the negative reviews that greeted some, although not all, of the six Star Trek movies, beginning with Star Trek: The Motion Picture in 1979, before the first Enterprise crew were replaced on the big screen by The New Generation. "We've heard it a hundred times, that Bill's getting fat and I'm looking like death," remarked Kelley, who was 71 when he was beamed down for the last time. But the last of the series grossed a healthy $70 million.

Sadly, someone else has to pronounce the words that he uttered on so many occasions. "He's dead, Jim."

Ronald Bergan

DeForest Kelley, actor, born January 20, 1920; died June 12, 1999

Making history at the OU

David Englander

The Open University's David Englander, who has died from cancer aged 49, was a brilliant historian who made a specific study of housing and social reform, poverty and poor relief. Among the subjects his work reflected were the experiences of soldiers in both world wars and of immigrant Jews in Britain.

With his wife, Rosemary, he set up the Charles Booth Centre for the History of Social Investigation, producing publications such as Retrieved Riches (1995) and the forthcoming edition of Henry Mayhew's Victorian survey of London Labour And The London Poor.

There was a CD-Rom database of the Booth Poverty Notebooks, and a CD-Rom-based undergraduate course on Booth's work in investigating poverty in the 19th century.

Englander was born in Chicksand Street, Whitechapel, the son of a cabinet-maker, and he was regarded as backward at school. After attending the Brick Lane Talmud Torah, the Brady Club, Hanbury Street, and Robert Montefiore Primary School, he failed the 11-plus, and went to Robert Montefiore Comprehensive School in Vallance Road.

There he blossomed under the attention of the headmaster Rhodes Boyson and of other influential teachers. When Boyson told his mother that her son should have a bright future at university, she blurted out: "Are you sure this is my David you're talking about?"

In 1970, David graduated in history and politics from Warwick University, where he had been greatly influenced by the historian EP Thompson. After study at London University's Institute of education, he taught history at Dame Alice Owens school, returning to Warwick in 1972 for his MA and doctorate. In 1976, he won a junior research fellowship at Corpus Christi College, Oxford. He was an enthusiastic member of the Labour History Society and of the board of its bulletin.

David joined the history department of the Open University in 1979, rising to become reader. He loved the variety of the work, from studies of Rabelais and the 16th-century to the comparative economic history of Britain and the US, and from Jewish history to the study of the wars of this century: he enjoyed the excitement of researching and writing.

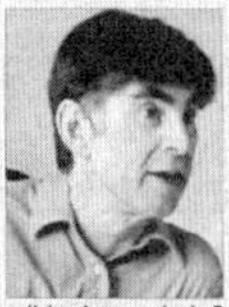

Englander ... past societies

It was at the OU that he met the historian Rosemary O'Day. Theirs was an exceptionally happy marriage: they shared the same sense of humour and scholarly concerns and outside interests in art, music, literature, and wildlife.

Rosemary survives him, as do his stepson, and two sons.

Arthur Marwick

David Englander, historian, born June 3, 1949; died April 7, 1999.

Birthdays

Rod Argent, rock musician, 54; **Dr Sir James Black FRS**, Nobel laureate, pharmacologist and medical researcher, 75; **Paul Boateng MP**, minister of state, home office, 48; **Mike Bradwell**, founder, Hull-Truck Theatre Company, 51; **Stuart Evans**, rugby player, 36; **Julie Felix**, singer, 60; **Boy George**, pop singer, 38; **Steffi Graf**, tennis player, 30; **Edna Healey**, writer, 81; **Dorothy McGuire**, actress, 80; **Yvonne Moores**, chief nursing officer of England and Wales, 58; **Lily Savage (Paul O'Grady)**, drag queen, 44; **Jonathan Raban**, novelist, travel writer, 57; **Kathleen Raine**, poet, 91; **Dame Rosemary Rue**, former president, BMA, 71; **Pierre Salinger**, journalist, former White House press secretary, 74; **Antony Sher**, actor and writer, 50; **Prof Lord (Trevor) Smith**, vice-chancellor, University of Ulster, 62; **James Wright**, vice-chancellor, Newcastle University, 60; **Mike Yarwood**, impressionist, 58.

Letters

David Evans writes: I was disappointed to read your recent obituary (May 13) on John Anstey, with its references to his "fortune".

John and I were born and grew up together in the same street in Hendon. In adult life, John worked for my firm for a short period before he began to set out on his career as the leading expert on rights of light and on party walls.

John was not a man to whom money was of great interest and certainly he never sought wealth for himself.

He believed in sharing his success by donating lifeboats and by supporting many other charities, as your obituary pointed out.

He will not be remembered for making money, but for his generosity and for his strong personal convictions, as well as for the eminence he rose to in the surveying profession.

Death Notices

THOMAS, Katrina

Slavko Curuvija

Silencing the insider

SLAVKO CURUVIJA, who has been murdered in Belgrade aged 50, was telephoned a week ago by another Belgrade journalist and asked whether he had had any problems since the start of the Nato bombing. "I'm just waiting," he said. His death may be considered the first political assassination of the war in Serbia proper. It is the culmination of a campaign against the press which has been underway since last autumn, when the Belgrade regime imposed its draconian information law and began silencing non-conformist media.

In the days before the October agreement on Kosovo between Milosevic and the US envoy Richard Holbrooke, Curuvija had used his monthly magazine, European, to publish a scathing attack on the regime's 10 years in power. "Serbia," he wrote, "is dead already." He was fined $240,000.

Curuvija was also editor of Dnevni Telegraf, which he launched in 1996, and which boasted a circulation of 100,000. He had been sentenced to five months in prison for an article about a scandal involving the Yugoslav United Front (JUL) of Mirjana Markovic, the wife of the Yugoslav president. But he had yet to be arrested — instead he was gunned down in front of his house by masked youths who also beat his wife, the historian Branka Prpa. They had a son, Ivan.

However, Curuvija was not part of the clique of independent media and democracy activists. In fact, he was the consummate insider, a sometime member of the establishment close to the regime and the security forces who played the game and lost. A former policeman, he was a large and attractive man who liked to dress well. As a journalist, he was skilful and stubborn. Only a few months ago, he boasted that he spoke on the telephone with Mirjana Markovic once a week, and he fitted in easily with the Belgrade moneyed set.

But his real alliance was with Jovica Stanisic, former head of state security and heavily involved in the military campaigns in Croatia and Bosnia. This past autumn, Curuvija published an article praising Stanisic as a moderate, against violence in Kosovo and in favour of good relations with the renegade republic of Montenegro. But the inside power games shifted and Stanisic was sacked shortly after. Curuvija's telephone calls with the president's wife came to an end.

DNEVNI Telegraf was essentially a tabloid scandal sheet. With big headlines, which the small texts could not exactly justify, it was among the first papers in Belgrade to run sensational "exclusives" on the "terrorist UCK" — the Kosovo Liberation Army. But Curuvija's inside sources meant his paper was also highly informed about the ins and outs of the establishment, and could sometimes touch a nerve.

With his links to the JUL broken, Curuvija adopted an increasingly maverick stance, taking on the profile of a fighter for press freedoms in Serbia. He moved the publication of Dnevni Telegraf to Montenegro, but distribution within Serbia was patchy.

A week ago the regime newspaper, Politika Express, published an article reporting a statement attributed to Markovic that one newspaper owner in Serbia supported the American bombing. A few days later the statement was broadcast on television, and Curuvija was identified as this newspaper owner. A few days later, he was dead.

Tony Borden

Seada Vranic writes: Slavko Curuvija was an outstanding journalist and editor on the newspaper Borba from the mid-1980s till 1994. He was based in Belgrade when I was its Croatian editor, based in Zagreb. I met him for the last time in the summer of 1992, when the situation was deteriorating. On being asked whether he was worried about being a Serb in the Croatian capital, he displayed a characteristic disregard for personal safety, saying, "My family comes from round here — why should I worry?"

A brave, intelligent and perceptive man, he well understood the real reasons for the coming war: it was utterly clear to him that Serbian interests were never imperilled in Bosnia, and that the whole strategic point of the exercise was to build a greater Serbia. At the time of our discussion, he had just come from a meeting in London, where he heard about plans for Serbian aggression from Nikola Koljevic, a leading member of the Bosnian Serb political leadership who later committed suicide. Slavko was only frustrated that he could not do everything that he wanted to with this knowledge, but remained as critical as circumstances permitted.

Slavko Curuvija, newspaper owner and journalist, born 1949; died April 11, 1999

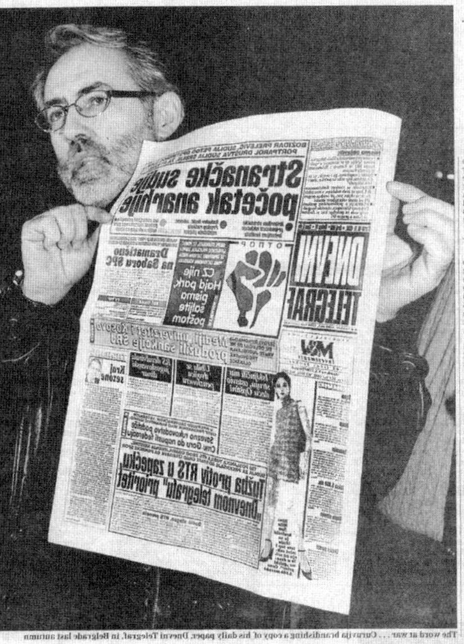

The word at war . . . Curuvija brandishing a copy of his daily paper, Dnevni Telegraf, in Belgrade last autumn

Elie Kagan

Camera campaign

HIS long-time friend, the writer and editor François Maspero, described a first sight of the French photographer Elie Kagan, who has died aged 70, at a demonstration on October 17, 1961 about the Algerian war of independence and the curfew imposed on Parisian North Africans. He was "a strapping great red-bearded fellow, with a kind of mad courage. He was at the head of the procession, using flash for his photographs. His head stuck out above the crowd, he burrowed through like an animal, he reacted viscerally." When Maspero attempted to publish Kagan's images with interviews, he was prevented from doing so, and only a few copies were circulated clandestinely.

Kagan became a victim of his own almost accidental success. He was the sole photographer to effectively cover the events of that night, when 25,000 North Africans responded to a call for a peaceful protest in defiance of the curfew imposed upon them via the hated chief of police Maurice Papon. Kagan's pictures were used to back accusations of police brutality, including indiscriminate beatings, shootings, even the dumping of bodies in the Seine. Since Kagan's death these images have returned to haunt Papon, now belatedly on trial.

An unrepentant left-winger and one-time communist party supporter, Kagan took his first professional pictures at a 1957 Latin Quarter demonstration, and Louis Aragon published them in his *Lettres Françaises*. Kagan's collaborator on his one book, *Le Reporter Engagé* (1989), Patrick Rotman, labelled him a "sentimental third worldist, a convinced left-winger", but he was also engaged by a sense of justice and by internationalist and humanitarian motives.

In the 1970s Kagan worked with Beate and Serge Klarsfeld to rout out clandestine Nazis. This was a means of using photography to express progressive politics, and also a return to his roots as a Jew born to a Russian father and Polish mother, who always regarded growing up under Vichy — wearing a yellow star — as formative of his identity as an all-time survivor.

LATTERLY he looked more and more the rabbinical redhead, with his strong features and tousled beard. In happier days he had taken his self-portrait alongside Charlie Chaplin, Jane Birkin and the philosopher Foucault, among many others. In Gallic fashion, he straddled cultural and political worlds, while remaining essentially a loner.

He was not above shooting mainstream artistes — such as Jean-Paul Belmondo and Brigitte Bardot, Johnny Hallyday and Sylvie Vartan, Alain Delon and Catherine Deneuve — and mainstream politicians, including a further famous self-portrait with François Mitterrand. And he was not averse to a little direct action, in true agit-prop fashion. Yet he also had an often surprising range of outlets of his own — including the Nouvel Observateur and Rouge, the Témoignage Chrétien (Christian Witness) alternating with Tribune and Juive (the Jewish Tribune).

Traditional in his working practices, using only black and white film and a 35mm camera, the one-time protégé of Jean-Paul Sartre fell out into anonymity. He died alone in the same small apartment in the 10th arrondissement where he was born. The last story he covered was of a demonstration by a group of disenfranchised citizens, the *sans-papiers*, at the church of St Bernard.

To the end, François Maspero maintained that all he talked about was that unpublished book about the 1961 demonstration. "That night," said Maspero, "was a painful return to his childhood". Kagan left an archive of more than 40,000 largely uncatalogued images.

Amanda Hopkinson

Elie Kagan, photographer, born 1929; died around January 24, 1999

Letter

Michael Randle writes: While Ntsu Mokhehle (Obituary, February 25) will chiefly be remembered for his role in the struggle for an independent and democratic Lesotho, he was also keenly interested in wider international issues, especially the threat posed by nuclear weapons.

In 1959, he participated in the Sahara Protest Team, in which 21 people from Europe, the United States and several African countries attempted to travel by Land-Rovers and lorries from Ghana, through French-controlled West Africa to the proposed French A-bomb test site near Reggan in the Algerian Sahara. Among other participants in that project were the Rev Michael Scott, equally renowned for his commitment to the cause of African freedom and his opposition to the bomb, and the African-American Bayard Rustin, an associate of Martin Luther King and the man who in 1963 co-ordinated the historic civil rights march on Washington.

Ntsu at that time was president of the Basutoland Congress Party, and all of us on the project were impressed by his commitment, powers of oratory and strength of character. I still have a photograph of Ntsu and several others in the team confronting the French officers who were blocking our passage. While the French authorities went ahead and exploded their bomb, the project did much to mobilise opposition to nuclear weapons in Africa, especially in Ghana, where the team's progress was marked by huge open-air rallies.

Anne Evans

Impatient with poverty

ANNE EVANS, who has died aged 69, was a London general practitioner, an early advocate of primary care and community nursing and a woman committed to seeking political solutions to problems of poverty and social neglect.

She witnessed such conditions at first hand on the fringes of St John's Wood, itself a prosperous area of north-west central London, where her father, mother and brother were all doctors in the same practice. Her mother was one of Labour's first women parliamentary candidates, and her brother became a leader of the Labour groups in Marylebone and Westminster. Like them, she believed that food, clothing and good housing were essential in the treatment of working-class families in post-war inner London. The National Health Service had no stronger advocate than Anne.

In 1980, she took a year off to become professor of family health at the American University in Beirut. After witnessing the ferocity of the war in Lebanon, she was drawn, when she returned to London, to the Medical Foundation for the Care of Victims of Torture.

Anne had battled with multiple sclerosis for a decade or more, but cancer took hold, a disease she was able to monitor and confront. Many women — in organisations and individually — are grateful for her humanity as well as her skills over five decades. The day before she died in a Hampstead hospice she insisted, concerned GP that she was, on medical information being found for a fellow patient whose discomfort worried her. In 1964 she was my proposer for the first Greater London Council elections. She remained old Labour — a political animal unafraid of confrontation. She leaves two children and a granddaughter.

Illtyd Harrington

Anne Evans, doctor, born November 3, 1929; died February 9, 1999

CORRECTIONS AND CLARIFICATIONS

THE Global village voice feature, page 13, Travel, April 10, should have referred to Glasgow not Edinburgh as the city where the work of architect Charles Rennie Mackintosh can be seen.

THE Hemingway Bar in the Ritz Hotel, Paris, was wrongly given a second m in an article on whisky (page 28, April 10).

THREATENING letters sent by the Mardi Gra bomber (page 7, April 8) to Sainsbury's were addressed to the company's head of security not Sainsbury family members as we said. Also, Lord Sainsbury of Preston Candover, mentioned in our report, had [illegible] as chairman at the time of the threats.

It is the policy of the Guardian to correct errors as soon as possible. Please quote the date and page number. Readers may contact the office of the Readers' Editor on 0171 239 9589 between 11am and 5pm Monday to Friday. Surface mail to Readers' Editor, The Guardian, 119, Farringdon Road, London EC1R 3ER. Fax 0171 239 9897. e-mail: reader@guardian.co.uk

A Country Diary

CHESHIRE: With so much happening in these early weeks of April, the pages of a country diary look like some sort of catalogue. Sand martins were seen at several of the large meres in the first few days of the month, and these were followed by the first swallows arriving back at their home farms over the Easter weekend. The warm, sunny weather produced a flush of chiffchaffs, so that on April 2 the single bird that had been in the northern woods since mid-March was joined by three more. On April 3 I heard my first singing blackcap, but it pays to be a little bit wary of assuming these are summer migrants — a good number of birds from eastern Europe are winter visitors to Britain and are just as likely to burst into song on a fine day before returning home. No such doubts about the willow warbler, and a colleague tells me he heard the unmistakable cascade of sweet, liquid notes from two of these migrants on April 4 — his earliest ever record. The butterflies also enjoyed the Easter warmth, with the first holly blues on the wing, and I watched a bright comma butterfly sunbathing on a riverside bank — in beautiful condition after spending the winter in some dark crevice.

J M THOMPSON

Brian O'Connor

The health of nations

BRIAN O'CONNOR, who has died aged 69, inspired a generation of orthopaedic surgeons. In 1968 he was appointed director of clinical studies at the Robert Jones & Agnes Hunt Orthopaedic Hospital in Oswestry, Shropshire, a town that had a reputation as the birthplace of orthopaedics. From the outset, O'Connor was determined to enhance it.

He established the Institute of Orthopaedics there as a model for the co-ordination of post-graduate education, research and patient care, and thus attracted talent, nurtured innovation and built a global reputation. With his fellow Australian Jack O'Brien he established the country's first centre for the study of spinal disorders. In 1978 Birmingham University appointed him the first Robert Jones professor of orthopaedics. One of his greatest legacies is the pioneering operating theatre complex that he conceived and brought to completion in 1991.

O'Connor was born in Brisbane, educated at the city's St Joseph's College, and in 1944, at the age of 15, fearing that the second world war would end without him, he briefly signed on with a Swedish merchant ship. Back at school he became a gymnastic champion, and while at Queensland University Medical School he worked as a professional acrobat. After qualification he worked with the Aboriginal communities of Australia's tropical north and then moved to the US and Sweden, where he began to specialise in orthopaedics.

In 1957 O'Connor arrived in Britain. He worked at Stanmore and Mount Vernon hospitals in west London and in 1959 took a master's degree in orthopaedic surgery at Liverpool University. Appointed as senior registrar to the Nuffield Orthopaedic Centre and Radcliffe Infirmary, Oxford, he worked on new hospital admissions systems, which became a national model.

In Sudan, from 1962 to 1964, he established an orthopaedic service and a training programme for Sudanese surgeons. Henceforth, he was dedicated to the creation of an ideal administrative and clinical environment and he continued to work in the developing countries.

O'Connor had an unforgettable sense of humour and tremendous presence. His unique style was expressed with eccentric sartorial flair, and his drive and energy were as memorable as his ability to slice through red tape with a sharply turned phrase. He leaves his wife, Lynette Hunter, four children and four grandchildren.

Katrina Morphet

Brian Thomas O'Connor, orthopaedic surgeon, born September 27, 1929; died January 21, 1999

Eric Stanton

Fetish and fantasy

HAILED as "the father of fetish", artist and strip cartoonist Eric Stanton, who has died aged 72, was America's most provocative and influential post-war illustrator of bondage and domination. For more than 50 years, he developed his imagery of sexually dominant, high-heeled, steely-eyed women for comics, magazines, book covers and to accompany the private fantasy stories commissioned by mail-order customers.

The only gallery exhibition of his artwork, in 1984, at the Danceteria club in Manhattan, attracted more than 4,000 fans. The British painter Allen Jones admires Stanton and his peers for their "expressionist intensity" and "sheer pictorial invention, draughtsmanship and humour". Madonna modelled one of her early images on the Stanton female.

From a Russian family, Stanton was born in Brooklyn. Drawing became his passion from the age of 12, when he started copying the scantily-clad heroines in early comic books. "Since I was only young and not very successful at the art of love, I invented my own little world of which I am king," he said. His tastes gravitated towards such strong female leads as the star-spangled Amazon *Wonder Woman* and *Sheena Queen Of The Jungle*. Damsels in combat and distress were staple ingredients of adventure comics and the pulp fiction magazines from which they evolved.

On leaving high school in 1944, Stanton enlisted in the US Navy and produced an information strip about aircraft recognition for a service newspaper. He would also entertain his fellow sailors by drawing glamorous girls on their handkerchieves.

After the second world war, his first break into paid illustration was assisting newspaper strip cartoonist Gordon "Boody" Rogers in his Long Island studio. Stanton pitched in on backgrounds, lettering and colouring and invented some of the characters for Rogers's idiosyncratic plain-clothes superhero *Sparky Watts* and his hillbilly blonde bombshell *Babe, Darlin' Of The Hills*. During this period, Stanton came across an advertisement by Irving Klaw, New York's self-styled pin-up king, offering "fighting girl illustrated serials" by mail. Confident he could do better, the 22-year-old Stanton offered his services; his 1948 *Battling Women* debut began a 10-year association with Klaw.

In his earliest works, such as *Diary Of A Lady Wrestler*, Stanton concentrated strictly on "fighting femmes", but by the early 1950s, on Klaw's instructions, he started specialising in the bizarre conventions and contraptions of bondage. Entirely self-taught, he studied comic art from 1954 to 1956 at the Cartoonist and Illustrators' School under former Batman artist Jerry Robinson. He later shared a studio with classmate Steve Ditko, co-creator of *Spider-Man* and *Doctor Strange* for Marvel Comics in the 1960s.

Stanton invented many memorable titles for Klaw, including *Girls' Figure Training Academy* and *Madame Discipline*, and scripted the occasional serial, but he mainly illustrated Klaw's and other people's stories. He also worked on Klaw's photographic shoots with their most popular model, Betty Page.

By the more permissive 1960s, Stanton was able to show men in action with his women and tackle homosexual and transvestite subjects. He painted some 300 paperback covers and numerous interior illustrations.

After usually being poorly rewarded and losing much of his artwork, he set himself up as his own publisher in the 1970s as an artist-for-hire to visualise the fantasies of his specialist clientele. In 1997 the German publishers Taschen issued a 330-page art book covering his career, edited by photographer Eric Kroll.

Stanton is survived by his second wife and their two children.

Paul Gravett

Eric Stanton, illustrator, born September 29, 1926; died March 31, 1999

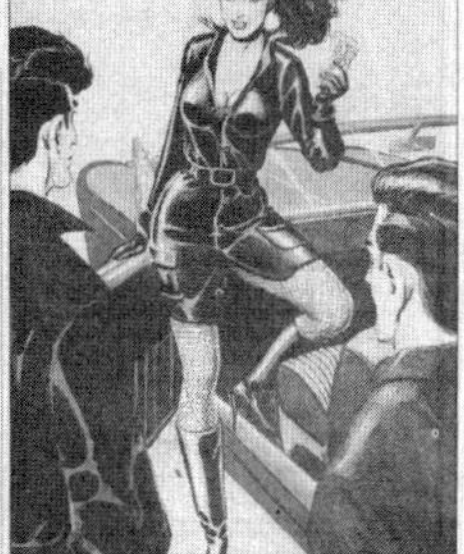
She who must be obeyed . . . fantasies of powerful women and submissive men characterised much of Stanton's work

Birthdays

Stephen Byers, MP, secretary of state for trade and industry, 46; **Alan Clark**, historian, diarist and Conservative MP, 71; **Stanley Donen**, film director and producer, 75; **Edward Fox**, actor, 62; **Prof A H Halsey**, sociologist, 76; **Rosemary Haughton**, writer, philosopher and theologian, 72; **Seamus Heaney**, poet, 60; **Garry Kasparov**, chess champion, 36; **Howard Keel**, singer and actor, 81; **Jonjo O'Neill**, racehorse trainer, 47; **Dame Margaret Price**, opera singer, 58; **Barbara Roche**, MP, financial secretary to the Treasury, 45; **John Swinney**, Scot Nat MP, 35; **Lord (Bill) Wedderburn**, authority on labour law, 72; **Eudora Welty**, novelist, 90; **Sir John Weston**, former ambassador to Nato, 61.

Death Notices

COLES, [illegible]

DANIELS, Geoffrey, [illegible]

ENGLANDER, Dr. David, [illegible]

GOUGH, John Brierley, [illegible]

GUY, Jacqueline Mary (née Needham), [illegible]

LUTTRELL, William, [illegible]

Births

HARDING AND HOLGATE. [illegible]

[illegible]

Obituaries

As deputy prime minister, he loyally defended Thatcher's revolution, but secretly lamented the Tory decline into meanness and greed

Viscount Whitelaw of Penrith

It is a doubly sad irony that Lord Whitelaw should have died, at the age of 81, just as the Northern Ireland peace talks were teetering on the brink of what Tony Blair has called "the abyss". For it was Willie Whitelaw, as the first politician to hold the post of Northern Ireland secretary, who came within a hairsbreadth of achieving a similar breakthrough a quarter of a century ago. The deal he negotiated only came unstuck after Ted Heath brought him back to London in the hope that his legendary skills as a conciliator could work similar magic with the striking National Union of Mineworkers.

As it turned out, even Willie's charm failed to win over the NUM. But many people — and they included Whitelaw — have since wondered whether the Troubles might not have ended if he had been left at Stormont long enough to chair the ill-fated Sunningdale conference.

Charm was the essence of the man: and it was recognised by thousands of people who never met him. They showed their affection by making him one of that relatively small band of politicians who become known by their first names alone. The one word, "Willie", came to conjure up a decent, slightly slow, endlessly courteous country squire, who liked his food and drink and got on with everyone he dealt with — no mean feat for someone educated at that supremely elitist institution, Winchester.

The crucial additional feature of his nature, however, was that the apparently guileless charm was accompanied by a razor-sharp shrewdness. He is widely acknowledged to have been the best Tory chief whip since the war.

Whitelaw might easily have been prime minister if he had been less of a gentleman. Ironically, his failure to do so transformed him into the crucial prop and lubricant of a government which transformed both the nation and the Conservative party in ways which he was later to find thoroughly distasteful. Mrs Thatcher once famously said that "every prime minister needs a Willie"; but for his loyalty, she might well have fallen much sooner than she did.

Whitelaw's whole character, upbringing and experience made him instinctively hostile to most of the values which underlay Thatcherism. His extraordinary loyalty to her accounts for the fact that many of his oldest party colleagues — especially those on its old-fashioned patrician wing — had serious reservations about him. A few were even prepared to accuse him of betrayal.

Whitelaw himself used to offer two explanations for his consistent dedication to his leader. The first was that he owed both Thatcher and the Tory party unswerving loyalty in the difficult circumstances created by the collapse of the Heath government. The second was that he believed he could exercise a moderating influence over the wilder flights of her radicalism — but only if his own conduct could be seen to be above reproach. Both arguments were typical of Whitelaw's emollient approach. But although each supplies part of the story, it cannot alter the fact that the rather unpleasant Britain created by the Thatcher revolution is almost as much a monument to him as it is to her.

Against this background, it can be seen that the watershed in Whitelaw's political career occurred in February 1975, when the so-called "peasants' revolt" on the Tory backbenches forced Ted Heath to stand for re-election as party leader. A senior member of the Heath team, Willie was by then Ted's party chairman in Smith Square. It was already obvious to everyone — save perhaps Heath himself — that the former premier was in serious trouble. The then Mr Whitelaw, though clearly the man best qualified to drag the party back to some sort of unity, decided that loyalty (that word again) disqualified him from standing against his revered boss.

When, to everyone's astonishment, Margaret Thatcher knocked Heath out of the bout in the first round, Willie climbed into the ring to carry on the fight in round two. But by then it was already far too late, even if Whitelaw's indecision had not made a poor impression on a party looking for someone tough enough to win them the next election. In the event, Thatcher beat Whitelaw by a two to one majority.

It remains possible, perhaps even probable, that Whitelaw would have won outright if he had had the ruthlessness to shoulder Heath aside and stand in the first ballot. In the event, he spent an anguished night contemplating his defeat, then pledged his total support to Britain's first woman party leader. It was a pledge he carried out to the letter, even if his famous oyster eyes were seen to water occasionally.

William Whitelaw was born at Nairn, in north-east Scotland. After Winchester he went to Trinity College, Cambridge, where he read history and law, and won a blue for golf. Golf remained a ruling passion throughout his life, and he once declared that he took more pride in becoming president of the Royal and Ancient than in anything he achieved in politics.

He served in the Scots Guards throughout the second world war, winning an MC in Normandy. In his very first battle he saw many of his close friends killed in a matter of minutes — an experience which ensured that he would become a dedicated supporter of European unity.

At first, there was no thought of going into politics. Instead, he resigned his commission in the Guards in order to run the family estates in Lanarkshire. But in those days possession of several thousand acres and an MC was seen in the Tory party as natural qualifications for a parliamentary seat, so before long he was approached to fight the hopeless seat of East Dunbartonshire. After two successive thrashings, he landed the safe seat of Penrith and the Borders, which he held from 1955 until Thatcher dispatched him to the Lords after the 1983 election.

He was soon recruited as a junior whip, and took his first step on the ministerial ladder as parliamentary secretary to the then minister of labour in 1962. Alec Douglas-Home quickly promoted him to the key post of opposition chief whip after Labour's narrow election win in 1964. Heath inherited him from Home, and made him leader of the Commons after his election victory in 1970. From that point onward, Whitelaw never looked back.

It was in 1972 that Heath handed him the government's hottest potato by making him the first-ever Northern Ireland secretary. His job was to run the province after the imposition of direct rule, and to try to find a solution to the running sore of sectarianism. He nearly succeeded.

He had become employment secretary by the time Heath began his fatal confrontation with the NUM over pay policy. When Heath eventually decided to put the issue to the people in a "who governs Britain?" election in February 1974, Whitelaw advised against it. The outcome, a psephological draw but a moral and political defeat, brought about the fall of the government, and led ultimately to the rise of Thatcher.

As runner-up to Thatcher in the eventual leadership contest, Whitelaw was clearly entitled to the post of deputy leader, and eventually to that of *de facto* deputy prime minister after the 1979 Conservative victory. Unusually, Thatcher acknowledged this special relationship by formally designating him as her deputy on taking office.

But as her first home secretary, it soon became clear that Whitelaw was not getting the same degree of loyalty from the prime minister as he was delivering to her. While Willie suffered the right-wing flak, she went out of her way to signal that, in her heart, she sympathised with them rather than with him.

Whitelaw's spell at the home office was a bumpy one, for it included the Brixton and Toxteth riots as well as a major backbench revolt over proposed new immigration rules. On the other hand, he will be remembered for a massive programme of prison construction, and for sharply increasing the size of the police force by the simple expedient of increasing police pay.

But it had become clear well before the 1983 general election that he wanted a change of employment. In the event, he was awarded the first hereditary peerage since the Macmillan years, and became leader of the Lords as well as deputy PM.

By now the government was getting a hard ride from their Lordships, who were playing all kinds of hell with its legislative programme. Their new leader's method of coping with this situation was to let them have their way when it didn't matter too much. In return, he sought support on key issues.

These conciliatory tactics did not immediately appeal to Thatcher, though she learned to swallow her belligerence. By now, she was coming to rely on Whitelaw to take on a whole range of ministerial functions, not least as an effective chairman of cabinet committees.

In particular, he had taken charge of the so-called star chamber committee, which adjudicates between the treasury and the great Whitehall spending departments at each year's pre-budget review of public expenditure. Even she seems to have noticed that he had a high success rate in reconciling the treasury's demands for cuts with the expectations of ministers — usually in the treasury's favour.

But if she recognised Whitelaw's usefulness in these relatively high-profile functions, it is questionable whether she ever acknowledged the role in which his service to her was greatest of all. For it was Willie's sensitive nose for trouble, combined with his talents as a discreet Dutch uncle, which often saved her from the disasters created by her own insensitivity. Indeed, at one stage, she made him chief of the entire government information service over the head of her own favourite, Bernard Ingham — a job which won him the title of minister for banana skins.

But whatever else he may have been, Willie Whitelaw was neither a coward nor a fool. Even those famous "Willie-isms", which sometimes sounded merely idiotic, often repaid careful analysis. Perhaps his most famous was uttered at a press conference at Belfast airport on his first arrival in Northern Ireland as chief minister. Bombarded with questions involving complex matters of Irish history, of which he was entirely ignorant, he discovered a gloriously Irish answer. "I always think," he said, "that it is entirely wrong to prejudge the past." In the context of Ireland, if nowhere else, it makes genuine sense. And so did his splendid complaint against Harold Wilson's attempt to win the 1970 election by boring the voters: "They are going up and down the country, stirring up apathy."

In the end, it was probably Thatcher's dependence on him which hastened Whitelaw's death. He might have managed just one job, like leader of the Lords. He might even have managed two jobs, including the chairmanship of the star chamber. But four or five full-time jobs proved too much even for his vast physique. Shortly before Christmas 1987, it precipitated a stroke, which persuaded Whitelaw, on medical advice, to retire as a minister.

He continued to travel to London from his Cumbrian home virtually every week, and faithfully attended and spoke to the House of Lords. His public utterances remained loyal as ever. But, in private, he made little secret about his distress at the extent to which his party was turning into a mean, greedy body composed of what Julian Critchley called "garagistes". Whitelaw continued to play golf for several years, though he was forced to give up his other pleasure, shooting, after an unfortunate incident in which a fellow gun got peppered.

There followed a number of further minor strokes, which finally incapacitated him. He was looked after to the end by his beloved wife, Celia, whom he married during the war when she was in the ATS. He is survived by her, and by his four daughters.

Ian Aitken

William Stephen Ian Whitelaw, CH, first Viscount Whitelaw of Penrith, politician, born June 28, 1918; died June 30, 1999

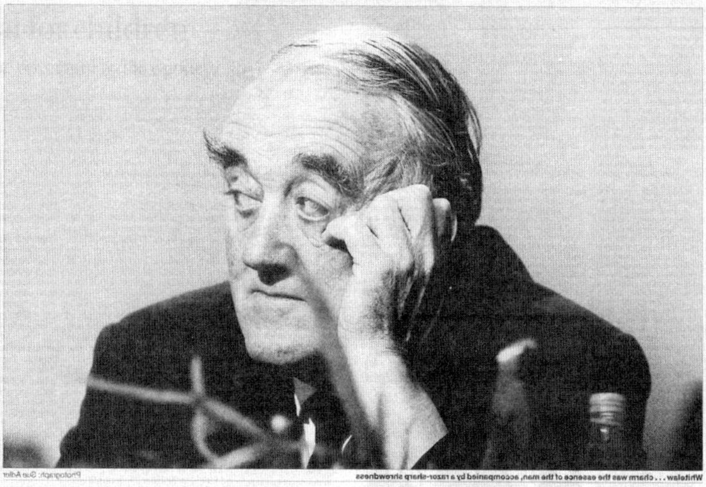

Whitelaw . . . charm was the essence of the man, accompanied by a razor-sharp shrewdness

Photograph: Sue Adler

Leader of Zimbabwe's freedom struggle whose dream was undercut by ethnic conflict

Joshua Nkomo

Joshua Nkomo, who has died aged 82 of prostate cancer, was the "father of Zimbabwe", but will be remembered as the man who did not become president of the nation he was so instrumental in bringing to independence. If Robert Mugabe won the political battle to become Zimbabwe's first president, Nkomo remained the unchallenged leader of the long struggle to achieve majority rule. Even Mugabe had to acknowledge that.

Nkomo was also the unofficial — but undisputed — king of Zimbabwe's Ndebele people. He was born and raised in rural Matabeleland, the third of seven children. His early years were spent shepherding the family's cattle. His father, a leader of the London Missionary Society, put a high value on education and young Joshua proved to be an outstanding student. He completed standard six and became a schoolteacher.

In 1942 he went to South Africa to continue his education, initially to study carpentry. Eventually, he earned a diploma in social science from Jan Hofmeyr School of Social Science. When, in 1949, he returned to what was then the British colonial territory of Southern Rhodesia, he became the first black African to be employed by Rhodesia Railways as a social worker. He continued his studies, through correspondence school, and won a bachelor of arts degree in economics and social science.

But Nkomo's true calling was the politics of African nationalism, and that career began in 1951 when he became secretary of the Railway African Workers' Union. Tall, handsome and with a commanding presence, eloquent in both Ndebele and English, he quickly made his mark. He was soon elected president of the Southern Rhodesian African National Congress (ANC).

He came to international attention when he stomped out of a London conference to protest at its endorsement of the Central African Federation, a fanciful piece of map manipulation designed by Britain to bring together the colonies of Northern and Southern Rhodesia and Nyasaland (now Zambia, Zimbabwe and Malawi).

Back home in Rhodesia, Nkomo put up a spirited and unflinching resistance to white minority rule. When the ANC was banned, he formed the National Democratic Party (NDP) — and became its president. When the NDP was banned in 1961, he founded the Zimbabwe African Peoples Union (Zapu) — and was elected president. He worked to make Zapu an all-inclusive party, but many of the country's Shona people, who make up more than 70 per cent of the population, were not comfortable under the leadership of an Ndebele.

Nkomo's high-handed, authoritarian manner did not help. In 1963 a group of mostly Shona members, including Robert Mugabe, split away to form the Zimbabwe African National Union (Zanu). Zanu became the nationalist party followed by most Shona people, while Zapu remained the party of most Ndebeles, with a small but significant Shona following. There were clashes between the two parties, which had overtones of ethnic violence. The Rhodesian authorities banned them both.

In the meantime, Nkomo became convinced that white Rhodesians would not voluntarily accept black majority rule. He travelled overseas to seek support for an armed struggle against minority rule. Although western countries rejected his appeal, the Soviet Union accepted.

When Ian Smith declared unilateral independence from Britain in 1965, Nkomo, like Mugabe, was held in detention for more than 10 years. Following his release he went into exile in Zambia, from where he led Zapu's armed battle against Rhodesia. Mugabe waged a parallel, and more successful, battle from Mozambique with Chinese assistance.

In 1979, Nkomo and Mugabe came together to negotiate Zimbabwe's independence at Lancaster House in London. The country's first free elections in 1980 largely split along the Shona-Ndebele ethnic divide: Nkomo lost the presidency to Mugabe and his Zapu party won just 20 per cent of the parliamentary seats.

Nkomo was appointed minister of home affairs in a government of national unity. But in 1982 Mugabe charged that Nkomo had plotted a coup and sacked him from the cabinet. Some of Nkomo's supporters carried out a series of violent anti-government protests, in which several people were killed.

Mugabe responded by sending in the army's Fifth Brigade, which is blamed for the deaths of more than 10,000 Ndebele civilians. Nkomo fled the country through Botswana and went to London, where he wrote his colourful autobiography, The Story Of My Life. He returned to contest the national elections in 1985, which kept the country divided along ethnic lines.

Sporadic ethnic violence continued until Nkomo and Mugabe signed a historic unity accord in December 1987, in which Nkomo agreed to merge his Zapu party into Mugabe's Zanu-PF. The violence stopped and Nkomo became one of Zimbabwe's two vice-presidents, but his political role was that of merely a figurehead.

Joshua Nkomo wanted desperately to be included in the ranks of the great African leaders who steered their countries from colonial subjugation to independence, and who became presidents. He achieved the lofty first goal, but he missed the second.

He is survived by his wife, Johanna, two daughters and a son.

Andrew Meldrum

Joshua Mqabuko Nyongolo Nkomo, politician, born June 7, 1917; died July 1, 1999

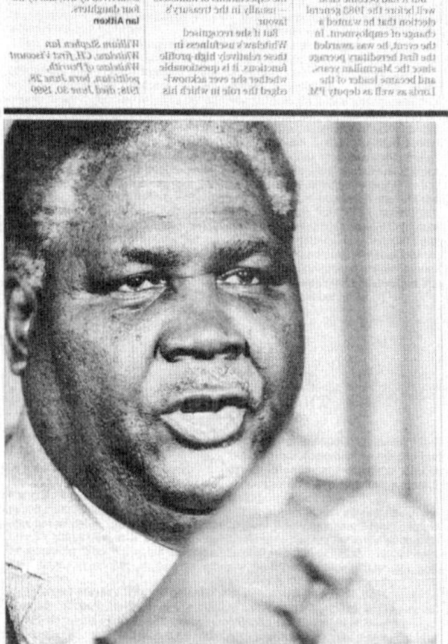

Nkomo . . . the father of his nation and undisputed king of its Ndebele people

Neil Libbert

Death Notices

ASHBY, John Henry Phil, devoted husband, loving father and besotted grandad, died quietly and pain-free on Tuesday 29th June at Bishops Wood Hospital, Northwood. He had finally had enough. Funeral service at St John's Parish Church, Pinner on Wednesday 7th July at 2.15 pm, and then at Breakspear Crematorium at 3 pm. Flowers to T A Ellement and Son Ltd, Pinner, telephone 0181 866 0834. Donations to Myrtle Currie Research Fund, Mount Vernon Hospital, Northwood, Middlesex.

HELLENDALL, Fritz, on 23rd June 1999, aged 98 at Hutton Village Nursing Home, Hutton, Brentwood, Essex; will be missed by Frank and his wife Marion, their three children, six grandchildren, the family of his late sister Mathilde, and many friends and acquaintances. Funeral at Chelmsford Crematorium on Wednesday 7th July at 2pm. No flowers, please, but donations if wished to World Cancer Research Fund c/o Gerretts (Brentwood) Ltd, 120 High St, Brentwood, Essex CM14 4AS, telephone 01277 211516.

■ To place your announcement telephone [illegible]

Obituaries

As political prisoner, party leader and eminent surgeon, he fought for the unity of Ethiopia

Asrat Woldeyes

Professor Asrat Woldeyes, who has died aged 70, was successively Ethiopia's most distinguished surgeon, physician and university dean, most controversial political party leader and best known political prisoner. He was also Haile Selassie's personal physician until his mysterious death in 1975 (in 1996 he was brought from prison to testify that the emperor had not died of natural causes).

Professor Asrat, who was the first Ethiopian to qualify as a surgeon in the west, after medical studies at Edinburgh University, devoted most of his working life to surgery at the two main hospitals in Addis Ababa, and to the deanship of medicine at the university. He could have practised in incomparably better conditions in the west — and for greater rewards — but he preferred to serve his people.

During the dark years of the military communist regime of President Mengistu Haile-Mariam (1974-1991), Asrat continued his medical and university practices. During the 1984-86 famine, his surgical skill saved the life of the Guardian correspondent, Jonathan Steele, who described the event in an eloquent article in the Guardian Weekend magazine last November.

Following the Eritrean-Tigrayan overthrow of Mengistu in 1991 and the independence of Eritrea, the Tigrayan-dominated government increasingly purged members of the Amhara ascendancy, which had dominated the Haile Selassie and Mengistu regimes. Asrat was among 21 Amhara professors dismissed from the university in 1993. In that year he became founder-chairman of the All Amhara People's Organisation (AAPO), dedicated to bringing back the unity of Ethiopia prior to Eritrean independence and the protection of Amhara interests under the ethnically-based constitution of president (now prime minister) Meles Zenawi.

Although AAPO remained nominally legal, its relations with the Meles government deteriorated and in June 1994 Asrat was arrested. He was imprisoned for two years on charges of planning violence against the state, although Amnesty International and other independent observers pronounced the evidence against him dubious and unsafe, and Asrat was on record as condemning violence for political ends. Further convictions followed, each on similarly unsatisfactory evidence, extending his sentence to five years. In 1996 he faced a new trial, repeatedly adjourned and never completed, clearly signalling the government's intention to keep him in prison beyond the expiry of his existing sentences.

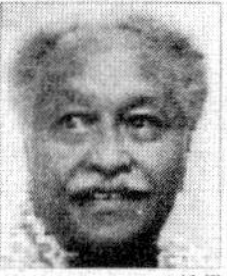

Woldeyes . . . courageous

By now in his late 60s, and with a heart by-pass, Asrat was incarcerated in a communal cell but forbidden to communicate with his fellow prisoners — a refined form of solitary confinement. His health deteriorated and in January 1998 he was transferred, under armed guard, to his old hospital, Tikur Anbessa (Black Lion). By November he was in intensive care. Medical details were kept secret, but news of his heart condition, the onset of diabetes, high blood pressure, deteriorating eyesight and a suspected blood clot on the brain caused growing anxiety. His government-appointed doctors reportedly said that to survive, Asrat needed treatment not available in Ethiopia.

On (western) Christmas Day, 1998, the government finally yielded to international appeals for him to be allowed to go abroad for treatment. Asrat was flown to London and then to Houston, Texas. He appeared to recover, but suffered relapses and died at the hospital of the University of Pennsylvania after less than five months of freedom.

Asrat was a man of great dignity and courtesy, stubborn to the point of cussedness, arguably politically naive. Throughout his five years' harsh imprisonment, Amnesty International, with other humanitarian organisations and numerous individuals, including now elderly Scottish doctors, campaigned for his release. Until very late, however, western governments, whose intervention might have carried weight with the Meles government, refused to go beyond occasional expressions of concern, apparently fearing to irritate a regime which, despite obvious shortcomings, was pro-western and a vast improvement on its predecessor.

It is hard to avoid the conclusion, though, that if those governments had worked harder and earlier, they might have averted the premature death of the most distinguished, and one of the most courageous, Ethiopians of our time.

Brian Barder

Asrat Woldeyes, doctor and politician, born June 12, 1928; died May 14, 1999

A pioneering woman athlete, her Olympic record stands unbroken

Betty Robinson

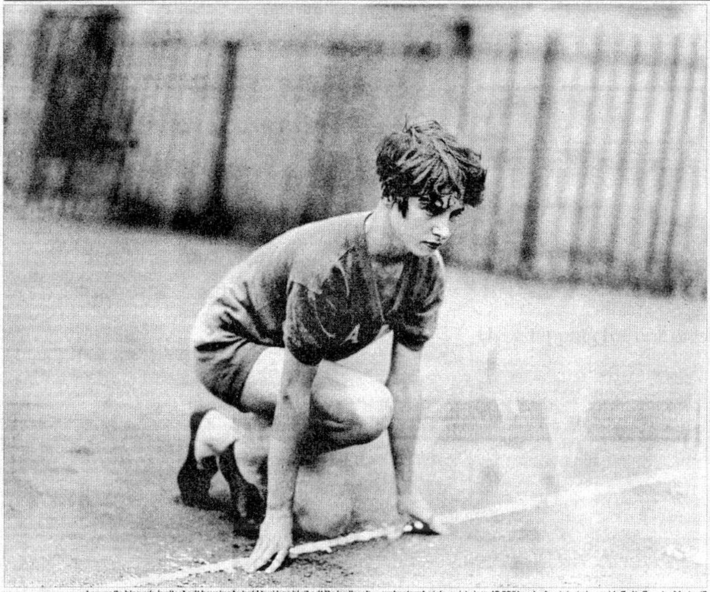

Fleet of foot . . . Betty Robinson in training for her 1928 Olympic triumph in Amsterdam — 'I walked off the field and just kind of enjoyed the feeling' she said afterwards

Betty Robinson, the first female athlete to win an Olympic gold medal for a track event, has died aged 87. She won the 100 metres in the 1928 Olympics in Amsterdam just before she was 17 — she remains the youngest ever winner of the event — and paved the way for modern superstars like Florence Griffiths Joyner, Gail Devers and Marion Jones.

The 1928 games were the first in which women were allowed to compete in track and field. Baron Pierre de Coubertin, founder of the modern Olympics, regarded their participation as unfeminine, suggesting they should stick to "genteel sports, such as tennis". But after much argument they were admitted to five events — and set world records in all five.

Robinson was a high school student in Illinois when her biology teacher saw her running to catch a train. Astounded at her speed, he suggested that they train together. Within weeks she made her racing debut, finishing second to Helen Filkey, the US 100-metres record holder. In her next meeting, she equalled the then world record of 12.0 seconds (Florence Griffiths Joyner's current record stands at 10.49.)

Robinson progressed so rapidly that at 16 she was selected to represent the United States at Olympic level, and the team sailed to Amsterdam working out on a quarter-mile linoleum track laid around the ship's deck. In what was only the fourth competitive race of her life, Robinson ran a world record of 12.2 seconds.

"I can remember standing in the middle of the field after the race and seeing the American flag raised, and hearing the Star Spangled Banner and all the people singing it," she said in a 1988 interview. "Then I walked off the field and just kind of enjoyed the feeling."

Robinson was nearly killed when a light plane in which she was travelling crashed near Chicago in 1931. Doctors said at first that she would not survive, then that she would not walk. After lengthy rehabilitation, she was eventually able to resume training, although as her ability to come out of the starting blocks was limited, she turned her focus to the relays. She won a second gold medal at the 1936 Olympic Games in Berlin as a member of the American 4 x 100-metres relay team, after which she retired.

She married Richard Schwartz in 1939 and often travelled the country speaking on behalf of the Women's Athletic Association and the Girls' Athletic Association. She is survived by a daughter and three grandchildren.

Duncan Mackay

Betty Robinson Schwartz, athlete, born August 11, 1911; died May 18, 1999

Veteran US submariner and naval hero

Rafael Benitez

Rear-Admiral Rafael Benitez, who has died aged 81, was the hero of a unique rescue operation when the United States navy submarine he commanded caught fire under the Arctic Ocean while spying on the Soviet navy in 1949.

USS Cochino was one of two USN submarines that left Portsmouth on August 12, officially on "exercises" but actually on dangerous intelligence gathering mission. The other boat was the Tusk and they were bound for the Barents Sea, north of Murmansk, the the main base of the Soviet northern fleet.

The Soviet Union was thought to be developing missiles, possibly fired from submarines. As the cold war intensified, the US and Royal navies sent submarines into far northern waters to spy on Stalin's fleet in a war of nerves involving several accidents and near-misses. The boats had snorkel breathing tubes, enabling them to stay underwater for long periods, and electronic eavesdropping devices.

The USN boats were lurking underwater about 150 miles north of Murmansk on August 25, when one of the Cochino's main, two-ton batteries caught fire, emitting poisonous chlorine fumes.

Benitez took his boat to the surface, where strong winds prevented the Tusk from coming alongside. The turbulent conditions made fire-fighting even more difficult, and Benitez ordered those of his crew of 77 who could not help to save the boat to lash themselves to the deck rails.

One man from the Cochino made for the Tusk on a raft, which turned over and knocked him unconscious. Hauled aboard, he was again washed into the sea and drowned, along with six men from the Tusk. Benitez fought for 14 hours to save the Cochino, at one stage ordering most of the crew to form a pyramid on top of the conning tower, designed to accommodate seven, to save them from inhaling gas.

The submarine followed the Tusk to calmer waters further south but was rocked by an explosion while Benitez — as skipper — was the only man left aboard. He refused to abandon his command until the Cochino began to list severely, forcing him to dash across the plank connecting the two boats, two minutes before his own vessel sank in 300 metres of freezing water 100 miles off Norway.

The Tusk took the crew to Hammerfest, where they were treated for exposure. The Soviet Union accused the boats of spying — just before it exploded its first A-bomb on September 23.

Benitez was born in Puerto Rico and enlisted as an USN cadet, graduating from Annapolis naval academy in 1939. He served in submarines throughout the second world war, winning the silver star and bronze star. Postwar he graduated from Georgetown law school in 1949, before returning to the submarine arm. He headed the US naval mission to Cuba from 1952 to 1954, and served in destroyers before retiring as a rear admiral in 1959. He then became Pan American Airways' vice-president for Latin America. He later taught international law at Miami University. He leaves a widow, Nancy, one son and two daughters.

Dan van der Vat

Rafael Celestino Benitez, submariner; born March 22, 1917; died March 6, 1999

Saudi leader who condemned women drivers

Abdul Aziz Ibn Baz

Sheikh Abdul Aziz Ibn Baz, who has died of cancer aged 87, was grand mufti of Saudi Arabia, a religious leader with ministerial rank in the government.

He was born into a family of traders, peasants and judges. His education was traditional religious, with intensive group tutorials led by a sheikh. His exceptional memory enabled him to learn the Koran by heart before he came of age — in spite of an eye infection which made him completely blind from the age of 16. He studied Arabic and Sharia, and said that the sheikh who influenced him most was Mohammad ibn Ibrahim, mufti of Saudi Arabia, who recommended him for his first job as judge in Al Kharj in 1938.

Sheikh Ibn Baz distinguished himself as both a student and a judge. He became a teacher at the religious institute in Riyadh in 1952 and an Islamic law lecturer at Riyadh University in 1953. In 1963, he was appointed head of the council of Islamic scholars and grand mufti, and by 1975 he was vice chancellor of the Islamic university at Medina. From 1978 until his death, he was chair of the prestigious permanent board of inquiry and fatwa, which carries ministerial status in the Saudi Arabian government.

The sheikh provided Islamic credentials for the policies of the custodian of the holy mosques. He made a fatwa in 1990 against the driving of cars by women — 50 working women defied the ban and drove their cars in Riyadh in June of that year. Earlier, in 1978, he had declared a fatwa that Viagra may could be prescribed to Muslim men. But he also supported the west in the Gulf war.

Sheikh Ibn Baz only spoke Arabic and never travelled outside the kingdom of Saudi Arabia, but he supported the principle of "peace with the Jews" and sanctioned Muslim-Christian dialogue. His forte was the ability to confront extremists with arguments which neither royalty nor the liberal middle classes possessed, mainly because he could not be dismissed as "secular" or "westernised".

Sheikh Ibn Baz is survived by two wives, four sons and several daughters, the youngest of whom is 10. The number of daughters is not revealed for traditional reasons

Khalid Al Mubarak

Abdul Aziz Ibn Abdallah Ibn Baz, cleric, born 1912; died May 13, 1999

Death Notices

FIGUEROA, Dorothy Grace Murray, née Alexander, [illegible]

HOLMES, John Edgar, [illegible]

MACKINTOSH, Aeneas James Douglas, [illegible]

POLLOK, Tom (J.G.), [illegible]

TAYLOR, James Douglas, [illegible]

Memorial Services

HERON, Patrick Heron, [illegible]

Births

DILLON, [illegible]

[illegible]

Birthdays

Liliana Archibald, expert on banking law, 71; **Kim Bailey,** racehorse trainer, 46; **Alastair Campbell,** prime minister's press secretary, 42; **Julian Clary,** comedian and actor, 40; **Barry Cox,** deputy chairman, Channel 4, 57; **Jeanne Crain,** actress, 74; **Prof Marianne Elliott,** historian, 51; **Prof John Ffowcs Williams,** engineer, master, Emmanuel College, Cambridge, 64; **Margaret Forster,** novelist and biographer, 61; **Livia Gollancz,** musician and publisher, 79; **Michael Harris,** cricket umpire, 55; **David Jenkins,** athlete, 47; **Sir Ian McKellen,** actor, 60; **Geoffrey Robinson,** MP, former Labour minister, 61; **Beverley Sills,** operatic soprano, 70; **Dave Lee Travis,** disc jockey, 54; **Anthea Turner,** broadcaster, 38; **David Wynne,** sculptor, 73.

Shirley Bury

An eminent Victorian

SHIRLEY BURY, who has died aged 74, was one of the most talented and inspirational of the post-war curators at the Victoria and Albert Museum. When she joined, the staff tended to divide between august male keepers and assistant keepers, with degrees from the older universities, and humbler assistants, again mostly men, who had joined the museum from school. Improved educational provision in Britain led to a new grade of research assistant, and in 1948 Shirley became an RA.

Born in Wimbledon, she read fine art at Reading University. She had a brief stint school-teaching, and then joined the V&A. It was an occupation that fitted her like a glove, and the loosening staff structure took her to the top. Shirley was not a militant feminist, but she wanted women to succeed in the V&A and, indeed, did much to make this possible.

She joined the circulation department, which (until its cessation in 1977) devised travelling exhibitions for regional museums and art schools in the 20th century; the V&A had increasingly withdrawn into antiquarianism, and there was general agreement that art stopped at about 1830. But because "the special requirements of art schools have naturally led to an emphasis on contemporary work", the circulation department ("circ") was allowed to take an interest in the present. All the same, when it came to establishing its academic credentials, "circ" turned to art historical studies, choosing the Victorian period, which was off-limits to the rest of the V&A. Shirley was certainly not out of touch with the contemporary — and later urged on the museum the patronage of modern designers — but she embraced the opportunity to specialise in Victorian art, becoming the V&A's doyenne of 19th-century studies.

Working alongside Shirley were two other young women with art-school training. Elizabeth Aslin was a big, stentorian woman; Barbara Morris was (and still is) more glamorous and effervescent; Shirley was smaller, softer, quieter, but had a special gift for instilling enthusiasm, bestowing encouragement and enlisting support. These "Three Graces", as they were sometimes known, together with Hugh Wakefield and John Lowry, were moulded by the department's keeper, Peter Floud, into a team which prepared a serious, penetrating exhibition of Victorian And Edwardian Decorative Arts in 1952.

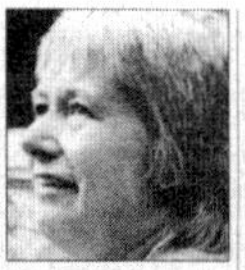

The fashion for the Victorians had derived a somewhat camp amusement from wax fruit, antimacassars, Baxter prints, papier-mache trays and such bric-a-brac. But, under the influence of H S Goodhart-Rendel, Nikolaus Pevsner and others, serious interest developed in Victorian architecture, and this was now extended by Floud to Victorian furniture and decorative arts. The exhibition was a turning point in the Victorian revival, which soon brought the foundation of the Victorian Society in 1958, with the Three Graces among the first members. At the museum, the team went on to set up new permanent galleries of Victorian art in 1964-66.

The path to success in the V&A required specialisation in a material, and Shirley chose metalwork, completing an MA in 1960 on the silver trade up to the industrial revolution. Promoted to senior research assistant in 1961, a year later, she obtained an assistant keeper post in the library. During her stay there, she organised an exhibition of Victorian church plate, Copy Or Creation, at Goldsmiths' Hall in 1967.

In 1968 she moved across to the metalwork department, where she truly wanted to be (becoming deputy keeper in 1972), and soon afterwards proposed the exhibition *Victorian Church Art*. Like the 1952 exhibition, this was exploratory — it was necessary first to trawl through contemporary sources for clues to possible exhibits, and then track them down, often subsequently smoothing their way into the museum's collections. For *Victorian Church Art*, many objects, forgotten in cathedrals and churches, were rehabilitated.

Shirley was also active in trade union matters. On becoming an assistant keeper, she arranged a quiet revolution

Shirley was also active in trade union matters at the museum, at first advancing the interests of lower grades and women. When, on becoming an assistant keeper, she joined the top people's union, she arranged a quiet revolution by getting younger people voted on to the committee.

One of the hot issues in the 1970s was whether senior staff should achieve promotion through "Buggins's turn" or by open competition. The latter was the progressive view, held by the director, Roy Strong, and by Shirley too. However, when the keeper of metalwork, Claude Blair, retired in 1982, only three years before Shirley was due to reach retiring age, Strong waived the open competition, and appointed Shirley by fiat to the keepership, to general approval.

In her writing, Shirley was a perfectionist. Her publications, refined so laboriously, tended to be on a smallish scale. However, after retirement, she published her big two-volume work *Jewellery 1790-1910: The International Era* (1991). Jewellery was her abiding interest, and she had re-displayed and re-catalogued the V&A's collection in 1982.

The V&A provided Shirley with a life-path in which her abilities were fully exercised. But institutional life can as easily be deforming as fulfilling: it all depends on the personal qualities you bring to it. Shirley brought humour, clear-eyed and open-minded common sense, gentle tenacity of purpose and moral strength — and the V&A was much the better for her influence.

She is survived by her husband, Morley, and her son Matthew.

Anthony Burton

Shirley Bury, museum curator, born February 27, 1925; died March 25, 1999

Peter de Normanville

Beams of light

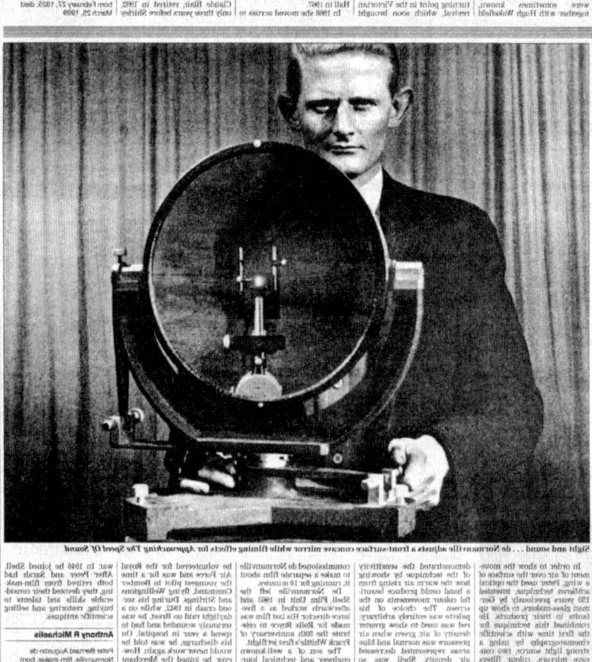

Sight and sound . . . de Normanville adjusts a front-surface concave mirror while filming effects for *Approaching The Speed Of Sound*

PETER DE NORMANVILLE, who has died aged 76, was a member of that elite group of film-makers who, between the 1950s and 1970s, pioneered jargon-free science documentary films.

Until 1963 he was the principal scientific director of the London Shell Film Unit, the best scientific film production centre in Britain. It was led by Arthur Elton, and among other members were Geoffrey Bell and Sarah Erulkar. In 1950 Sarah and Peter married, and together they directed the remarkable *Living City* (1975), a social documentary about the resurrection of the spirit of Calcutta. It won a Bafta award for the best short film in 1977.

Most of de Normanville's work for the unit received international awards, including *Man And Computer* (1967), *Let There Be Light* (1969), *Steel Research* (1973) and *Energy In Perspective* (1977). It was the policy of Shell to make films so that users of its products could understand the scientific principles behind them.

Although all the films were popular and in demand, it was the 1956 trilogy *High Speed Flight*, to which Peter contributed *Approaching The Speed Of Sound*, which became most famous for Shell intended the three films, total running time 70 minutes, to be used in the training of pilots transferring to supersonic flight. They proved immensely useful, not only for pilots but also for airline staff, air cadets and students of aerodynamics. They also became part of the training programme for Nato air forces because the diagrammatic explanations in colour were both timeless and a visual delight.

In order to show the movement of air over the surface of a wing, Peter used the optical schlieren technique, invented 150 years previously by German glass-makers, to show up faults in their products. He combined this technique for the first time with scientific cinematography by using a strong light source, two concave mirrors, colour filters and his cine camera. The effect was stunning. He demonstrated the sensitivity of the technique by showing how the warm air rising from a hand could produce beautiful colour movements on the screen. The choice of his palette was entirely arbitrary; red was used to show greater density of air, green when air pressure was normal and blue areas represented decreased air density. Shell was so impressed by the results of this new technique that it commissioned de Normanville to make a separate film about it, running for 18 minutes.

De Normanville left the Shell Film Unit in 1962 and afterwards worked as a freelance director. His last film was made for Rolls Royce to celebrate the 50th anniversary of Frank Whittle's first jet flight.

The son of a well-known engineer and technical journalist, Peter was educated at Ampleforth. At the age of 18 he volunteered for the Royal Air Force and was for a time the youngest pilot in Bomber Command, flying Wellingtons and Stirlings. During his second crash in 1942, while on a daylight raid on Brest, he was seriously wounded and had to spend a year in hospital. On his discharge, he was told he would never work again. However, he joined the Merchant Navy in which he served as a navigator until the end of the war. In 1946 he joined Shell.

After Peter and Sarah had both retired from film-making, they devoted their considerable skills and talents to buying, restoring and selling scientific antiques.

Anthony R Michaelis

Peter Bernard Augustin de Normanville, film-maker, born June 29, 1922; died March 7, 1999

Leonard Hancock

Music, maestro, please

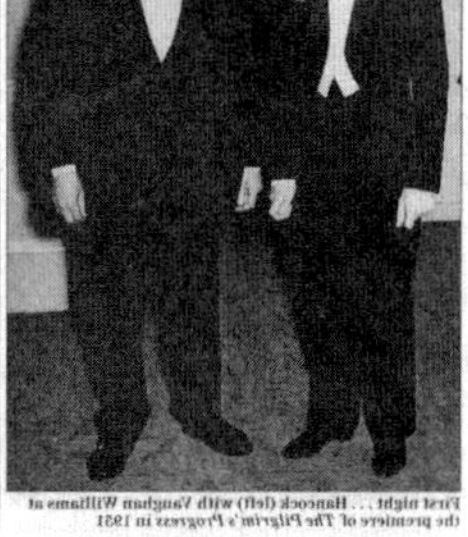

First night . . . Hancock (left) with Vaughan Williams at the premiere of *The Pilgrim's Progress* in 1951

LEONARD HANCOCK, who has died aged 77, was one of those conductors and musical coaches who form the engine-room of the best-run opera houses. At the age of 28, he was chosen by Ralph Vaughan Williams to conduct his opera, *The Pilgrim's Progress*, for the Festival of Britain — partly because the composer wanted someone who would turn up at all the rehearsals and not just swan in for the premiere. The same year Hancock worked with Benjamin Britten on the preparations for *Billy Budd*.

Despite these accolades, his most important work was probably done with Sadler's Wells in the 1960s and with Scottish Opera during its formative years in the 1960s and 1970s, acting as the safe pair of hands to the wayward genius of music director Alexander Gibson.

Hancock was born in Liverpool and brought up in Cambridge, where he learnt the organ and won a music scholarship to Jesus College, studying with Boris Ord and Patrick Hadley. After war service with the RAF, during which he won the DFC, he went back to Cambridge to gain his BMus and then moved to the Royal Academy of Music to study conducting with Richard Austin. In 1947, he was engaged by the then-resident, post-war Covent Garden company as a repetiteur.

By 1953 Hancock had already played a crucial role in helping operatic stars such as Elizabeth Schwarzkopf, Kirsten Flagstad, Victoria de los Angeles and Hans Hotter to learn their roles in English (most works then being given at Covent Garden in the vernacular). He left the Royal Opera House to increase his experience in Germany, working at the Cologne Opera for nine months in 1953. He then returned to Britain to work with the English Opera Group and helped Britten again, this time with the Venice premiere of *The Turn Of The Screw*.

Work followed with Glyndebourne, and the Carl Rosa Company, and when the latter merged with Sadler's Wells Opera, Hancock went with them. He did sterling work as a coach of young singers, among them the vivacious mezzo (later soprano) Catherine Wilson, who became his second wife. As head of music staff at the Wells, he was instrumental in the revival of the languishing career of Reginald Goodall (who had been a colleague of Hancock's at Covent Garden) when Goodall was invited to conduct *The Mastersingers* in 1968. He helped Goodall with the lengthy rehearsals and at one performance, as I well recall, stepped in to replace Goodall when he was unwell.

TYPICALLY, Hancock took over his senior's interpretation with the unassuming professionalism that was typical of him. He was also invaluable in teaching Alberto Remedios the roles of Walther, then that of Siegmund, when the company moved to the Coliseum, and eventually Siegfried. It was a template of the dedicated work he did to train singers and enhance the reputation of British opera.

At Scottish Opera, Hancock worked ceaselessly to develop the nascent company, rigorous in his training of artists and in the maintenance of musical standards over a wide repertory. There he met and worked with David Pountney, with whom he later collaborated on translating librettos. On his own, Hancock translated (and conducted) Nicolai's *The Merry Wives Of Windsor* for the 1976 Wexford Festival.

Latterly he worked both at the Royal Scottish Academy of Music, where he was in charge of the opera course, and at the Royal Academy of Music in London. He also taught at the National Opera Studio. He and his wife helped found Cheshire's Clonter Opera, a small company encouraging young artists in the county.

Hancock married his first wife, the soprano Iris Kells, in 1947 when both were working at Covent Garden. The marriage was dissolved in 1964, and in 1971 he married Catherine Wilson who survives him.

Alan Blyth

Leonard Hancock, conductor and musical coach, born September 11, 1921; died March 17, 1999

Penny Brohn

Quenching cancer's fire

AS a co-founder of the Bristol Cancer Help Centre, in 1983, Penny Brohn, who has died aged 55, inspired thousands of people to overcome their fear by helping change the way we think about the disease. She personified the heroic patient, and if the psychological challenges of cancer, the value of patient support groups and multi-disciplinary patient-practitioner partnership now seem obvious, she is among those we should thank.

Born in Bristol, she returned there with a sociology degree to take on child-care social work. She was 36, with three young children, when told she had cancer. The then medical approach left her feeling like a non-person, and her determination not to submit to conventional treatment became an affirmation that the disease was a part of her being. She had a life-long optimism and a faith in her own endurance; even, one sometimes sensed, in her invulnerability. But it was more than mere denial. She learned to draw nearer to the fear, sadness and disappointment cancer brought, and ultimately to speak with wisdom about wounds as well as triumphs.

Penny was a Christian and a churchgoer. She was an acupuncturist, too, and took to heart its ideas about psychological and spiritual causes of disease. She attended a healing circle held by Pat and Canon Christopher Pilkington, and, craving treatment that could embrace body as well as mind and spirit, she and Pat embarked on a grand tour of alternative cancer clinics.

Penny often used Auden's line about cancer being begotten by "foiled, creative fire". The new healing project into which she and the Pilkingtons began to pour their own creative fire became the Bristol Cancer Help Centre. The world saw her as the centre's representative. Critics said it was extreme in its regimes and notions. In the early days it was; increasingly though, it took a mainstream line on diet, while ever more emphasising counselling, art, coping skills and spiritual healing.

Penny chose alternatives to medicine and seemed to go from strength to strength. Yet in 1990 she had fought a recurrence and knew she should take a back seat. The centre's 10th anniversary conference event seemed appropriately triumphalist. Doubts were few and rarely addressed in public: the extraordinary strain on the centre's staff; feelings of guilt and failure among less than heroic patients; accusations that the centre was peddling a cure for cancer; and that conventional medics were being left to pick up the pieces. But sensitive to outside criticism, the centre was by then collaborating with the largest UK cancer charity, whose researchers Penny had confidently invited in as a way of spiking these guns.

The Chilvers Report made the dramatic claim that far from helping women, the centre was actually shortening lives. The world was suddenly confused, disappointed and indignant. At hostile press conferences, Penny defended the centre, but its reputation was ruined in the months it took to re-group and restore shattered morale. Eventually an incisive re-analysis of the statistics by Dr Tim Sheard revealed deep flaws in the original study, and subsequently the centre's patients' support group forced those involved to admit serious errors.

The following year Penny developed secondary bone tumours. Surgery and radiotherapy were unavoidable, but by then she could make the best of both therapeutic worlds and had found cancer specialists prepared to deal with her as a whole person.

For the last two years she and her husband David spent their summers renovating a ramshackle cottage on a Cretan mountainside, where Penny loved to make mosaics. Returning to Somerset this winter, she died peacefully, supported by her husband, son, two daughters and closest friends.

David Peters

Penelope Jane Brohn, alternative medicine practitioner, born July 18, 1943; died February 3, 1999

Birthdays

Admiral Sir Michael Boyce, First Sea Lord and Chief of Naval Staff, 56; **Sir Jack Brabham**, racing driver, 73; **Linford Christie**, athlete, 39; **Larry Coryell**, jazz guitarist, 56; **George MacDonald Fraser**, poet and author, 74; **Paul Gambaccini**, disc jockey, 50; **Myra Green**, director, British Emergency Action to Russian Republics, 61; **Raymond Gubbay**, classical music impresario, 53; **Sir Alec Guinness**, actor, 85; **Penelope Keith**, actress, 59; **Sir Peter Middleton**, chairman, Barclays Bank, 65; **Prof Camille Paglia**, writer, 52; **Andrew Puddephatt**, director, Charter 88, 49; **Dermot Reeve**, cricketer, 36; **Michael Rizzello**, sculptor and coin designer, 73; **Teddy Sheringham**, footballer, 33; **Sue Townsend**, author, 53; **Denis Tuohy**, broadcaster, 62.

CORRECTIONS AND CLARIFICATIONS

A CAPTION on page 11, G2, March 29 described the building in the accompanying picture as "a medieval mosque in Mali, Timbuctoo." It should, of course, have read "in Timbuktu, Mali."

BURGHCLEAR, referred to in a letter to the editor from Shirin and Unity Spencer, page 23, March 30, should have been Burghclere, home of the chapel containing Stanley Spencer's murals. Our mistake in transcription; sorry.

THE BIRDS' eggs seized by police (News in brief, page 9, March 31) were recovered from houses in Brixham, in Devon, not Brixton.

It is the policy of the Guardian to correct errors as soon as possible. Please quote the date and page number. The office of the Readers' Editor is closed until Tuesday. After that, readers may contact the office on 0171 239 9589 until Friday. Surface mail to Readers' Editor, The Guardian, 119, Farringdon Road, London EC1R 3ER. Fax: 0171 239 9897. e-mail: reader@guardian.co.uk

A Country Diary

NORTHUMBERLAND: Last week I spent a day with Jim Martin, the Northumberland Wildlife Trust warden at Hauxley on the coast. Within minutes, from the hide overlooking pools created from open-cast mining, he identified eight species — coot, black-headed gull, shelduck, canadas, teal, greylag, redshank, mallard, widgeon and gadwall. Greyland and shelduck were looking for nesting sites, mallard are already sitting on eggs. Jim got excited when two yellowhammers flew by, and the binoculars were up again to identify the three ringed plovers.

A volunteer called to report toads and a green frog on the flooded pools in the meadows, where wild flowers now flourish. "We have marsh and pyramid orchids, and last year I found a dusky cranesbill," said Jim. "An artist visited and spent two days painting our unusual vetches." We looked at frog spawn and the little black tadpoles now a rarity for me, although I am always peering hopefully into dykes and streams. Another volunteer was completing the bird census, which she does every week, and I saw others repairing one of the hides.

Sadly the water voles here have been lost to mink; Jim caught four on the reserve last year. Resident families of stoats and weasels are welcome. Jim sees them on his dawn walk, when he checks the hides are intact from storm damage or vandalism. This broad sandy beach, the sand dunes and fresh brackish water ponds provide vital feeding ground for large numbers of terns.

VERONICA HEATH

Death Notices

ALDIS, Philip Michael, beloved husband and father, died on 26th March after a short illness. Local government officer and county councillor, he worked tirelessly for what he believed in, practical socialism, protection of the countryside and integrity in public life. 40 years a cricketer, he always walked when he had touched the ball. Funeral service on Tuesday 6th April at St John the Baptist Church, Aldbury, Hertfordshire at 2.00 pm.

FLEISCHMANN. Suddenly on 26th March 1999 at Midtown House, Carlisle, formerly of Brooke Road, Carlisle, Marianne, dearly loved sister of the late Grete. Funeral service and cremation at Carlisle Crematorium on Friday, 9th April, at 11.40 am. Family flowers only please, donations, if desired, to The Royal National Institute for the Blind, c/o J. Hill and Sons, Funeral Directors, Station Road, Wigton.

HARRIS, Richard, Sinologist and former Deputy Foreign Editor of the Times. Died peacefully on 28th March 1999, after a long illness, aged 84. Much loved husband of Rachel and father of Gregory and Deborah. Funeral service will take place on Friday 9th April at St. Marylebone Crematorium, East End Road, East Finchley N2 at 11.30 am. No flowers but donations in his memory if desired to Action For Dysphasic Adults, 1 Royal St, London SE1 7LL.

In Memoriam

MARSHALL, J. Richard, died April 2nd 1995, aged 44. Loved and missed always, with love Olya.

Marriages

WORMLEIGHTON:JENKINS. Vicky and Duncan are getting married on Saturday 3rd April 1999, near Bury St Edmunds.

■ To place your announcement telephone 0171 713 4567 or fax 0171 713 4721 between 9am and 3pm Mon-Fri.

The Minnesota Declaration:

TRUTH AND FACT IN DOCUMENTARY CINEMA

by Werner Herzog

1. By dint of declaration the so-called Cinéma Vérité is devoid of vérité. It reaches a merely superficial truth, the truth of accountants.

2. One well-known representative of Cinéma Vérité declared publicly that truth can easily be found by taking a camera and trying to be honest. He resembles the night watchman at the Supreme Court who resents the amount of written law and legal procedures. 'For me,' he says, 'there should be only one single law: the bad guys should go to jail.' Unfortunately, he is part right, for most of the many, much of the time.

3. Cinéma Vérité confounds fact and truth, and thus plows only stones. And yet, facts sometimes have a strange and bizarre power that makes their inherent truth seem unbelievable.

4. Fact creates norms, and truth illumination.

5. There are deeper strata of truth in cinema, and there is such a thing as poetic, ecstatic truth. It is mysterious and elusive, and can be reached only through fabrication and imagination and stylization.

6. Filmmakers of Cinéma Vérité resemble tourists who take pictures amid ancient ruins of facts.

7. Tourism is sin, and travel on foot virtue.

8. Each year at springtime scores of people on snowmobiles crash through the melting ice on the lakes of Minnesota and drown. Pressure is mounting on the new governor to pass a protective law. He, the former wrestler and bodyguard, has the only sage answer to this: 'You can't legislate stupidity.'

9. The gauntlet is hereby thrown down.

10. The moon is dull. Mother nature doesn't call, doesn't speak to you, although a glacier eventually farts. And don't you listen to the Song of Life.

11. We ought to be grateful that the Universe out there knows no smile.

12. Life in the oceans must be sheer hell. A vast, merciless hell of permanent and immediate danger. So much of a hell that during evolution some species—including man—crawled, fled onto some small continent of solid land, where the Lessons of Darkness continue.

Walker Art Center, Minneapolis, Minnesota
April 30, 1999

TALES FROM LITTLE DIPPER

by Steve Rushton

Name______________________________

Can you connect the stars in number order?

Make the Little Dipper.

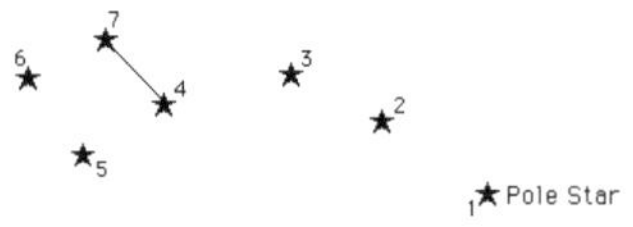

Make Draco, the Dragon.

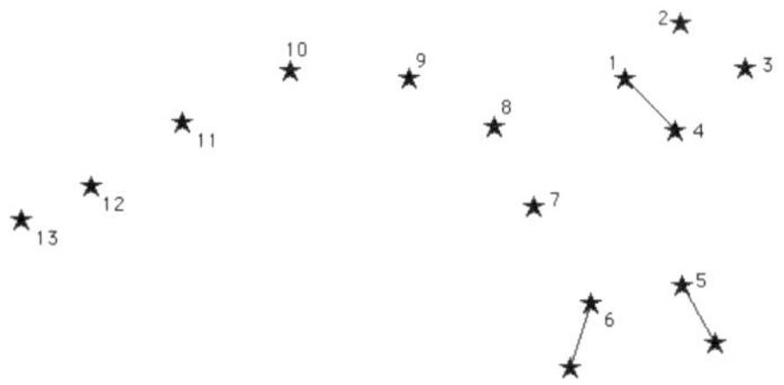

1

You enter an empty room. You throw a hand full of the dried beans into the air. They fall in a chaotic mess on the floor. After a little time, once you have become used to the way the beans happened to have fallen, their configuration acquires a meaning for you—the beans remind you of a constellation of stars. You begin to look at one group of beans in relation to another, an arbitrary 'line' or 'string' of beans becomes a 'bridge' between one 'cluster' and another. You have begun to develop a terminology for the things you see. Alone in the room and with little else to occupy your mind you give names to each group of beans within the 'constellation'. You even go so far as to christen the whole 'the bean system' and you set yourself the task of eventually giving a name to each individual bean and measuring the distance between each. Only then will the whole bean system be known.

2

You hold a piece of grey cardboard measuring 2cm by 1cm between your thumb and index finger. The edge of the object, which is about 2mm thick, curves to form lagoons and rounded peninsulae—in fact the piece is wholly comprised of such lagoons and peninsulae. It is a uniform box grey on one side whilst on the other a thin piece of paper has been glued; this piece of paper follows the contours of the piece of cardboard exactly. On the surface of the paper a small fragment of a picture is printed. You could get to know this object, every contour of its edge, the thickness of the paper in relation to the thickness of the cardboard on which it is mounted, you could get to know every colour and tone of the reproduction of a few flecks of paint, rendered in the impressionist style, or maybe a detail from a Pieter Bruegel painting.

In the jigsaw puzzle business the piece you are holding is called a 'little chap' because it suggests the outline of a man with his arms and legs stretched out like a blobby Vitruvian Man. Other pieces that make up the jigsaw system are called the 'crossbars' and 'double crosses'. Once the piece fits into place, when the peninsula slides effortlessly into its predestined lagoon, everything you know about the particularities of the piece, or indeed whether it is a 'little chap' or a 'crossbar' or a 'double cross', becomes irrelevant. Once this piece finds its place it becomes a fragment of a whole.

The fragment you are holding is part of a reproduction of a picture that Frans Hals painted in 1636. The painting has the long-winded title of Officers Of A Company Of The Amsterdam Crossbow Civic Guard Under Captain Reynier Reael And Lieutenant Cornelis Michielsz Blaeuw, but it is more economically known as The Meagre Company. It depicts a group of over-confident Dutchmen in fine, flamboyant cloths. The flecks of paint on the piece of cardboard you are holding find their place on the most central of the sixteen figures depicted in that painting—the piece clicks in where the scalloped lace fringes of a pair of trousers fold over the edges of a leather boot. The boot is worn on the left leg of a figure that stands with his back to us, his head turned casually in our direction. His waist is girthed by a red sash, he has his hand on his hip, in a manner which in his day would have displayed a cavalier charm but to the contemporary eye seems comically camp—as if he is rehearsing the lines, 'I'm a little teapot short and stout / here's my handle, here's my spout'.

You remember an ancient Aunt who framed each jigsaw puzzle she completed: the vigorous brush-strokes of a Van Gogh; the golden light embracing the pyramids at sunset; the stolid solemnity of Queen Victoria's funeral; a kitten popping its head out of an old top hat; a rosy-cheeked boy in a velvet suit staring at a soap bubble; the risen Christ displaying the Sacred Heart; 007 in a tuxedo holding a Beretta. All were cut through by the curvilinear matrix of those little chaps, cross-bars and double crosses. This same matrix now conspires to become an invisible grid through which we see Captain Reael and his assembled company. You consider how curious it is, this ability to shift effortlessly from one system to another, to shift so easily from the kind of reading required to look at a picture to the type of attention needed to look at a puzzle, just as easy as the move from scanning a telephone book to leafing through an encyclopaedia, and to shift again to the mode of attention required when reading a novel.

3

The starting point for Mariana Castillo Deball's exhibition Estocastic Archive was a group of ten books by writers who were obsessed with ordering the world—an obsession she has shared with them for some years now. For Castillo Deball the fascination seems to be in how systems change and how the busy and messy business of real life can occupy a given system, stepping on the cracks between the regular paving stones, betraying an understanding that every system has its exception.

A few years ago Castillo Deball made a book called Penser/Classer. This made reference to Georges Perec's book of the same name in which Perec exercised his own obsession with cataloguing the arbitrary and everyday. Castillo Deball's version consisted of a collection of photographs of her bedroom kitchen and toilet—a portrait of a relationship with a particular species of space. Ironically this catalogue of space proved difficult to place on the shelves: how should it be categorised, as the parasite of an existing title? Curiously, there is no record of the author's name on Castillo Deball's edition—it stands as an anomaly that only has the APPEARANCE of being part of a system—like a look-alike who gains entry to the club of which he is not a member. The book's very existence requires the reader to make a readjustment, to re-catogorise.

For Interlude: The Reader's Traces (2005) Castillo Deball invited a number of artists and writers to add to existing books—to provide traces in the spirit of those incidental additions which lenders unconsciously or accidentally add to library books—the pale pink stain from a jam sandwich, the bus ticket serving as a bookmark, hastily scribbled notes in the margin of the page... The contributors dealt with the challenge in different ways, some making abrupt interventions that changed the register of reading, whilst others disguised their addition by adding an extra chapter or page in the style and format of the original. The pieces were placed in libraries in Berlin, New York and Paris and now lie in wait for some future reader to happen upon them. There is no way of knowing what their effect might be or what pleasures or irritations they might solicit.

For Castillo Deball's next project Never Odd Or Even (2005) contributors were invited to invent the blurb for non-existent books which were then made into real book jackets—these work most convincingly when wrapped around existing publications and include: a pornographic book jacket to be used as a dummy cover by shy philosophy students; the account of Roland Barthes' collection of totally black negatives; the biography of the inventor of the photocopy machine who believed that the innovation would aid our ability to communicate with the spirit world; the mind-numbing Records Of Employment Requests 1992–95; a book devoted to finding defective components in TV set; a catalogue of Stalinist monuments on display in Lithuania's Grutas Park; the tale of the memorial statue of Harry

Houdini which constantly goes missing; the autobiography of a 17th century sectarian mystic repackaged for the new age market. The 24 titles span a wide range of genres representing individual publications that could find their place in the infinite and expanding library, speaking to the promise that every particle of knowledge can be gathered safely into the library.

4

> ... the Gnostic gospel of Basilides, the commentary on that gospel, the commentary on the commentary on that gospel, the true story of your death, the translation of every book in all languages, the interpolations of every book in all books.
> (Jorge Luis Borges, The Library of Babel)

Georges Perec's Life: A User's Manual comprises 179 chapters about the inhabitants of a ten-storied building in Paris. The structure of the book is dictated by a famous chess problem: how to visit every square on the board using only the knight's move. The system alludes to the jigsaw puzzle or patchwork of the building and accords a structure whereby the everyday and arbitrary can find their place within the series of L-shaped steps from room to room. The system allows the author to scrutinise objects in great detail, to release the memories they hold, to travel through them to meet those who occupied the building decades before, charting a chronology that stretches from 1833 to 1975. Although the book is systematic and structures the disparate elements it also opens up the promise of infinity—that every aspect of life can be recoded and catalogued. The absurdity of this promise is highlighted in Borges' parable 'The Library of Babel', in which an infinite library takes up the whole universe providing an over abundance of texts which renders life meaningless and in which certain knowledge is impossible.

Text informed by Georges Perec, Life: A User's Manual, translated by David Bellos (Vintage, London, 2003)

Rolling heads at the top of DDD11's recto pages: NEVER ODD OR EVEN Summary, a project by Mariana Castillo Deball (Marres, Center for Contemporary Art / Revolver, 2005)

WRITING MY LIFE

by Ryan Gander

For some time now I have been collecting obituaries. Some I find, some I am given. Most are cut from newspapers, but a few take more unusual forms: an inscription in the front of a book, a few words rendered in graffiti, a story over a bar-room table. Those obituaries are moulded by the makeup of everyday life and although harder to record, are equally valid.

I have come across three main types of obituaries. The first and most common is the type of obituary that has been written in advance of death. Nearly all newspaper obituaries are like this, prepared to be published in the days following the passing away of a public figure. They are generally written by a journalist, drawn from a stock of objective and factual news coverage throughout the subject's lifetime. At times they are so clinically removed from any sense of mourning that they seem to be written about a fictional character rather than a real person.

The second type, less common, is an obituary that has not been written in advance among the stockpile of others in the newsroom libraries, despite being a subject with a life or work of public interest. The usual obvious reason for this is because the subject is young, or at least young enough to have died unexpectedly by accident or catastophe. Not only are these almost always tragic, but they are also usually written by a writer with intimate knowledge of the subject or their work; on many occasions, a friend or a colleague of the deceased. They tend to be more intimate, emotional, subjective, often anecdotally humorous, and always painfully touching to read.

The third type, and most magical of all, is the self-obituary prepared by the subject themselves. This is the form I am most interested in. They are extremely rare exercises in unabashed egocentricity. For someone to write their own obituary in advance of death suggests the person is either aware that they are about to die, immensely preoccupied with their own death and anxious about their influence in the world, or concerned that a posthumous obituary written by someone else would represent them badly (through being either factually accurate or inaccurate, depending on the nature of the particular character).

The music video of the song 'Hurt' by Johnny Cash is one such attempt at a self-obituary. Cash died on 12 September 2003 from complications associated with diabetes. He was 71 years old and had been warned he was about to die. The media stated that Cash had been working up until only a few weeks before his death together with a music video director, Mark Romanek, in an attempt to finish the promo for the single. Following his death, music video channels played 'Hurt' in heavy rotation, making it Cash's most popular song in commercial terms. The film is a medley of both still and moving images of the singer at different moments and different locations throughout his life, like a live photo album. At one point Cash is represented as Christ, at another we see images of a museum dedicated to his life. Although genuinely saddening, I can't work out if it's his death or the size of his ego that makes me melancholy.

The English-born American journalist and radio correspondent Alistair Cooke died on 30 March 2004. I was a fan of Alistair Cooke's weekly radio show 'Letter from America', played on BBC Radio 4 every Sunday morning. When I heard of his death I was naturally saddened, but also intrigued to hear that he had prepared a sort of 'last letter from America' to be played after his death. Due to some stupid mistake I missed its initial airing, but the following week I was driving from one side of London to the other when the radio announced it was about to be repeated. This is a recording of the re-airing of the self-obituary I heard that day:

> Its two minutes past eight, and we are broadcasting now a tribute to Alistair Cooke whose death was announced last Tuesday. A man considered one of the greatest broadcasters in the world, Alistair Cooke's weekly Letter From America has been running on the BBC for over half a Century, but Alistair Cooke was a man of many talents and passions as Jane Nockety now remembers …
>
> 'I am sure you expect me to say I am sorry not to be with you. Well on the whole I am not sorry. I believe that Radio broadcasters should be heard and not seen. I don't want to disturb any pleasing image any of you may have of me. So you see why I am not over-anxious to be with you.'
>
> THANKS DUNCAN, SEE YOU SOON.
>
> Alistair Cooke was the quintessential radio broadcaster, but he was more than just a journalist, he was a Renaissance Man whose world encompassed newspapers, television and even Hollywood in its heyday. A man to whom Jazz piano and golf were as much of life as poetry, he was an Englishman who became an American, an institution on both sides of the Atlantic.
>
> OH, IT'S ALRIGHT, I WAS JUST, ERM … I WAS JUST LISTENING TO ALISTAIR COOKE, I WAS INTERESTED TO SEE WHAT HE WAS GOING TO SAY THEN, ABOUT, ERM, BEING SORRY NOT TO BE WITH US, SO I'VE JUST GONE OFF ON A LITTLE … SO ANYWAY, PRESUMABLY YOUR JUST ON A LITTLE MEAL BREAK ARE YOU? SO YOU'LL JUST BE GOING HOME AFTER THIS?
>
> OH REALLY?
>
> OH BLIMEY, OH WELL I HAD A VERY GOOD AFTERNOON BEFORE, BECAUSE MY HUSBAND WON HIS BET ON THE GRAND NATIONAL AND GOT NINETY QUID.
>
> YOU BET! I SHOULD THINK I SHOULD AT LEAST GET A GOOD OLD DRINK OUT OF IT, ANYWAY. ANYWAY SEE YOU SOON, BYE.

A technician had left a microphone switched on during the live airing. I find this portentously delightful.

Now there is a box in the corner of my studio where I keep my newspaper obituaries, and it is overflowing. The pile is getting higher and higher and is really in the way, but I don't feel ready to move it into storage just yet because this research hasn't quite reached fruition. A piece of work is waiting to be made, but the idea of its production is a perfect paradox. You see, I want to write my own obituary, but for that to happen I will need to write my own death, and for that to happen first I'll have to finish writing my life.

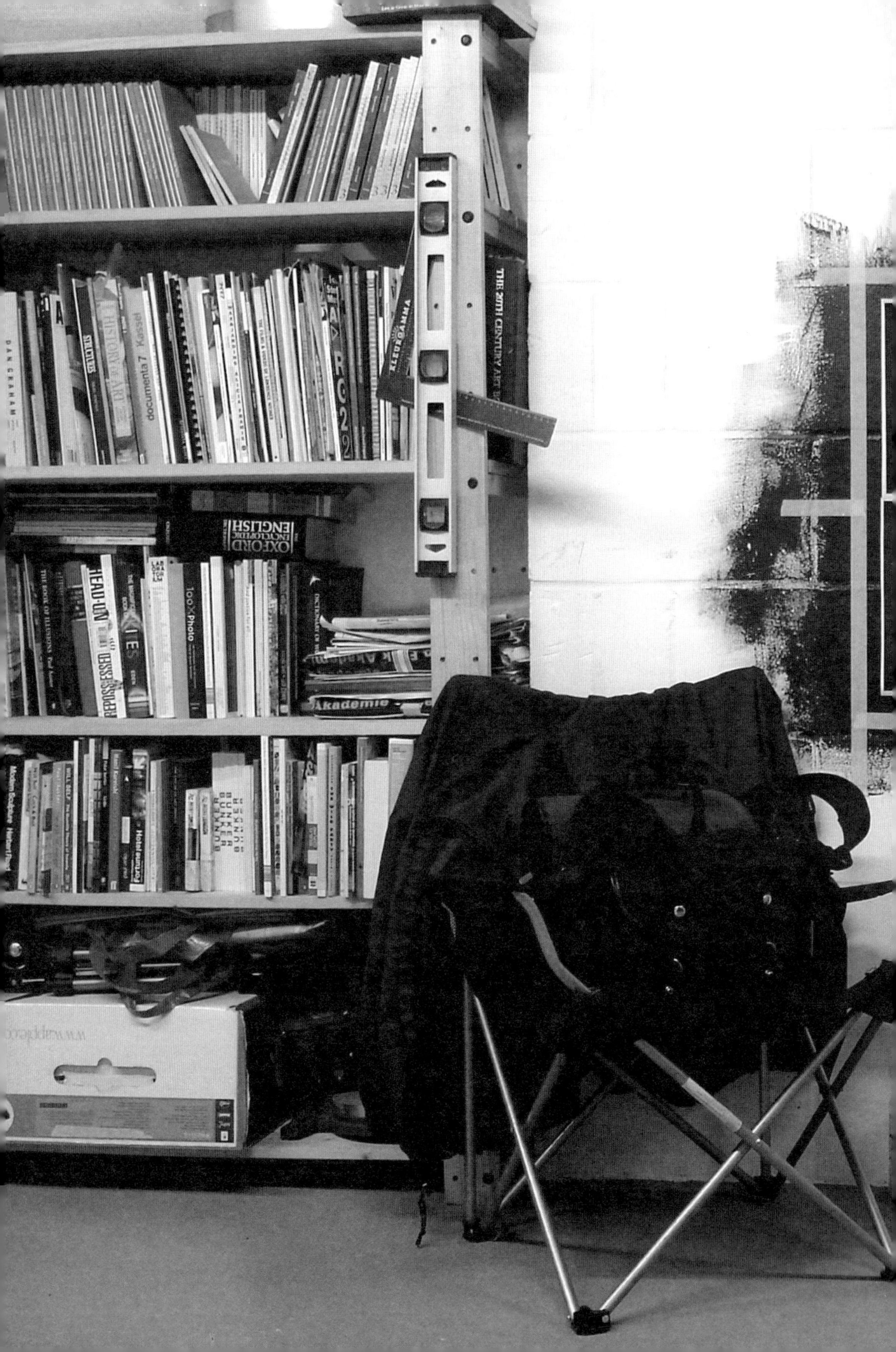
DAN GRAHAM
documenta 7 Kassel
OXFORD ENCYCLOPEDIC ENGLISH
THE 20TH CENTURY ART BOOK
HEAD-ON
REPOSSESSED
100 x Photo
Akademie
Modern Sculpture Herbert Read

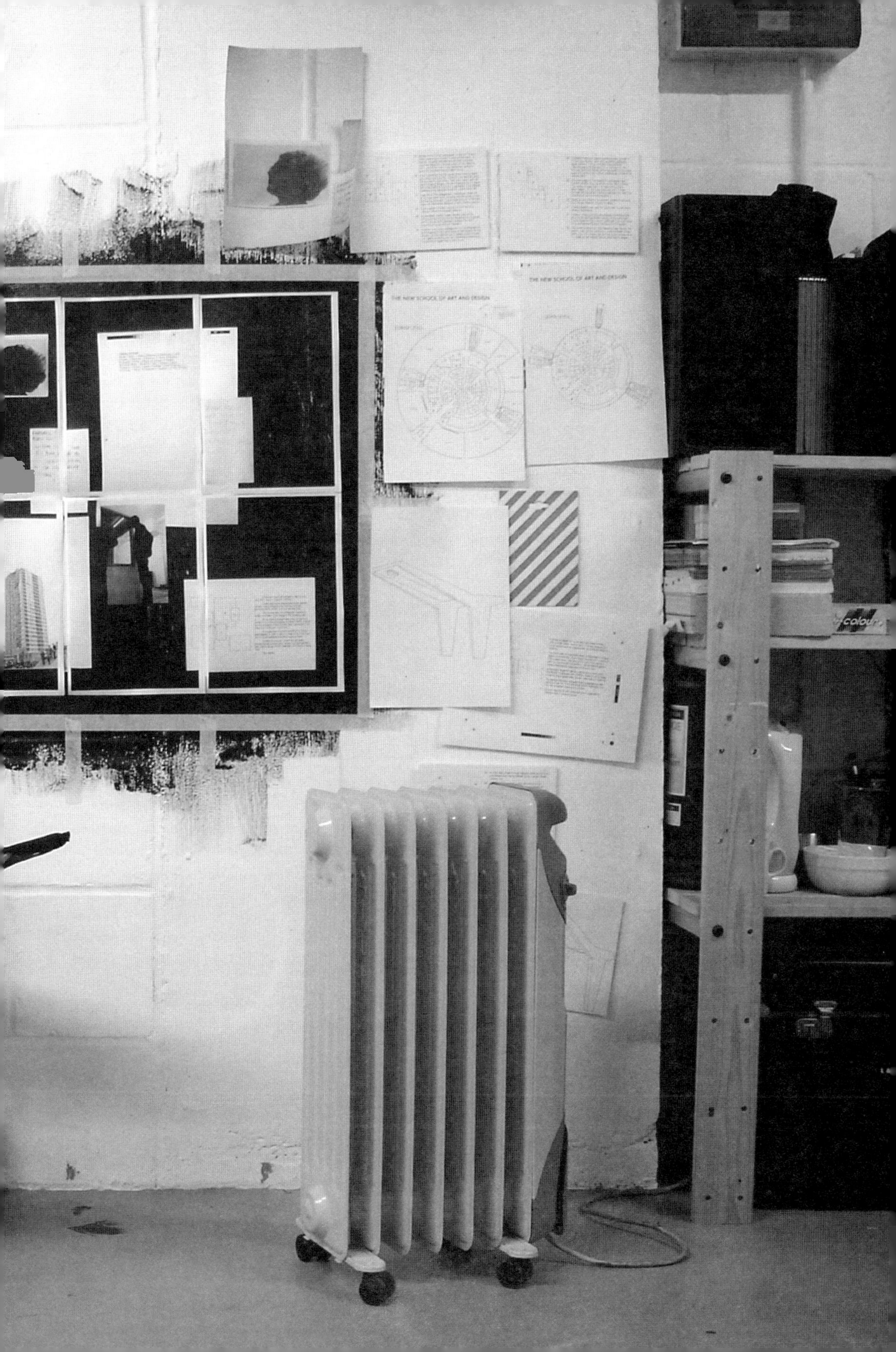
THE NEW SCHOOL OF ART AND DESIGN
THE NEW SCHOOL OF ART AND DESIGN

TOWARDS ASSUMPTION

by Emmanuelle Dauplay

50 stars and 5 points on each star, it's 55, said Alex with a malicious grin. He was referring to the American flag in the picture we were looking at. He was also compassionately mocking my ongoing, sweetly perverse relationship with the number 55. Everyone has probably had an encounter with a certain number that appears everywhere you set your eyes—an expression of chance, a demonstration of that which is eventual. I may have developed a stupid fixation. I shall never know until I reach some sort of conclusion, of closure, or else become too busy with actual tangible matters to always find magic every other hour in happenings that I most probably invent anyway, to bother looking for the significance of pseudo-poetic encounters, which are born and buried everyday.

Ah yes, 55. I used to live in an apartment at number 55, then I moved out to settle into another. I had two jobs at the time, and the address of both offices were numbered 55. To get to both places from both apartments, I had to take the 55 bus.

I cannot remember how it all started, or how I came to notice. I forgot about the beginning. All I know is that in a period of at least five years, the time was always something-55, my phone, credit card, social security numbers, the job centre and walk-in clinics' queue numbers, any routes, any stops, and so much more besides, all featured these two digits. In trains, airplanes, I was daydreaming at seat number 55. Once I was even relocated from window seat 43, there had been a mistake, the agent said, I hope you won't mind. Driven by a need to find meaning through my creation of a sign, with enthusiasm and ardour I began a process of delusional interpretation. A sign that took the form of a number—when it could have been a word, a sound, an object or a flavour—a number with no intrinsic meaning until I invested it with significance.

About a year ago, I decided to leave 55 and all the rest behind. I arrived in Toronto and found an apartment at number 123 Mutual Street. It sounded like it could be a new beginning, 123. The number felt fresh, it was set against a solid black wooden door, it was safe and cosy. I arrived on the tenth of a cold, dry and deserted January. There wasn't much for me to do, so I got busy reading manuscripts for a modest living and getting familiar with my surroundings. At this point I didn't know I was soon to find a job at number 55 Front Street East—I was patiently waiting for something to show up, to happen. I must confess this strong tendency to defer action, to be dilatory. I used to think I was a passive perfectionist, but in fact I'm a procrastinator, thwarted by an uncontrollable fear of making mistakes. It had crossed my mind that 55 was a discreet chaperone, leading me, reassuring me, perhaps even showing me the way. It had crossed my mind, too, that I could simply be a little off in the head.

Searching for my truth, constructing my own semiosis, being the author of my reality, I adopted the simplistic method of defining a sign as something that implies something in some respect, which, for me, stands for something in a way, for what it's worth. I gave it value, granted it reliability, I was seeing every and anything that could support my intuitive theory, that could fit tightly, nicely into my evolving narrative. I decided to overlook reason, to suppress it in favour of a quest for discovering meaning; ad infinitum. I thought my beliefs were real, I cherished them as a source of truth, sadly aware that truth should be independent of anyone's beliefs. Facts are what make things real, and I didn't have any. Was I looking for them only to authenticate the scheme I wished to entertain?

--

One weekend, I visited my cousin in British Columbia. I had never met him before, so I felt a little anxious, apprehensive, but also surprisingly careless. He picked me up at the airport and we drove to his velvet cottage, cottoned up in a mantel of snow. Fabian turned out to be a nice, amicable and well-rounded individual in his mid-forties, a joyous loner with the occasional boy- or girlfriend. His prominent belly, carefully protected by extra thick wool-knit sweaters, gave him a comforting allure, and his plump lips were inherited for him to hold a pipe. We had a heartening dinner, we introduced ourselves at great length, got tired and went to bed. We left early the next day. With his mind firmly set on making me enjoy the scenery, the beauty and the tranquillity that he had found in this pocket of Canada, he took me to Vancouver Island's Butchart Gardens—an odd, domestic choice—or so it seemed. I feared it would be closed at this time of year, he said, but you seem to be in luck: here are 55 acres of wonderful floral displays open for your eyes to see. As we walked towards a Japanese garden, my cousin contemplated my pensive expression, and wondered what was troubling me. Nothing, I said, then briefly explained my insignificant story of 55. Plants illustrate the Fibonacci series in the numbers and arrangements of petals, leaves, sections and seeds, uttered a friendly voice. Is that what you're talking about? The gardener, who was working on the layout and arrangement of some pale smooth stones, was also eavesdropping.

Daisies have 55 petals, for example, and a sunflower seed has 55 clockwise spirals, he continued. Yes, I know, I replied, I read something about it; it's funny. Yes, funny, he repeated; it deserves a smile. Somehow spooked by this surprising intervention, I grabbed my cousin's arm and we progressed along the promenade. I felt like a lost body investigating the environment it had wilfully corrupted. Give me a consistent theory of quantum gravity, I thought, arouse me with compelling evidence of the premises of causality, define the nature of time for me, and I'll stop it all. But if I can perform 27 steps before I reach the blue iron gate and the exit sign, then I'll continue to search for the unseen factor, I'll connect all occurrences, I'll find a worthy link between any two incidents.

Well into the evening, as we were finishing dinner by the rustic fireplace back at the cottage, Fabian mentioned that in the I-Ching the sum total of heavenly numbers and earthly numbers is also 55. It is this which completes the changes and transformations, and sets demons and gods in movement. But I suppose you know that too, he said. Yes, I've done my research, I replied. I was getting a little irritated, perhaps even ashamed, by the affair, by its redundancy, but was careful not to show any sign of impatience. It was warm, it was quiet, all was peaceful and docile, I was calmly getting drunk. We cheered to the truths we originate in order to find some wonder in ordinary existence, we saluted the sense of wonder that loosens the mind's restraint.

As Fabian got up to fill two more generous glasses of whisky, I noticed a little book on the antique coffee table. It was protected by the creamy shade of the lamp, inundated by the glare of the flames. Naturally, I picked it up. Ah, yes, you'd like that, Fabian said. Well, actually I read it a long time ago, I remarked, but I had never seen this edition before. The thin, light object I was holding was a collection of Paul Auster's writing. The cover displayed a group of jazz musicians who were celebrating the perfect rhythms of the stories. Well, let's see what's on page 55, said Fabian with an almost innocent smile as he bounced back in his upholstered armchair. Like alcohol, he added, coincidences enfold a burst of vitality and spawn a new lust for life. The desire to create them is only natural. I opened the book, soothed my throat with a poignant sip of whisky, and stared at the first sentence on that page. It read:

My first novel was inspired by a wrong number.

DEAR DEAR DEAR KIPPENBERGER

by Maxine Kopsa

Dear Writer,

Let's start at the end: 'Forget him, he's dead.'

Like an English Terrier with a stick, I'm not going to let this go. Throw it as far as you like and I'm going to bring it back to you again and again and again, even from the lake (though I'm anticipating you're grudgingly fond of dogs). The thing is, the whole idea about having this piece about Kippenberger has become more pertinent because slowly, almost without me noticing, the upcoming issue has become saturated with Biography. Not necessarily a series of straight monographs, of course, more a series of inquiries into the nature of Biography itself, which—by extension—implies a series of inquiries into the nature of this thing called History itself, which is something DDD has always been covertly interested in. The issue is also full of Repetition, and I'm curious about what happens in whatever that mysterious crossover area in venn diagrams is called where these two—Biography and Repetition—bleed into each other.

There's something that fundamentally connects here with Kippenberger, in the sense that I think he endures repetition more gracefully than any other artist currently experiencing overkill. The tritest but truest thing to say is that this is because he was so prolific and so varied. But Kippenberger WAS trite and true, and my feeling is that here we should be too.

So I just reread the year-old original piece you wrote—let's christen that the SLOW PIECE—and then the second six-month-old writing-in-fifteen-minuites exercise you did six months on, hereafter known as the QUICK PIECE. My idea now is that we construct something to be published by tacking together those two pieces with this letter, and this glue is visibly part of the final sculpture too. As ever, the trick is knowing when to stop—and doesn't that seem to be Kippenberger's greatest talent (aside from some obvious retort about alcoholism, and even then I can't help but wonder: knowing when to stop in terms of life, too)?

Last month in New York there were three simultaneous Kippenberger shows, and anyone might be excused for thinking they were by three different artists. The locations were telling too, as if implying some further meta-biography about Manhattan. The first, the Chelsea one (the Populist) was an exhaustive show of self-portraits, the quantity and quality overwhelming already in the foyer which was a wall of whichever of his posters included himself in one way or another. The second, on Madison Avenue (the Specialist) was the exhibition 'Dear Painter, Paint For Me', the collection painted by a billboard artist to his specifications, then signed as a compound of their names, Werner Kippenberger. And the third, at the independent Nyehaus among the faded elegance of Gramercy Park's National Arts Club (the Elitist) collected documentation of his global Metro-Net project—videos, models and other paraphenalia of the life-size metro entrances in Greece, Canada and their related air vents elsewhere.

All this: isn't it just describing different faces, moods, characters of the same person, artist, art scene, city; some barely fathomable psychogeography (or geopsychology)? That's why I suddenly thought that constructing the piece like this was the most appropriate form of monograph. But let's get back to where we started this piece more than a year ago:

> Maxine, I want an excuse to show some of the Kippenberger hotel letterhead notepaper drawings in DDD, to point to how they distill all the usual Kippenberger reference points—the hotel nomadism, the alcoholism, the generosity, the roughness, the brutality, the non-style, the personality, the signature etc. etc.—how they were the perfect found form to piss all over.

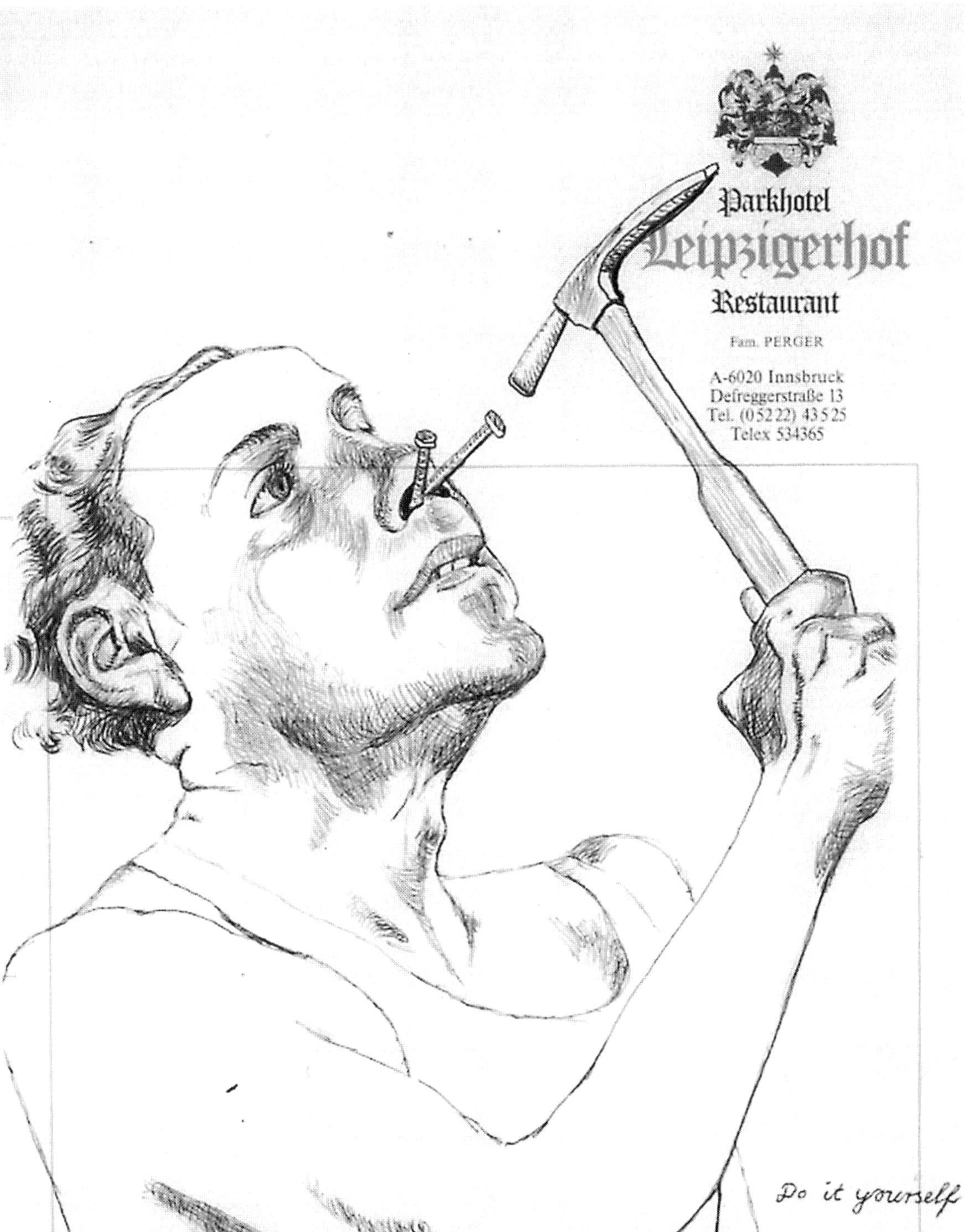

Untitled, 1993, Pencil, ballpen on hotel stationery, 29 × 21 cm

So: ladel on some contextualising text for me. Dear Writer, Write For Me. Discuss.

NOW I realise that you, Maxine, arrive at exactly the same point as I do here when you describe the video of him and Robert Ohrt in the FAST PIECE, that THIS is the single event, work, which captures—or embeds—everything else for you. So: is Kippenberger ALL THINGS TO ALL PEOPLE? Or at the very least (I'm less excited at this prospect, so no capitals): all things to all art writers?) My question to you isn't really that one punctuated by the 'Discuss' above, then, it's this:

Is the reason you arrive at that interview, me at the hotel notepaper, and Meuser in your SLOW PIECE at his 'Forget him: he's dead', as our respective distillations of this man, precisely because you're an art writer, me a graphic designer, and Meuser a friend?— that Kippenberger is a container, to be filled, completed, with whatever we bring to him?

Regards, Editor

QUICK PIECE

Dear Editor,

I'm awfully self conscious about writing for DDD. Especially since I was asked as the—how should we put it?—person-who-knows-something-we-don't, the, uh, art historian. Or the critic. Or the knower of some things made. In any case, even though I would never title myself art historian, I'm the OUTSIDER. And you're all INSIDE somewhere... The stinging avoidance (and shameless pull, I must add) to write had to do quite simply with the idea that you were expecting me to know more about one thing than you. I'd have to supply some goddamn-ly bright answers, some brainy, also astute and even shifty never-before-heard analysis. Purpose-full and completely pertinent. Without doubt it had to be one step removed from regular art historical missives because 'regular' is of course not purpose-full nor apply-able.

So you see you're asking me to be me but be 'more'. I say 'more' and put it between quotation marks because I obviously have a chip on my shoulder. The proof: ever since Paul Elliman asked me why I kept saying 'artist'—was I being euphemistic?—I find myself swallowing the term or entirely replacing it with 'maker', even in conversation with my own kind... So hold on. Right there. There's the root of reserve: turn it around.

I think you know more about something I know less about. You're closer. I underwrite the cliché that you all, you insiders, you makers, have experienced it and we haven't... IT being some kind of primary making thing. Hail the non-applied the autonomous ahhhh the freedom the real thing the non-dependent. Now we're getting down down down to the fundamental difference between makers and writers about makers again. Again. We do have to do this again and again and again. We do. So dear editor, my apprehension to write or not to write to you and for you, with you in my head, on my chipped shoulder, leans on a bored truism: you're better than me. And that there's an inside and an outside. Players and watchers.

But to be fair, if we really must get down to ground rules then we should really also question whether writing about makers is in itself as secondary—as not primary—as we (I?) believe? Quickly, quickly then slowly: On a good day, I'd have to answer that there are at least two manners of writing about, about. And one is less worthy, and the other on par. On a bad day I'd say it's all parasitical, no matter how well cut.

Enough. Today's a good day, and let's leave it at that, for now.

This all as a miserable intro fully substantiated until I read one of the articles, the first no less, in the latest issue of DDD. And felt better. I didn't actually finish it. I lost interest. That's why I felt better. So I've decided to employ a technique a writer friend told me about: all you can write in 15 minutes. Just like a Sunday dim sum brunch. Here goes my chestnut (and there is a link with all the above, I swear):

Kippenberger sits in a beige raincoat, sunglasses on next to Robert Ohrt, in a jacket, sunglasses on. They're both smoking. The studio is plain. Just a studio. Plenty of microphones, electrical cords

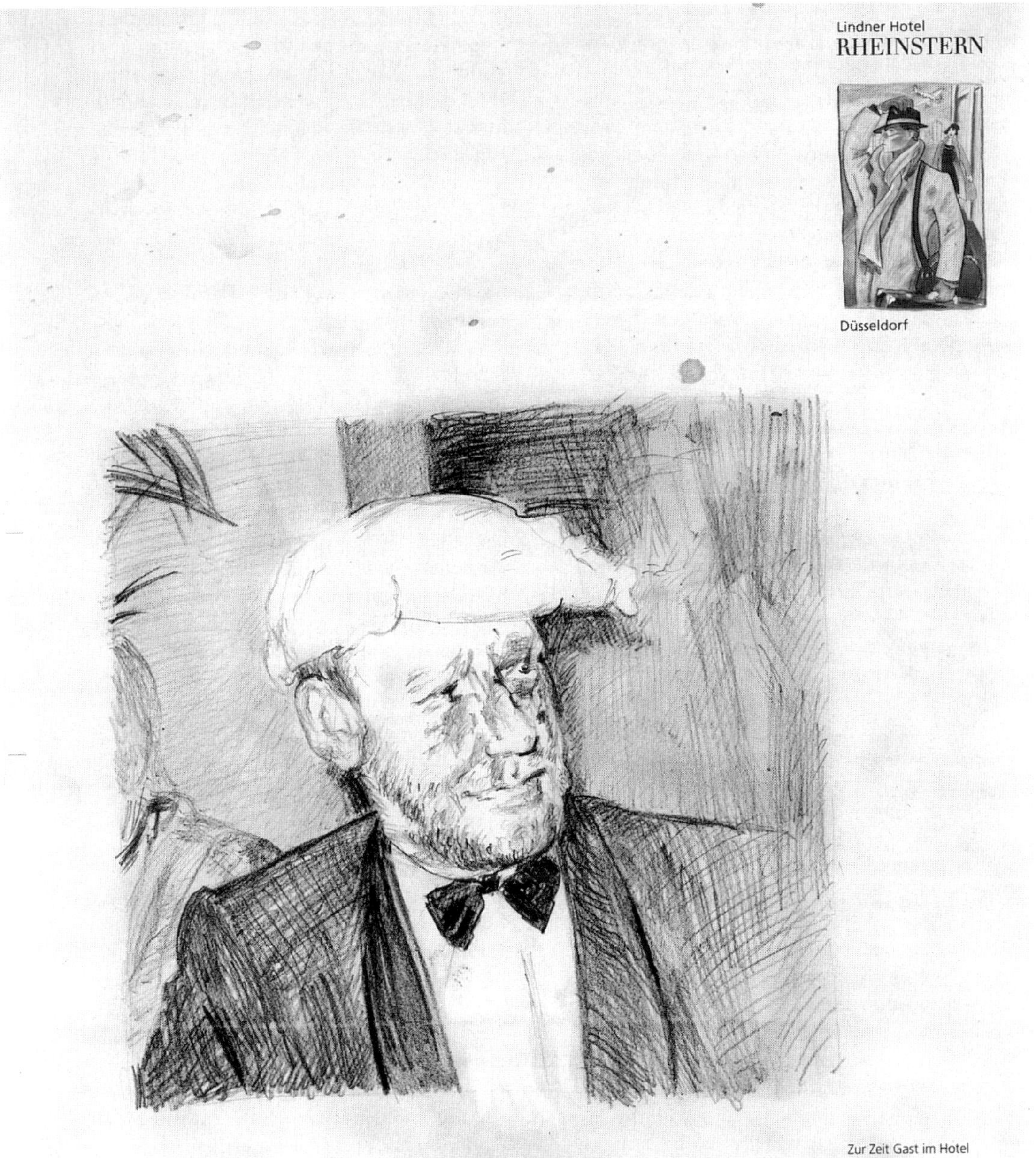

Untitled, 1992, Pencil on hotel stationery, 29.7 × 21 cm

making their way from behind our camera view into view, along the chairs' legs and back to the blue backdrop. There's a small table, I think, and I think also that the chairs, though not exactly bar stools, are slightly higher than the regular chair, forcing them to lean over awkwardly for the ashtray. Which I think they do, which is why I think they were sitting high, and I think I remember Kippenberger had one leg straightened out forward to keep him up and balanced. But they do both slouch, that I recall. And grin, or even a giggle, if you can say that men in their late 40s giggle. The equivalent, at least. And it is awkward, the whole thing, the higher chairs, the small coffee table, the sunglasses, the raincoat, somehow Ohrt's late 1980s jacket, certainly his oversized vuarnets.

This live interview marks the beginning of an international art market, of globalism before we started using the term all over the place and for everything. Even though after WWII, what with all the moving from Paris to New York, there was plenty of internationalism—which really took off in the 1960s—there wasn't in effect an even, international (i.e. Europe/USA) art market. The fact that we're watching them play at it, Kippenberger and Ohrt, with it, marks its true birth. They know it so they can afford to appropriate its aspects. They're playing at being global players (while still oh so German) without being about, about.

See, what we watch for six and a half minutes is Ohrt asking Kippenberger questions from a Jörg Immendorf catalogue—he's actually holding it and reading the questions to Kippenberger—questions some other interviewer, some other critic, asked Immendorf some other time. And what we see is Kippenberger answering—countering, really—with his own answers from a previous published catalogue—also in hand—from a previous interview with a different critic altogether. In French. The thing is, Ohrt can speak French, at least he seems to be understanding what he's saying—there's a good amount of proper pronunciation—but Kippenberger doesn't. We're watching Kippenberger reading his own words, his own answers about himself, what he's doing, how he does it, his own explanations of his making as though he has no clue of their content. So there's subtitles, in French, a transcript of what's being said, following the two speakers, demonstrating their logic. The new FOUND logic, happening right there, in front of us, at that moment, in that very studio, and these subtitles, these verifications, pull us, the happy onlookers, into the whole circuitous affair—the 'interview'—by helping us to comprehend and not comprehend at the exact same time. The utter disorder of about. The downright pure, primary, autonomous, non-dependent, purposeless rendering of making.

Sure I could mention the posters, the invitation cards, the hotel drawings, the countless books, but it's all there, all in this interview. All the irony, the happy cynicism, the failure, all the crossing of the line of making and not-making, all the avoid-making, the letting of the gaps, the refusal. The plain refusal. And not even on the making level alone. On all possible levels. Kippenberger and Roberto on Kippenberger and Roberto within a big big version of the world, conscious of the bigness of the world and conscious of Kippenberger and Roberto in this big world.

That's it. It was a lot of fun.

SLOW PIECE

Dear All,

There's a story about Martin Kippenberger that goes like this: Invited to Yale for a day of guest teaching Mr Kippenberger takes his students to the favourite local pub where he drinks breakfast with them. In the afternoon the entire merry band returns to Yale where, instead of doing the usual lecture and studio visits, he holds a drawing contest: whoever can draw the best portrait of Frank Sinatra wins his or her portrait done by Kippenberger himself. Apparently, when everyone was finished, Kippenberger couldn't decide on a winner—'you all have too much talent!' he exclaimed. He sat down to draw each student's portrait, and so it goes.[1]

I don't know what made me think I could write about Martin Kippenberger ...

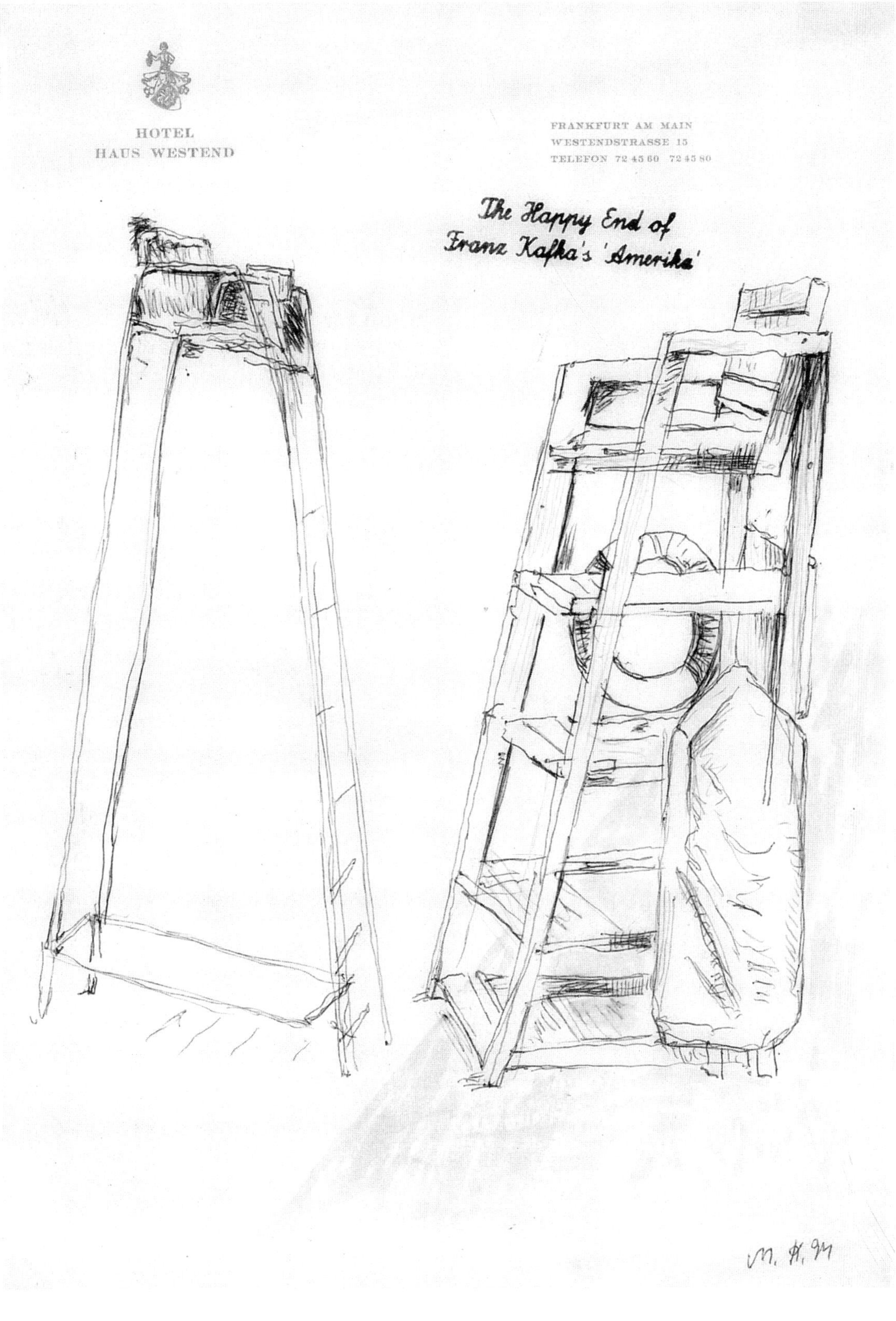

Untitled, 1994, Ballpen, colour pencil on hotel stationery, 29.7 × 21 cm

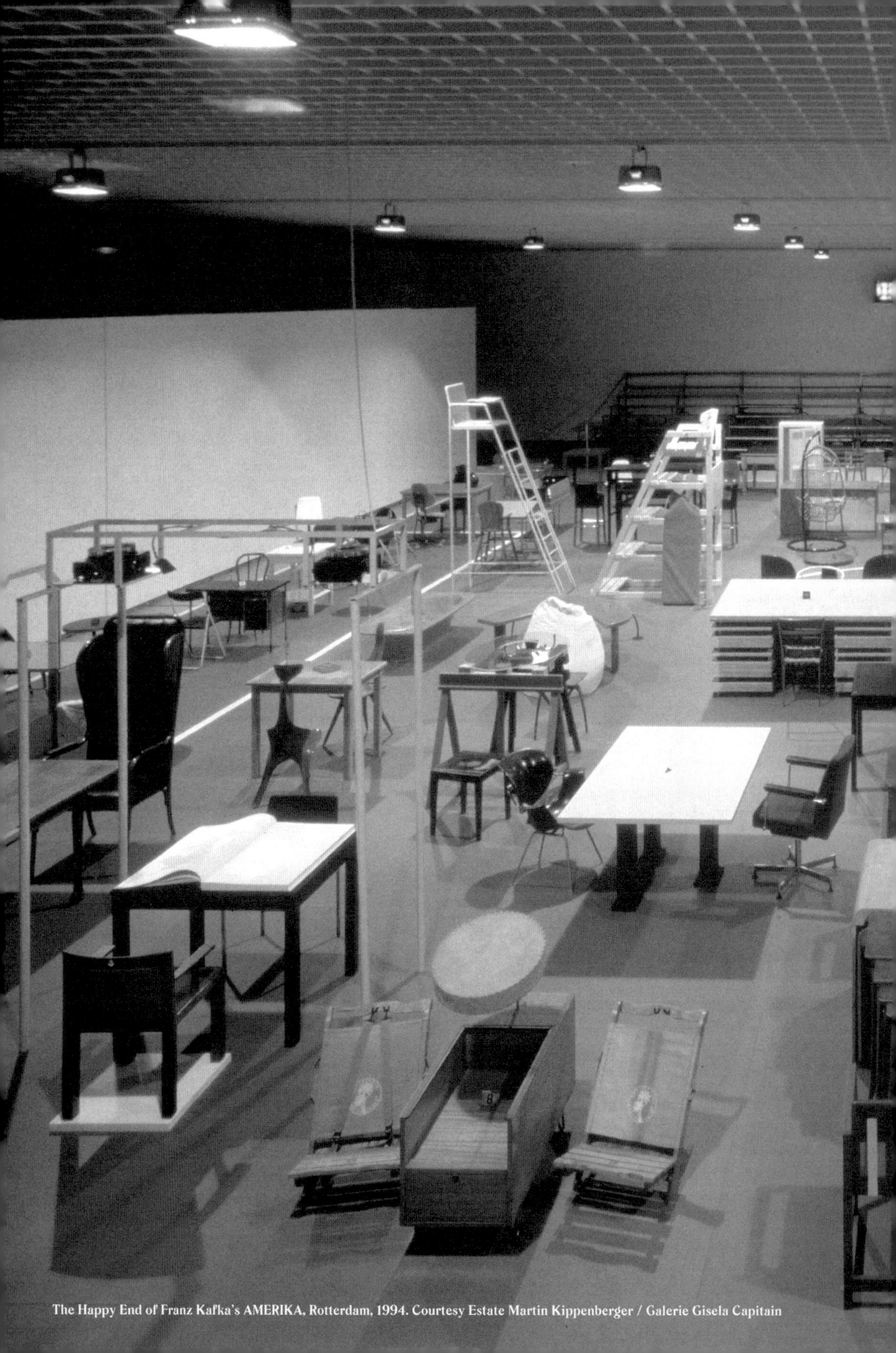

The Happy End of Franz Kafka's AMERIKA, Rotterdam, 1994. Courtesy Estate Martin Kippenberger / Galerie Gisela Capitain

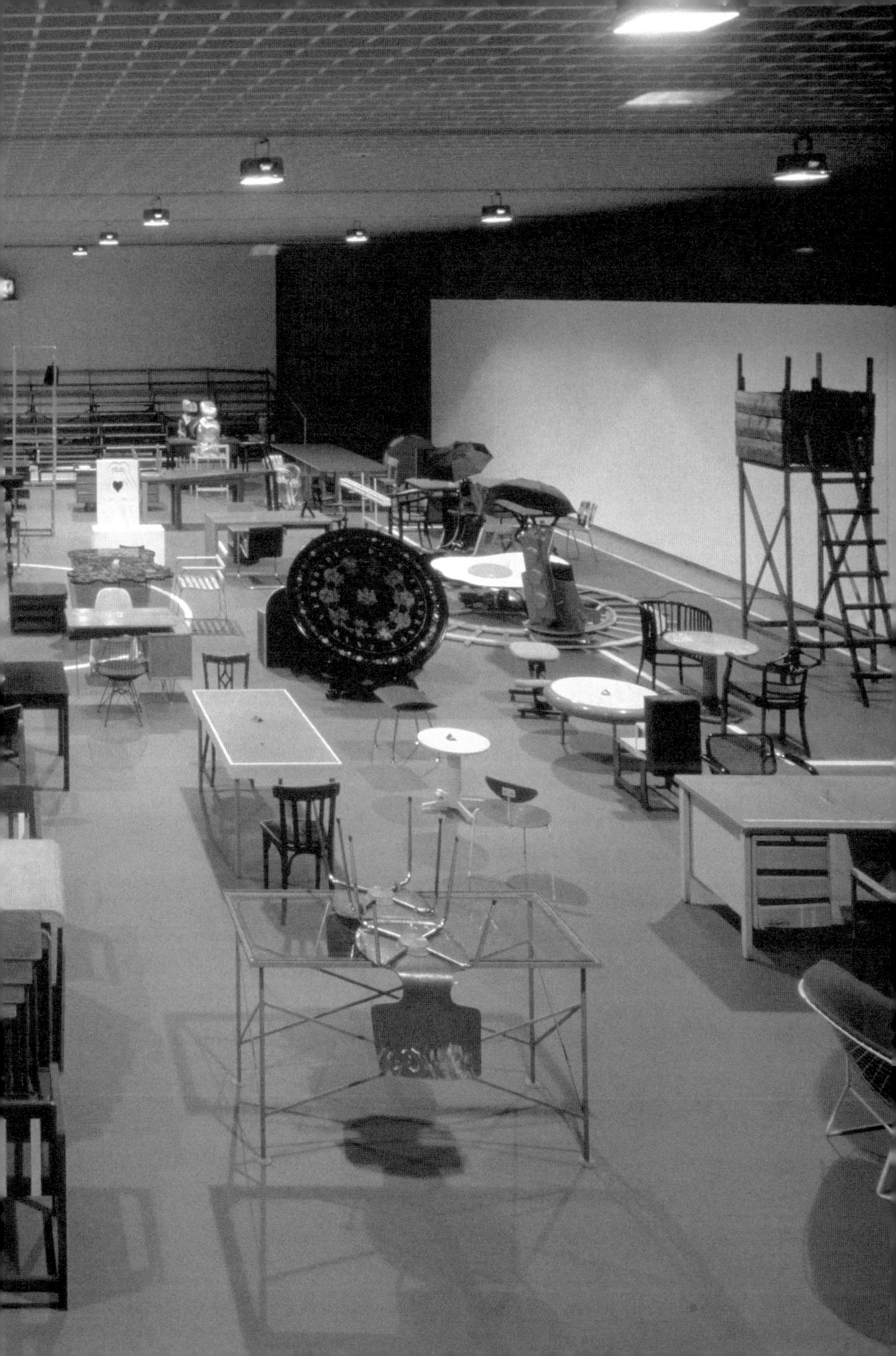

A bit of a lie, actually. I do: there was a solo exhibition opening in honour of what would have been his 50th birthday, at the Museum für Neue Kunst in Karlsruhe and I knew that many people would see it and that many people were talking about it because it was the first major retrospective since his death in 1997. And above all, I knew I was curious, but that I had little grounds. I was curious to see why so many people I have spoken to recently about Kippenberger, artists, gallerists, curators, why they all seemed to get the same glint in their eyes, give the same corroborative, sympathetic nod and then say not much more on the matter, really. And I was shocked to see myself do the same. I glint, I nod and then I look down. As if my companion and I feel the same, know the same, and know we don't have to add to what it is we know about Martin Kippenberger. Or do we? Shouldn't we? Speaking for myself, I certainly needed to polish up (validate?) the reasons why I glint and nod and smile and look down because, frankly, I don't imagine I have much more reason to react this way than the simple belief in his large reputation and my ardent wish to follow this rumour.

I asked a German museum director a couple of weeks ago at an opening of a young painter show what it is he thought young artists now saw in Martin Kippenberger's work. 'Kippi.' He said 'They all call him Kippi.' Kippi as if they knew him, as if they had worked with him, and as if they still do. His answer was short but I understood. We glinted, I nodded, he looked down.

'Kippi' is what his friends—and it seems he had many—had called him.

If you look at the literature on and listen to stories about Kippenberger you will quickly realise that most is anecdotal. Stories of how he got drunk with X and then with Y and then really drunk with Z. Or, more specifically and closer to home, of him teaching at the Rijksakademie and trying out the Yale trick. It was Michael Raedecker who put his foot down when he got a call from a fellow participant who told him to come instead to the bar where they were all holding their 'studio visits'. 'No way' he thought, 'I want Kippenberger to see my work.' And so he did. Forced back into the proper rules of teaching, a couple hours later Kippenberger enters Readecker's studio. He enters with one glass and a bottle of wine in hand. Pouring Michael a glass and keeping the bottle for himself, like a good teacher should, he proceeds to instruct the young participant as to where to make the necessary (formal) changes. And then there are better, more curious stories, ones like how he bought shares in a restaurant in Venice, California, called 'Capri',[2] of how he ran the inspiring exhibition space called Kippenberger's Office[3] and later the S.O. 36 hall (both in Berlin), organising concerts and shows, film screenings and even recording records himself. One also reads sadder stories of his mother dying in an accident and bequeathing him 750,000 DM at the age of 23,[4] or crazier stories of unfinished and or unrealised plans—often deliberately partial—of a museum of contemporary art with himself as director, called the MOMAS (Museum Of Modern Art, Syros, Greece),[5] or of the ongoing imaginary metro system called 'Metro-Net' that spanned the world, linking cities and desolate places, Kippenberger's way of commenting on the inevitable guzzling movement of globalisation.[6] Stories which slip easily into work or works which easily become stories: A chair stands at a table, a completely different chair at the other side. They are empty and seem to wait, their mis-matchedness somehow relaying their anthropomorphism. They have conversed, one could almost say. A job interview has taken place. And he got it, whoever he is. Let's call him Peter. Peter got the job. And Peter's administration will follow. This was the happier end to Franz Kafka's Amerika, according to Martin Kippenberger. A novel he chose to elaborate upon and change, change into a large playing field punctured by tables and chairs, desks and watchtowers; punctured by the promise of endless social encounters, ones controlled by (bureaucratic) regulations and silent, general consent, but ones, nonetheless always 'successful'.[7]

Finished and unfinished stories, anecdotes which become allegories. Allusions, citations, puns, one-liners, political annotations, social refutations, art historical de- and reconstructions, ironic plays and countless cruel mockeries of himself (most of all) but also of others. These are the many ingredients of Kippenberger's complex body of work. Although, undeniably—albeit cynical—it is his insolence towards colleagues which is perhaps the most revealing. Within the ridicule, and, above all, amongst the titles of

Courtesy Estate Martin Kippenberger / Galerie Gisela Capitain

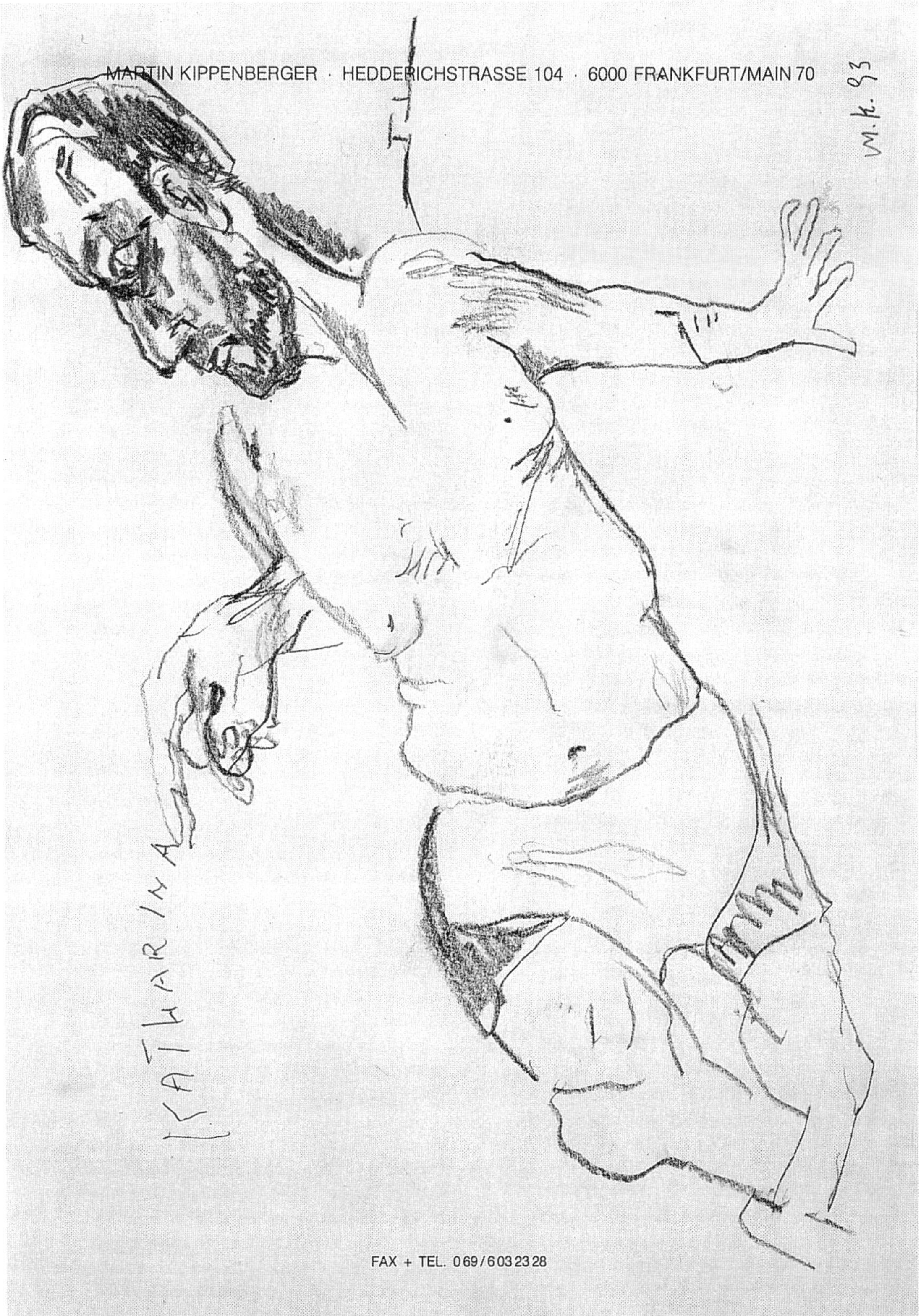

Untitled, 1993, Pencil on hotel stationery, 21 × 29.7 cm

this ridicule, Kippenberger's affiliation to his own time can be read quite fluently. The neo-expressionists were first on his hit list: Walter Dahn and Jiri Dokoupil got it in his series called the 'I.N.P. Pictures' (1984). 'The Is Not Embarrassing Pictures' parodied Dahn and Dokoupil's romantic vision of primitivism which went a bridge too far in Kippenberger's eyes in their 'Africa' catalogue. Next was Thomas Schütte, Harald Klingelhöller, Reinhard Mucha, the so-called 'Model-Builders' from Dusseldorf. Kippenberger's models (quasi mock-ups) of various 'politically correct' buildings with titles like 'Student Hall Riad' (1985) and 'Design for the administration building of resort for recuperating mothers in Güutersloh'[8] (1985) are a harsh review of such model attitudes. The point of the parody developing from the combination of the excessively didactic and contrived titles and the desperately bare, low-fi materials (all models were made from wooden pallets).

Even god himself, Joseph Beuys, was not left holy. A particularly rude portrait of his mother, The mother of Joseph Beuys (1984) attests: Beuys' mother is rendered as a very sober, very bleak, incredibly serious, a Malevich-like farmer-cum-soldier, an unattractive she-man, to put it bluntly. The meaning here is, I think, clear: Beuys's crusade was just that: an anachronistic battle. Anselm Kiefer was of course an even easier target, one Kippenberger liked to combat together with his friend Albert Oehlen. They apparently discovered the cool effects of painting with porridge oats, effects as affected as Kiefer's mushy moralistic material, though, much like with the wooden pallets, clearly low-grade enough to counter Kiefer's highbrow, heavy-handed ethical and historical magnanimity. Their quasi-historical paintings made with porridge oats were often of a Ford Capri. And finally, it was Gerhard Richter who got it as much for his own reputation as for the workings of the art market itself. A small coffee table made of one of Richter's grey painting from 1977 which Kippenberger had acquired knowing full well once placed into his work, made into the actual top of the table, would never fetch the selling price of the Richter ohne Kippenberger itself, Modell Interconti (1987) fetishizes the fetishist. It is a work in which the synthetic value placed on a Richter—Richter standing in here for many a famous artist—is paradoxically both lessened and increased. 'Heil Hitler, You Fetishists'[9] you almost hear Kippenberger say, as he sits centre stage demanding attention. Looking around himself it seems he saw an (upsetting?) expanse of the here and now punctured too feebly by these colleagues, these colleagues, in his mind either too serious, too ascetic, too stuck-up, too slow, too bourgeois, too lazy, or simply too their-time to make a difference.

He, the unhappy hedonist, through all these feisty manoeuvres, succeeded in doing the near impossible, succeeded in achieving the ultimate two-step, succeeded in, simply said, taking himself seriously and taking the piss AT THE SAME TIME. Or more poetically put, destroying the world (killing all his darlings), loudly and softly with a bang and a whimper. There's a picture of him at the back of a catalogue[10] which tells a befitting story. Next to a very serious Jurgen Klauke in his studio and a close up of Anselm Kiefer lighting a modest sized cigar, Kippenberger is shown standing in a bank, at the teller's counter, smiling smugly while putting away a wad of cash. Underneath, a brilliant coincidence, is the title of one of his works illustrated in the book: Not Knowing Why, But Knowing What For (1994).

Reading the stories, looking at the pictures, listening to tales of the good old Kippi days causes you to do something you were taught not to. All this information coupled with the abundance of works makes you read the works as though they were made for you, as though he and you had a special thing going. Worst of all, as though you knew him. They make you equate the maker and the made, producing a naggingly incorrect series of deductions: 'to understand Kippenberger is to understand Kippenberger' becomes 'to understand Kippenberger is to understand art' and leads to: 'to appreciate Kippenberger is to understand life.'

These dodgy deductions continue along a train of thought which stops at a text called 'In the Name of Picasso' by Rosalind Krauss. It's an article about the workings and misgivings of Proper Name Art History, a decree, really about how ridiculous it is to associate the maker—his name, his reputation, his life—with his work. Many writers on Picasso practice 'Art as Autobiography'

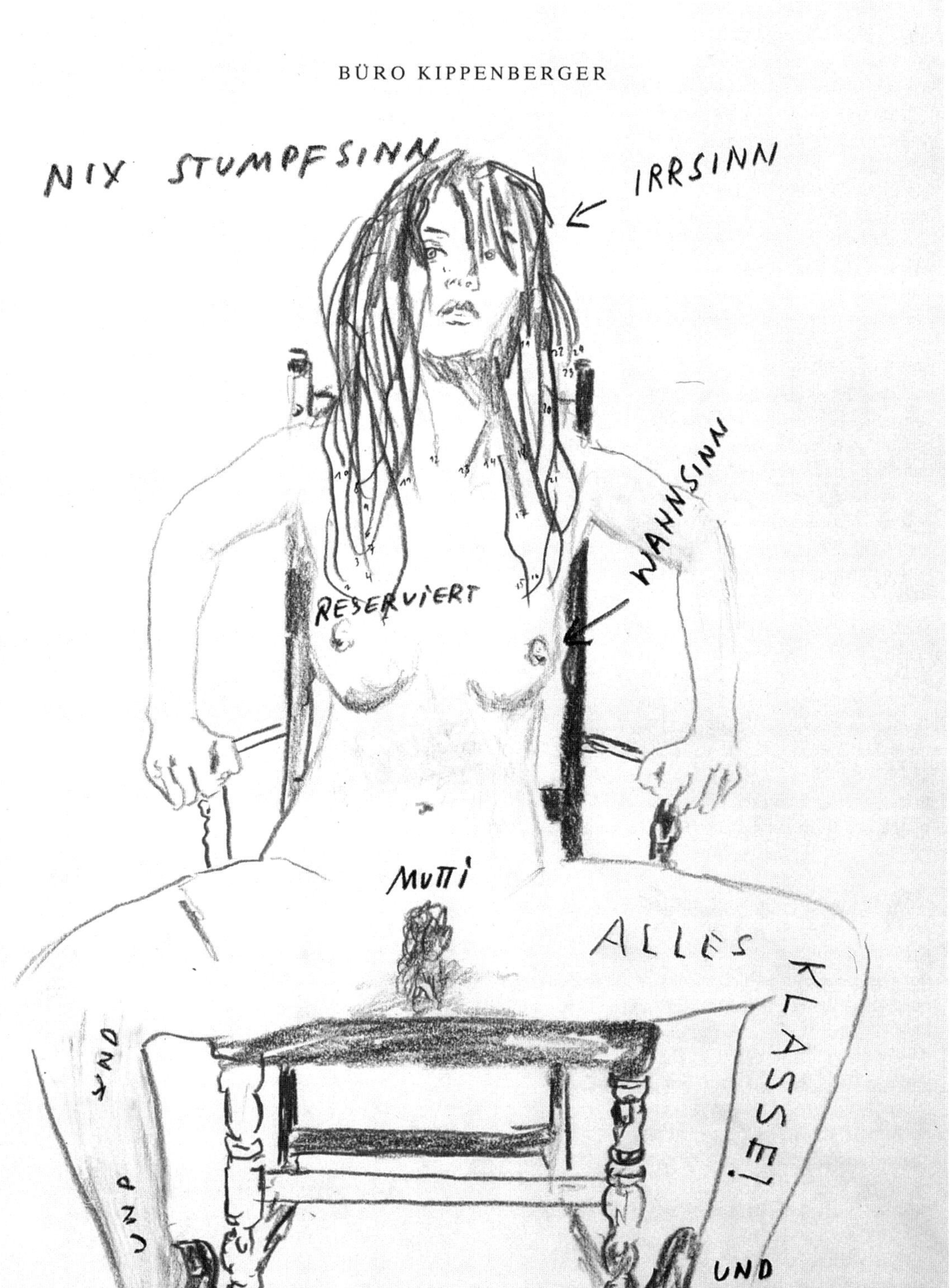

Untitled, 1993, Pencil, colour pencil on hotel stationery, 29.7 × 21 cm

she explains, and she tells of how absurd it is to analyse an oeuvre according to encounters the maker may or may not have had, experiences in his/her personal life s/he may or may not have undergone which may or may not have filtered into his/her work. Krauss pleads for a complete disassociation of personal history from transpersonal history claiming the utter impossibility of intelligently combining the two. And perhaps she's correct, to a certain degree: to analyse Picasso's different periods according to who he was sleeping with at the time does get a bit dull and, needless to add, leads to dumb theory. But to ignore the maker in all cases and under all circumstances leads to the kind of art historical methodology which also infers the dangerous notion that we, the viewers, must make up our minds about a work without prior knowledge, or, worse, ensuing knowledge of s/he, the maker, where s/he is coming from (literally and figuratively) what s/he is intending, in short, what the maker may mean by this or that work. The no-to-the-proper-name! kind of attitude begs the modernist belief that a work must be understood immediately and virginally. That its worth lies more or less entirely—give or take a few obvious social, historical and contextual factors—in its intrinsic nature. Death of the author and all that. So why the major slip up when it comes to Kippenberger, why the subjective history and all the theories peppered with personal anecdotes at every turn, in every book?

A day before the opening I'm sitting with Franz and we're talking about the exhibition and about the way in which it seems they had set it up. 'He's no more of a painter than I am' Franz spits out indignantly. 'They've made a painter show of his work.' He heaves an annoyed sigh and looks down at his glass. 'But Franz, they all think of you as a painter too.' I point out. 'I Know!' He almost yells. And then goes quiet. Indeed, how could Kippenberger be a painter if he showed such disrespect for its modernist ('true') values by asking someone else to paint the pictures he wanted to see. Dear Painter, Paint For Me (1981) is a series of large canvases painted only according to his instructions. How could he be a sculptor, for that matter, if he made an entire series of 3-D works titled Familie Hunger (1985) based on one very Henry Mooresque 'sculpture' shown briefly in Hitchcocks's Rear Window, in a scene where one of the neighbours James Stuart is spying on greets another neighbour who is apparently sculpting away in her garden on a work she says is titled 'Hunger'.

How could he? The funny thing—the difficult thing—is, that he is in fact both and more. The main point of concern and confusion with Kippenberger lies not in the fact that he was exceptionally prolific and diverse in terms of subject and form, as most will tell you (because once you learn to read the signs you inevitably understand their meaning[11]), the difficulty with Kippenberger lies in the fact that the works also possess a virtuous material quality. Though irrefutably conceptual, they are at the same time, simply said, well done. The viewer is locked into admiring their surface. Locked in, seduced, and made to look seriously at the work at hand in a manner of observation which can only be said to make him/her the dummy by any conceptual standpoint. And, conversely, by looking only at the works' conceptual significance, the viewer might get the joke but not the punchline. There's really no two ways about it, or, better still, there are exactly two ways about it: Kippenberger the rumour feeds off of Kippenberger the artist. His work is his reputation: to understand Kippenberger is to understand Kippenberger. 'Down with the bourgeoisie'[12] he says with a smug smile folding the wad of crisp cash in his hand. Whether through posters, invitation cards, artist books, installations, sculptures, paintings or drawings, through the very specific or the unbelievably generic, be it banal or clichéd, Kippenberger did not merely tell others off. He tells us a story. His works read like a massive public diary. A monolithic, ear-splitting address in which he tells us of himself, and—more quietly—through himself, of his time, and through all time—more faintly—of love, of politics, of control, of convention. Of endless social interactions.

'Would Kippenberger have been happy with this show?' I ask everyone I can at the opening. I wasn't sure myself whether I was happy with it. 'No, I don't think so,' someone related to his Estate answers. 'They rebuilt Deep Throat, made all the effort, spent all the money, but put it way at the back of the main space. They should have put it right at the entrance, where it could

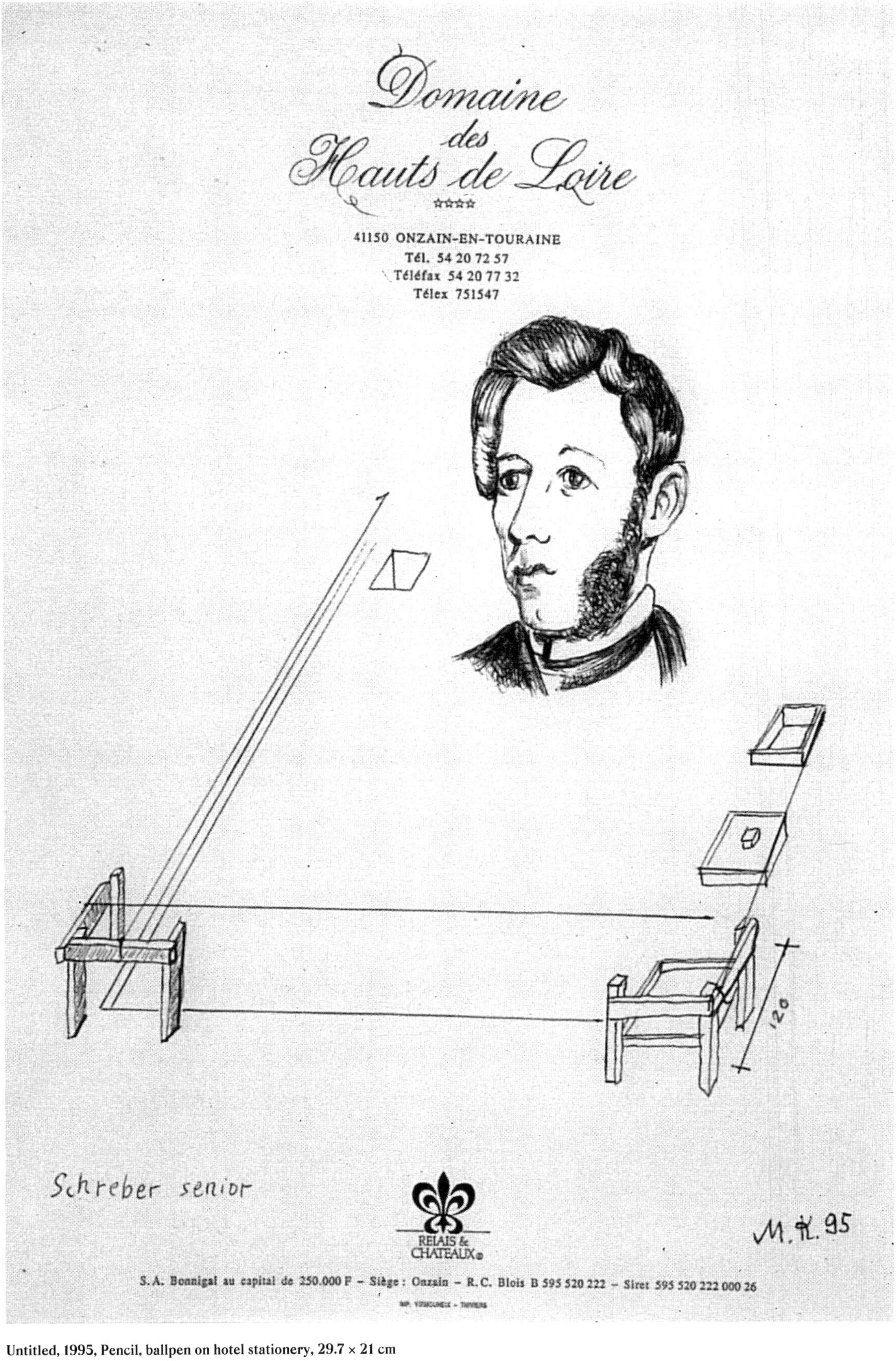

Untitled, 1995, Pencil, ballpen on hotel stationery, 29.7 × 21 cm have made a strong point. Made the point it should be making.' Make a strong point. That's what it was about. It's not about the actual point itself.

But about making it. 'Put your eye in your mouth'[13] you hear him say. I bumped into the museum director again and asked him the same. 'I doubt it. There's no friction between the works. Everything is too neat, too clean. Paintings over here, sculptures and installations over there, posters hung here.' 'The dissemination of mediocrity',[14] you almost hear him curse, and then, out of desperation add: 'I'm going into the birch forest as my pills will be taking effect soon.'[15]

Later, we've move to the dinner where Kippenberger's favourite food is being served: Noodles ('social pasta') and jello. Meuser, his friend and colleague sits smoking and looking somewhat peevishly around this large room punctured with guests. 'An endless band of successful social interactions', you hear him say softly. Meuser wasn't listening to us, he was drinking, and I guess had gotten smarter since the good old Kippi days because I watched him consistently take one glass of red wine, and then one glass of mineral water, one glass of wine, one glass of water, wine, water. What is it they say about water and wine? Long ago, that Jesus turned one into the other and now that we've learned to add one to the other. Transformation, mythification, conciliation. I asked Meuser what I had been asking the rest. His answer was clear: 'Forget him, he's dead.' He was glintless, I nodded, he looked away.

NOTES

1. As told by Ronald Jones in his article, 'Swizzle Shtick', in Artforum, October 1997.
2. Hence the obsession of the Ford Capri in the Capri series done together with his friend Albert Oehlen?
3. Bureau Kippenberger was established in 1978 with Gisela Capitain who now oversees the Kippenberger Estate.
4. Enough money with which he was able to finance his early trips abroad to Florence, for example, and later the Bureau; money which he is said to have spent very quickly.
5. MOMAS was founded in 1993 and shows did take place these by such as Christopher Wool who made direction signs for MOMAS, Herbert Kiecol, Cosima van Bonin, Stephen Prina, Michel Majerus. 'Shows' consisted mainly of posters and invites but never of works that actually in any way altered the make-up of the actual structure—a supposed slaughter house never put to use—for which 'they' (he and his band of mischievous bad boys) had not received a proper licence.
6. Metro-Net is a series of entrances or vents complete with sound A total of five are completed: one on the Greek island of Syros; one in Dawson City, Canada; the third, Transportable Subway-Entrance (1997) at documenta X; another in Munster now in Karlsruhe; and in Leipzig.
7. The Happy Ending Of Franz Kafka's AMERIKA is an incredibly involved installation which was first shown in Rotterdam in 1994, then in 1999 at the Deichtorhallen Hamburg and most recently during the Carnegie International '99 –'00 at the Carnegie Museum of Art. Kippenberger was a great collector, not only of art but also of books, cartoons, magazines and furniture.
8. Studentenwhonheim Riad; Entwurf Verwaltungsgebäude Für Müttergenesungswerk In Gütersloh.
9. Title of painting of a bank machine, Heil Hitler, Ihr Fetischisten (1984).
10. Klaus Honnef, Kunst Der Gegenwart, Taschen, 1988.
11. Kippenberger developed his own patois, so to speak, by way of themes which recur pictorially in various forms and recur literally in his titles. Subjects are returned to like Santa Claus, the frog prince, the lamp post for drunks. They repeat and change but also interact, each time more pregnant with implication: Santa Claus, the frog prince and even the lamp post are symbols of or for the small, pitiful hero ('I want to be first in the second class'); as were eggs, fried or boiled, egg-men, pasta, the Ford Capri; the idea of mediocrity, the notion of the joke, the workings of pills, of drunkenness, of assistants–all called Peter, (his own) nomadism, (his own) studio, (his own) failure.
12. Title of painting, Nieder Mite Der Bourgeoisie (1983).
13. Title of the installation at the San Francisco Museum of Modern Art, 1991.
14. Title of painting, Die Verbreitung Der Mittelmässigkeit, 1994.
15. Title of an installation, Jetz Geh Ich In Den Birkenwald, Denn Meine Pillen Wirken Bald, 1990.

THE JOHN PEEL EFFECT

by Robert Garnett

Always the same, always different.[1]

We have long become accustomed to the familiar refrain that artists are the new rock 'n' roll stars just as we have long become myopically accepting of the idea that NEW-NESS = YOUNG-NESS. But something happened in the UK last October that should make us pause for thought. This was the premature and untimely death, at the age of 65, of undoubtedly the most vital champion and facilitator of new popular music. In the year in which he became of pensionable age he still personified everything that was genuinely new and radical about popular musical culture.
John Peel was a figure whose attitude and taste confounded any conceptions of age. Throughout his career, spanning over five decades, he continued to exceed the cyclical temporality of pop's fashion system. His example is one that both foregrounds and confounds the ageists that prevail within our culture to the extent that it should force us to seriously rethink the relations between culture, newness and the cult of youth.

NEW!

Nevertheless, within the art world, the increasing privileging of youth has without doubt been one of the key shifts to have taken place over the past decade or so. This is particularly the case in post-yBa London where, if you're the wrong side of 40, attending an opening can occasionally make you feel like the proverbial Dad at the school disco. It may not be the same case everywhere, but in an intense scene-economy such as this, if you've not made it as an artist by 30 it's time to start thinking about another career.
Many have already been and gone by this age, have won the Turner Prize and faded into obscurity. The main determinant of this privileging of the figure of the young is, of course, the market and the media. Art's increasing alignment with style culture, since at least the time of Pop Art, has meant that novelty has by now become almost totally equated with YOUNG-NESS.
That this has occurred has in no doubt been aided and abetted by the lack of any adequate conception of THE NEW within advanced art theory and criticism. This has left us in something of a double bind, where an aloof 'critical' theory dismisses THE NEW as an ideological myth, leaving the art market's novelty machine free to turn over at an ever-accelerating rate in its cycle of IN-NESS and OUT-NESS as the perpetual construction of commodity-equivalence.

In both art and pop this state of affairs is more than taken for granted, to the extent that it is difficult, if not impossible, to disassociate the frisson of the new from the vitality of youth.
But I wish to speculate here that all this might not be as inevitable and immutable as it might appear, because I think it is becoming clearer that something has changed within popular culture, and particularly the culture of pop music.
While art has been busy sidling up to pop (or at least its own projected image of it), pop itself might be seen to have been undergoing something of a shift in direction. Consumers of pop music today, whether 18 or 80, are every bit as discerning as those of art, and is becoming clear that in pop The New might no longer be the exclusive preserve of the young. If one consults any reliable barometer of avant-garde taste in pop music over the past decade—take the UK-based Wire magazine for example—one will see that its conception of what is cutting edge is far less exclusive than that of the art world's.
What would be surprising for most denizens of the latter is the lack of any real generation gap within a context that is itself synonymous with the postwar invention of the category of YOUTH.
This emerging transformation offers us—indeed forces us—to begin to rethink the relations between art and pop, the category of THE NEW and our unthinking equation of it with the virility of the young.

HOMEWORK!

Before going any further, let's look at some of the implications—not at all totally negative—

of our worshipping at the fount of youth in recent years. Not long ago it was assumed that an artist had to undergo some kind of apprenticeship, and there was generally a distrust of something that hit the scene too early. Even though today this might be a timely reminder, there are numerous instances of work made by very young artists that have since become canonical and explode this myth. Frank Stella's black paintings, produced when he was only 22, or Jasper Johns' flags, made around the same time, along with later figures such as Joseph Kosuth: all made significant breakthroughs while still in their twenties.

Furthermore, the kind of conception of artistic intelligence that prevailed pre-yBa, the 1980s/90s Neo-Conceptual conception of art as applied theory, of art's MANAGEMENT of it by a prior theoretical notion of it as CRITICAL WORK IN AND ON REPRESENTATION (as the jargon of the time went) pre-supposed a certain way of practicing, appearing and learning. A young artist, it was assumed, had to do his or her theoretical homework. This, it could be argued, served to infantilise the young artist, and indeed any artist who refused to conform to this.

Subsequently, we saw an inevitable reaction to this: a return of the repressed, where young artists, along with quite a few older ones responded by actively dis-identifying with this SERIOUS image of art and the artist. It was an art of so-called ATTITUDE that productively exploited the irresponsible licence of youth to betray theory, rather than passively apply it. In doing so it actively created new problems for theory that we are still in the process of thinking through. But when the media got hold of it, it immediately branded it as YOUNG British art and thus contributed to the very same cultural climate that almost kept someone like Paul McCarthy hidden from our view. McCarthy had the last laugh though, by abjectly reminding us of the remaindering of the old and incontinent in his own work.

CRISIS!

If there are indeed positive dimensions, there are manifold negative implications to all of this too. It would be unthinkable today, in London anyway, for somebody to do what Marcel Broodthaers did back in the 1960s and embark upon a career as an artist when he was 40. It is unlikely that an artist such as Raoul De Keyser, for instance, could have found the space, could work long enough, to be 'discovered' only after he'd passed through middle-age. With the institutionalisation into art of a CAREER PATH, the emergence of such late developers is extremely exceptional; the development of younger artists is a better INVESTMENT PROPOSITION. However, younger artists today are subject to the accelerated cycle of currency that is catching up that of the pop charts. This leads to the all-too-often phenomena of overproduction-to-order, and Damien Hirst-style premature burnout.

Nevertheless, there have been attempts to redress this imbalance, most notably at the last documenta exhibition (no. 11, 2002). Explicitly—and on the whole laudably—it sought to counter mainstream, market-led ageism in an exhibition within which the average age of the participants was over 55. In this respect, it probably broke all records. However, what it ultimately ended up achieving was less a transcending of the generation gap than an inadvertent reinforcing of it, and this via the implications of its own critical agenda. The overall moralist tone of the show, its assumption of a RESPONSIBILITY in the face of the aftermath of 9/11, after which it was now time for art to GET SERIOUS, to become ADULT, so to speak, has contributed in no small way to the widening of the schism we face in the art world today: that between a MATURE, neo-political, socially-engaged art, and its binary, the ostensibly widespread outbreak of a YOUTHFUL, truculently irresponsible posturing.

In the context of pop music, however, we have a different kind of situation which is almost the inverse of this. If one looks at a mainstream pop publication such as the weekly New Musical Express, which was for over half a century the contemporary-musical bible for a number of generations of British consumers, it is apparent that a significant shift is underway. For some time now it seems that younger artists are seen and heard to be the defenders of REAL music, the guardians of the canon of the CLASSIC ROCK

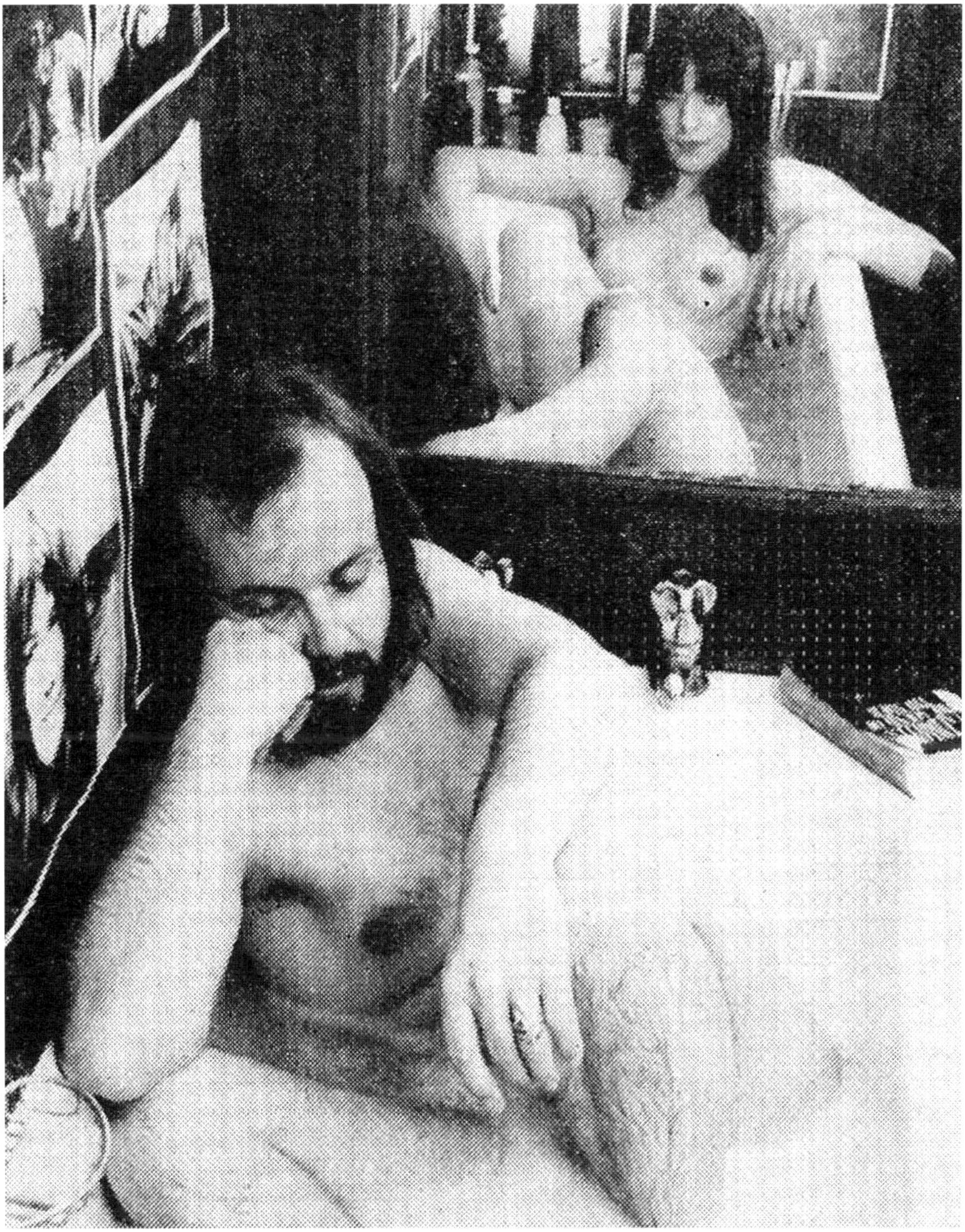

aesthetic. Hence, we see a widespread conservatism amongst the young and retroism as the dominant mode. After the so-called CRISIS IN DANCE MUSIC in the 1990s, there has been a back to basics revival of a guitar music that strikes all the RIGHT emotional chords and consists of riffs upon all the conventional Rock clichés. The most acclaimed and hyped of the new guitar bands are Franz Ferdinand, after whom a writer at the NME coined the term ART POP, yet this band's music sounds barely different to how art pop sounded 30 years ago, in its almost note-for-note reiteration of bands like Television and Wire. If the postmodernism of the 1980s ironically celebrated the return of the same as farce, here we see bands such as The Strokes, The Kaiser Chiefs, Bloc Party, The Kills and a host of others barely distinguishable from each other, tragically renouncing everything Peel had once stood for. What mainstream pop today amounts to is what Michael Hardt and Toni Negri refer to as the COLONISATION OF THE AFFECTS, the total processing, circumscription and reining-in of the affective energy that once empowered an entire generation, and made the category of YOUTH a social force to be reckoned with.

BASTARDS!

But, this is not the end of the story. If Rock is dead there is still Postrock, or what the Wire refers to as Avant-rock. This was a neologism coined a decade ago to refer to musics that were within the rock tradition but at the same time didn't seem to quite fit there, didn't sound like conventional rock music because it was too formally complex or unconventional, or either too fast or too slow, or both at the same time. Its advent amounted to something like a hinging point, a hiatus, maybe even a COMING OF AGE, that is still forcing us to rethink the status of pop music. Initially Postrock referred to certain bands from the USA such as Tortoise, Slint and Labradford, who along with their European counterparts such as Stereolab, used electronics in combination with conventional instruments in musics that deployed repetition combined with sudden structural shifts and new layer of complexity. It was subsequently genealogised, linking it to precedents such a Sonic Youth, and further back to the Krautrock pioneers, Neu!, Faust, Can and Kraftwerk. It was then further expanded to encompass new kinds of non-functional, i.e non-danceable, forms of electronic music that came out of Techno. Postrock is ultimately, I would argue, neither a style nor a condition but rather a PROCESS. And, it is one that is forcing us to rethink and rewrite the history of pop as a process of the BETRAYAL OF ITSELF, rather than a VH1-style CLASSICAL canon. This is a process of an ongoing BASTARDISATION of pop, within which mutations and contaminations create new, affective sonic collisions that will always remain IMPURE. Maybe this is what good pop music has always done, though. Maybe it was always the product of the affirmative attitude of desiring to hear something different, to be taken somewhere else. In this sense it is less a POST phenomenon, than the PRE-POSTEROUS process that good pop always was and will continue to be.

All this is still being done by these artists, and a big shift of the past 10 years, and something unprecedented in the history of pop, is that the above are still doing radical things in their 40s; Sonic Youth are all around 50. This is possible because music is no longer about TEENAGE KICKS; it is no longer the VOICE OF YOUTH. Rather, it gives voice to an unavowable, fluid community that is constantly shifting, always in the process of DE-TERRITORIALISATION in tune with the music. It is what Lyotard referred to as a CLOUD OF COMMUNITY, a moving target resistant to definition in terms of industry demographics of age groups or any existing social classifications. A current instance of this might be the Grime and the related Dub-step scene in London, which is largely ignored by the mainstream even though artists such a Plasticman, Mark One and The Slaughter Mob are producing some of the newest and most vital music anywhere. This may be because it is undanceable, despite coming out of dance culture; it is primarily instrumental rather than vocal, unlike that of their more successful peers such as Dizzee Rascal and Lady Sovereign. Also, the scene and its participants extend across all age and cultural demographics and resists being patronisingly—but potentially profitably—labelled as the voice of young Black, or otherwise, Britain.

PREPOSTEROUS!

What this all amounts to is an ongoing process of the collective dis-identification with prevailing images of music and the musician, being worked out right now by musicians from the ages of 18 to 80. It is the product of ATTITUDE and is in many ways similar to the YOUNG art referred to above; and we can no longer take for granted that it is attributable to any one GENERATION. It is furthermore an attitude that is not amenable to the gaze of a Cultural Studies that conceived of it as a SUBCULTURE, as Dick Hebdige in his pioneering eponymous account put it. Rather, it is going elsewhere, overground, and constitutes the process—to cite an overused Deleuzianism—of a RHIZOMATIC practice of creating new elsewhere in the here and now. It is a process both too fast and too slow for the fashion cycle it nonetheless parasitically rides upon. It frustrates the cycle of what Lyotard refers to as TIMELY, PERPETUAL INNOVATION, the production of a novelty that paradoxically always remains the same. In contrast, it becomes testament to the possibility in pop of what he called ART'S EXPERIMENTATION, that is the creation of the UNTIMELY NEW, as opposed to the MERELY NOVEL, that is simultaneously the creation of what we might call a SCENE-EVENT on the margins of pop as we know it.

In London today, however, mainstream pop is still tuned into an image culture that fixes and packages it as a phenomenon of the fashion cycle. Once the world centre of the creation of new YOUTH CULTURES, it is in danger of becoming the victim of its own success. The yBa scene passively aligned itself with style culture, but in so doing created a problem for itself in that there is no new, YOUNGER generation to succeed it as part of timely process of linear succession. There have been attempts to package newness, such as ad-man Charles Saatchi's branding of NEW-NEUROTIC REALISM, NEW LABOUR, and now, THE TRIUMPH OF PAINTING, but as we have seen, real EVENTS don't happen that way. It is also the reason why they will always exceed and outlive attempts at packaging them. Good pop like good art neither grows gracefully old, nor stays forever young, but remains forever PRE-POSTEROUS.

A version of this piece first appeared (in Dutch) in Metropolis M, no.3, 2005. It is reproduced here with thanks to the editors.

NOTES

1. John Peel describing The Fall.

WYNDHAM LEWIS

by Stuart Bailey

BLAST
years 1837 to 1900
Curse abysmal inexcusable middle-class
(also Aristocracy and Proletariat).
BLAST
Pasty shadow cast by gigantic Boehm
(imagined at introduction of BOURGEOIS
VICTORIAN VISTAS).
WRING THE NECK OF all sick inventions
born in
that progressive white wake.

Our vortex is not afraid of the past:
It has forgotten its existence.

(Wyndham Lewis, BLAST 1, 1914)

As with Joyce, Beuys and Mark E. Smith, the historians will be arguing about (Percy) Wyndham Lewis until the kingdom comes. 20th century culture has been kept alive by the irritants which work their way under its skin. In this much, McLuhan's call for 'the need for a counter-environment as a means for perceiving the dominant one' required a new century to prove its accuracy. Wyndham Lewis, who could so easily be the subject of a myriad quarterly reviews, has remained a shadowy and mistrusted figure, silhouetted on the banks of the cultural mainstream. As our times appear to demand art terrorist outsiders, Lewis has called the era's bluff by refusing easy routes to fashionable and commercially-lucrative acceptance. While Marinetti caught, peeled and ate the orange thrown at him in public disgrace, Wyndham Lewis—unknown to many—continues to ply his trade as a novelist, satirist, poet, critic of literature, philosophy and art, magazine editor, painter and fly-in-the-ointment.

Lewis formed the Vorticist group (as the point of maximum energy) in London in 1914. At the time he was painting and writing around the fringes of London's Bloomsbury, later from the Rebel Art Centre which he co-founded with Kate Lechmere. This was a time when most of Europe was largely unsuspecting of the imminent war, only a few months away. The studied neurosis of Realism and Impressionism was about to give way to the deliquescing anarchy of Cubism and Expressionism. But the Vorticists had no place—nor wanted one—in either camp. From their inception, Lewis's Vorticists were bloody-minded outsiders, possessing an extraordinary ability to get up noses. At a time when Post-Impressionism was about to disgrace itself with the saccharine posturing of Abstraction, Lewis appeared equally comfortable in the regulation uniform of trench warfare, as much as the louche smoking jacket of his gentleman's club. In 1914 art was reinventing itself as a minefield of carefully stylized factions; the Vorticists, immovable in their determination to remain aloof from the posturing of their peers, quickly earned not only incomprehension but also hostility. In an early appearance at one of Marinnetti's London speeches at the Doré Gallery, Lewis and company brought the volatility of a working men's club to a scene which believed itself to be self-contained and self-policing. The rhetoric of the Vortex was similar to suddenly finding onesself in a slanging match with a chauvinist, fascist, intellectual drunkard. For this invective Lewis has never been forgiven. Challenged with the notion that the Vorticists drew their menace from the seismic detonation of Futurism, Lewis replied with a dismissive sniff, 'Automobilism—Marinnetteism—bores us. We don't want to go about making a hullo bulloo about motor cars, anymore than about knives and forks, elephants or gas-pipes. Elephants are VERY BIG. Motor cars go quickly.'

Like Marinetti's Futurist Manifesto, Lewis's BLAST magazine was regarded as the alarm call of the pre-war years; this was polemic which seemed to deal with personal and political dissatisfaction in a manner which was both sinister and confrontational. By the end of the decade the Futurists resembled a self-parodic cabaret turn fit only for the history books. The Vorticists, on the other hand, made their sense of alienation part of their art, laying the foundations for a creative process which was almost immediately disrupted by a war which saw them divided, dispersed and, in some cases, killed in action.

Portrait by Chris Evans

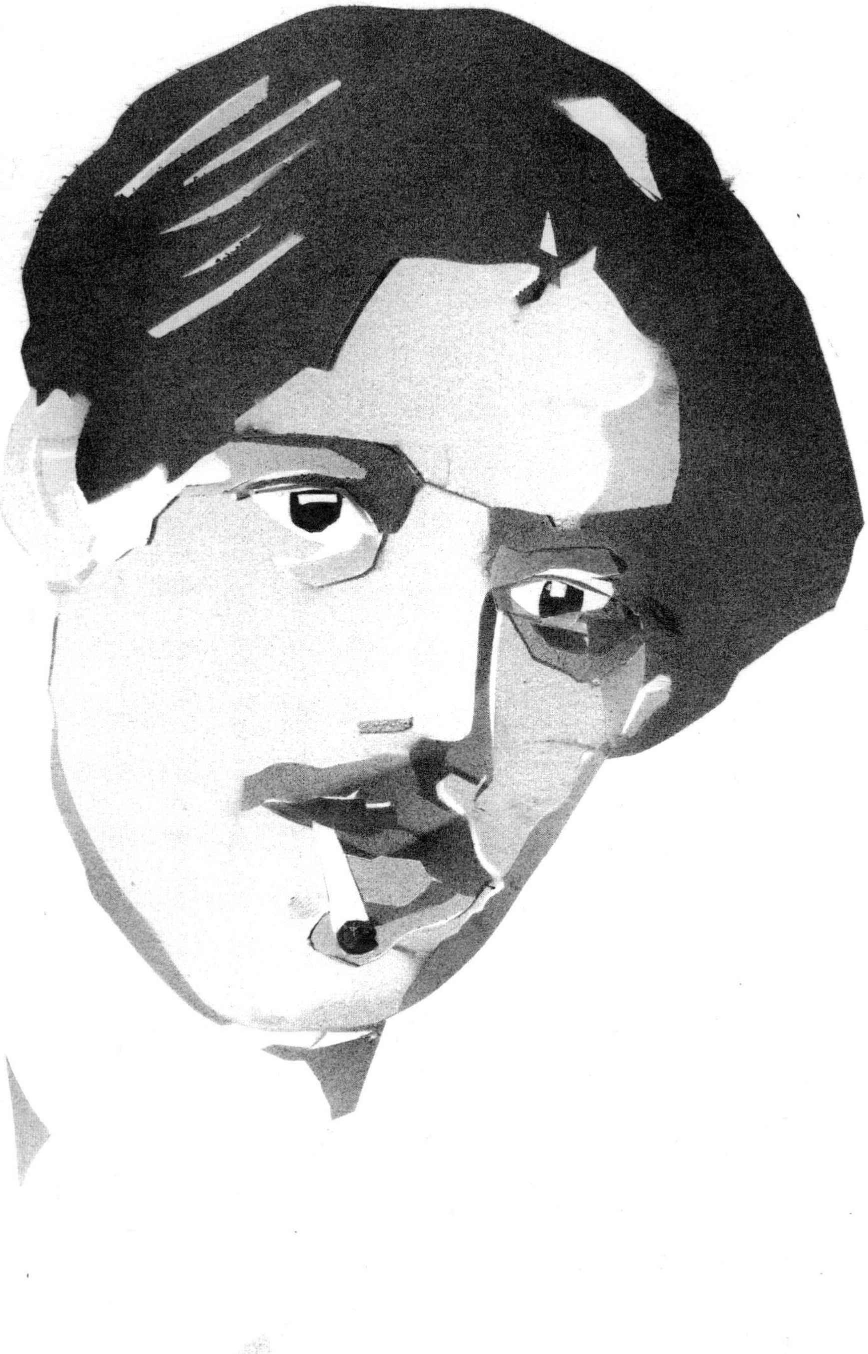

For Wyndham Lewis, irreverance was put to work for Vorticism. As the self-titled 'Enemy', he would parade around London's art and literary circles shouting random insults at the bewildered cognoscenti. The Futurist statue will move: then it will live a little: but any idiot can do better than that with his good wife, round the corner, 'This war talk, sententious execution and much besides, Marinetti picked up from Nietszche' or, 'I loathe anything that goes too quickly. If it goes too quickly it is not there' when delivered with the correct mixture of urgency and forethought, could obtain an effect that bordered on the sinister.

It was only a short step, aesthetically, from confusing Marinetti and the Futurists with dismissive put-downs to offending the art cognoscenti by challenging their self-satisfaction. BLAST was jarring and disjointed, making a virtue of its graphic appearance, faithfully set according to The Enemy's bombastic wishes by an alcoholic ex-printer between startling puce covers: 'The "Poor" are detestable animals! They are only picturesque and amusing. The "Rich" are bores without a single exception, En tant que riches! / We want those simple and great people found everywhere / BLAST presents an art of Individuals'.

Already, Lewis's campaign bore marked similarities to the Live At The Witch Trials phase of Mark E. Smith's and The Fall's assault on the post-punk new wave. Smith was a Renaissance Man without a culture vital enough to support the fulfilment of his talents. Similarly, Lewis is locked in a position of terrorist warfare, cerebral and caustic against a fashion driven society which is indurate to all attitudes save its own conservative 'non-conformity'. Thus Lewis is cast (again like Smith) as a cat amongst pigeons, stalking the effette by saying the unspeakable. In 1914 Lewis wrote: 'OH BLAST FRANCE! / pig plagiarism / BELLY / SLIPPERS / POODLE TEMPER / BAD MUSIC / SENTIMENTAL GALLIC GUSH / SENSATIONALISM / FUSSINESS / PARISIAN PAROCHIALISM'. Or again: 'As to women: wherever you can, substitute the society of men. Treat them kindly, for they suffer from the herd, although of it, and have many of the same contempts as yourself. But women, and the processes for which they exist, are the arch conjuring trick: and they have the cheap mystery and a good deal of the slipperiness, of the conjuror. Sodomy should be avoided, as far as possible. It tends to add to the abominable confusion already existing.'

Whist Lewis's polemic continues to affront every notion of political correctness, his audience recognize that his contrariness is merely a facet of a far more complex, and engaging, world vision. The ability to provoke and doubt, simultaneously, has often been cited as being fundamental to great art. Lewis himself went some way to acknowledging this in 1917: 'You must be a duet in everything. For the individual, the single object, and the isolated is, you will admit, an absurdity. Why try and give yourself the impression of a consistent and indivisible personality?'

From the very beginning, Vorticism has been Wyndham Lewis's medium for expressing his unique world view: everything outside the Vortex is meat for his stew. Within the chaos of Vorticism, and within the oblique, humorous code of Lewis's writing, there are precise patterns and a finely focused lucidity. He assembles his words in such a manner that found language, narrative, slang, double-talk, trigger phases and rapid juxtapositions are combined to create a discourse which describes as it commentates. The style is not artless, as it may seem, but the product of careful design. 'Life is what I have gone out to get' says Lewis, '—life where it is merging with something else, certainly. But I catch it just before it goes over into the fastuous element. The fish is still in the stream. Or if you like, this is the raw meat in the kitchen—destined, perhaps, for the Banquet of Reason, but as yet highly irrational.'

Like Mark E. Smith, Wyndham Lewis will suggest the existence of a conspiracy behind most manifestations of modern culture. In texts such as 'Enemy of the Stars', 'Life is the important thing', 'Policeman and artist', 'Orchestra of the Media, 'Tarr', and 'Code of a Herdsman', Lewis appears to endorse what Smith meant by 'the war against intelligence'. In 1937 Lewis stated: 'Do not play with political notions, aristocratisms or the reverse, for that is a compromise with the herd. Do not allow yourself to imagine "a fine herd though still a herd." There is no FINE HERD. The cattle that call themselves "gentlemen" you will observe to be a little cleaner. It is merely cunning and produced with a product called SOAP. But you will find no serious difference between them and those vast dismal herds they avoid. Some of them are very dangerous and treacherous.'

If Vorticism is both Lewis's vision of the world and his means of describing it, then the Great British Vortex is peopled with grotesque characters whom Lewis has invented. These would include BRITANNIC AESTHETE, WILD NATURE CRANK, DOMESTICATED POLICEMAN, GAEITY CHORUS GIRL, AMATEUR, SCIOLAST, ART-PIMP, JOURNALIST, SELF-MAN, ORGANIST, and THE HAIRDRESSER. One gets the impression that Lewis's imagination was incubating this cast since before Vorticism began. In many ways his writing has served to fill the biographies of these characters; at the same time Lewis will write pseudonymously under their names. In a later autobiographical piece entitled 'The "Author of Tarr"' he begins, 'So much for Mr Cantleman. Need I repeat that this hero of mine is not to be identified with me? But to some extent, in the fragments I have just quoted, you get the lowdown on the editor of BLAST. That is why I used them.'

When asked to clarify this assessment of these characters, Lewis cautiously sips his beer before replying 'Never fall into the vulgarity of assuming yourself to be one ego. Each trench must have another one behind it. Each single self—that you manage to be at any given time—must have five at least indifferent to it. You must have a power of indifference of five to one. All the greatest actions in the world have been five parts out of six impersonal in the impulse of their origin. To follow this principle you need only cultivate your memory.'

'In order to live you must remain broken up,' Lewis announced in 1917. Whilst critics have yet to agree whether the Vorticists, artistically, are drab or dynamic, the roots of mesmeric intensity lie in the practice of contradiction. In the most compelling Lewis texts, the language and typography merely provides an open structure through which Lewis roams like a suspicious caretaker, flashing his torch from one empty dark room to another. This is best illustrated in BLAST's 'Manifesto', signed by ten others. The seven-part polemic begins with a ten-point prologue in which Lewis declaims:

> Beyond action and reaction we would establish ourselves
> We start from opposite statements of a chosen world. Set up violent structure of adolescent clearness between two extremes
> We discharge ourselves on both sides
> We fight first on one side, then on the other, but always for the same cause, which is neither side or both sides and ours.

As Lewis explains, the idea of the Vorticists was always to create a violent central activity, attracting everything to itself, absorbing all that is around it. 'Vorticism was an intellectual eruption, productive of a closely-packed, brightly-coloured alphabet of objects with a logic of its own. The doctrine which is implicit in this eruption is to be looked for in the shapes for which it was responsible ... I should have encouraged the shaping, in clay or in wood, of objects conforming to these theories. In other words, a world of not-stone, not-trees, not-dogs, not-men, not-bottles, not-houses, etc.'

Initially, the received idea of the Vorticists' audience was that of pale, tall, exceedingly romantic-looking fellows. The obscurity of The Vortex appeared to demand supporters who were socially dysfunctional—the weird cousins of the Bloomsbury Group. In time, however, the Vorticists have achieved a certain following alongside fellow modernists such as James Joyce, Ezra Pound and T.S. Eliot.

'It was scarcely our fault that we were a youth racket. It was Ezra who in the first place organized us willy nilly into that. For he was never satisfied until everything was organized. And it was he who made us into a youth racket —that was his method of organization.

'All politics today, and all the "Youth-racket" element in politics are put across by men-of-letters, journalists, philosophes, or the propaganda of intellectualist sects, groups and philansteries, rather than via the Clubs or the floor of the House of Commons. And as I have already indicated, there was a tidy bit of political contraband tucked away in our technical militancy. But I was not the responsible party.

'Yes Mr Joyce, Mr Pound, Mr Eliot—and, for I said that my piety was egoistic, the Enemy, as well—the Chiricos and Picassos, and in music their equivalents—will be the exotic flowers of a culture that has passed. As people look back at them out of a very humdrum, cautious, disillusioned society, the critics of the future day will rub their eyes. They will look, to them, so hopelessly avant-garde! so almost madly up-and-coming!

'What energy!—what imposssibly Spartan standards man will exclaim! So heroically these "pioneers" will stand out like monosyllable monoliths—Pound, Joyce, Lewis. They will acquire the strange aspects of "empire-builders", as seen by a well-levelled and efficiently flattened out Proletariat, with all its million tails well down between its shuffling legs!'

But, despite their position as a 'difficult' group already at odds with shifting cultural fashions, the Vorticists' Luddite tendencies have brought them into the focus of serious debate about contemporary art.

'The Arts with their great capital A's are, considered as plants, decidedly unrobust. They are the sport, at the best, of political chance: parasitically dependent upon the good health of the social body.

'A few arts were born in the happy lull before the world-storm. In 1914 a ferment of the artistic intelligence occurred in the west of Europe. And it looked to many people as if a great historic "school" was in process of formation. Expressionism, Post-impressionism, Vorticism, Cubism, Futurism were some of the characteristic nicknames bestowed upon these manifestations, where they found their intensest expression in the pictorial field. In every case the structural and philosophic rudiments of life were sought out. On all hands a return to first principles was witnessed.'

Wyndham Lewis's writing anticipates and rejects academic criticism, although he has offered analyses of his work. Of his various BLASTs (1914) Lewis says, concisely: 'Take the first BLAST, "Blast Humour". That is straightforward enough. The Englishman has what he calls a "sense of humour". He says that the German, the Frenchman, and most foreigners do not possess this attribute, and suffer accordingly. For what does the "sense of humour" mean but an ability to belittle everything—to make light of everything? Not only does the Englishman not "make a mountain of of a molehill"; he is able to make a molehill out of a mountain.' The more ambitious Tarr (1914–15), a terse first novel of verbal economy, was summarized by Lewis as displaying 'a certain indifference to bourgeois conventions, and an unblushing disbelief in the innate goodness of human nature.'

Lewis, spokesman of 'The New Egos', maintains a similar single-mindedness towards the traditionally sensitive subject of politics. 'I am trying to save people from being "ruled" too much —from being "ruled" off the face of the earth, as a matter of fact.'

But would Lewis invest, seriously, in politics? 'Really all this organized disturbance was Art behaving as if it were Politics. But I swear I did not know it. It may in fact have been politics. I see that now. Indeed it must have been. But I was unaware of the fact: I believed that this was the way artists were always received; a somewhat tumultuous reception, perhaps, but after all, why not? I mistook the agitation in the audience for the sign of an awakening of the emotion of artistic sensibility. And then I assumed too that artists always formed militant groups. I supposed they had to do this, seeing how "bourgeois" all Publics were—or all Publics of which I had any experience.'

'Anyhow, in 1926 I began writing about politics, not because I like politics but everything was getting bogged in them and before you could do anything to deal with the politics with which it was encrusted. And I've got so bepoliticked myself in the process that in order to get at me, today, you have to get the politics of me first. However, when politics came on the scene I ring down the curtain; and that was in 1926. That was when politics began for me in earnest. I've never had a moment's peace since.'

Inevitably, Lewis is in danger of becoming as marginalised as Mark E. Smith became in his later and most prolific years. As yet, however, the Vorticists remian a quesion mark in the history of art. But Lewis continues to rant.

'Peace is a fearful thing for that countless majority who are so placed that there is no difference between Peace and War—except that during the latter day they are treated with more consideration. In war, if they are wounded they are well treated, in peace, if struck down it is apt to be nothing like so pleasant.

'You will be astonished to find out how like art is to war, I mean "modernist" art. They talk a lot about how a war just-finished effects art. But a war about to start can do the same thing. War, art, civil war, strikes, coup d'états dovetail into each other. it is somewhat depressing to consider how as an artist one is always holding up a mirror to politics without really knowing it. My picture called The Plan of War painted six months before the Great War "broke out", as we say, depresses me. A prophet is a most unoriginal person: all he is doing is imitating something that is not there, but soon will be. With me war and art have been mixed up from the start. It is still.'

This piece, originally published in Metropolis M, no. 2, 2005, is an inversion of a piece by Michael Bracewell and Jon Wilde, 'Mark E. Smith', originally published in Frieze, no. 6, 1992.

Lewis's 'conversation' is drawn from his various writings, particularly his autobiography Blasting And Bombadiering (1937).

MARK E. SMITH

by Michael Bracewell & Jon Wilde

Yer got sixty hour weeks and stone toilet back-gardens
Peter Cook's jokes, bad dope, check shirts, lousy groups
Point their finger at America
Down pokey quaint streets in Cambridge
Cycles our distant spastic heritage
Its a gay red, roundhead, army career, grim head
If we were smart we'd emigrate

(The Fall, The English Scheme, 1980)

The Fall have always been at arm's length. That's our mentality.

(Mark E. Smith, 1980)

As with Joyce, Beuys, and Wyndham Lewis, the historians will be arguing about Mark E. (for Edward) Smith until the kingdom comes. 20th Century culture has been kept alive by the irritants which work their way under its skin. In this much, Wilde's late-Victorian aphorism, 'To be great, one must be misunderstood' required a new century to prove its accuracy. Mark E. Smith, who could so easily be the subject of a myriad Sunday supplement profiles, has remained a shadowy and mistrusted figure, silhouetted on the banks of the cultural mainstream. As our times appear to demand art terrorist outsiders, Smith has called the era's bluff by refusing easy routes to fashionable and commercially lucrative acceptance. Whilst Damien Hirst prepares to suspend his Turner prize in a vat of formaldehyde, Mark E. Smith —unknown to many—continues to ply his trade as an independent musician, philosopher, historian, writer, wit and fly-in-the-ointment.

Smith formed the group, The Fall (after the Camus novel), in Manchester in 1977. At the time, he was working in Manchester Docks as a customs clerk. This was a time when the metropolitan impetus of punk rock was being challenged by the provinces. The deliquescing anarchy of the Sex Pistols and The Clash was giving way to the studied neurosis of Joy Division and Cabaret Voltaire. But The Fall had no place—nor wanted one—in either camp. From their inception, Smith's Fall were bloody-minded-outsiders, possessing an extraordinary ability to get up noses. At a time when postpunk fashionablilty was about to disgrace itself with the saccharine posturing of new romanticism, The Fall looked like a cross between a class outing from Please Sir! and a crew of chagrined pipe-fitters on their afternoon off. In 1980, pop music was reinventing itself as a kaleidoscope of carefully stylised factions: The Fall, immovable in their determination to remain aloof from the posturing of their peers, quickly earned not only incomprehension but also hostility. In their early performances, they brought the volatility of a bad night in a Wakefield Working Men's Club to a scene which believed itself both to be self-contained and self-policed. The rhetoric of The Fall was similar to suddenly finding oneself in a slanging match with a vituperative Mancunian lorry-driver. For this invective, The Fall have never been forgiven. Challenged with the notion that The Fall drew their menace from the twilight of punk rock. Smith replied with a dismissive sniff, 'Punk? I 'ate that stuff. I wouldn't have it in the 'ouse!'

Like Public Image's Metal Box, The Fall's debut LP, Live At The Witch Trials, was regarded as the death rattle of the 1970s; this was music which seemed to deal with personal and political dissatisfaction in a manner which was both sinister and confrontational. By 1981, Public Image resembled a self-parodic cabaret turn fit only for the chicken-in-the-basket circuit. The Fall, on the other hand, had made their sense of alienation a vital part of their art, laying the foundations for a creative process which has seen them through 15 LPs in as many years.

For Mark E. Smith, even irrelevance could be put to work for The Fall. As a teenager, he would ride around Manchester on the top deck of a bus, shouting random words in a pointed manner at bewildered passers-by. LEPER, PENGUIN or, GRANDMOTHER! when delivered with the correct mixture of urgency and forethought, could obtain an effect that bordered on the sinister.

It was only a short step, aesthetically, from confusing Mancunian pedestrians with ordinary language to offending the music cognoscenti by challenging their self-satisfaction. Live At The Witch Trials was jarring and disjointed, making a virtue of its Northern bloody-mindedness: 'We are The Fall! Northern white crap that talks back; we are not Black; tall; no boxes for us / do not fuck us ...'

Already, Smith's campaign bore marked similarities to the BLAST phase of Wyndham Lewis and the Vorticist assault on inter-war Bloomsbury. Lewis was a Renaissance Man without a culture vital enough to support the fulfilment of his talents. Similarly, Smith is locked in a position of trench warfare, blasting and bombardiering against a fashion-driven society which is indurate to all attitudes save its own conservative 'non-conformity'. Thus, Smith is cast (again like Lewis) as a cat amongst pigeons, stalking the effete by saying the unspeakable. Interviewed in 1979, Smith said: 'Nuking Russia might not be a bad idea as far as the bleedin' world is concerned. They've plunged a lot of people into miserable lives. You've only got to be in East Germany to see it. It's a horrible way to live. It's like Middlesborough.' Again, in 1985: 'Live Aid? I smell a lot of Victorian bloody do-gooding about the whole thing. There are people in Hulme (Manchester) who are half starved, so why not send the aid to them? Never in a million years. And any country that can be invaded by the Italians must be a load of crap. Am I right?'

Whilst Smith's polemic continues to affront every notion of political correctness, his audience recognise that his contrariness is merely a facet of a far more complex, and engaging, world vision. The ability to provoke and doubt, simultaneously, has often been cited as being fundamental to great art. Smith himself went some way to acknowledging this in 1988: 'Whenever I say anything, I often think that the opposite is true as well. Sometimes I think the truth is too fucking obvious for people to take. The possibilities are endless and people don't like that. They go for the average every time. Well, that doesn't interest me in the slightest.'

From the very beginning, The Fall has been Mark E. Smith's medium for expressing his unique world view: everything outside The Fall is

Portrait by Chris Evans

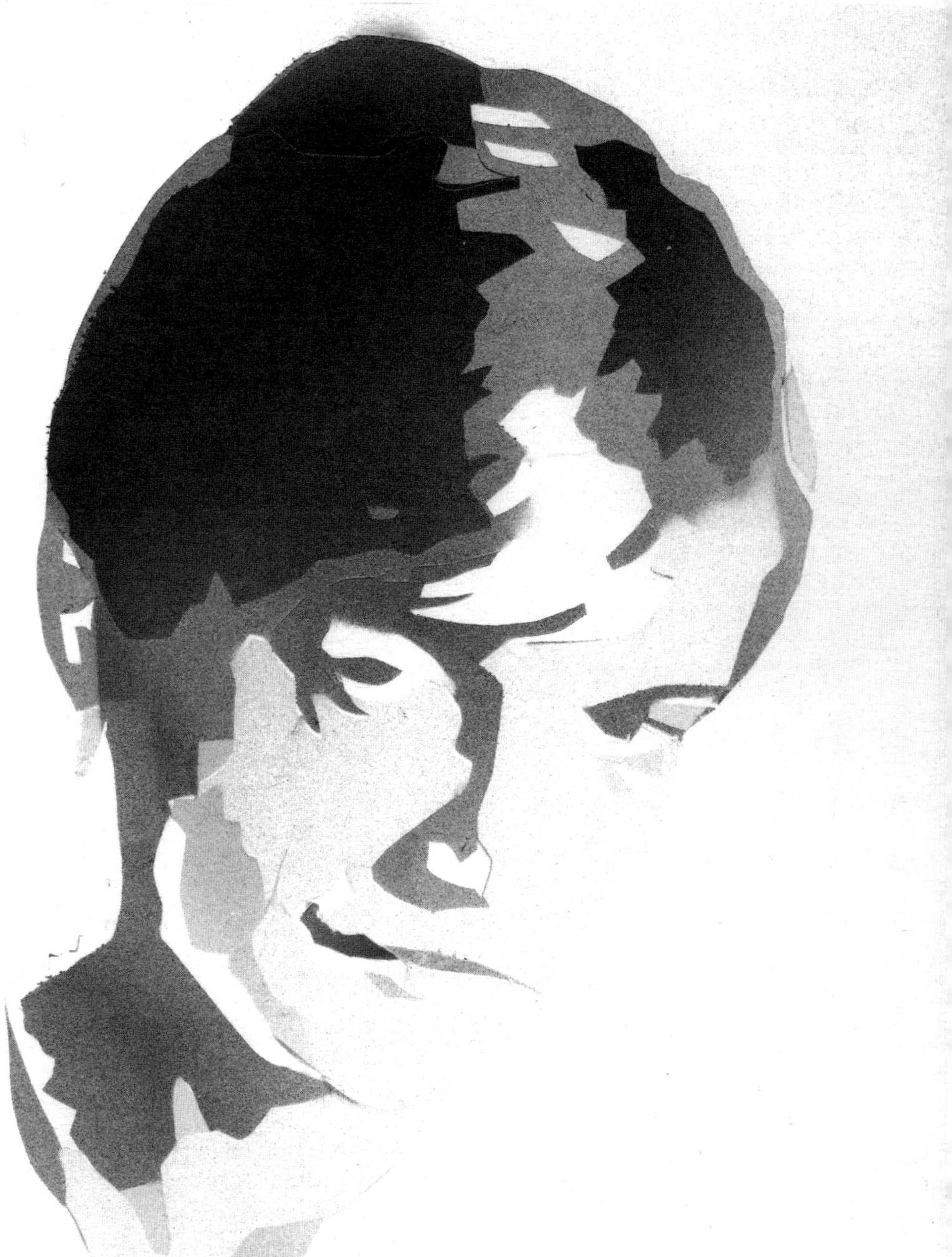

meat for his stew. Within the chaos of The Fall, and within the oblique, humourous code of Smith's writing, there are precise patterns and a finely focused lucidity. He assembles his lyrics in such a manner that found language, narrative, slang, double-talk, trigger phrases and rapid juxtapositions are combined to create a discourse which describes as it commentates. The style is not artless, as it may look. but the product of careful design.

'It's just precog,' says Smith. 'You write things down and you don't know what they mean but you know they're true and they come true later. It's not prophecy as such. It makes me laugh actually. I see things happening and I think: "Oh, that reminds me of something." Turns out it's something I wrote five years ago. I wrote a song called Zagreb Daylight two years ago. We were playing in Zagreb and I could feel this horrible, murderous shit in the air. I had a feeling that yobs were going to rule the earth. I'm half one myself you see. Anyway, I wrote this thing about a man in a shop with a dwarf behind the counter. It didn't go down well at all. If it came out a month from now, people would say it's topical.'

Like Wyndham Lewis, Mark E. Smith will suggest the existence of a conspiracy behind most manifestations of modem culture. In songs like 'Oswald Defence Lawyer', 'Kicker Conspiracy', 'Bug Day', 'The War Against Intelligence', 'Rowche Rumble' and 'Riddler!', Smith appears to endorse what Lewis meant by, 'the immense false-bottom underlying every seemingly solid surface.' Interviewed in 1990, Smith stated: 'It's natural to gripe at things like British Telecom. One time I was using the phone a lot and I dialled a number, and I could hear people munching sandwiches and talking about my last phone call. I actually rang the operator and said, "Look. I'm trying to dial a fucking number here and I can't get through because your people are talking about my phone calls. Have you got a bloody license to do this?" And she slammed the phone down on me!'

If The Fall are both Smith's vision of the world and his means of describing it, then the strange and frightening world of The Fall is peopled with grotesque characters whom Smith has invented. These would include Joe Totale, J.Temperance, Wireless Enthusiast, Fiery Jack. The Man Whose Head Expanded, Hip Priest, Man With Chip, Carry Bag Man and Slang King. One gets the impression that Smith's livid imagination was incubating this cast since before The Fall began. In many ways, his writing for The Fall has served to fill in the biographies of these characters: at the same time, Smith will write pseudonymously under their names. On the sleeve of 1980's Totale's Turns, R. Totale XVIII pens a note entitled, 'Call Yourselves Bloody Professionals?' and concludes with the comment, 'This is probably the most accurate document of The Fall ever released, even though they'll have a hard time convincing their mams and dads about that, ha ha.' Interestingly enough, the remains of R. Totale's ancestor are described elsewhere as being found buried on a Welsh hillside complete with instructions to unleash the content of certain tapes upon the world.

When asked to clarify this assessment of these characters, Smith cautiously sips his beer before replying, 'Man With Chip still going strong on the chat show. Cheap TV stance, yeah. Oprah Winfrey. Heh! Heh! Magnus fucking Pyke!'

'We've got repetition in our music and we're never gonna lose it,' Smith announced in 1978. Whilst critics have yet to agree whether The Fall, musically, are a din or a sublime symphony, the roots of The Fall's mesmeric intensity lie in the practice of repetition. In the most compelling Fall songs the group merely provide an open structure through which Smith roams like a suspicious caretaker, flashing his torch from one empty dark room to another. This is best illustrated in 1988's Dog Is Life/Jerusalem, a lyric which featured the unique songwriting credit of William Blake/Mark E. Smith. As the song approaches a narrative passage, the music is pared down to an unflinching pulse over which Smith declaims:

> I was walking down the street when I tripped up on a discarded banana skin
> And on the way down I caught the side of my head on a protruding brick, chip
> It was the government's fault
> I was very let down with the Budget
> I was expecting a one million quid handout
> I was very disappointed
> It was the government's fault.

As Smith explains, the idea of The Fall has always been to write intelligent lyrics over a raw, basic beat 'That's never changed really. One thing we always get is, "this is their most commercial album for ages". In fact, the LPs have become less and less commercial over the years and I'm quite proud of that. The problem with that is, people get this idea that we're determined not to do well. Which isn't the case at all. So we get Top 30 singles and they won't even consider us for Top of the Pops. It's the last thing they want. I think there's a fear of The Fall in that respect. If people heard us, they'd find us entertaining and stimulating. Intelligence is actively discouraged these days though isn't it?'

Initially, the received idea of The Fall's audience was that of pale, spotty, adolescent males—bedroom misfits and train-spotters who wore anoraks with elasticated cuffs and lived off white bread sandwiches. The obscurity of The Fall appeared to demand supporters who were socially dysfunctional—the weird cousins of Clash fans. In time, however, The Fall have achieved a massive European following which covers all social groups from art world fashion victims to pot-bellied middle-aged rockers.

'Fall audiences have always been a bit weird,' says Smith. 'Well, not weird actually. I think they're the salt of the earth. I get letters from kids in Wales. Their lives have been transformed by The Fall. I suppose if you're on the dole in Wales there's nowt else to do unless you're out burgling.

'These guys in Wakefield, miners and all that, they've all grown up with wives and kids, and they've been with us since 1978. They don't buy records anymore but they're still into The Fall. It means a lot to me. They read interviews I've done and write me postcards saying, "Reel 'em in, cock—the lads in the Wakefield Pit." Actually, we've always caught the individuals. In Germany, we played this gig and the oldest man in the world was there. He must have been about ninety. Had grey hair down to his arse. He looked like God with a Fall LP under his arm.

'It always annoys me when I hear other bands going on about how they're not a student group like The Fall. Student group? You must be fucking joking! I don't mean to sound prejudiced but if you go to university, you're a bit daft anyway. I've nothing against students, mind. We play student places quite a lot You walk into the disco and there's all these kids on the dancefloor jigging around to Lynyrd Skynyrd records. When Slates (1981) came out, we lost our student audience overnight. I was fucking glad about that.

'I feel a bit sorry for kids these days. They're obsessed with animals and all that. That's quite nice I suppose. I've got two cats myself. But they're putting the frighteners on kids these days. Giving them anxieties they don't need. I saw something yesterday. It was horrible. These kids in tears about elephants. I blame the fucking teachers.'

But, despite their position as a 'difficult' group already at odds with shifting musical fashions, The Fall's Luddite tendencies have brought them into the focus of serious debate about contemporary art. 'Some of our stuff is art and some of it isn't,' Smith shrugs. 'We get it and we lose it. I like that as it happens. I think a lot of my writing is art but I'm a bit shy about it and that's why it's not printed. I couldn't be so precious to force it on the public. I've seen too many rock bands go out and pretend they're art. You get classed with them. I've always been careful to keep away from all that.

'I'd like to be considered as an artist But I don't want to get into David Byrne territory. I'm not knocking the guy, but he was never any good to begin with. They go for him in a big way out in America. He's not an artist like John Waters is an artist. I suppose Waters is a bit like me really; he takes trash, puts it together with what he thinks and does it very well. But basically, my attitude to life is to live. It's more important to be a man than an artist. I don't believe in the artist syndrome. I think I stimulate people's brains by saying what I think. Always have done. But, when we tour America, we get people coming up to us saying, "If only you could be a bit more like Talking Heads." Well we always had better backdrops than Talking Heads.'

Mark E. Smith's writing anticipates and rejects academic criticism. Also, he has famously avoided offering analyses of either his records or his collaborative projects in theatre and dance.

Of his play, Hey! Luciani (1986) Smith says, concisely: 'It's like a cross between The Prisoner and Shakespeare. There's even bits that rhyme and stuff.' The more ambitious I Am Curious Orange (1986), a ballet with Michael Clark, dealing with the ascendancy of William of Orange to the British throne, was summarised by Smith as, 'The English get pissed off with their king, kick him out and get some Dutch bloke in.' As an historian, Mark E. Smith possesses the self-assurance of A.J.P. Taylor: 'You don't hear much about Cromwell these days, despite the fact that he built England up to what it was. There used to be this Statue of Cromwell outside Victoria Station, in Manchester, but they moved it and put it in some fucking park in Wythenshawe, behind some bush. Nobody knows about it!'

Smith, spokesman of the 'prole art threat', maintains a similar single-mindedness towards the traditionally sensitive topic of money. 'Fear is relative to how much you're earning and what kind of threat you're under. But I can live on a fucking quid a week, me. And I have done. But, if I suddenly made a load of it, I'd buy a house. I don't like shopping and all that but I like nice clothes. A good pair of trousers when you can. You usually find in Britain that the scruffiest people are the richest. Have you noticed that?'

But would Smith invest, seriously, in art? 'Course I would. Italian stuff mainly. Chairs and stuff like that. If I had an awful lot of money, I'd buy some of that Catholic stuff—Tintoretto, El Greco. I like the colour in those paintings. But what would I do with it all? I've got the books and that anyway. I'm well into Venetian art. They always had a bit of humour about them. Like, they'd put a German soldier in the middle of The Last Supper. Stuff like that.

'I look at some of the things in Frieze, like the stuff with the tin cans. I did all that in the fifth year at School. You'd get these sixth formers with Pink Floyd sleeves under their arms doing this stuff with green blobs and brown blobs. They'd be going, "Oh, it's about the economy and the Third World debt." Then they'd tell me that my stuff wasn't art but it were miles better than their fucking horrible blobs. Ten years later, they're doing it for themselves down in Chelsea. That's the tragedy of being a self-taught artist.'

Inevitably, Mark E. Smith is faced with the danger of becoming as marginalised as Wyndham Lewis became is his later and most prolific years. As yet, however, The Fall remain a question mark in the history of art. But Smith continues to blast.

'Manchester council had this "Bring Art to the People" Day, he concludes. 'They're all raving socialists that lot. There were five exhibitions in bars around the city. It was a kind of art pub crawl. They wanted me to kick it off, snip the ribbon and all that. I thought our fame was going down last year so I decided to do my bit. You've got to keep a high profile. It's that kind of business. Anyway, we were dragged around these bars and showed all this art. There was all this Factory stuff done by some bloke who won't get our of bed for less than £5,000. These sub-Warhol drawings of Carry On characters. I'm thinking, "This is crap!" but you don't want to be rude about it 'cus it's all middle-aged people. They're saying, "Oh Mark. I never knew you were into art" I was going, "Oh yeah, I love a bit of art. me. I'm into Tinzeretto and all that," and their mouths dropped.

'So, we got to the third bar. By this time, the band were dropping off one by one and going home for a bit to eat. I stuck around and I was trying to make an effort 'cus there were all these art writers from the famous papers. I was talking to one woman about Wyndham Lewis and she went into this rant for about twenty minutes about how he was a fascist and all that I was saying, "Alright luv, we all know that. But at least he apologised for his mistakes." Then they were asking me which ones I liked. So I pointed to this painting on the wall—a black and white thing with barmen wearing leather coats and all these grotesque characters hanging about. It looked a lot like an Otto Dix. Then this bloke from the Council ambles over and says, "Actually Mark, that's not part of the exhibition". Turns out it's just part of the wall. Heh! Heh! It was easily the best though.'

This piece, originally published in Frieze, no. 6, 1992, is an inversion of a piece by Stuart Bailey, 'Wyndham Lewis', originally published in Metropolis M, no. 2, 2005.

Reproduced with thanks to the editors, and to the authors for their help and consent.

LIAM GILLICK ON REPEAT

Interview by Mark Owens

Liam Gillick is a British artist whose work cuts across multiple domains, including sculpture, writing, curation, architecture, and graphic design. Pressing the late-modern visual language of wall texts, supergraphics and architectural surfaces into service, Gillick's work creates spaces for potential action that call into question contemporary ideological, economic, and political formations and processes. Alongside his artistic commissions Gillick has also completed a number of architectural and design projects in the world outside the gallery. Inserting himself into the gaps of the client/designer/artist matrix, Gillick pursues ways of working that test the implied limits of managerial practice.

--

1. RECENTLY YOUR WORK HAS INCLUDED A RANGE OF APPLIED PROJECTS, SUCH AS THE LOGO FOR THE FRANKFURTER KUNSTVEREIN, PUBLIC SCULPTURES, AND ARCHITECTURAL COMMISSIONS. APPLIED WORK, PARTICULARLY IN THE REALMS OF ARCHITECTURE AND GRAPHIC DESIGN, GENERALLY REQUIRE A FAIR AMOUNT OF NEGOTIATION AND DISCUSSION, BOTH OF WHICH ARE CENTRAL CONCERNS IN YOUR ART PRACTICE. HOW HAS WORKING ON THESE PROJECTS AFFECTED YOUR THINKING ABOUT THESE KINDS OF PROCESSES?

Strangely enough, I have often been the one pushing the notion of discourse as a functional rather than instrumental tool. Management is the large unspoken aspect of all this. Micro-management and the excess of analysis that is at the heart of most organized operations leads to a situation where there is often the semblance of discussion and openness but most things have been pre-decided. Of course there is a big difference between working with the Frankfurter Kunstverein and Deutsche Bank. But there is a pre-decision level that I often try and unpack. This sounds rather mannered in a way, but it effectively means assessing the situation and often trying to find 'real' discursive points and looking at where these people have decided the edge of their decision-making is located. My interest in the notion of discourse as a valid and challenging political tool is applied when that theoretical aspect is tested in real situations. There are times when I use techniques of refusal too. Closing down discussion as much as opening it up for its own sake.

2. WHAT IS IT ABOUT A MORE TRADITIONAL DESIGN-TYPE APPLIED PROJECT THAT INTERESTS YOU, AS OPPOSED TO AN ART COMMISSION, FOR INSTANCE? PERHAPS YOU COULD GIVE A SPECIFIC EXAMPLE.

Right now I am in the middle of working on a project for a bank in Switzerland, along with Daniel Buren, Robert Barry and John Armleder. As you can imagine this is not a standard bank, however a great deal of its interest in the legacy of conceptual art really resides in knowing where the art ends and their processes of exchange begin. About half way through the project the curator mentioned to me that the bank is dissatisfied with their logo. So I stopped the art part and shifted into a new set of thinking that could try and address this lack or loss of contact between the organization and the designers. I am an uninvited guest at this point. Pushing forward ideas that somehow activate the other 'art' work that I am doing for the new building. The logo I have worked on is relatively indistinguishable from any other bank logo. The issue is not so clearly tied to the form of the idea itself, more connected to claiming territories. I am treating the project as a practical exercise like designing a chair because people need somewhere to sit down. I am taking over a territory and occupying it, which will call into question the status of the apparent artworks I am doing alongside this. I am not sure that Daniel would be so interested in designing the bank logo. And this is a crucial difference which attests to the elegance of his theoretical position. But for me it is often necessary to abandon the more esoteric or abstract elements of the work to pursue truly

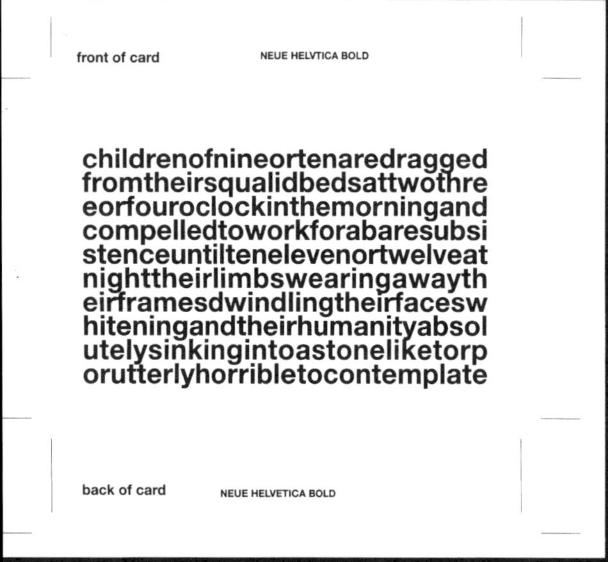

1

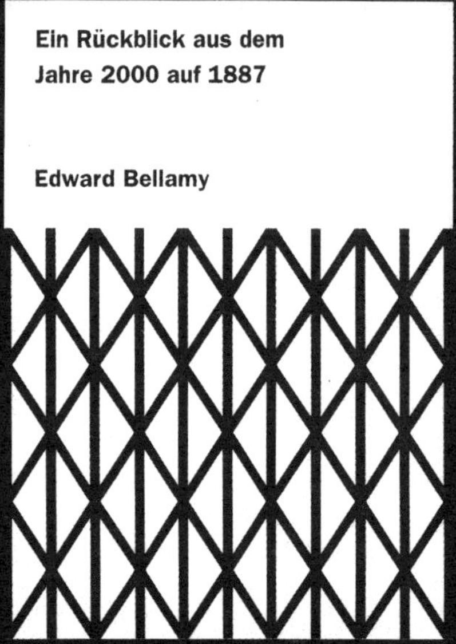

2

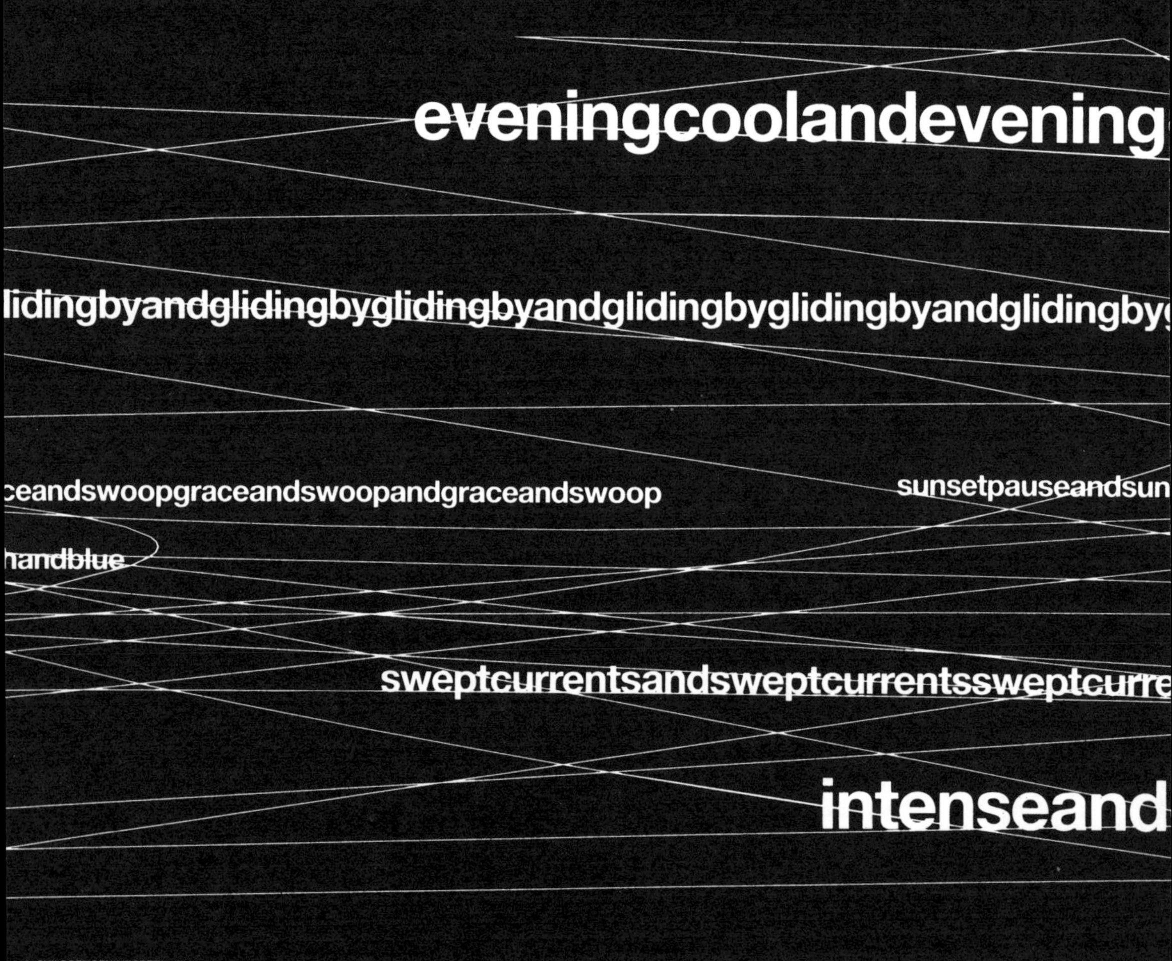

1: **CHILDRENOFNINEORTEN**, 2002
Postcard design
2: **Book Cover** 1998 (with Matthew Brannon)
3: **Book Cover** 1997 Züich
4: **IDEA HORISONS**, 2002
Curtain Wall for Ft. Launderdale/Hollywood International Airport, Florida.
フロリダのラウンダーテール国際空港のカーテンウォール
image 1, 4 taken from *Liam Glllick: The wood way*, Whitechapel Art Gallery 2002, exhhibition catalogue.
image 2, 3 taken from *Liam Glllick*, Lukas & Sternberg, New York, 2000, exhibition catalogue

practical issues that are absent or evaded by the cultural aspect of the situation.

Asked a few years ago to make a commission for some of the earliest public housing in Brussels I opted to improve the lobbies of each block, making new mailboxes, Entry-phone systems and lighting. I vigorously claimed that this was not an artwork. And that politically it was important for the commissioners of the project to understand the shift I was making. They continued to assert the art-ness of the project, so I abandoned it in terms of artistic authorship. The residents of the building still have the great lobbies, but they curators of the project don't have the chance to claim the 'work' as some kind of neo-Duchampian reference point. This kind of socio-political schizophrenia is common in my work, as there is no consolidation of form and content taking place. The work is a sequence of parallels interrupted by delusion, distraction and moments of refusal or reversal.

3. I HEARD SOMEWHERE THAT ONE OF YOUR PARENTS WAS A DESIGNER—DOES YOUR INTEREST IN DESIGN ALSO STEM IN PART FROM YOUR FAMILY BACKGROUND?

My mother used to work at home as a graphic designer. A low paid, pre-computer job, pasting up designs for books and brochures and catalogues. It is possible that the prolific side of my work might be connected to the speed with which I can work with computers, a situation which both put her out of work in the end and led to a temporary demise of pragmatic graphic talent. I certainly understood from the beginning by watching her work that there were many gaps in the managed and organized capitalist system that could be played with by people who interact extremely closely with its visualisation. She was extremely skeptical about her own work in that context but very good at it and maybe some of my deluded skepticism and enthusiasm simultaneously is a result of that experience. As she didn't value her work very much, she didn't attempt to teach me. So it was more the whole aesthetic of working at home, Rotring pens, drawing boards and paste-up that appealed to me. If you ever see my 'works on paper' in a gallery context you see the legacy of that early experience. She was quite into Scandinavian and French graphic design but that only came out by default in a general critique of lumpy British everyday design. It is the everyday that disturbed her rather than the edges of what was possible being truly interesting and that sense of related backwards to the experienced world of design continues to fascinate me.

4. YOU HAVE DESCRIBED YOUR WORK AS DISPLAYING 'AN ATTACHMENT TO A CERTAIN FORM OF NAIVE UTOPIAN MODERNISM WITH SOME OF THE DNA REMOVED' AS A WAY OF AVOIDING THE PITFALLS OF IRONY OR FATALISM. I LIKE THIS IDEA OF A WILLFULLY NAIVE UTOPIANISM THAT IS STILL SOMEHOW POLITICALLY ACTIVATED. CAN YOU TALK A BIT MORE ABOUT THE VALUE YOU SEE IN THIS KIND OF APPROACH, PARTICULARLY IN THE CURRENT POLITICAL CLIMATE?

It is quite clear to me that certain artists and other cultural workers found some aspects of postmodern theory quite convenient. Instead of focusing on the critical and analytical aspect of post-modern theory, they either used it as a source for illustration or as cultural permission for a super-ironic relationship to the apparent failures of modernism. I have always been a little disturbed by the continued use of the word utopian in relation to any progressive movement of the last hundred years or so. Any time people got together to try and make things better the forces of capitalism, as it were, accused them of being utopian and if that failed, crushed them with their boots. I know this sounds out of control until you think about pre-war Germany; the Vietnam war; the struggles of the late 1960s and recent fights against the suppression of human rights in light of the battle to control oil in the middle-east and even the boom and crash of new technologies in the US. But we have to say naïve utopianism because postmodernism taught us to be suspicious of certainties and determinism and the ongoing endless progress of the modern world. But that doesn't mean that postmodernism is not a theory of the left. It is still possible to engage in a form of self-conscious utopianism in order to reclaim the phrase—almost to piss people off who keep thinking that rational utopianism has been crushed or marginalized. Right now I would say that the use of pretty much

Literally No Place
Communes Bars
and Greenrooms
Liam Gillick
Book Works
London

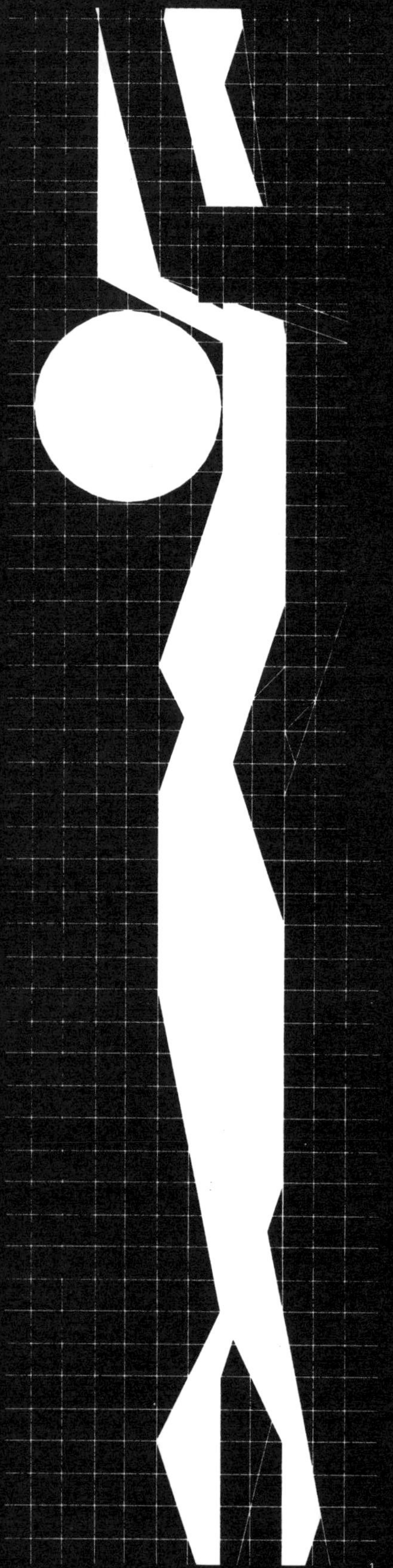

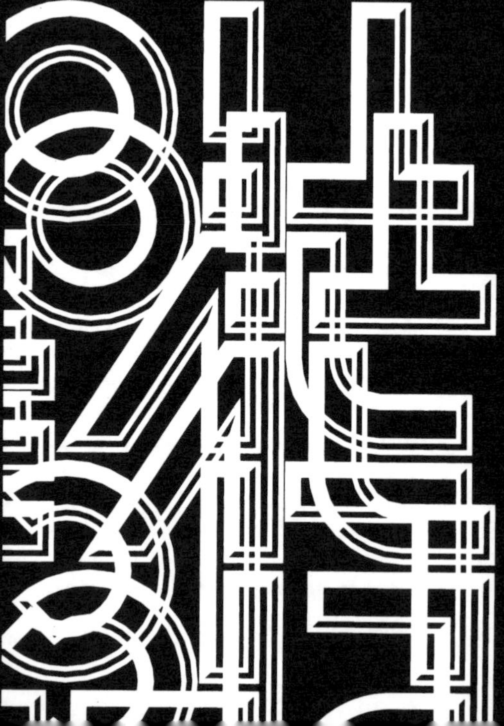

any kind of progressive analysis or action is worth a try. I would steer clear of the word utopian, but if it creates space to think and plan and work freely then there is no reason to deny it.

5. ON THE SUBJECT OF MODERNISM(S), I WONDER IF YOUR WORK HASN'T BEEN MISREAD, IN PART, AS A RELATIVELY STRAIGHTFORWARD APPROPRIATION OF A CORPORATE MODERNIST AESTHETIC ASSOCIATED WITH THE EXPORTATION OF THE SWISS NEUE GRAFIK AND THE POPULARIZATION OF HELVETICA IN THE LATE 1960S AND EARLY 1970S. PERHAPS THIS IS PARTIALLY A FAILURE IN HOW DESIGN HISTORY GETS WRITTEN. IF ANYTHING, THAT PERIOD SAW A PROLIFERATION OF VARIOUS MARGINAL 'SOFT' OR 'BASTARD' MODERNISMS THAT WERE BY NO MEANS SIMPLY COMPLICIT WITH CORPORATE OR POLITICAL POWER.

Absolutely. And good designers are the first to notice this. The whole corporate aesthetic misreading is coming directly from the art criticism community. I am interested in the way ideology leaves its traces in the built world and how things get decided and aestheticised in a post-consensus environment. This is not an issue of appropriation but instead it is a question of inserting yourself into an implicated position and trying to make work about a very visible aspect of our time. I am really interested in finding ways to decode and understand certain processes rather than reflect them. I think my ideology is quite clear from the work but it doesn't matter to me that some people try to filter out the rhetoric around the projects. I am not trying to overdetermine or completely telegraph ideas all the time. As I have often said, I am frequently interested in making work to turn your back on. Work that is activated by your sense of seeing other people in relationship to it. Things that set a scene or create a setting for a certain kind of thinking to take place. The key ideas in the work are not always in the most apparent objects or things. That stuff might just be a backdrop to something quite complex or glib.

On the other hand, however, I don't want to deny my continued interest in those moments in the last century at Ulm for example where people really tried to get involved in making things better for other people in a somewhat dour way. The processes of discussion around those periods haven't really been transcended. I am not looking for a paradigm shift in my own work, but I am using the role of the artist as one that can enter into the culture without the presence of the clearly defined 'client' or judgment system. Some people might find that a strange statement, but a collector is not a client. There is a crucial difference here about self-imaging being out of sync with what's possible in terms of how people self-censor and how they create feedback loops of their own making in relation to what their fellow designers or artists are getting up to.

6. SINCE THE MID-1980S GRAPHIC DESIGN HAS SEEN A SUCCESSION OF FORMAL CHANGES AND TECHNOLOGICAL INNOVATIONS, INCLUDING THE DEMOCRATIZATION OF TOOLS WITH THE ADVENT OF THE MAC, FORMAL EXPLORATIONS INFORMED BY FRENCH THEORY AND A SUBSEQUENT REVISITING OF CERTAIN KINDS OF MODERNIST MINIMALISMS THROUGH THE 1990S, AND MORE RECENTLY A PREOCCUPATION WITH THE HAND-DRAWN AND VECTOR-BASED ILLUSTRATION. HAS THE RELATIVELY RAPID DISSEMINATION OF DESIGN TOOLS SUCH AS ILLUSTRATOR, FOR EXAMPLE, INFORMED YOUR ART PRACTICE OR YOUR ABILITY TO GET WORK DONE?

I have used Apple computers since 1986 and my first exhibition made use of one of the drawing packages that came with the computer. It had nothing to do with the idea of the computer. It was just a convenient way to do fast clean-lined drawings. At that time I was really doing what I think of now as parallel activities, at that point working pretty much like an architect, but designing maybe 200 buildings a day instead of one every week, month or year. I have a typical intuitive relation to software like Illustrator. Finding the same things frustrating that everyone else finds frustrating, like the dopey 3D part of Illustrator CS.

I think that the great American contribution over the last years has been software. And at every point this has challenged the power structures that are already in place. Of course

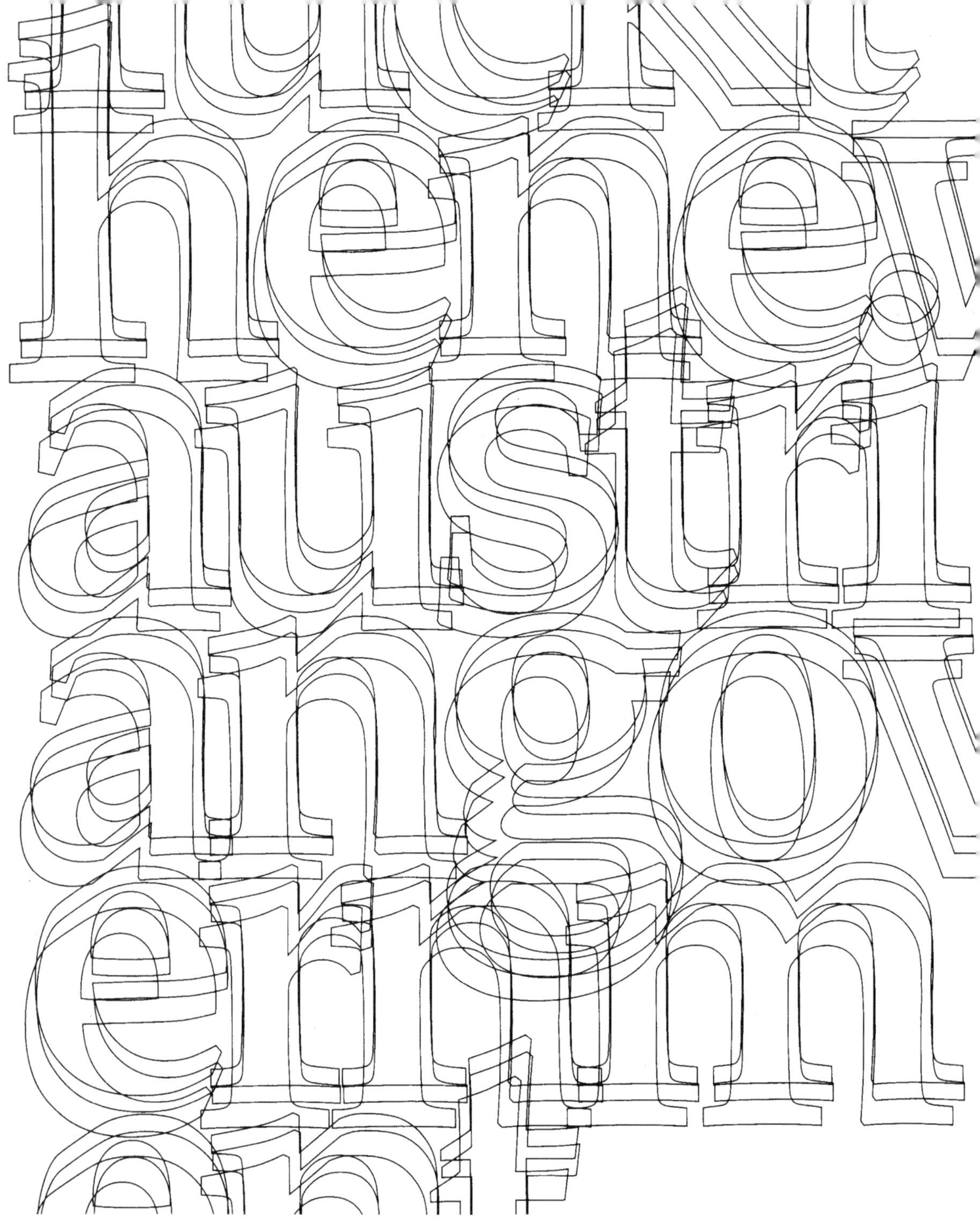

FUCKTHENEWAUSTRAINGOVERNMENT, 2000
Schipper & Krome, Berlin

from *Liam Gillick: The wood way,*
Whitechapel Art Gallery 2002, exhhibition catalogue

this rather practical aspect of software writing has been swept away by super-capitalised play with the marketing of the idea of having an idea that culminated in the tech-market crash. But the truth of the matter is that the functional effect of graphic software is often closer to the impact that the invention of the modern pencil had on some forms of French art and accounting at the same time. It is a multiple effect that feels extremely specific to each layer of the culture that is using it. The ideological message within the work is the dominant feature that shouldn't be allowed to evade scrutiny. For me none of this has felt like a rapid dissemination as I have had to wait for nearly 20 years for a decent vector based drawing programme that works as fast and efficiently as I would like it to work.

7. WHEN I WAS VISITING LONDON RECENTLY I WAS STAYING IN BLOOMSBURY AT THE BRUNSWICK CENTRE, A SORT OF FANTASTICALLY SHABBY SECOND COUSIN TO THE BARBICAN THAT IS CURRENTLY UNDERGOING MASSIVE RENOVATIONS. WHAT DO YOU MAKE OF THE RENEWED INTEREST IN LATE MODERNIST PUBLIC ESTATES ARCHITECTURE, THAT PARTICULAR SPECIES OF 'UGLY' LATE 1960S/EARLY 1970S BRUTALISM? OVER THE YEARS THESE KINDS OF BUILDINGS HAVE BEEN OPENED UP TO AN INTERESTING MIX OF COMPETING INTERESTS—FROM ARCHITECTURAL PRESERVATIONISTS TO URBAN OPPORTUNIT-STS, SUCH AS THE SKATEBOARDERS IN LONDON'S SOUTHBANK.

I was always appalled growing up by the way amazing things got built and then abandoned by the city. It seemed absolutely perverse to build some great looking place from the near-future and then let it get trashed by people who rightly took out their frustration with their marginalized place in society on the mega-structural symbols of their oppressors, if you see what I mean. Not that people really completely destroyed things, it was more a process of boredom and a lack of education. The cities often took a defensive approach in the first place, which lead to a general pulling out of the social contract. Not trusting the residents, not opening the bar they said they would open. Not encouraging good times, parties or social interaction beyond the most basic.

A few years ago I went back to Thamesmead in south London. An enormous brutalist housing project built on a swamp. It was used as the setting for A Clockwork Orange and I wanted to see if it could still work as a place to film in. Of course the silhouette of the structures is still incredible, and really works off the surrounding area. Kubrick was worried that if people saw A Clockwork Orange there might be moments of social collapse so he pulled the film from distribution in the UK. Part of the subplot of my distracted visit that day was to see what I would make of his form of apolcalytic narcissism. The situation there is much worse than he thought it could be. Nothing has happened. Absolutely nothing at all. You can still park for free in the free underground parking, walk by the six-inch-deep lake, wander past the empty 'social club'. The interest some of us have in these structures from the recent past is connected to the moment of initiation combined with the potential that they have to form an appropriate place for the people who want to live there now. If we don't examine what went right with these places, it will be much easier for people in the future to avoid making extensive social gestures for the good of everyone and instead leave the future to the opportunist chaos of the market, which might be fine for a lot of people but will further divide up the culture and create new problems for the near future that won't look like the ones from the recent past.

This text is repeated from The Blow Up magazine, no. 3, 2005. The images are repeated from Idea magazine, no. 297, 2003.

COMIC MARXISM : PUNK'S DAY-GLO AND THE BASH STREET KIDS

by Ben Watson & Esther Leslie

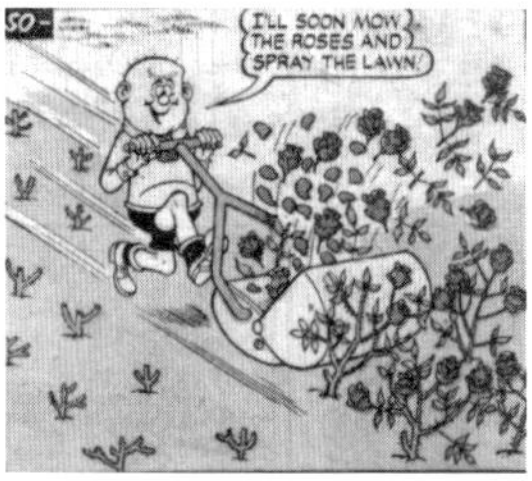

Bodily functions meet analytical philosophy

The great discovery of the Surrealists was not shock, sex and blatancy (all of which have been technically superseded by advertising), but the strange and unavoidable attraction of coincidence—or what looks like coincidence to those positivists who believe in a Cartesian separation between the realms of soul and body, thought and the universe. Such positivism was mocked at its inception. Take Tristram Shandy, a work by the Irish-born writer Laurence Sterne published between 1760 and 1767. Tristram Shandy mocks burgeoning philosophies of rationalism and empiricism by pointing out that humans are physical beings before they can be mental ones. Like James Joyce, Sterne used sexual materialism to explode bourgeois morality and rationalism, introducing digestive and body functions in the most unlikely places. Tristram Shandy begins his biography—logically enough—with his own conception. His parents' sexual congress is interrupted when his mother asks his father if he has remembered to wind up the clock: the protest against mechanical reason could not be more graphic. Tristram Shandy trashes notions of propriety. This read is not 'improving'. It is hilarious, convulsive. For the materialist that makes Tristram Shandy all the more true.

From the absurdism of Tristram Shandy it might seem some way to the methods of Karl Marx. However, Marx did not think that comical books and light reading of the same inhabited a different universe to his lofty philosophical project. The young Marx read Tristram Shandy and loved it. In the late 1830s he wrote an emulation of it named Scorpio Und Felix, and the outrageous satire of his Eighteenth Brumaire and Capital would not have been possible without Sterne's literary example. In chapter 37 of Scorpio und Felix, Marx satirises the wannabes who creep up the hierarchy on the back of genuine innovation as an illustration—contra David Hume's empirical philosophy—of the importance of cause and effect. The bourgeois world is topsy-turvy and honours mediocrity.

> David Hume maintained that this chapter was the locus communis of the preceding, and indeed maintained so before I had written it. His proof was as follows: since this chapter exists, the earlier chapter does not exist, but this chapter has ousted the earlier, from which it sprang, though not through the operation of cause and effect, for this he questioned. Yet every giant, presupposes a dwarf, every genius a hidebound philistine, and every storm at sea—mud. As soon as the first disappear, the latter replace them, sitting down at the table and sprawling arrogantly with their long legs.
>
> The first are too great for this world, so they are thrown out. But the latter strike root in it and remain, as one may see from the facts, for champagne leaves a lingering aftertaste which is repulsive. Caesar the hero leaves behind him the play-acting Octavianus, Emperor Napoleon the bourgeois Louis Philippe, the philosopher Kant the carpet-knight Krug, the poet Schiller the Hofrat

> raupach, Leibniz's heaven Wolf's schoolroom, the dog Boniface this chapter.
>
> Thus the bases are precipitated, while the spirit evaporates.[1]

Marx's recent biographer Francis Wheen is correct to see in this passage an anticipation of the famous opening lines of the Eighteenth Brumaire, where Marx used similar phrases to mock Napoleon III as a farcical repetition of Napoleon Bonaparte. Sterne's debunking satire, which contrasts grand ideals with shabby reality, made a permanent impression on Marx.
This contrast is contained in the Marxist insult 'epigone'. It describes the degradation of the presentday politicians and cultural figures compared to the illustrious history to which they appeal for legitimacy. 'Spirit', true 'genius' sets everything going, but is chased from the world, in order that banality might reign. Such Marxist satire reappears in Clement Greenberg's dialectic of avant-garde and kitsch. Mainstream mass culture circulates a kitsch reproduction of innovative culture, and it leaves a repulsive after-taste. Marx's conclusion—'thus the bases are precipitated, while the spirit evaporates'—accuses the current ruling class of being the dregs, applying to them the insult they direct at the proletariat. Marx's satire concludes with a dog named Boniface (apparently the 'one and the same as Saint Boniface, the apostle of Germany', citing in proof his Epistles no. 105, where he describes himself as a barking dog) being given an enema of oil, salt, bran, honey and clyster.

> 'Poor Boniface! You are constipated with your holy thoughts and reflections, since you can no longer relieve yourself in speech and writing!'
> 'O admirable victim of profundity! O pious constipation!'[2]

This is no prissy appeal to transcendental spirit with no bodily functions. Spirit and body are not separate entities for a materialist, and 'profundity'—which is invariably codswallop—like all that pretends to be holy, must be profaned. Marx's equation between literary production and the moving of the bowels was also one made by James Joyce. It is not only scatological satire of the high and mighty, but insistence on the human agency in literary production, refusal to allow the text's productive source in the writer's bodily being to be obscured by transcendental concepts. Marx's satire on David Hume is based his own productivity as a thinker and writer: he attacks Hume's scepticism by accusing it of an a priori certainty that what he is writing at the minute will only be the lifeless residue of previous ideas. For Marx, vulgarity, in its many senses, is a key component of cultural development, even of the most elevated philosophy and social theory. Vulgarity (of the vulgate, from the people, from 'below'), even when it outrages those who claim to speak for the people, sets something in motion.

Blasting culture

In the last fortnight of 1913 a group of London based artists, led by Wyndham Lewis, produced a periodical. Its name was BLAST, and its emblem was a vortex. Lewis's BLAST was supposed to be a celebration of the blast furnaces of the industrialized Midlands and North. Blast also suggests a hygienic gale from the North. The emblematic representation of the vortex on the first pages of Blast is a figuration of a storm-cone with the

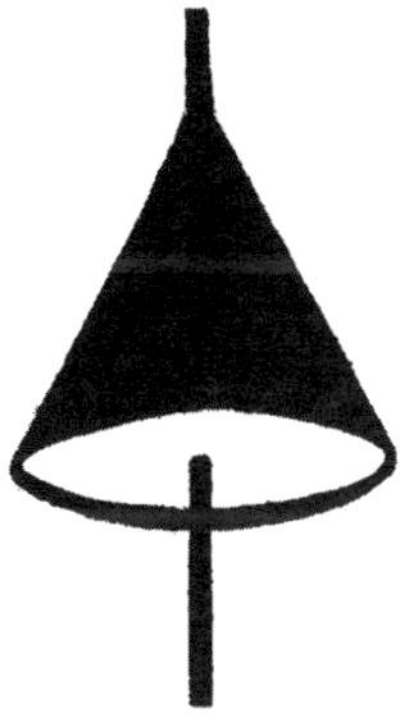

apex up: a signal used by coastguards to represent strong winds from the north. With its glorious outrageously luridly pink cover and heavy anonymous blockish black typography and polemical rants BLAST was as shocking as the Sex Pistols' Never Mind The Bollocks LP cover some 60-odd years later.

Designed in 1913, printed in 1914, BLAST was designed to be a verbal expression that could be adequate to the 'stark radicalism of the visuals' that Lewis had been developing in the previous years.[1] The journal's cover was almost a foot's length of lurid pink, and its paper thick and rough. It was a fat pink slab of invective and black ink and it appeared with a date, 20 June 1914, to specify the very moment of its interruption of art history. BLAST reeked of assertion and industry. Its typography was black and solid, evoking newspaper headlines rather than tasteful art-salon brochures. Apart from the cover's diagonal rip of language, the type sat squarely on each page, blockish and dark. This was in sharp contrast to futurism's parole liberta, twisting and twirling across the pages. But it was the cover's colour that issued the first shock. Lewis 'planned and launched the hugest and pinkest of all magazines, BLAST, whose portentous dimensions and violent tint did more than would a score of exhibitions to make the public feel that something was happening'.[4]

In a letter to Lord Carlow, in July 1914, Lewis described BLAST as a 'puce monster'.[5] In his autobiography Blasting and Bombardiering in 1937, he recalled that it had 'a page area of 12 inches by 9 1/2' and was of a 'puce colour', adding that 'in general appearance it was not unlike a telephone book'.[6] No one could ignore the cover; the critics all mentioned it. Ford Maddox Hueffer called it purple in Outlook. The Times, in its edition of 1 July 1914, deemed it 'bound in purple paper'. The Athenaeum, New Weekly and New Statesman decided upon magenta. Poetry called it cerise. The Morning Post considered it 'a vast folio in pink paper covers, full of irrepressible imbecility'.[7] The Little Review decided on 'something between magenta and lavender, about the colour of a sick headache'. The Egoist called it pink. The Pall Mall Gazette coined 'chilled flannelette pink', and noted that the colour 'recalls the catalogue of some cheap Eastend draper, and its contents are of the shoddy sort that constitutes the Eastend draper's stock'.[8] The Observer's reviewer settled on 'a peculiarly aggressive pucey pink'.[9] The colour screamed vulgarity.

BLAST was written by self-styled 'Primitive Mercenaries'.[10] It spoke for the savage artist mingling in the 'enormous, jangling, journalistic fairy desert of modern life', which 'serves him as Nature did more technically primitive man'.[11] The journal was designed to crash into the European art scene and cause a stir.

In the glorious pink volume of BLAST no.1 (of only two) Ezra Pound presents some condensed Imagist poems on colour, artifice and chemicality:

> Women Before a Shop
> The gewgaws of false amber and false
> turquoise attract them,
> Like to like nature. These agglutinous
> yellows.

Or again:

> L'Art
> Green arsenic smeared on an egg-white cloth,
> Crushed strawberries! Come let us feast
> our eyes.

Or again:

> The New Cake of Soap
> Lo, how it gleams and glistens in the sun
> Like the cheek of a Chesterton.[12]

These slogan poems cough up the major concerns of London Vorticism. In the first poem, consuming women are attracted to baubles, to the fakery of the commercial. It's all a cheap trick to pull in the punters. They are attracted because they themselves are no different: like eyes up like, each as artificial, false and hideous as the other. The second poem vituperates against art—in the modish French sense—as a mélange of poisonous tint and damaged nature on canvas. A feast for the eyes indeed bitterly evokes a deadly mess, of faked and ruined nature for those who know no better. The third poem parodies formal appreciation on the part of art lovers, by conceiving the aesthetic pleasures of a bar of soap, cleanliness being its aim, just like the good clean English middle-class fun of G.K. Chesterton. Lewis asked Pound to submit some 'nasty' poems to BLAST. The nastier the poems the better. How does Pound get nasty? By reference to the modern age's fakery and chemical inauthenticity. BLAST insisted on negation and maliciously mocked the 'culture-loving' classes. It eschewed culture as affirmative. It did this from the vulgarity of its cover to the viciousness of its lyric. Vile bodies asserted themselves, not least in the death-laden figures of no. 2, the War Issue. This culture outburst negates a negative world. The barbarians from BLAST exposed in jagged outlines truths known but suppressed.

Biffo the Bear meets Adorno : The Bash Street Kids meet Punk

In the black and white world of post-WWII Britain, colour was what made the Beano comic so attractive. It is used sparingly, to keep the price down. Simple black-and-white is alternated with black-and-red-and-white. There is colour for the front and back pages, and the magnificent centre-fold of 'The Bash Street Kids'. All of which describes a certain pecking order: the funnier strips with the stronger characters get the extra red, and everyone agrees that 'The Bash Street Kids' are the comic's high point.

These comics emerged in an era before newspapers were printed in colour, though by the 1960s there were glossy 'Sunday supplements' with colour photographs and advertisements featuring sexy models, cars, liquor and cigarettes—none of which were of interest to children. Instead, bliss was a Beano and a packet of sweets: Refreshers, Opal fruits, Wine Gums or a handful of four-a-penny Fruit Salads. Back then a child's pocket money purchased riches unknown to parents and older siblings. In this sense, the Beano provided the same kind of infantile pleasure as the multicoloured beads strung across a baby's pram.

In shops the Beano tended to be kept at ground level—it could be located quickly even in an unknown newsagent. The infant consumer pushed past grown-up legs to find the printed treasure. The Beano's stories are told from the point of view of children, continually at war with parents, teachers and policemen.

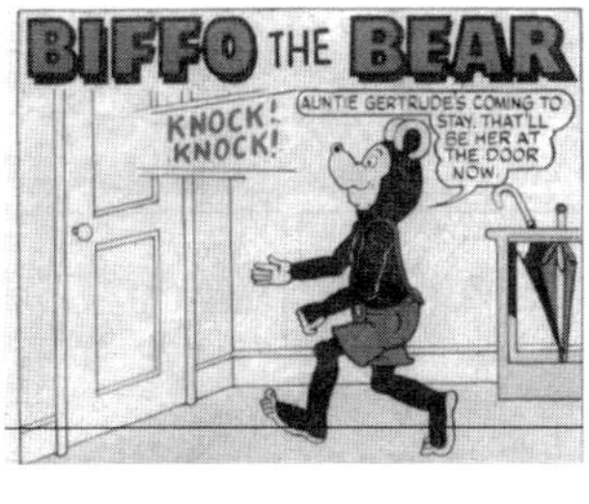

The Beano did not only express a child's point of view. It also performed the Brechtian 'art of thinking in other people's heads'. In the early days, the cover featured 'Biffo The Bear', an unaccountably petit-bourgeois character who was forever fussing about his carpet, curtains and pictures. No less than Odysseus, 'Biffo The Bear' acts out civilizational dilemmas whose significance for philosophy could far outweigh his picaresque adventures. Here Biffo goes to answer the door. His Auntie Gertrude is coming to stay (unlike most characters in the Beano, Biffo The Bear is a character of strict routine and social arrangement). Unfortunately, she has brought with her a pet spaniel named Bowsie.

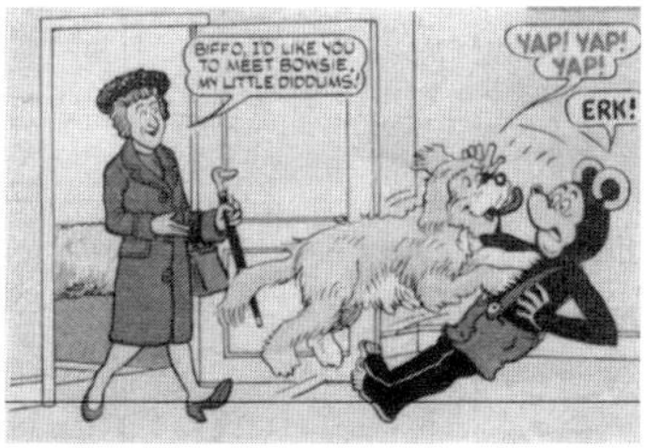

In his unbridled canine enthusiasm, he not only knocks over poor Biffo, but threatens his precarious status as petit-bourgeois and semi-human. After all, Biffo wears shorts and braces (though no shirt), but the dog is naked! Biffo resorts to the standby of human beings who do not wish to communicate with each other, and switches on the TV, handing over his consciousness to be administered by the mass culture industry.

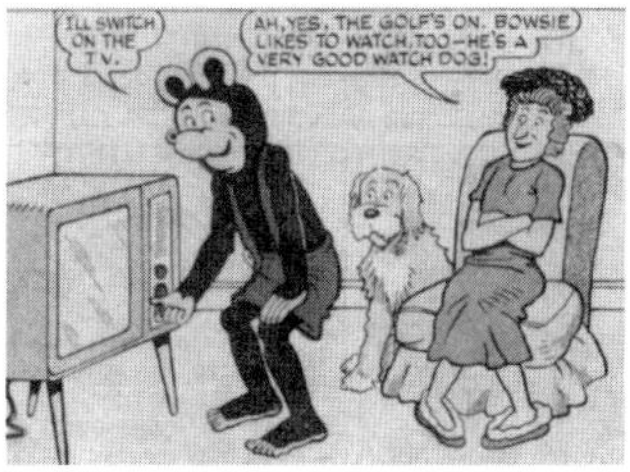

Auntie is pleased that they can watch golf, probably the most boring sports programme possible. She also makes a pun: the dog likes TV, he is a very good 'watch dog'. The change in status between the working dog of the countryside—whose task is to 'watch' the sheep—and the ornamental 'little diddums' is indicative of the petit-bourgeois milieu inhabited by Biffo and his Auntie. Biffo occasionally works as a keeper in the zoo, but for a householder he has an inordinate amount of leisure. One suspects a private income or stipend of some kind. This distance from regular employment makes him subject to numerous neuroses, often centred on housework. Unfortunately, the dog enjoys watching golf on TV so much, he begins barking. Biffo wonders why the 'flop-eared fool' does not deafen itself.

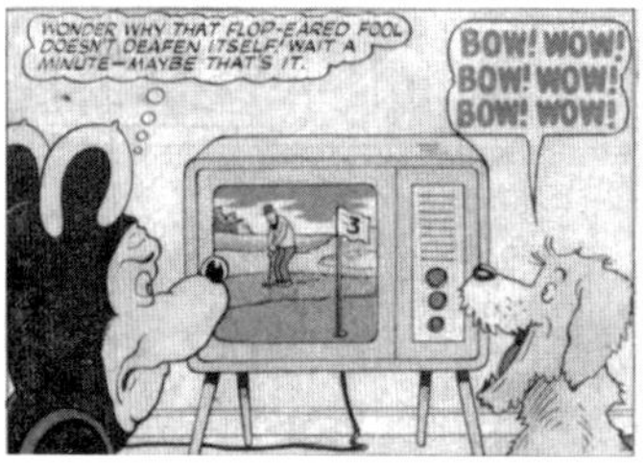

However, this gives him an idea. He takes a rubber band and puts it on his head, pressing his ears down against his head.

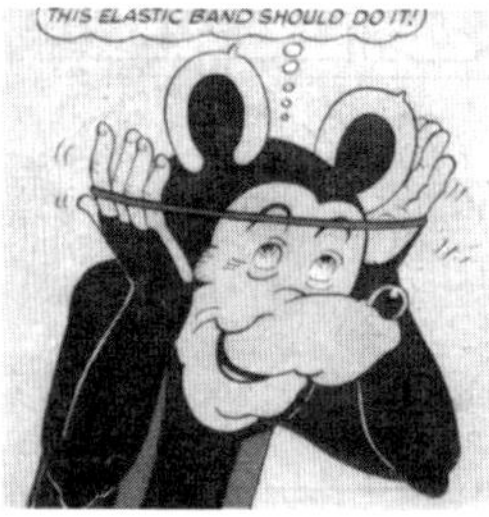

Biffo's solution to the TV-dog problem is fraught with paradox. He prevents himself hearing the dog, but he also cannot hear the commentary coming from the TV. The totality of the golf game will now become incomprehensible, its narrative and dramatic logic made incomprehensible. On the screen, the golfer is missing the ball and instead sending up pieces of turf. It is as if the game itself has got caught in Biffo's self-defeating logic.

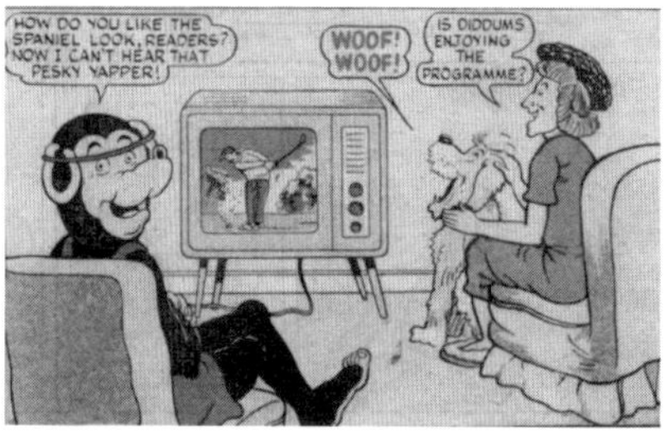

Biffo has closed his ears to the voice of nature in order to concentrate on mass-cultural delusion, but in so doing has rendered that delusion incomprehensible, reduced it to an endless series of missed strikes. He asks the readers if they like his 'spaniel look'—spaniels are famous for their ingratiating, fawning characters—but has made himself deaf to any reply (he has also turned himself into the very thing he hates in this self-harming act). This is surely symbolic of the petit-bourgeoisie, deaf to criticisms of their own self-inflicted limitations, yet still confident they are 'doing the right thing'? Any resemblance to Adorno and Horkheimer's famous tale of Ulysses in Dialectic Of Enlightenment is obviously a 'coincidence', of a kind that only a materialist explanation of bourgeois society's relationship to nature (and itself) could explain.

Biffo was deposed from the front cover in late 1974. 'Dennis the Menace', which had previously been on the back page, now occupied both front and back. Dennis has a dog Gnasher, an extraordinary prosthesis, seemingly an autonomous bundle of Dennis's wild hair. They are prototypical Punk rockers, allergic to 'softies', flowers and perfume—though Dennis sprouted his dreadlocks in the late 1960s, far in advance of The Sex Pistols. Benjaminites will be upset to learn that the prototypical softie is called Walter. He has a friend with the upper-class name Bertie Blenkinsop, and he has a pet poodle named Foo Foo. The war against them is one of urchin versus posh kid, mongrel versus thoroughbred.

The black scribble which represents Dennis's hair and Gnasher beautifully sets off the rest of the colours in this strip. In Goethe's Faust, Mephistopheles first appears to Faust and Wagner in the shape of a black poodle. Faust is fascinated by the multiple colours and sparks that fly around him. The point is not that the designers of 'Dennis The Menace' were making a reference to Faust, but that Goethe was interested in perceptual phenomena, and a large area of black is just the thing to make colours shine bright. The Beano artists use the same device.

The Bash Street Kids are an anarchic collective, each with a distinct character. They have regular confrontations with the Blob Street gang. When the Sex Pistols named themselves Johnny Rotten and Sid Vicious, and presented the appearance of a bunch of naughty street kids playing at pirates, it is difficult not to see an influence stemming from the Bash Street Kids. What was amazing with Punk was that these characters had somehow leapt out of the comic and were scandalising newspaper columnists, royalists and police officers up and down the country.

The Bash Street Kids insist on fun and transformation and constantly come into conflict with authority. They particularly love it when figures of speech become actualities, and phrases that refer to wild animals or overgrown jungles or which have double meanings suddenly become entities in real life. As in a dream or a poem, the distinction between images and what they refer to keeps being dissolved. This is because the strip is predicated upon jokes—an involuntary response on the part of the reader—not upon maintaining the conditions of illusion. Any artist who can take this aesthetic seriously is keeping open a channel of communication with the utopian delight of childhood. This insistence on libidinal gratification rather than organised culture consolidates one of Marxism's fundamental drives: to shape and transform the world, and pursue a dialectic between 'mere ideas' ('images') and reality. That is because Marxism is not mere 'philosophy'. It is revolutionary praxis. So was Punk.

Day-Glo vs. Taste

A century before Punk emerged as rebel youth movement, the word itself meant something else: it meant something worthless, foolish, rubbish, empty talk, nonsense: such that Lord Carlyle could speak of 'phosphorescent punk and nothingness'. However, when it came to future dreams for colour schemes, Punk preferred fluorescence's immediate shock to phosphorescence's postponed illumination in the darkness. Fluorescence holds nothing back for later—like Punk, its mode is the mode of anti-interiority, denial of romantic self, a cheap trick, a cheap trip without innerness, an upfront slap in the face of public taste. One way of blowing apart the dead inevitability of history written with hindsight—its placid affirmation of the status quo—is Walter Benjamin's habit of seizing on a significant detail. This came from a reading of Capital. Benjamin's hallucinogenic focus on a single detail jolts a moment from its place in a preordained sequence of events, and lets in the multivalent possibility inherent in human action. As Hegel said in the smaller Logic, para. 143, 'Viewed as an identity in general, Actuality is first of all Possibility'.[13]

The Punk story told in terms of chart placements and fame slots Punk back in the pop logic it was a protest against, whereas reveries about shopping schemes, council tenancies, bondage and Day-Glo plunge us into the first moments of Punk's immediacy, its shock and exhilaration—the heretical idea of living historically instead of according to the needs of capital accumulation. No past, no future, no capital, no mortgage payments? Punk emerged out of an amalgam of Situationist high theory and anarchist practice, and anti-muso rock n roll. It fused the critical negational energies of Debord and Vaneigem with the positive expressions of youthful creativity and generational revolt that had been incubated by a thousand working class American rock 'n' rollers and a trashy culture of B-movies, garish cartoons, low-budget pornography and screaming tabloids. This is not at all the same as saying that it merged high and low—that was the culture-affirming principle of a later mode of postmodern art.

Punk's mix was confusing, hot-tempered and disruptive. Its mode of attack was splitting, making impossible (ie. ridiculous) certain previous cultural forms, upsetting and contaminating certain cultural signifiers, notably swastikas, which were sprinkled over monarchs, hippy businessmen, such as Richard Branson, and punks alike. Punk made a mark that looked like a wound or a rip, self-harm or social harm, no future or one built up anew from below, shambolically—contradictory in its very gesture. Punk destroyed the capitalist recuperation of the 1960s called rock culture. Its ludicrous and uncontainable contradictions align it with true revolutionary interruption of culture as business as usual, the only culture visible to the sociologists and cultural analysts of the academy.

Day-Glo was the colour of choice for Punk, except it is not a colour, or more than a colour: it is a twist on the volume control. Day-Glo had been around for some time when Punk appropriated it. In the 1930s, after one of them received a bonk on the head and a spell of recuperative treatment under ultra-violet light, Bob and Joe Switzer, eager young experimenters, were mucking around with dyes and resins to make colours that were brighter than normal and glowed under u.v. light. They used these new fluorescent colours in their hokey little magic shows. The new fluorescent colours were eye-catching. They leapt out to the eye more than other colours. These were colours keen to assert themselves. It was as if a new part of the spectrum had been discovered.

Colour arises in ordinary objects through selective absorption, so something that is green absorbs all colours, except green. A cherry reflects back only red, emitted at the same wavelength as that absorbed. Ordinary paint absorbs some of the spectrum from white light and reflects the rest; it absorbs and reflects light from the visible part of the spectrum. Fluorescent paints, however, do not simply scatter light back from the visible part of the spectrum. They can also soak up shorter wavelengths (such as ultra-violet), which are invisible to our eyes, re-emitting the energy by transforming it into photons of longer wavelength. The energy in ultra-violet light is converted into visible light emitted by the chemicals in the paint. Fluorescent pigments absorb photons and the high-frequency ultra-violet radiation excites electrons into a higher energy vibrational state. Agitated, these send off waves and a glow is seen. This is what produces their extraordinary brightness.

So fluorescent paint lets more of itself as colour be seen; it shines brighter, seeming as if it holds within itself a source of illumination. Fluorescence buzzes in ordinary light, but it positively fizzes under other light types, such as blue light, short wave ultra-violet light, long wave ultraviolet and x-rays. Fluorescent colours are up to three times brighter than conventional colours. They shine more brilliantly, more vibrantly.

In 1936 the Switzer brothers set up a firm in Cleveland. War came, and their new colours found military application in bright signal panels used by troops in North Africa to identify themselves as friendly to Allied dive-bombers. Fluorescent paint also enabled pilots to land warplanes at night on aircraft carriers in the Pacific, an advantage not possessed by the Japanese. The Switzer brothers developed fluorescent inks that bombardiers used during blackouts and fluorescent penetrants to find hidden flaws in machined parts, such as engine pistons and rockets' liquid oxygen tanks. So fluorescence could help win wars, but peace put them back into civilian use on billboards, in safety signage and promotional publicity, and soap powder boxes. In 1946 the Switzers' firm was incorporated as Switzer Bros. Inc. and they called their dyes Day-Glo. The North American postwar landscape zinged with brighter than bright colours, many of which were now in the service of advertising. In 1947 Canadians saw the first Day-Glo colours on a billboard, and Chesterfield cigarettes used fluorescent colours on packaging. In 1959 fluorescent colours appeared on a soap powder box when Proctor and Gamble made their first box of Tide in shrieking colours, seeming to leap off the supermarket shelf into the shopper's basket. Once outside the military context, Day-Glo was associated with vulgarity, the too obvious, the screamingly evident.

In the 1950s the name Day-Glo was trademarked and in the late 1960s the company formally changed its name from Switzer Bros Inc to Day-Glo Colour Corp. Vulgarity, cheapness and commercialism dogged Day-Glo, but its manufacturers' aspirations seemed limitless and sublime. The names given to Day-Glo Color Corp's palette of colours ring with the poetry of science, industry and space exploration. The full trademarked pigment set comprises:

NEON RED
ROCKET RED
FIRE ORANGE
BLAZE ORANGE
ARC YELLOW
SATURN YELLOW
SIGNAL GREEN
HORIZON BLUE
AURORA PINK
CORONA MAGENTA

Each one fizzes in its optical attack, saturating vision, soothing and alerting simultaneously. The cosmic utopianism of space travel, as well as the love of the alien-sounding letter X, permeates the product line names: Starfire, Filteray, Velex, Optex. Fluorescent colours decorated a world in which space exploration had advanced. Earth had been imaged by rockets in space in 1947, and then, sharper and more spectacularly from the US Navy Viking II rocket in May 1954. And these rockets headed for the moon or launched satellites that were man-made moons.

Despite this utopianism, Day-Glo remained a bad taste product, acceptable only to commercial art, where Psychedelia found a use for it in posters: Day-Glo fluorescent paint was easy to get hold of in the 1960s—it became a household word through Tom Wolfe's book on Ken Kesey and the Merry Pranksters, The Electric Acid Kool-Aid Test (1968). Then Day-Glo found its way into film: in the entry on the word Day-Glo the OED quotes an article from The Listener, from 1968, which condemns the use of flashing Day-Glo colours as vulgar signal of an orgasm in Girl On A Motorcycle, a film by Jack Cardiff. The hippies used Day-Glo in their cultural artefacts, and even on their bodies, but theirs was an attempt to paint over the world in the colours of their hallucinogenic trips. Day-Glo was being taken into the student bedroom, the kids' blacklit den where individual mediation could hinge on the wonders of a perceptual trick that disappeared when normal electricity resumed. It took Punk to fully assimilate Day-Glo without transforming it—or rather it took Punk to sublate it (accepting, negating and raising it to a higher level), vulgarity and all. Punk exploited Day-Glo's bargain-basement, eye-catching impudence. Jamie Reid's cover for Never Mind The Bollocks modelled itself on crude signs in budget off-licences and cut-price supermarkets. This was consumer society staring itself in the face. Fine, gallery art was behind the times when Peter Halley began to use Day-Glo paints in his abstractions in the 1980s. Punk had already camouflaged itself in the colours of the antagonist.

BLAST's acerbic squeal found an echo 60 years later in the singer Polystyrene's lyrical rejection of germ-free adolescence and postwar plastics, engine of a new economy. Her band X-ray Spex's single 'The Day the World Turned Day-Glo' was a chemical retort to the internalized hippy-trip of 'Lucy in the Sky with Diamonds':

> I clambered over mounds and mounds
> Of polystyrene foam
> Then fell into a swimming pool
> Filled with fairy snow
> And watched the world turn
> Day-Glo you know you know
> The world turned Day-Glo you know
>
> I wrenched the nylon curtains back
> As far as they would go
> Then peered through Perspex window panes
> At the acrylic road
> I drove my polypropylene car
> On wheels of sponge
> Then pulled into a Wimpy bar
> To have a rubber bun
>
> The x-rays were penetrating
> Through the Latex breeze
> Synthetic fibre see-thru leaves
> Fell from the rayon trees

Polystyrene woke up in a world that was synthetic, just as the Vorticists had woken up in a world that was machinic. While Lewis publicly scorned Marinetti's 'Futurist gush over machines, aeroplanes, etc.' he was impressed by Marinetti's idea that humans are changed by living in cities with communications and transport at their disposal, and he affirms a Dada manifesto from 1918 which describes the Dada sound poem as the sheer noise of urban existence, the screech of tram brakes, which wipe out traces of old-style individuality. Punk's post-war version of Lewis's material desideratum forwarded not the machinic society but the plastic consumer society. Polystyrene again:

> I know I'm artificial
> But don't put the blame on me
> I was reared with appliances
> In a consumer society
>
> My existence is illusive
> The kind that is supported
> By mechanical resources
>
> I wanna be instamatic
> I wanna be a frozen pea
> I wanna be dehydrated
> In a consumer society

Despite its lurid appearance, the cover of Never Mind The Bollocks was no cheap and easy, thrown-together item—it relied on modern painterly technologies. The printing process was difficult, because yellow is a 'notoriously bad colour to print as it shows up any impurities in the process very clearly. And, although the sleeve gives the impression of being simple, it uses a series of complex overlays. Fluorescent colours are hard to print as well, which doubled the difficulty'.[14] Reid also says: 'It was a feature of the finished sleeve that it deteriorated very quickly: if left out in the sunlight, the yellow and the pink faded, just leaving the black of the overlays.'

Evanescence and the mystique of fleeting intensity was arguably a core modernist theme, and Lewis had affirmed it already in a comment of his in the essay 'Futurism, Magic and Life',[5] where he notes how the most perishable colours in painting (such as Veronese green, Prussian Blue, Alizarin Crimson) are the most brilliant. So that which burns brightest burns most briefly, and in true modernist fashion brilliance must be but fleeting, timely, not eternal, a coincidence of moment, viewer and object. Lewis proclaims of this: 'This is as it should be: we should hate other ages, and don't want to fetch £40,000 like a horse'—asserting the desire not to be commodified and not to become a part of the archive.

For Reid and the Sex Pistols, the painstaking work on the cover paid off, for the sleeve caused a fuss when it came out. Mainly because it appeared to be the opposite of what it was —shoddy, cheap and nasty—and also because it had an anonymity as its theme: not only the cut out newspaper lettering (so reminiscent of BLAST), but also the lack of 'stars' on the cover. No phosphorescent stars sending back their celebrity light to illuminate the gloom of adolescent fantasy as The Clash, getting it so wrong, would do on their first LP. The Sex Pistols, of course, did enstage themselves, not on the covers but elsewhere. However this self-display refused interiority, turning their selves into mannequins, for Westwood's clothes, McLaren's game.

The Day-Glo coloured vinyl Punk record is not a black hole or empty meaning, but a circular assertion of anti-nature, of synthetic actuality. The record, which had been forgotten as item, as disc, is brought back into visibility, by the coloured vinyl—of course in combination with the miniature artwork of the picture cover. This should not be confused with later attempts to stimulate collectability and sales with picture discs or limited editions. The coloured disc hoped to detonate a mini-shock as it was slipped from the cover. The record stopped being natural, a hippy dream where the listener gazes at beautiful band members photographed against shrubs and trees, the hippy dream of an unsullied life. Punk devastated the romantic idyll. It made pop music historical and artificial once more. With Punk the single came back into its own—famously ousting the concept album's languor. It was an assertion of vinyl importance, before or beyond the concept. It understood itself as the short sharp shock, just as Wyndham Lewis before it had understood the end of painterly duration in BLAST:

> The surfaces of cheap manufactured goods, woods, shell, glass etc already appreciated for themselves and their possibilities realised, have finished the days of fine paint.[16]

Punk's equivalent was vinyl, Day-Glo and cardboard. The point was not to represent such materials, but to make consumers look at what they held in their hands. Punk was a populist modernism which reached a mass audience: punks could only look on with amused contempt as the academic epigones, who had never been to the gigs and never dyed their hair pink, took on the philosophy of postmodernism and took over the academy, declaring that 'high modernism' was an enemy of the people, and that consumer culture provided audiences with everything they need. Giants had been replaced with dwarves, and the champagne left an aftertaste that was repulsive.

A properly materialist account of culture must recognise how social hierarchy humiliates the ego and damages the psyche. Ignorant of this hurt, culture is set up as something external to the self, an oppressive set of maxims and rules. The 'victims' of culture, in turn, turn on it, angry and frustrated by culture's cheery ambivalence. Culture philistines and avant-gardists alike trash cultural aspirations. Hans Richter, both a participant and annalist of Dada, named its dialectic 'art and anti-art'. Rather than targeting a subordinate race or nation as the object of destruction, Dada targeted the educated person's own culture and refinement, deriding the pretensions of culture and allowing the recovery of a universal humanity, the laughing body.

It is our contention that a new revolutionary Marxism, uncontaminated by the compromises of Stalin's idea of 'socialism in one country', needs to recover this levelling, non-affirmative aspect of Dada. Its coruscating influence can be witnessed elsewhere—for example, in the vicious satire of Vorticism's BLAST, in the ludicrous nihilism of kids' comics, and in the seizure of the vulgar colour-stuff of Day-Glo by Punk. When, at the height of the Punk furore, the manager of the Sex Pistols, Malcolm McLaren, was accused of provoking violence and destruction at Punk gigs, he replied 'you've got to be able to destroy to create'. And it is not for nothing that the Beano, the most widely read children's comic of the 1970s, expresses a continual animosity to civilisation in favour of jokes, chaos and transformation. If such cultural moments remain unappreciated, the doldrums and hypocrises of 'improving' culture beckon.

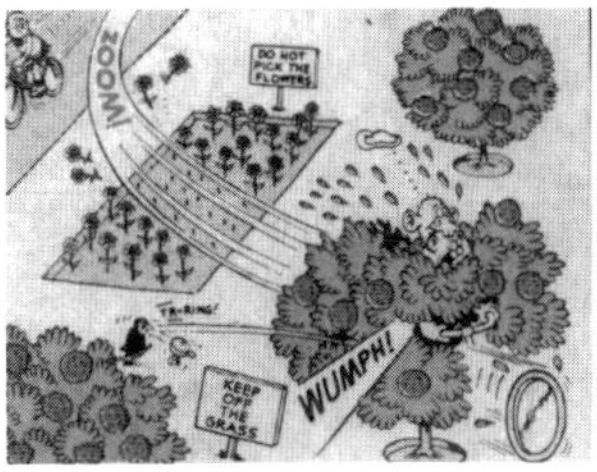

If truth is 'objective, not plausible', as Adorno put it,[17] then the most astonishing thing for the active imagination is not the special leisure garden of the soul set aside by an administered society, but the moment when actuality—human needs, rude reality—breaks in and jolts conceptual systems. The philistine gatecrashing the culture-party and stamping on the precious flowers of cultural existence could well be the harbinger of a revived vitality, a new social order. That which is external to culture, that which is valueless—the contingent, the coincidence, the non-cultural—is crucial for its existence.

Aspects of this article (on Vorticism and Day-Glo) find another form in: Esther Leslie, Synthetic Worlds: Nature, Art and the Chemical Industry, Reaktion, London, 2005.

NOTES

1. Karl Marx/Friedrich Engels, translated by Alick West, Collected Works, Vol. 1, Lawrence & Wishart, London, 1975, chapter 37, p. 628.
2. ibid., p. 632.
3. Letter to Partisan Review, from Lewis, 1949, quoted in Richard Cork, Vorticism, I, p260.
4. Wyndham Lewis, Rude Assignment: An Intellectual Autobiography, 1950, republished by Black Sparrow Press, Santa Barbara, 1984 p. 135
5. Richard Cork, Vorticism And Abstract Art In The First Machine Age, vol. 1, 'Origins and Developments', Gordon Fraser, London, 1976 p. 235.
6. Wyndham Lewis, Blasting And Bombardiering, 1937, republished by Calder and Boyars Ltd., London, 1967, p. 37.
7. As reported in an advertising blurb in BLAST 2: War number, John Lane, London, 1915.
8. See Paul O'Keefe, Some Sort Of Genius: A Life Of Wyndham Lewis, Jonathan Cape, London, 2000 p. 157.
9. Richard Cork, Vorticism And Abstract Art In The First Machine Age, vol. 1, 'Origins and Developments', Gordon Fraser, London, 1976 p. 263.
10. BLAST: Review Of The Great English Vortex, John Lane, London, 1914, p. 30.
11. ibid., p. 33.
12. ibid., p. 49.
13. G.W.F. Hegel, Logic, 1817/1827, translated by William Wallace, republished by Oxford University Press, Oxford, 1975, p. 202.
14. Jamie Reid, The Incomplete Works Of Jamie Reid, Faber & Faber, London, 1987, p. 79.
15. BLAST: Review Of The Great English Vortex, John Lane, London, 1914, p. 134.
16. ibid., p. 142.
17. T.W. Adorno, Negative Dialectics, Routledge & Kegan Paul, London 1973, p. 41.

DOT DOT DOT 11
Winter 2005/6
ISBN 90-77620-05-2

Published twice a year
by Dot dot dot
Zwaardstraat 16
2584 TX The Hague
The Netherlands

www.dot-dot-dot.nl
<editor@dot-dot-dot.nl>

EDITORS
Stuart Bailey
<molecule@dds.nl>
New York
and
Peter Bilak
<peterb@peterb.sk>
The Hague

THANKS
Tom Benson
Anniek Brattinga
Mariana Castillo Deball
Galerie Gisela Capitain
Rob Giampietro
Liam Gillick
Sven Herzog
Will Holder
Ryan Holmberg
Idea magazine
Robin Kinross
David Lillington
Louis Lüthi
Philomene Pirecki
David Reinfurt
Domeniek Ruyters
Ian Whittlesea

DDDB: Peu Importe Les Conneries (par Jamie Reid) was designed and edited together with Sven Herzog and originally published as part of Dutch Resource, a project and book by the Werkplaats Typografie, Arnhem. Reproduced with many thanks to all involved.

All other pieces designed by editors/authors.

CONTRIBUTORS

Gerry Beegan
New York

Michael Bracewell
Heysham

Simon Critchley
New York

Emmanuelle Dauplay
Toronto

Chris Evans
Berlin

Ryan Gander
London

Robert Garnett
Brussels

Liam Gillick
New York

Katrine Herian
London

Maxine Kopsa
Amsterdam

Esther Leslie
London

Mark Owens
New York

Radim Pesko
Amsterdam

Steve Rushton
Berlin

Frances Stark
Los Angeles

Anu Vahtra
Tallinn

Ben Watson
London

Jon Wilde
Brighton

SUBSCRIPTIONS

1 year (2 issues):
€29 in Europe
€44 everywhere else
Worldwide exchange rates subject to change.

Contact:
Bruil & Van de Staaij
Postbus 75
7940 AB Meppel
The Netherlands
T: +31 522 261 303
F: +31 522 257 827
info@bruil.info
www.bruil.info

Distribution Europe:
Coen Sligting Bookimport
Van Oldenbarneveldtstraat 77
1052 JW Amsterdam
T: +31 20 673 2280
F: +31 20 664 0047
sligting@xs4all.nl

Distribution UK:
Central Books
99 Wallis Road
London E9 5LN
T: +44 (0)845 458 9911
F: +44 (0)845 458 9912
orders@centralbooks.com
www.centralbooks.com

Distribution Americas, Asia, Africa, Australia:
Princeton Architectural Press
37 E 7th Street
New York, NY 10003
T: +1 212 995 9620
F: +1 212 995 9454
sales@papress.com
www.papress.com

Advertising:
<peterb@peterb.sk>
DDD11 adverts paid per greyscale %

Printing:
Lecturis, NL

Diminutive quotes on p. 2 and p. 96 are drawn from the lyrics of Mark E. Smith.

FRONT COVER

FÉMININ IMAGE PUBLIC OR BIOGRAPHY LIMITED
The cover girl is Sue Lyon who played the title role in Kubrick's adaptation of Nabokov's Lolita. Someone has punched holes in the transparency, leaving three dots to censor the excessiveness of an inappropriately erotic mouth.

BIOGRAPHY FÉMININ OR PUBLICITY LIMITED
Someone with an interest in Lolita stole this image of the actress who played her from a celebrity photo agency, thinking herself justi fied on account of its having been rendered useless by the hole punch which was clearly employed with the intention of saving her future embarrassment. Besides it wouldn't be of use to any of the stupid magazines like People and Hello that the agency was in the business of selling images to.

FÉMININ BIOGRAPHY OR BIO NOT YET GRAPHED
A woman writer, not to say a feminine one, promised Dot Dot Dot a text that would fit snugly under this heading. She didn't commit sufficiently to writing the piece, incidentally giving higher, if undeserved, priority to texts promised to periodicals of larger circulation. She did, though—in lieu of the essay intended to argue for a renewed interest in biographical aspects of strong women—supply Stuart Bailey with the image used on the cover because she thought it was 'perfect for him'.

(Frances Stark)

The same again, sir? How can you have the same again?

The problem is : to get back to zero
– Jean-Luc Godard

Stuart Bailey: “The second in a proposed series of site-specific exhibitions, DDDB is an hour-long walk through a collection of objects in a garage somewhere in the French town of Chaumont on the longest day of 2005.

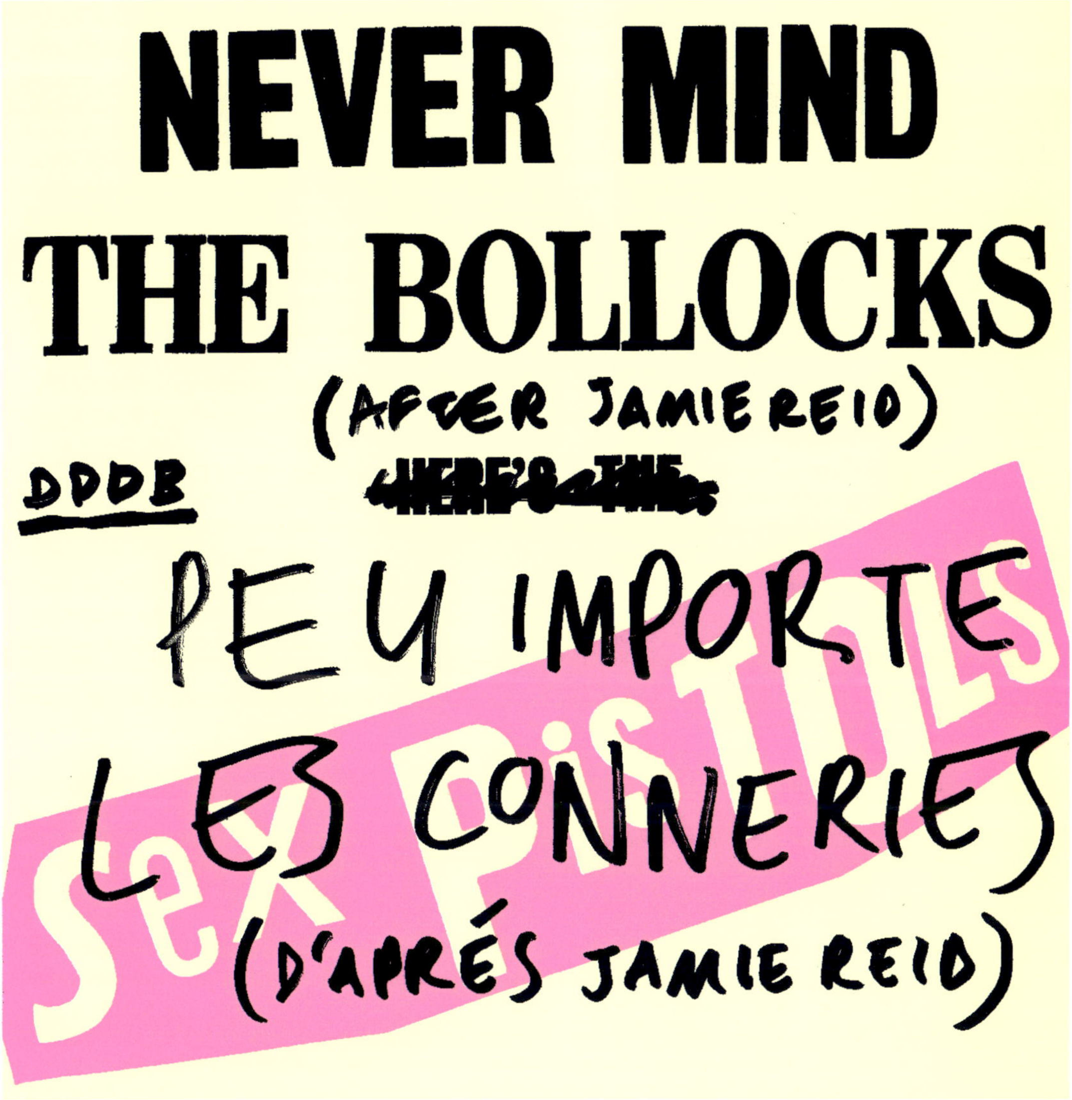

Le problème est : revenir à zéro
– Jean-Luc Godard

Stuart Bailey: “DDDB est la deuxième dans la série d'expositions proposées par nos soins sur un emplacement spécifique. DDDB est une promenade d'une durée d'une heure à travers une collection d'objets dans un garage de la ville française de Chaumont et cela le jour le plus long de 2005.

1
The Sex Pistols, NEVER MIND THE BOLLOCKS HERE'S THE SEX PISTOLS, cover by Jamie Reid, 1977

"A couple of years ago I was invited to give a talk at some event in Barcelona, replacing Jamie Reid, who had pulled out at the last minute. I decided to use the opportunity to present a collection of friends' work I admired. Upon realising this didn't amount to very much, the idea stretched to encompass a general collection of work from the past century by a gang of both dead and living spirits who made work with some common link; a bond – like an umbilical cord – stretching through the twentieth century from some anonymous modernist mother. I might reluctantly describe this work as being cerebral, rigorous and worthy, if those words weren't so cerebral, rigorous and worthy-sounding. So instead maybe: charged, luminous and illuminating, like a series of momentary cartoon light bulbs flashing on and off above my head.

"I always find talking about my own work is a problematic and deflating experience. This is partly just the awkward feeling of being on some election rally, magnifying something quite ordinary and everyday out of all comfortable proportion, and partly because I always seem to end up describing the mistakes and failures in the work – what went wrong, why, and how it should and could have been. When talking about other people's work, on the other hand, it's a relief to skip over these incessant disclaimers to just focus on the good parts – the pub anecdotes rather than the dull mess of business meetings. At its most fundamental level, then, this talk is just a collection of work I'd like to have made myself. It represents what I'm trying to do better than anything I've managed to do. They are *ideas*, ways of looking at things, and as such, maybe even charged with philosophic potential. This collection doesn't necessarily conform to what would conventionally be considered graphic design – there's as much music, film, art and literature here – but the common denominator is always language, and how language is designed.

"So I started by deciding to name the talk *Never Mind the Bollocks*, in direct homage to Jamie Reid, and to use the Pistols' cover as a title page. I never even intended to say anything about the way the cover looked, but it gradually dawned on me that it single-

1
The Sex Pistols, NEVER MIND THE BOLLOCKS HERE'S THE SEX PISTOLS, coverture par Jamie Reid, 1977

"Il y a quelques années, j'ai été invité pour faire une présentation à un événement à Barcelone pour remplacer Jamie Reid, qui s'était désisté au dernier moment. J'ai décidé de profiter de cette opportunité pour présenter une collection de travaux d'amis que j'admirais. Me rendant compte que ça donnait pas grande chose, l'idée s'est étendue pour englober une collection générale d'œuvres d'esprits vivants aussi bien que morts du dernier siècle et dont les œuvres étaient liées d'une manière ou d'une autre; un lien – comme un cordon ombilical – qui s'étend à travers le vingtième siècle depuis une mère moderniste anonyme. Je pourrais éventuellement décrire ce travail comme étant cérébral, rigoureux, méritant, si ces mots n'étaient pas aussi cérébraux, rigoureux ou comme méritants. Alors peut-être, chargé, lumineux, illuminant, comme une série d'ampoules de dessin animés qui clignotent au dessus de ma tête.

"Je le trouve toujours problématique et décourageant de parler de mon propre travail. C'est en partie juste ce sentiment maladroit comme si on était en campagne électorale, qui grossit quelque chose d'assez ordinaire et quotidien dans une proportion qui n'est plus confortable, et en partie parce que je finis toujours par parler des erreurs et des échecs dans le travail – ce qui n'a pas marché, pourquoi, comment ça aurait dû ou pu être. Par contre, quand je parle du travail des autres, c'est un soulagement de sauter ces démentis incessants et ne parler que des parties réussies, des histoires de comptoir; la surface plutôt que le fouillis ennuyeux des réunions de travail d'en dessous. Sur son plan le plus fondamental alors, la présentation est juste une collection d'œuvres que j'aurais aimé faire moi même. Elle représente ce que j'essaie de faire mieux que tout ce j'ai réussi à faire. Ce sont des *idees*, des manières de regarder, et en tant que telle peut-être même chargées de potentiel philosophique. Cette collection ne se conforme pas forcément à ce qui serait normalement considéré comme design graphique – il y a beaucoup de musique, des films, de l'art et de la littérature – mais le dénominateur commun est toujours la langue et comment la langue est conçue.

"J'ai donc commencé et j'ai appelé la présentation *Never Mind the Bollocks*, en handedly embodied a lot of what I was trying to say elsewhere. Not unlike Jamie Reid's second-hand Situationism, I was hijacking an iconic style for my own purposes; a Russian doll of tribute. In a recent conversation the writer Michael Bracewell described to me how he increasingly found himself observing the world from the vantage point of 1977. He didn't mean this in a sentimental or retrospective way, more that this was a personal lens through which other aspects of culture could be viewed, like a homemade pinhole camera, or a magnifying glass to channel the sun and burn a few ants. He meant looking from the past forwards as well as the future backwards: he meant 1977 as an ongoing present tense.

"On the occasion of presenting this second DDD exhibition in Chaumont, I'm offering a direct literal translation of the title into French. Unlike many nationalities, the French stubbornly insist on translating the titles of foreign films, often resulting in the ridiculous or misleading (though not without charm; I prefer it to the arrogance of Dutch voice-overs or German overdubbing). It reminded me how graphic design is always translation – in its broadest sense, from a cerebral idea into a physical object – and something is always lost in that translation. The work here seems to me to come about as close as possible to forging a direct link between the intial idea and its eventual communication. Anthony Froshaug wrote: 'design consists [...] in translating all the problem, set of problems, into another language, another sign system, with love.' The majority of what passes as graphic design doesn't really stick to any reasonable notion of form following function. On the contrary, I would say form generally *fucks* function. And to proceed with such a dubious line of thought, I'll turn it around again and say that, contrary to this, the examples here show form and content having great sex, mutual and inseperable, or at least French kissing.

"No matter how much I try to keep it at bay, all this comes out of failure anyway: Jamie Reid pulled out, and in the end I pulled out too. But here, two years on, the idea has settled and enough work has gathered in the corners of my mind to be able to make a reasonable attempt. As I began to stick it together I came across a piece of writing which described an attractive paradox in

hommage directe à Jamie Reid, et j'ai utilisé la couverture des Pistols comme première page. Je n'avais jamais l'intention de dire quoi que ce soit sur la couverture mais il m'est apparu soudain qu'elle incarnait beaucoup de ce j'essayais de dire par ailleurs. Un peu comme Jamie Reid et le situationisme, je prenais un style iconique en otage à mes propres fins; c'était comme une poupée russe d'hommage. Dans une conversation avec l'écrivain Michael Bracewell l'année dernière il racontait comment il se retrouvait de plus en plus en train d'observer le monde depuis la position avantageuse de 1977. Ce n'était pas dans un sens sentimental ou rétrospectif, mais plutôt comme un objectif pour lui à travers lequel on pouvait voir d'autres aspects de la culture, comme un sténopé fait-maison ou une loupe à travers laquelle on canalise les rayons du soleil pour brûler quelques fourmis. Il voulait dire regarder depuis le passé en avant et depuis l'avenir en arrière. Il voulait dire 1977 comme un présent continu.

"A l'occasion de la présentation de cette deuxième exposition DDD à Chaumont, je propose une traduction directe, littérale du titre vers le français. Contrairement à d'autres nationalités, les français insistent sur la traduction des titres de films étrangers, ce qui donne souvent des titres ridicules, trompeurs (mais non dénués de charme; je le préfère à l'arrogance des voice-overs hollandais ou au doublage allemand). Cela me rappelle comment le design est toujours une traduction – dans son sens le plus large, d'une idée cérébrale en un objet physique – et quelque chose se perd toujours dans une traduction. Le travail ici me semble s'approcher le plus possible à la création d'un lien direct entre l'idée initiale et sa communication par la suite. Anthony Froshaug a écrit: 'le graphisme consiste à [...] traduire tout le problème, une série de problèmes en une autre langue, un autre système de signes, avec amour.' La plupart de ce qui se passe dans le graphisme ne colle pas vraiment à une notion raisonnable de forme selon la fonction. Au contraire, je dirais que la forme généralement *encule* la fonction. Et pour continuer avec cette métaphore douteuse, je la retournerai et dirai qu'au contraire, ces exemples montrent la forme et le contenu en train de faire l'amour, ensemble et inséparable, ou au moins en train de s'embrasser.

"Peu importe comment j'essaie de le contenir, tout ceci provient d'un échec quand the *Bollocks* cover. While Reid's signature amphetamine typography gobs an easy cartoon degeneracy, the sleeve was actually quite difficult to make. Fluorescent pink and yellow are difficult colours for a printer to hold flat and consistent over a large print run, so the apparent cheap simplicity of Reid's design betrays an expensive luxury. As someone else somewhere else at some other point in time wrote: *The simple things you see are all complicated*, and there's another key to unlock the work here: they are all products of care, commitment and attention to detail, with second and third-hand stories and anecdotes behind each surface which not only complement but *complete* the design. And before getting around to actually beginning, I'll quickly just emphasize the obvious fact that these are merely poor illustrations of real-life objects, which should be sought, found and held. Their function here is merely to sit on the page and vibrate.

2
Daniel Spoerri, with Robert Filliou, Dieter Roth, Emmett Williams & Roland Topor, AN ANECDOTED TOPOGRAPHY OF CHANCE, Something Else Press, New York, 1966, (originally published as TOPOGRAPHIE ANECDOTÉE DU HASARD, Paris, Editions Galerie Lawrence, 1961)

"The structure of this talk is well described by this first piece of work.The French artist Daniel Spoerri began his *Topography of Chance* by mapping the breakfast table of his Paris apartment one morning. He laid a sheet over it, traced all the objects and made a brief description of each one, then added further notes, subjectively supplementing the original objective facts. He asked Roland Topor to draw each item from memory, another friend, Robert Fillou, to annotate the first set of annotations, and when it

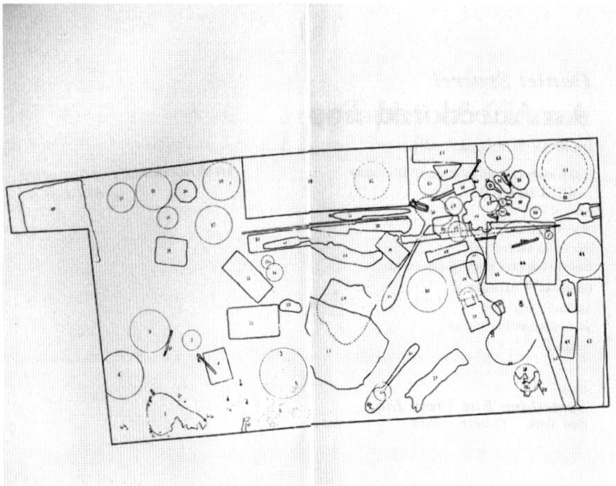

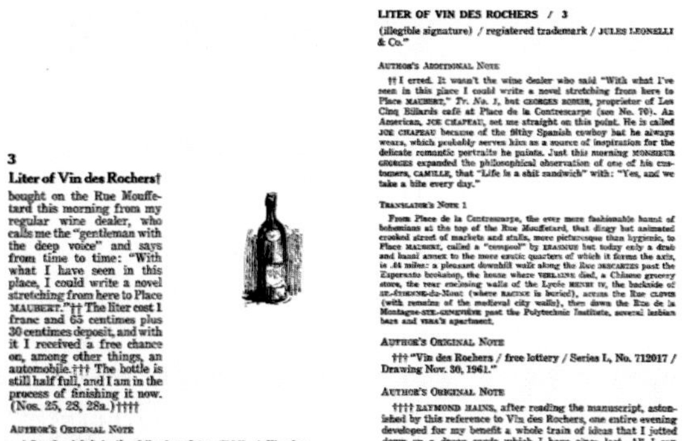

3
Liter of Vin des Rochers†
bought on the Rue Mouffetard this morning from my regular wine dealer, who calls me the "gentleman with the deep voice" and says from time to time: "With what I have seen in this place, I could write a novel stretching from here to Place MAUBERT."†† The liter cost 1 franc and 65 centimes plus 30 centimes deposit, and with it I received a free chance on, among other things, an automobile.††† The bottle is still half full, and I am in the process of finishing it now. (Nos. 25, 28, 28a.)††††

AUTHOR'S ORIGINAL NOTE

† On the label is the following data: "11% / Vin des Rochers / Lines your stomach with velvet / I guarantee this wine is made from wholesome and dependably pure juice /

—8—

LITER OF VIN DES ROCHERS / 3

(illegible signature) / registered trademark / JULES LEONELLI & Co."

AUTHOR'S ADDITIONAL NOTE

†† I erred. It wasn't the wine dealer who said "With what I've seen in this place I could write a novel stretching from here to Place MAUBERT," *Tr. No. 1*, but GEORGES ROMER, proprietor of Les Cinq Billards café at Place de la Contrescarpe (see No. 70). An American, JOE CHAPEAU, set me straight on this point. He is called JOE CHAPEAU because of the filthy Spanish cowboy hat he always wears, which probably serves him as a source of inspiration for the delicate romantic portraits he paints. Just this morning MONSIEUR GEORGES expanded the philosophical observation of one of his customers, CAMILLE, that "Life is a shit sandwich" with: "Yes, and we take a bite every day."

TRANSLATOR'S NOTE 1

From Place de la Contrescarpe, the ever more fashionable haunt of bohemians at the top of the Rue Mouffetard, that dingy but animated crooked street of markets and stalls, more picturesque than hygienic, to Place MAUBERT, called a "cesspool" by ERASMUS but today only a drab and banal annex to the more exotic quarters of which it forms the axis, is .44 miles: a pleasant downhill walk along the Rue DESCARTES past the Esperanto bookshop, the house where VERLAINE died, a Chinese grocery store, the rear enclosing walls of the Lycée HENRI IV, the backside of ST.-ÉTIENNE-du-Mont (where RACINE is buried), across the Rue CLOVIS (with remains of the medieval city walls), then down the Rue de la Montagne-STE.-GENEVIÈVE past the Polytechnic Institute, several lesbian bars and VERA'S apartment.

AUTHOR'S ORIGINAL NOTE

††† "Vin des Rochers / free lottery / Series L, No. 712017 / Drawing Nov. 30, 1961."

AUTHOR'S ORIGINAL NOTE

†††† RAYMOND HAINS, after reading the manuscript, astonished by this reference to Vin des Rochers, one entire evening developed for my benefit a whole train of ideas that I jotted down on a dozen cards which I have since lost. All I can remember is that he started out with an analysis of an essay by ETIEMBLE, "PAUL CLAUDEL et le Vin des Rochers," to which

—9—

2

même. Jamie Reid s'est désisté, et enfin, je me suis désisté aussi. Mais ici, deux ans plus tard, l'idée a fait son chemin et suffisamment de travail s'est déposé dans les recoins de ma tête pour que je puisse faire un essai. Quand j'ai commencé à recoller le tout, je suis tombé sur un écrit qui décrivait un paradoxe attrayant sur la couverture Bollocks. Alors que la typographie amphétaminé signée Reid crache une dégénérescence de bande dessinée, la jaquette était en fait assez difficile à réaliser. Du rose et du jaune fluo sont des couleurs qu'un imprimeur a du mal à imprimer de façon régulière pour un grand tirage, donc l'apparente simplicité du dessin de Reid trahit un luxe très cher. Comme quelqu'un d'autre a dit ailleurs à un autre moment: *Les choses simples que vous voyez sont compliques*, et voilà une autre clé pour déchiffrer le travail ici: ce sont tous des produits issus de soin, engagement et d'attention aux détails, avec des histoires et des anecdotes de plein de gens derrière chaque surface, qui ne font pas que complémenter mais *completent* la création. Et avant de commencer à parler du début, je voudrais juste souligner le fait évident que ce ne sont que des illustrations pauvres d'objets de la vraie vie qui devraient être cherchés, trouvés et gardés. Leur fonction ici n'est que d'être posé sur la page et vibrer.

2
Daniel Spoerri, avec Robert Filliou, Diether Roth, Emmett Williams et Roland Topor, AN ANECDOTED TOPOGRAPHY OF CHANCE, Something Else Press, New York, 1966 (publication originale sous le titre TOPOGRAPHIE ANECDOTÉE DU HASARD, Paris, Editions Galerie Lawrence, 1961)

"La structure de la présentation est bien expliquée par la première œuvre de l'artiste français Daniel Spoerri. Ce sont des pages de *Topographie Anecdotée du Hasard*, was later translated from French to English, Spoerri also invited the translator, Emmett Williams, to add further notes. So the book traces this series of ever-branching anecdotes, and its graphic translation clearly mirrors this, from the double column of the original description and accompanying image, down through the ever-decreasing sizes of footnotes. From this visual analogue the reader grasps the process immediately. The project represents how the apparent banality of an everyday table contains an infinite potential of stories and interpretations. It recalls a scene in Godard's *Deux ou trois choses que je sais d'elle* [*Two or three things I know about her*] where the camera hones in on a just-stirred cup of coffee as a deadpan voiceover intones philosophy and the universe, and the silently spinning bubbles in the centre of the cup seem suddenly choreographed as atoms and planets.

3

Raymond Queneau, EXERCISES IN STYLE, Gaberbocchus Press, London, 1958 (originally published as EXERCISES DE STYLE, Éditions Gallimard, Paris, 1947)

"Another angle on this talk is to consider it a series of exercises in style, after the title of the next example, in which French author Raymond Queneau conceives a throwaway incident based on an altercation between two men on a Paris bus, then rewrites it in 99 different rhetorical styles, from 'Exclamations' to 'Spectral', 'Dog Latin' to 'Haiku'. It emphasizes the compact efficacy of language, and the same is true of graphic language: like Spoerri's *Topography of Chance*, the design of each new edition of this book significantly adds or detracts from its content, being more or less in tune with the intentions of its author, and so more or less inspired, appropriate, interesting and communicative. This one was designed by Stefan Themerson, a Polish writer-designer-philosopher who lived and worked most of his life in London. The brilliance of his graphic interpretation begins on the cover, a photograph of the author cut up and rearranged according to a simple mathematical pattern – a direct graphic translation of one of Queneau's 99 categories,

la manifestation d'un projet qu'il a commencé en dressant la carte de sa table de petit déjeuner un matin dans son appartement parisien. Il l'a recouverte d'une feuille, a tracé tous les objets, fait une brève description de chaque objet, a demandé à Roland Topor de la dessiner de tête, et a pris encore des notes, pour compléter de façon subjective les faits objectifs d'origine. Ensuite, il a demandé à un autre ami, Robert Fillou de faire la même chose, en annotant ses annotations, et plus tard, une fois que c'était traduit du français en anglais, il a invité le traducteur, Emmett Williams d'y ajouter ses notes aussi. L'œuvre devient finalement une série d'anecdotes avec des arborescences continues, et sa traduction graphique le reflète clairement, depuis la double colonne de la description initiale et l'image qui l'accompagne jusqu'à des notes de pied de page qui deviennent de plus en plus petites. Le lecteur comprend le processus immédiatement avec cette analogie visuelle. Le projet représente la façon dont la banalité apparente d'une table ordinaire contient un potentiel infini d'histoires et d'interprétations. Il rappelle une scène dans *Deux ou trois choses que je sais d'elle* de Jean-Luc Godard, où la caméra s'approche d'une tasse de café en train d'être remuée pendant que la voix-off parle de philosophie et du monde. Le tournoiement, les bulles au centre de la tasse deviennent des planètes et des atomes, simultanément.

3

Raymond Queneau, EXERCISES IN STYLE, Gaberbocchus Press, Londres, 1958 (publication original sous le titre de EXERCICES DE STYLE, Éditions Gallimard, Paris, 1947)

"Un autre aspect de cette présentation est de le considérer comme un exercice de style, d'après le titre du prochain exemple ou l'auteur français Raymond Queneau imagine un fait divers d'une altercation entre deux hommes dans un bus à Paris, et ensuite le réécrit dans 99 styles rhétoriques différents, de 'Exclamations' à 'Spectra', 'Latin de cuisine' à 'Haiku'. Cela souligne l'efficacité de la langue en modifiant la signification ou l'effet, et bien sûr la même chose est vraie pour la langue graphique. Comme *Topographie Anecdotée du Hasard*, le design de chaque nouvelle édition de ce livre ajoute sensiblement à ou détracte de son contenu, étant plus en moins en phase avec les intentions de son auteur, et donc plus ou moins inspiré, approprié, intéressant ou communicatif. Celui-ci a été conçu par Stefan Themerson, un auteur-graphiste-philosophe polonais qui a vécu et travaillé une bonne

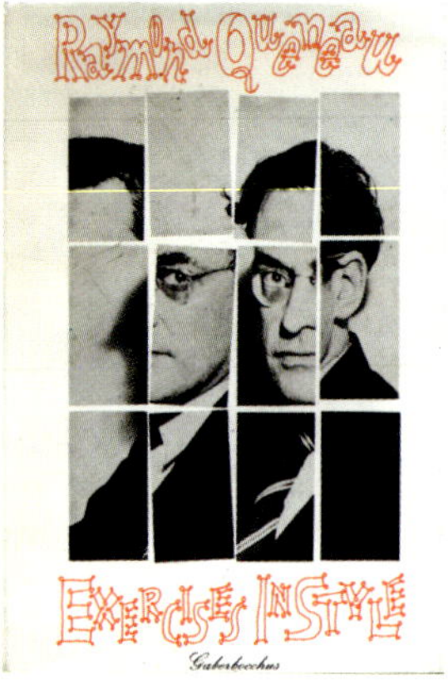

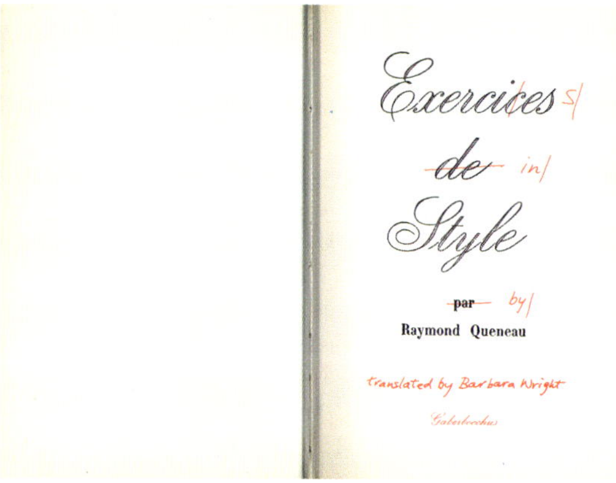
Exercices ~~de~~ in/ Style
~~par~~ by/
Raymond Queneau
translated by Barbara Wright
Gaberbocchus

'Permutations'. Passing over the reflexive title page and the contents list of Queneau's attempted styles, the spread of 'Surprises' and 'Dream', with Themerson's absurd initials, demonstrates the rest of the book's flippant virtuosity. In her introduction, Queneau's translator Barbara Wright describes her initial surprise on learning how keen Queneau was on having what seemed to be a particularly untranslatable French text translated, until realising 'in the same way that the story *as such* doesn't matter, the particular language it is written in doesn't matter *as such* [...]' She goes on to suggest that 'Queneau's attitude of enquiry and examination can, and perhaps should? – be applied to every language.' A graphic language translation of Queneau's exclamation marks in the 'Surprises' text, then, might be Reid's fluorescent yellow and pink, or the treatment of the title on the cover of the next example.

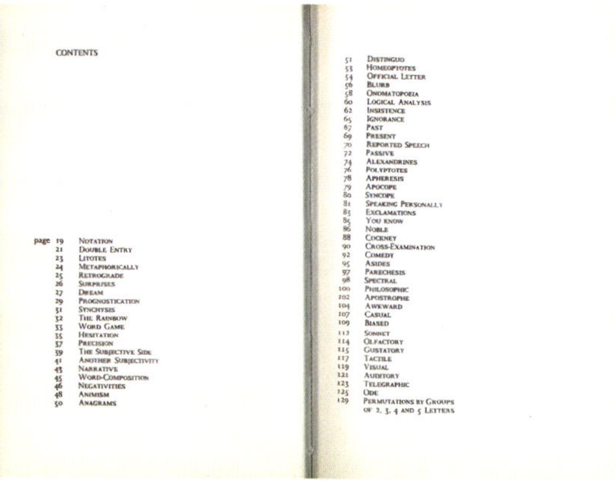
CONTENTS

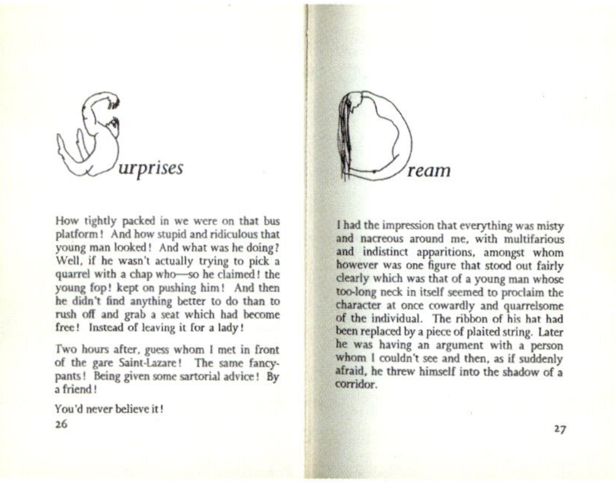
Surprises

How tightly packed in we were on that bus platform! And how stupid and ridiculous that young man looked! And what was he doing? Well, if he wasn't actually trying to pick a quarrel with a chap who—so he claimed! the young fop! kept on pushing him! And then he didn't find anything better to do than to rush off and grab a seat which had become free! Instead of leaving it for a lady!

Two hours after, guess whom I met in front of the gare Saint-Lazare! The same fancy-pants! Being given some sartorial advice! By a friend!

You'd never believe it!

26

Dream

I had the impression that everything was misty and nacreous around me, with multifarious and indistinct apparitions, amongst whom however was one figure that stood out fairly clearly which was that of a young man whose too-long neck in itself seemed to proclaim the character at once cowardly and quarrelsome of the individual. The ribbon of his hat had been replaced by a piece of plaited string. Later he was having an argument with a person whom I couldn't see and then, as if suddenly afraid, he threw himself into the shadow of a corridor.

27

partie de sa vie à Londres. La brillance de son interprétation graphique commence à la couverture, une photo de l'auteur découpée et redisposée selon un schéma mathématique simple expliqué à l'intérieur, sa propre traduction d'une des 99 méthodes de Queneau, 'Permutations'. En passant par la première page réfléchie et la table des matières des styles tentés par Queneau, la mise en page de 'Surprises' et 'Rêve', avec les initiales absurdes de Themerson, montre l'équilibre impeccable entre la désinvolture et la précision dans le reste du livre. Dans son introduction, la traductrice de Queneau, Barbara Wright, était surprise d'apprendre à quel point Queneau voulait que ce texte tellement français soit traduit jusqu'à ce qu'elle se rende compte: 'de la même façon que l'histoire *en tant que telle* n'avait aucune importance, la langue dans laquelle elle est écrite n'a pas d'importance *en tant que telle* [...]'. Elle continue et suggère: 'L'attitude d'interrogation et d'examination de Queneau peut et peut-être doit? – s'appliquer à toutes les langues.' Une traduction graphique des points d'exclamation de Queneau dans les texte 'Surprises' pourrait être le jaune et rose fluo de Reid ou alors le traitement du titre sur la couverture du prochain exemple.

4
Wyndham Lewis, BLAST, London, 1914

"This is the first of two issues of a journal edited and mainly written by the English artist-writer-agitator Wyndham Lewis which appeared just before the First World War. The original publication had the awkward stature of a telephone book, designed to expose itself on the coffee tables of the pre-war London intelligentsia. Like Lewis's public persona, its bright pink exclamation was a conscious pose, impossible to ignore, forcing opinion and reaction. Lewis was gleefully scratching the same public unease as the Sex Pistols would sixty years later, even sardonically dubbing himself *The Enemy* (anticipating John Lydon's *I is the enemy / I is anarchy...*), and it hardly seems coincidental that both these debuts of public agitiation share the same graphic strategy: delinquent brother and sister *BLAST* and *Bollocks* dressed up in violent pink, spitting an economy of language in tall grotesque black block capitals. These examples burn on so vividly today because their site-specific production remains so firmly embedded in their respective forms, whether via Reid's hand-me-down pop-Situationism, or Lewis's chance encounter with an alchoholic

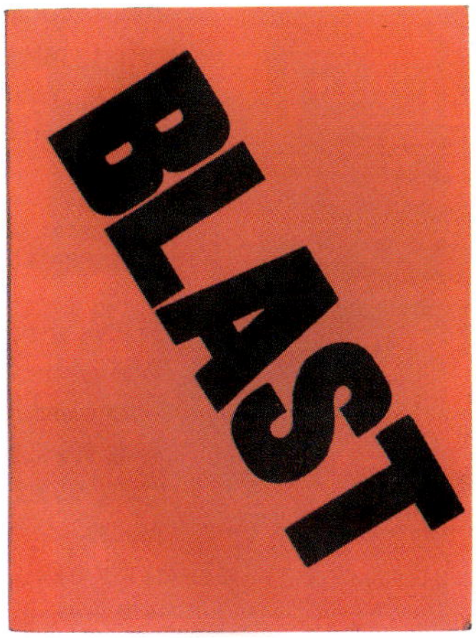

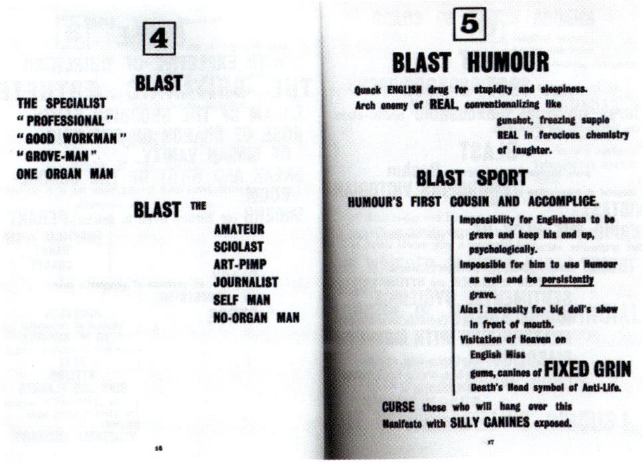
4

BLAST
THE SPECIALIST
"PROFESSIONAL"
"GOOD WORKMAN"
"GROVE-MAN"
ONE ORGAN MAN

BLAST THE
AMATEUR
SCIOLAST
ART-PIMP
JOURNALIST
SELF MAN
NO-ORGAN MAN

5

BLAST HUMOUR
Quack ENGLISH drug for stupidity and sleepiness.
Arch enemy of REAL, conventionalizing like gunshot, freezing supple REAL in ferocious chemistry of laughter.

BLAST SPORT
HUMOUR'S FIRST COUSIN AND ACCOMPLICE.
Impossibility for Englishman to be grave and keep his end up, psychologically.
Impossible for him to use Humour as well and be persistently grave.
Alas! necessity for big doll's show in front of mouth.
Visitation of Heaven on English Miss gums, canines of FIXED GRIN
Death's Head symbol of Anti-Life.
CURSE those who will hang over this Manifesto with SILLY CANINES exposed.

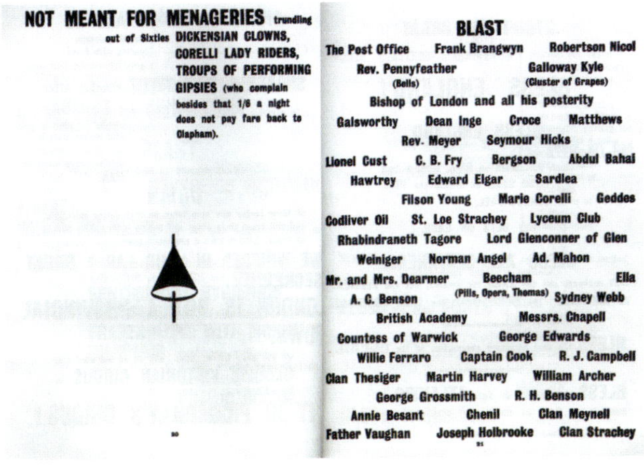
NOT MEANT FOR MENAGERIES trundling out of Sixties DICKENSIAN CLOWNS, CORELLI LADY RIDERS, TROUPS OF PERFORMING GIPSIES (who complain besides that 1/6 a night does not pay fare back to Clapham).

BLAST
The Post Office — Frank Brangwyn — Robertson Nicol
Rev. Pennyfeather (Bells) — Galloway Kyle (Cluster of Grapes)
Bishop of London and all his posterity
Galsworthy — Dean Inge — Croce — Matthews
Rev. Meyer — Seymour Hicks
Lionel Cust — C. B. Fry — Bergson — Abdul Bahai
Hawtrey — Edward Elgar — Sardlea
Filson Young — Marie Corelli — Geddes
Codliver Oil — St. Loe Strachey — Lyceum Club
Rhabindraneth Tagore — Lord Glenconner of Glen
Weiniger — Norman Angel — Ad. Mahon
Mr. and Mrs. Dearmer — Beecham (Pills, Opera, Thomas) — Ella
A. C. Benson — Sydney Webb
British Academy — Messrs. Chapell
Countess of Warwick — George Edwards
Willie Ferraro — Captain Cook — R. J. Campbell
Clan Thesiger — Martin Harvey — William Archer
George Grossmith — R. H. Benson
Annie Besant — Chenil — Clan Meynell
Father Vaughan — Joseph Holbrooke — Clan Strachey

4

4
Wyndham Lewis, BLAST, Londres, 1914

"C'est la couverture du premier de deux numéros d'un magazine publié et principalement écrit par l'artiste-auteur-éditeur-agitateur anglais Wyndham Lewis, qui est sorti juste avant la première guerre mondiale. La publication originale avait la stature maladroite d'un annuaire, faite pour être exposée sur des tables de salon d'une intelligentsia londonienne d'avant guerre. Comme Lewis lui-même, son exclamation puce était une pose consciente, ne pouvant passer inaperçue, poussant à prendre position et à réagir. Lewis grattait joyeusement ce même malaise public que le Pistols allaient toucher 60 ans plus tard, allant jusqu'à s'appeler *The Enemy* (en anticipation de *I is the enemy / I is anarchy...* de John Lydon), et il ne semble guère être une coïncidence que ces deux débuts d'agitation publique partage la même stratégie graphique: frère et sœur délinquants, *BLAST* et *Bollocks* habillés en rose violent, crachant une économie de langage en grandes lettres noires grotesques. Ces exemples sont encore tellement brûlants de nos jours, parce que leurs spécificités locales sont tellement gravées dans leurs formes respectives, que ce soit à travers le Pop

5

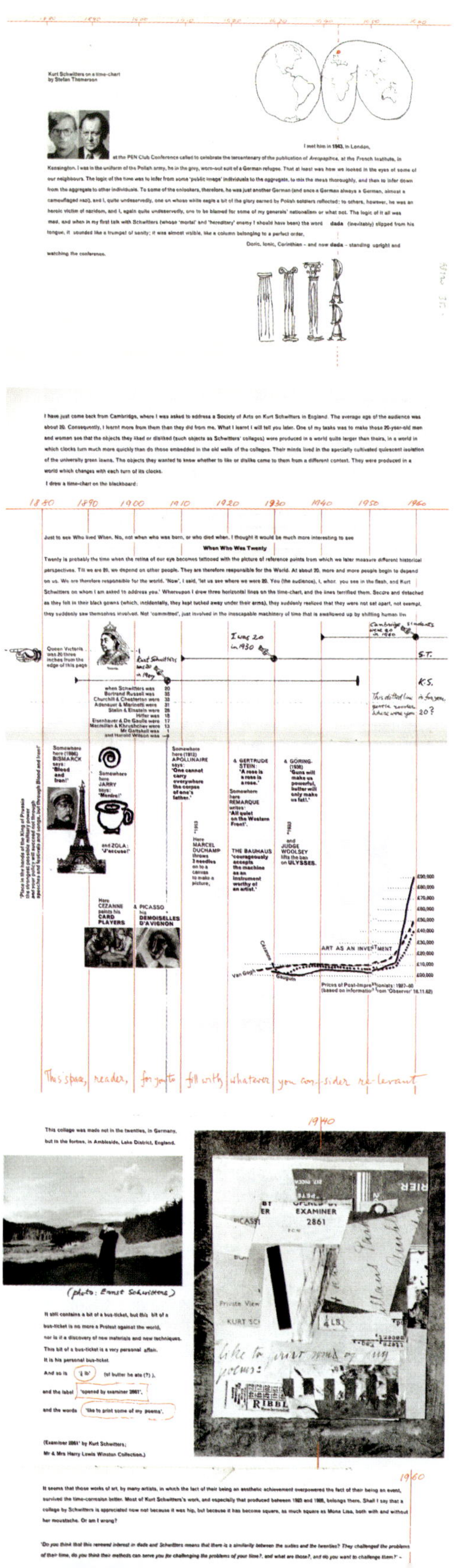

ex-printer, the only person who consented to typeset according to Lewis's incendiary typography. Rather than *Bollocks*'s glue and scissors ransom note or *BLAST*'s drunken metal type *passively* setting the text after its conception, it seems closer to the truth to imagine Lydon or Lewis or *actively* writing at the source, wired and lucid, where form & content = chicken & egg.

5
Stefan Themerson, KURT SCHWITTERS ON A TIME CHART, in TYPOGRAPHICA no. 16, London, 1967

"Here's another piece of work by Themerson, but this time he wrote as well as designed it. Together with his artist wife Franciszka in the 1950s, he established a small publishing imprint called the Gaberbocchus Press, as well as an irregular art salon called The Common Room. Both were important channels for the European avant-garde to bleed slowly into Britain. This particular piece of work has a lengthy history, again rooted in failure. One of the early publications of the Gaberbocchus Press was a particularly well-crafted book about the life and work of Kurt Schwitters. Compiled, edited and designed by Themerson, this publication was an

situationisme de récup de Reid ou la rencontre fortuite de Lewis avec un ancien imprimeur alcoolique, la seule personne qui voulait bien travailler avec la typographie incendiaire de Lewis. Plutôt que la note de rançon découpée et collée de *Bollocks* ou la typo saoul métallique de *BLAST* qui pose le texte *passivement* après la création, il semble plus vrai d'imaginer Lewis ou Lydon écrivant *activement* sur place, branché et lucide, ou la forme et le contenu sont la poule et l'œuf.

5
Stefan Themerson, KURT SCHWITTERS ON A TIME CHART, dans TYPOGRAPHICA no. 16, Londres, 1967

"Voici une autre œuvre de Themerson, mais cette fois il l'a écrite et créée. Avec sa femme-artiste Franciszka dans les années 1950, il a fondé une petite imprimerie d'édition qui s'appelait la Gaberbocchus Press, ainsi qu'un salon d'art irrégulier appelé The Common Room. Les deux étaient des canaux importants pour l'infiltration de l'avant-garde européen en Grande Bretagne. Cette œuvre a une longue histoire, encore une fois enracinée dans l'échec. Une des premières publications de Gaberbocchus Press était un livre bien fait sur la vie et l'œuvre de Kurt adventurous, particularly tactile attempt to capture the nature and sensation of Schwitters' work through chaotic, collaged layout; scraps of text and image combined with different textures and colours of paper. Some years after its publication, however, Themerson was unhappy with it, feeling he'd fundamentally failed to capture the artist's true spirit. He denounced it as being closer to parody, mimicking certain material but ultimately superfluous aspects of his subject's work. Rooted in Schwitters-like idiosyncracy himself, Themerson despised the inevitable distortion inherent in any conventional idea of biography, but his dogged reflection and determination to work out a satisfactory antidote resulted in a major revision and two further pieces of work. The first was a lecture, delivered to a group of 20-year old students in Cambridge three years later. He began by drawing a timeline on an overhead projector on which he then marked that year, 1960, when his audience were 20 years old; then the year he was 20; then the year Schwitters was 20. This deceptively simple opening salvo immediately situated the students *in time*, as active participants, collapsing any comfortable anaesthetic of history as something that merely happened in the past, detached. The timeline then receded to a template on top of which which Themerson added relevant people and events – the World Wars, Hiroshima, Hitler, Queen Victoria, Picasso, Duchamp – situating Schwitters' work in the various explosive contexts of his life and, by implication, on into in the present. Then Themerson submitted a graphic translation of the lecture to Herbert Spencer, editor of *Typographica* magazine, though it wasn't published until almost a decade later. Here the time chart was redrawn laterally over twenty pages, transposed from 3D to 2D, and accommodating the necessary shifts in speed, cadence and technique. Apart from everything else, this piece of work is vital as a representation of the idea that design is a fluid, ongoing thought process that can carry on even after the cut-off point of an initial deadline or publication. Themerson's perpetual inquiry and humility are constantly chasing a way of working in the *spirit* of his subject matter rather than making a simple pastiche of it. In a postface he wrote: 'Perhaps the reader must endure this book, (together with its time-chart and other nonsense), and then throw it away. Perhaps that is what he must do in order to enjoy K.S.'s work rightly.'

Schwitters. Compilé, édité et créé par Themerson, cette publication était une tentative aventureuse et particulièrement tactile de capture de la nature et la sensation du travail de Kurt Schwitters à travers une mise en page chaotique en collage; des bouts de texte et d'images avec différentes textures et couleurs de papier. Quelques années après sa publication cependant, Themerson n'en était pas content, convaincu qu'elle n'avait pas réussi à capter le véritable esprit de Schwitters. Il l'a dénoncée comme étant plus proche de la parodie, imitant de la matière mais finalement que des aspects superflus du travail de Schwitters. Enraciné dans la particularité à la Schwitters lui-même, Themerson détestait la distorsion inévitable qui est inhérente à toute biographie conventionnelle, mais sa réflexion et détermination pour trouver un antidote satisfaisant a engendré une grande révision et deux autres œuvres. La première était une présentation faite pour un groupe d'étudiants de 20 ans à Cambridge. Il a commencé par dessiner une ligne de temps sur un rétroprojecteur sur laquelle il a inscrit l'année, 1960, lorsque les étudiants avaient 20 ans. Ce début, d'une apparence simple a immédiatement situé les étudiants *dans le temps*, en tant que participants actifs, réduisant toute anesthésie confortable de l'histoire comme quelque chose qui s'est déroulé dans le passé. La ligne de temps s'est ensuite réduite à un modèle sur lequel Themerson ajoutait des événements et personnages importants comme les guerres mondiales, Hiroshima, Hitler, la reine Victoria, Picasso, Duchamp – situant le travail de Schwitters dans les contextes explosifs de la vie et, par extension dans le présent. Il a fallu encore dix ans pour que Themerson soit satisfait d'une autre traduction graphique de sa présentation pour le dernier numéro du magazine *Typographica* à la fin des années 1960. Ici, la ligne de temps a été dessiné latéralement sur vingt pages, transposée d 3D à 2D en aménageant le déplacement nécessaire dans la vitesse, les cadences et la technique. Sans parler du reste, cette œuvre est vitale en tant que représentation de l'idée que le design est fluide, un processus de pensée continu qui peut continuer même après le la coupure de l'échéance. L'humilité tenace de Themerson finit par évoluer en une manière de travailler dans l'esprit de son sujet plutôt que d'en faire qu'une simple pastiche.

6
Ryan Gander & John Morgan, ON CAMOUFLAGE poster, 2001

"Leaping forward another forty years or so, here's a very graphic demonstration of lateral thinking from a project initiated by the artist Ryan Gander. As an exercise in relinquishing any aesthetic control of his work, he asked around ten designers to make posters for fictional events or products based on a series of formal briefs. His brief to John Morgan was to make a poster advertising a lecture titled *On Camouflage* for an international intellectual panel discussion in a Belgian theatre hall. John's reaction was to take a poster from the street – one which might be described as the most poster-like poster imaginable – for a travelling circus, and to apply the details of the lecture on the blank panel typically reserved for the local information. In doing so he created his own act of camouflage, with the poster literally enacting the title.

7
Ryan Gander, installation view from THE DEATH OF ABBÉ FARIA, Stedelijk Museum Bureau, Amsterdam, 2003

"Here's another piece of Gander's work; by this time he'd had enough of designers,

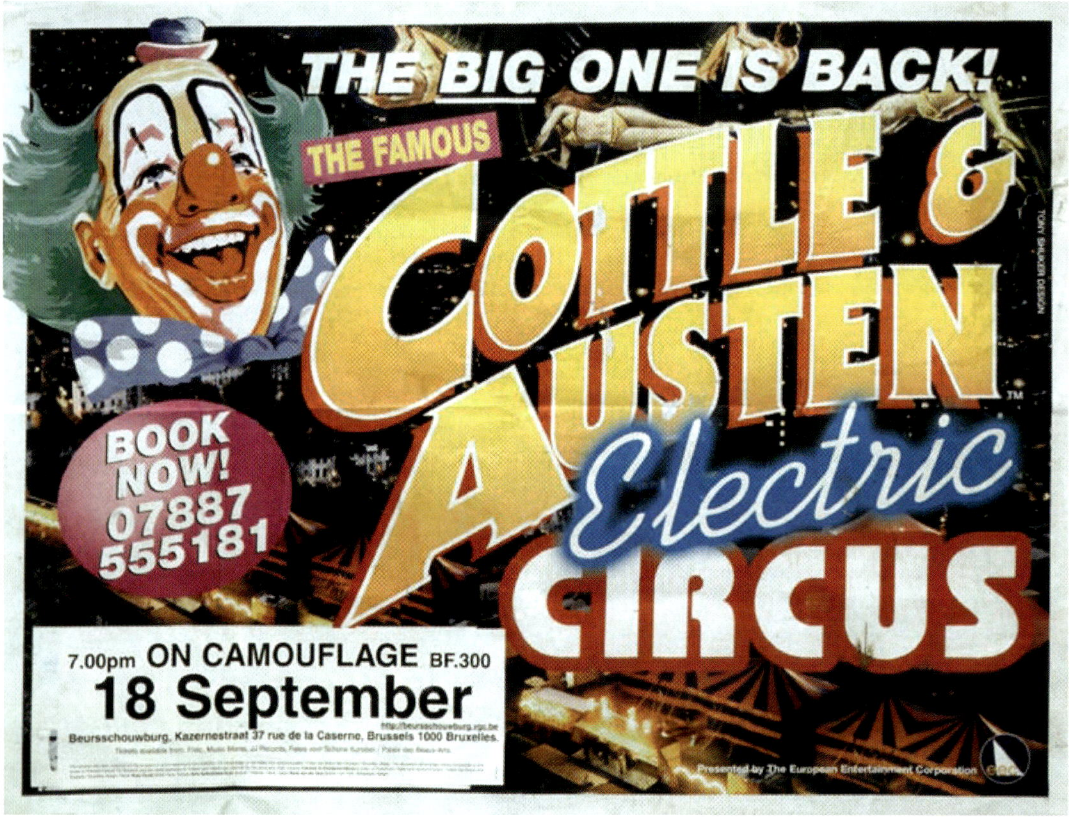

6

6
Ryan Gander & John Morgan, ON CAMOUFLAGE affiche, 2001

"En sautant encore une quarantaine d'années, voici une démonstration très graphique de la pensée latérale d'un projet initié par l'artiste Ryan Gander. Il a demandé à une dizaine de graphistes de créer des affiches pour des événements ou produits fictifs sur une série de communiqués formels, en guise d'exercice sur l'abandon de tout contrôle esthétique de son travail. Son communiqué à John Morgan était de faire une affiche publicitaire pour une présentation appelée *On camouflage* pour une sorte de débat intellectuel dans une galerie belge. La réaction de John était de prendre une affiche dans la rue – une qui serait une affiche ressemblant le plus à une affiche – pour un cirque itinérant, et d'appliquer les détails sur le débat sur le panneau blanc qui est normalement réservé à l'info locale. Par là, il a ainsi créé son propre acte de camouflage, l'affiche incarnant le titre.

7
Ryan Gander, vue d'une installation de THE DEATH OF ABBÉ FARIA, Stedelijk Museum Bureau, Amsterdam, 2003

"Voici une autre œuvre de Gander; arrivé à ce point, il en avait assez des graphistes, et a and went back to solving the aesthetics himself. You can see why I'm not distinguishing between art or design or music or film or literature here, because the pieces all share an *approach* and an *attitude*, and that similarity is far stronger than any difference in discipline or media. There are a number of aspects which resonate (or maybe feedback) across Gander's practice. One is the appropriation, transfer and reconfiguration of everyday aesthetics, visual signs and symbols which are generally overlooked or unnoticed (such as the result of months' worth of street posters pasted over and torn away from each other). Another might be described as an aesthetic of melancholy, a subtle filtering of an almost human sadness possessed by inanimate objects (such as a broken flip-dot bus sign which can no longer form texts, only drip random dots like tears). Both aspects combine in this piece of work, an almost-overlooked piece in the corridor of a larger installation. The show was loosely concerned with the death of a fictional character called Abbé Faria. A couple of months before the show, Gander and various friends began sending letters, packages and junk mail to the gallery addressed to Abbé Faria, so by the time the show opened, a large pile of mail had amassed as a sculptural illustration of death by an essentially mundane but direct symbol of absence.

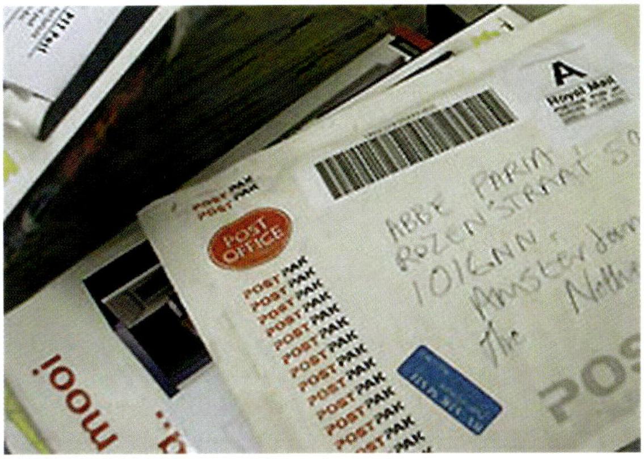

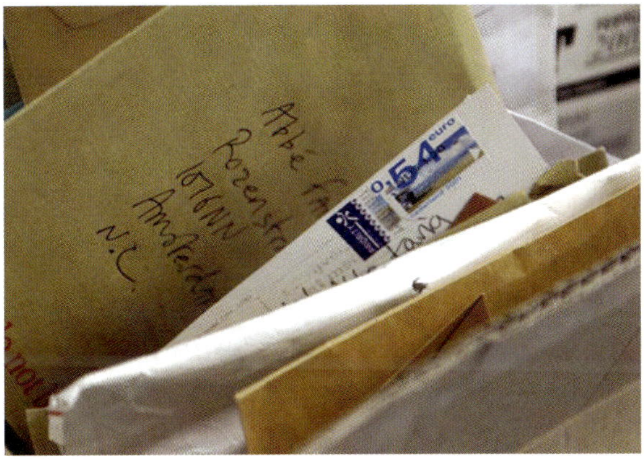

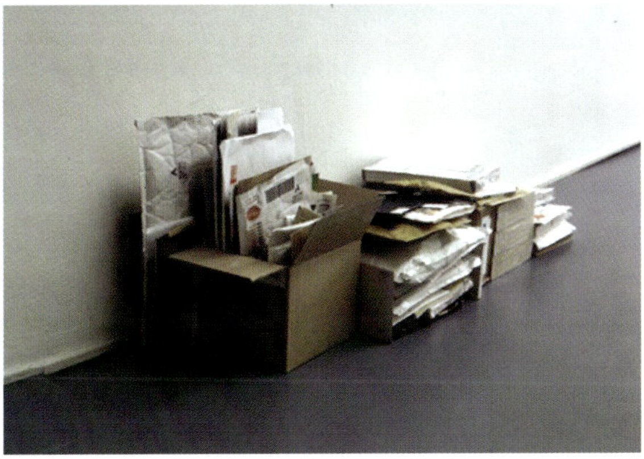

7

recommencé à résoudre l'esthétique par lui-même. Vous pouvez voir pourquoi je ne fais pas la distinction entre l'art ou le design ou la musique ou le cinéma ou la littérature ici, parce qu'ils ont tous une même *approche* et une *attitude*, et cette similitude est de loin plus forte que toute différence de discipline ou de média. Il y a de nombreux aspects qui résonnent (ou peut être des retours) dans la pratique de Gander. Un est l'appropriation, le transfert et la reconfiguration d'une esthétique ordinaire, des signes et des symboles visuels qui ne se remarquent pas, comme le résultat de la collecte d'un mois d'affiches collées et recollées et déchirées. Un autre pourrait être une esthétique de la mélancolie, un filtrage subtile d'une tristesse presque humaine que possèdent des objets inanimés comme un affichage cassé de bus qui ne forme plus des textes, mais seulement des points arbitraires comme des larmes. Les deux aspects sont réunis dans cette œuvre, une œuvre presque pas remarquée dans le couloir d'une installation plus grande. L'exposition parlait vaguement de la mort d'un personnage fictif nommé Abbé Faria. Quelques mois avant l'exposition, Gander et des amis ont commencé à envoyer des lettres, des colis et des pubs à la galerie en les adressant à l'Abbé Faria, et donc lorsque l'exposition a ouvert, une pile de deux ou trois cent courriers s'était amassé, comme une illustration sculpturale de la mort à travers un symbole d'absence mondain mais direct.

8
Will Holder, SAFE HAVEN, invitation card, 2003

"This is a flyer for an exhibition subtitled *The Aesthetics of Safety*. Like the previous two works, Holder appropriates an existing form, a found aesthetic of safety: the 'stylised hawk' silhouette sticker often found on large areas of glass and plastic in public to prevent birds from flying into the panes or panels. What turns a good idea into a great one, however, is Holder's further use of the yellow circle usually found in combination with the bird on the plexiglass of Dutch railway platform windows, where they appear in a chest-high row to stop humans making the same mistake as the birds. When combined the circle becomes a sun, and the whole scene is further aestheticised into a new form: a landscape. Other details spin off from and compound this idea: a gloss laminate around the two symbols which fake the appearance of a sticker sheet (again referring to the *aesthetic* of functionality, of safety – the *flavour* rather than the reality of it); and on the reverse an overload of information from the curator set tight, with a nod to User's Guide typography. This kind of rigorous supporting detail is what I meant elsewhere by the statement 'God is in the footnotes'.

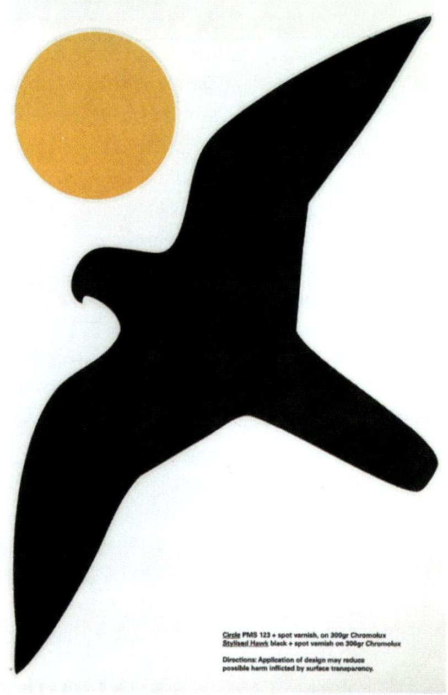

SAFE HAVEN
... or the æsthetic of safety

A project organised by De Vleeshal and Guus Beumer, in collaboration with the Dutch Institute for Architecture (NAi) and the Premsela foundation for Dutch design.
With contributions by: goodwill, Marjo Kranenborg, Herman Verkerk, Lucas Verweij and Tobias Woldendorp. And lectures by: Aaron Betsky, Dingeman Kuilman, Mark Wigley and Anna Tilroe.

Safety has an æsthetic all of its own. The project 'SAFE HAVEN... or the æsthetic of safety' is an attempt to illuminate our desires & fears with regard to safety by examining the æsthetic employed.

The project 'SAFE HAVEN... or the æsthetic of safety' consists of three components:

1. EXHIBITION AT DE VLEESHAL
24 JANUARY THROUGH 23 MARCH 2003

Central to 'SAFE HAVEN... or the æsthetic of safety' is the exhibition with the same title at De Vleeshal. This exhibition consists of two parts.

The first part of the exhibition endeavours to provide a historical context for the present æsthetic of safety by means of a number of 'settings'. The focus of these settings is not so much on any one style or designer, but rather on the development of the æsthetic aspect - and in particular the use of materials: from the velour covered interior of the 19th century to the steel and glass of the 1930's.

The second part is a 1:1 model of an inside and an outside space. This model forms an illustration of how the æsthetic of safety has led to a radical transparency of materials, resulting in the increasing blending of inside and outside spaces.

The model was designed by Herman Verkerk, architect and one of the founders of sloom.org, while Marjo Kranenborg created the different 'settings'.

Elucidation Guus Beumer
& lecture Dingeman Kuilman
At the exhibition's opening, curator Guus Beumer will comment briefly on the exhibit. Following this, Premsela director Dingeman Kuilman will argue that the demand for safety is an expression of individual fears and collective distrust.

The publication 'Directions for use' (designed and edited by goodwill), which accompanies the exhibition, will be presented at the opening.

Programme 24 January
17.00-19.00: Opening exhibition
20.00: Elucidation Guus Beumer
20.15: Lecture Dingeman Kuilman
21.00: Close

2. COACH TRIP AND LECTURES
BY AARON BETSKY AND MARK WIGLEY
8 FEBRUARY 2003
The second component of 'SAFE HAVEN... or the æsthetic of safety' is a coach trip from Rotterdam to Middelburg during which various projects exemplifying the current view on safety will be visited. This trip has been set out in co-operation with Tobias Woldendorp, advisor to the DSP-group on socially safe design. He will also be one of the tour guides.

The coach trip will commence with a lecture by Aaron Betsky, director of NAi. Betsky will address the banality of safety and the codification of security. The lecture will be held at the NAi and can also be attended by those not wishing to take part in the coach trip.
US resident Mark Wigley, author of (among others) 'White Walls, Designer Dresses', will further examine the current æsthetic of safety and the philosophical and societal background to the exhibition. This lecture can also be attended separately from the coach trip.

Programme 8 February
15.00: Lecture Aaron Betsky at the NAi
16.00: Coach trip leaves from the NAi
18.00: Supper
20.00 Lecture Mark Wigley at De Vleeshal (this lecture will be delivered in English)
21.30 Return coach trip to Rotterdam (arr. 23.00)

Admission to both lectures is free. The coach trip costs 40 euros, which includes supper.
By reservation only:
0118 652200 (De Vleeshal, Jacqueline Cijsouw) or
010-4401200 (NAi, Iris Knapen)

3. LECTURE ANNA TILROE & PUBLIC DEBATE
1 MARCH 2003

The third and last part of 'SAFE HAVEN... or the æsthetic of safety' will be a lecture by Anna Tilroe at De Vleeshal. The lecture will be followed by a public debate between Tilroe and the other participants in the project. The debate will be chaired by Lucas Verweij.

Anna Tilroe, art critic and author of (among others) the collection of essays 'Het Blinkende stof, op zoek naar een nieuw visioen', will address the feelings of fear, longing and want that bring the issue of safety into the realm of art and culture.
Verweij is one of the founders of Schie 2.0 and was recently appointed 'domain keeper' at Premsela, foundation for Dutch design.
Start lecture: 20.00. Admission is free.

For more information, please contact
Jacqueline Cijsouw on +31118 652200

Thanks to: Museum Boijmans van Beuningen, Rotterdam; Historisch Museum, Rotterdam; MPK, Leiden; Pilkington and the University Archives, Utrecht.
De Vleeshal: Markt 1 (Postbus 6000) 4330 LA Middelburg. www.vleeshal.nl
From February through March 2003 Guus Beumer will be project director at De Vleeshal

CE

goodwill

8

8
Will Holder, SAFE HAVEN, carton d'invitation, 2003

C'est un flyer pour une exposition intitulée *The Aesthetics of Safety*. Comme les deux œuvres précédentes, Holder s'approprie une forme existante, une esthétique de sécurité trouvée, l'autocollant d'un oiseau qu'on trouve souvent sur les grands panneaux de vitrage ou de plastique pour éviter que les oiseaux s'y perdent. Ce qui fait d'une bonne idée une grande idée, est l'utilisation que Holder fait avec l'oiseau sur le plexiglass, du cercle jaune qu'on trouve sur le plexiglass des fenêtres des quais de gare aux Pays Bas, où ils apparaissent alignés à hauteur de poitrine pour empêcher les humains de commettre la même erreur que les oiseaux. Réunis, le cercle devient un soleil, et toute la scène est esthétisée en une nouvelle forme : un paysage. D'autres détails se développent de et composent cette idée: une plastification brillante autour de deux symboles qui donnent l'impression d'un autocollant, mais ne le sont pas tout à fait – encore un portrait subtil de l'*esthetique* de la fonction, de la sécurité, de la *saveur* plutôt que sa réalité; et sur le verso, une surcharge d'informations serrées de la part de l'organisateur, imitant la typographie d'un manuel d'utilisation.

9
Robin Kinross (editor), Jaap van Triest & Karel Martens, KAREL MARTENS, PRINTED MATTER \ DRUKWERK, London, Hyphen Press, 1996, designed by Jaap van Triest & Karel Martens

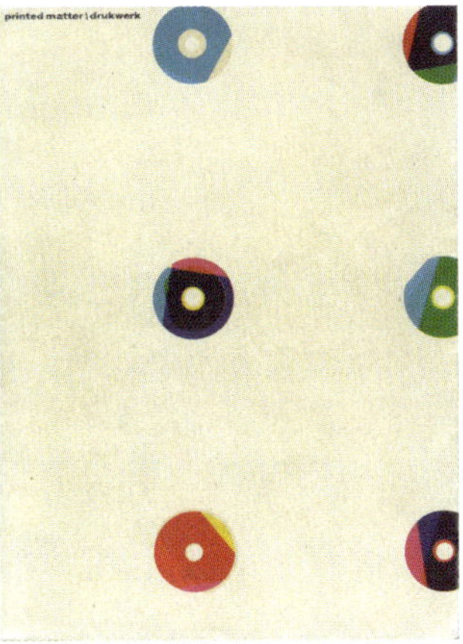

“I’m showing both the cover and an inside spread of this Karel Martens’ anthology to point out the similarities between his so-called free and applied work, specifically the way the abstract and the representational feed off each other. The cover is a collection of Karel’s personal prints: homemade experiments in overprinting colour with pieces of found metal, combining pattern and chance. Inside, his commissioned work is loosely arranged on an underlying grid; a running, chronological arrangement of small reference covers on the far edges of Japanese-bound pages, setting off the free arrangement of supporting sketches and larger reproductions of the more important or telling work. The phonecards on this spread obviously demonstrate the influence of the free work, now applied with reason: the quantity and density of the numbers and colours increases in relation to the value of the cards. Both the cover and interior pages of *Printed Matter* perform their respective jobs of attraction and articulation within the same intimate, personal style. And zooming in even further,

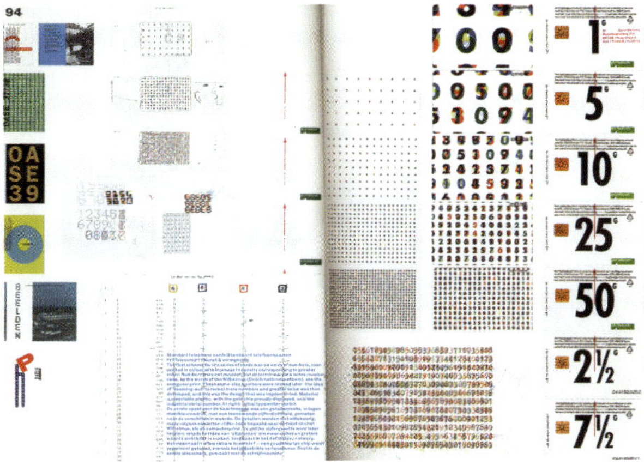

9

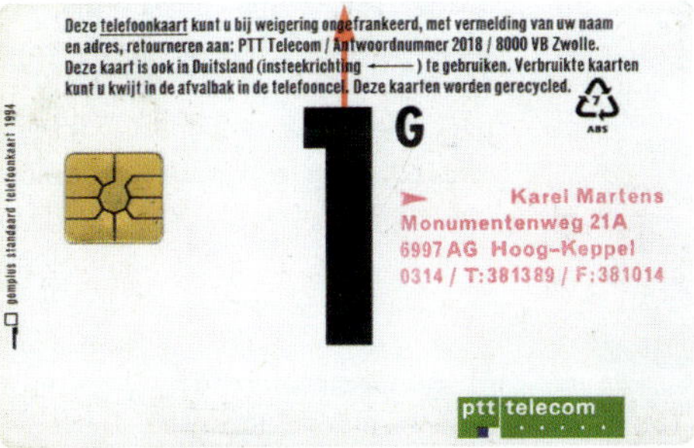

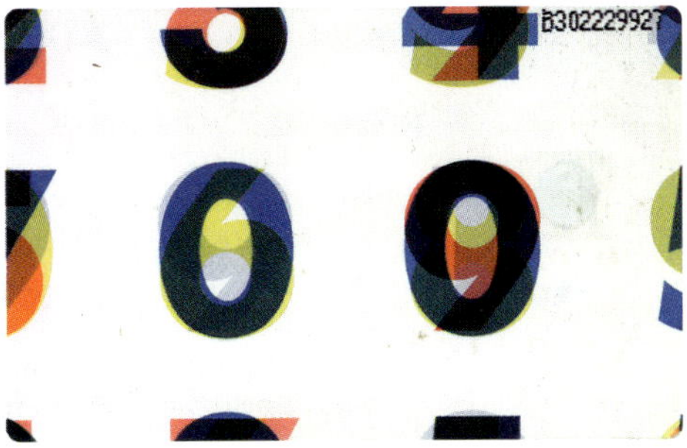

Cette sorte de détail rigoureux illustre ce que je voulais dire ailleurs par la phrase ‘Dieu est dans les notes de pied de page’.

9
Robin Kinross (éditeur), Jaap van Triest et Karel Martens, KAREL MARTENS, PRINTED MATTER \ DRUKWERK, Londres, Hyphen Press, 1996, conçu par Jaap van Triest & Karel Martens

“Je veux montrer la couverture et la page intérieure d’une anthologie du travail de Karel Martens pour souligner les similitudes entre son travail dit libre et appliqué, particulièrement la façon dont l’abstrait et le figuratif se nourrissent mutuellement. La couverture est une collection des ‘druksels’ de Karel – des expérimentations maison sur la surimpression de couleurs avec des morceaux de métal trouvés, mêlant des motifs et le hasard. A l’intérieur, son travail est présenté de façon espacée sur une grille de fond, un arrangement continu, chronologique de petites couvertures de référence sur les bords éloignés de pages reliées à la japonaise, accentuant la disposition libre d’esquisses et de plus grandes reproductions du travail plus important ou plus parlant. Les cartes téléphoniques sur cette mise en page montrent de façon évidente l’influence du travail libre, ici appliqué raisonnablement: la quantité et la densité des chiffres et des couleurs augmen-

Martens bought a supply of the cheapest 1 Guilder cards and rubber-stamped his address to create a composite of address card and portfolio on top of the wry bonus gift of communication.

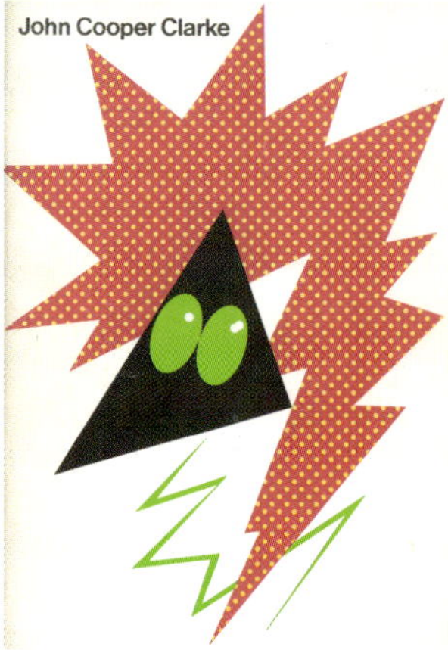

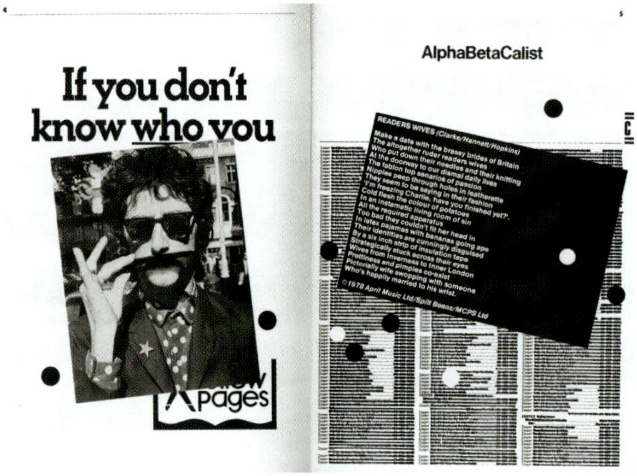

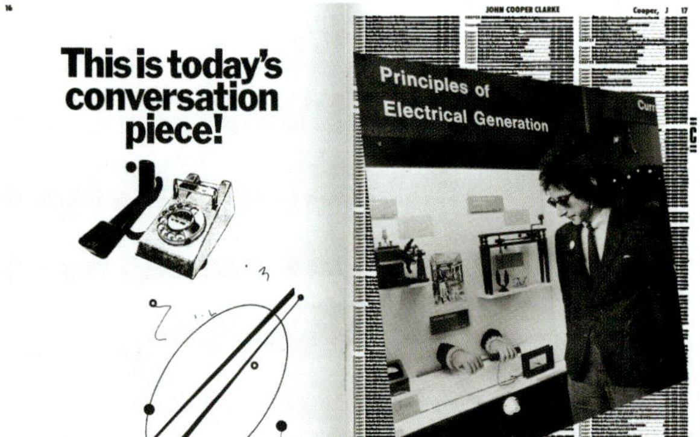

10

10
Barney Bubbles & John Cooper Clarke, songbook, 1979

“Most of the work shown here results from a designer and an artist (or writer, whatever) collaborating to producing a new piece of work, rather than a merely documenting an existing one. Contrary to the general (and generally accepted) situation of a designer working at least one step removed as a detached *form-giver* (to borrow from the Dutch), these works push for a resolution which neither designer nor artist could have achieved alone, something greater than the sum of their constituent parts. Here are the cover and two spreads of what is essentially a book of lyrics by post-punk poet John Cooper Clarke. Cartoonish abstract character portraits were a recurring motif in the work of Barney Bubbles, and the one of Cooper Clarke here typically captures multiple facets of his style and character: contrary, electric, day-glo, pop and punk. Inside, Bubbles took every page of Coopers and

tent en fonction de la valeur des cartes. La couverture aussi bien que l’intérieur du *Drukwerk* jouent leur rôle respectif d’attirance et d’articulation à l’intérieur d’un style intime et personnel. En se rapprochant encore plus, Martens a acheté un stock des cartes les moins chères à 1 Guilder et a tamponné son adresse en haut, créant ainsi une carte de visite composite, un book, un cadeau.

10
Barney Bubbles/John Cooper Clarke, livret, 1979

“La plupart du travail montré ici provient d’un graphiste et un artiste (ou écrivain, comme vous voulez) qui collaborent pour produire une nouvelle œuvre, plutôt que de documenter une œuvre existante. Ils poussent pour obtenir une résolution que ni l’artiste, ni le graphiste aurait pu faire seul, quelque chose de plus grand que la somme de leurs constituants, contrairement à la situation générale (et généralement acceptée) où le graphiste travaille à côté, comme un donneur de forme détaché de l’œuvre. Voici la couverture et deux pages de ce qui est en fait un livre de textes de chansons du poète punk John Cooper Clarke. Un motif récurrent dans le travail de Barney Bubbles sont

Clarkes in the phone book, crossed them all out and used them as a background wallpaper on which to compose a series of formal collages incorporating fragments of angular poetry and judicious photography. This freeform invention is carried over onto the phone book's advertising pages, subverted by Bubbles into a series of cryptic announcements.

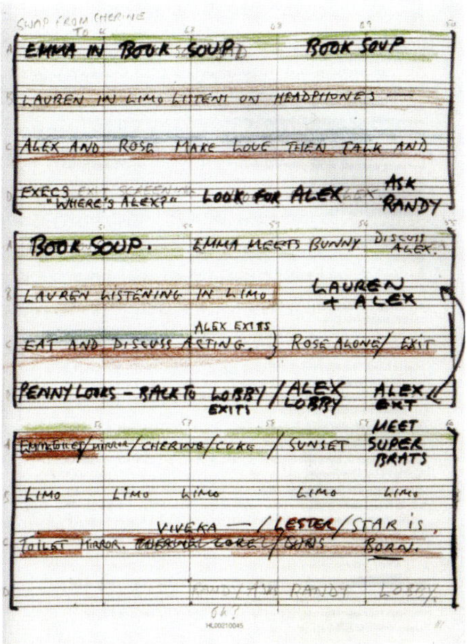

11

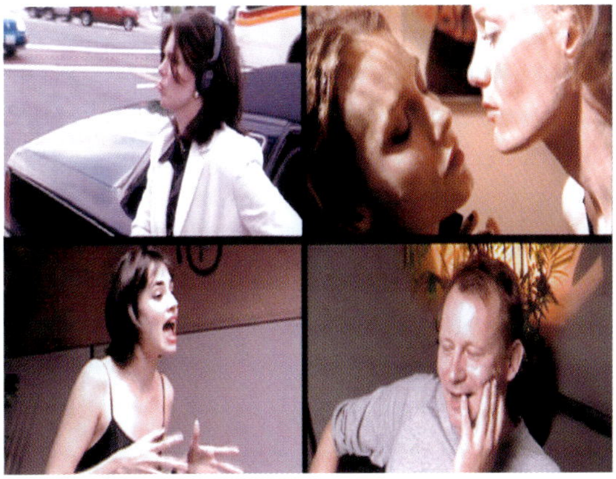

11
Mike Figgis, camera script for TIMECODE, 2003

"This is one of a number of sheets which outline the screenplay of Figgis's film *Timecode*, another example of transposing the particular qualities of one medium to another – but on demand, through necessity rather than originality for its own sake. *Timecode* was conceived from the outset as a quadruple split-screen film, with four cameras following the simultaneous action of various characters in different locations across Los Angeles. Midway through writing the screenplay, Figgis came across some standard music notation paper which sparked the light-bulb of using the music staves and bar divisions as a basis on which to work out his story and transcribe the synchronicity; to score the film for four cameras rather than four instruments. He proceeded to write the film and distribute instructions to the cameramen in this way, developing an elaborate colour coding system, with each bar of notation representing a minute of action. Regrettably, the resultant film is awful.

des portraits abstraits des facettes de son style et caractère: à la fois contradictoire, électrique, day-glo, pop et punk. A l'intérieur, Bubbles a pris toutes les pages des Cooper et Clarke dans l'annuaire et a rayé toutes les entrées pour les utiliser en papier peint de fond sur lequel il compose une série de collages formels avec des fragments de poésie angulaire et des photos judicieuses. Cette invention en forme libre s'étend aux pages publicitaires de l'annuaire, détournées par Bubbles pour devenir une série d'annonces cryptées.

11
Mike Figgis, scripte de caméra pour TIMECODE, 2003

"Ceci est une des nombreuses feuilles qui exposent le scénario du film de Figgis, *Timecode*, un autre exemple de la transposition de certaines qualités d'un média à un autre – mais sur demande, par nécessité plutôt que par un désir fallacieux d'originalité. Depuis le début *Timecode* a été conçu comme un film à 4 écrans divisés, avec quatre caméras qui suivent l'action simultanée de plusieurs personnages dans des lieux différents de Los Angeles. A mi-chemin de l'écriture du scénario, Figgis est tombé sur du papier à musique standard et a eu l'idée lumineuse d'utiliser des portées de musiques et des séparateurs de mesures comme base pour construire son histoire et transcrire la synchronisation. En effet, d'arranger le film pour quatre caméras plutôt que pour quatre instruments. Il a écrit le film et a distribué les instructions aux caméraman de cette façon, en développant un système de codes couleur assez élaboré, où chaque mesure de notation représentait une minute d'action. Malheureusement, le film qui en résultait est mauvais.

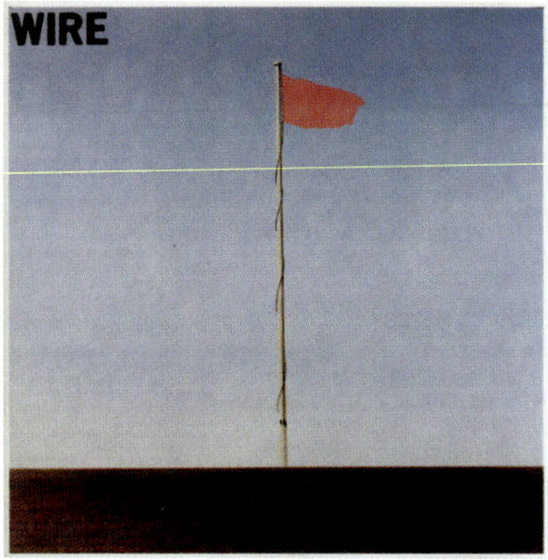

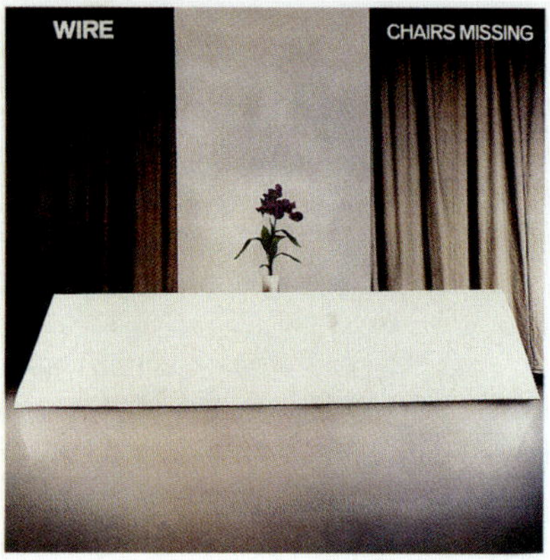

12
Wire, PINK FLAG, 1977; CHAIRS MISSING, 1978; 154, 1979; ON RETURNING (compilation), 1989

"These are Wire's first three albums from the end of the 1970s, plus one compilation from a decade later. Each of the first three has its own independent anecdote. For example, immediately after the band had decided on *Pink Flag* as the title for their debut, they played a gig in the British seaside town of Plymouth, and were walking along the seafront the following morning when they came across a perfect solitary pink flag flapping against a spotless blue sky, which they photographed immediately (a good example of designing backwards rather than laterally). But the best thing about these albums is the Best-of, *On Returning*, compiled ten years after *154*. Although Wire had an extensive output inbetween, this compilation collected tracks exclusively from those first three, and so the cover similarly montages all three orginal covers together to form a new composite. It's a good example of one of those ideas so perfectly obvious that it's almost reflexively overlooked.

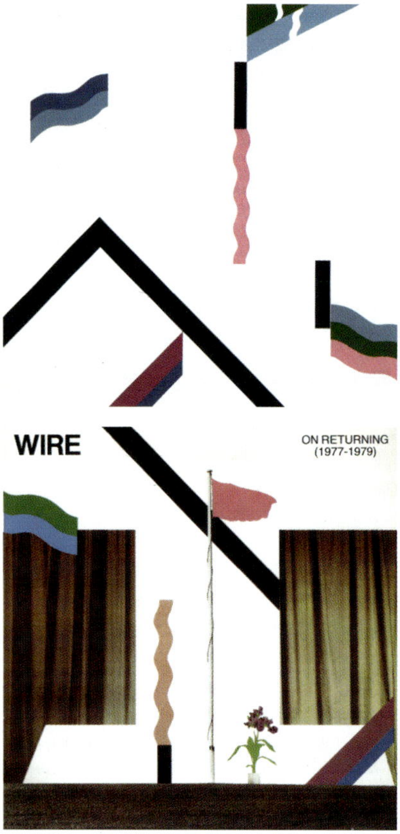

12

12
Wire, PINK FLAG, 1977; CHAIRS MISSING, 1978; 154, 1979; ON RETURNING (compilation), 1989

"Ce sont les premiers trois albums de Wire de la fin des années 1970 ainsi qu'une compilation qui date de dix ans plus tard. Chacun des trois premiers a sa propre anecdote: après que le groupe ait décidé du titre *Pink Flag* pour leur début, par exemple, ils avaient tapé le bœuf dans une petite ville de bord de mer, Plymouth, et se promenaient au bord de cette mer le lendemain matin, lorsqu'ils ont vu un drapeau rose solitaire et parfait qui flottait devant un ciel d'un bleu immaculé, ce qu'ils ont pris en photo; un bon exemple de conception à l'envers plutôt que latérale. Mais le meilleur est encore le Best-of, *On Returning*, compilé dix ans plus tard. Bien que Wire avait fait beaucoup d'autres disques entre temps, cette compilation réunissait que des chansons de ces trois premiers albums, et donc la couverture était un montage des trois couvertures originales pour former un nouveau composite. C'est un exemple parfait d'une idée qui est tellement évidente qu'elle passe presque inévitablement inaperçue.

A friend recently related how it was only a few years ago – well into his twenties – that he consciously realised that the two World Wars actually took place in colour, as if the world was monochrome before colour TV. Now we're entering a black and white section, or a grayscale section, as if stepping forward into the 1930s. I had a hard time cutting down this section to make it equal to the full colour one as dictated by the particular limitations of this book. The work shown here is economically inventive, drawing maximum effect from minimum means, turning limitations into benefits, and the first of those limitations is usually printing with a single colour. That's what's happening here too, of course: the given 16 CMYK / 16 BW is being used to structure the talk, forcing us to consider how the beginnings and endings of the piece work, this crossover point, or the implied symmetry at work. (I like to think the talk is reversible.)

13
Jimmy Cauty & Bill Drummond, THE MANUAL (HOW TO HAVE A NUMBER ONE THE EASY WAY), London, 1988

"Cost has such a direct bearing on graphic design, yet is rarely mentioned when describing and critiquing it. Although at first glance *The Manual* might have little in common with *Never Mind the Bollocks*, graphically they share some kind of debut aesthetic – the archetype of the first release: rough, basic, probably flawed in terms of technics and technique, but with an authenticity and integrity manifest in years' worth of honed, compressed ideas. Cauty and Drummond worked as the KLF around the early 1990s, created a string of hits, notoriously burnt £1 million on a remote island, announced their withdrawal from the music industry,

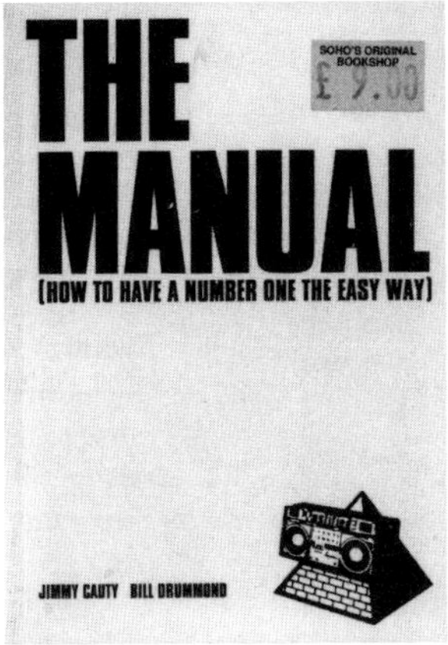

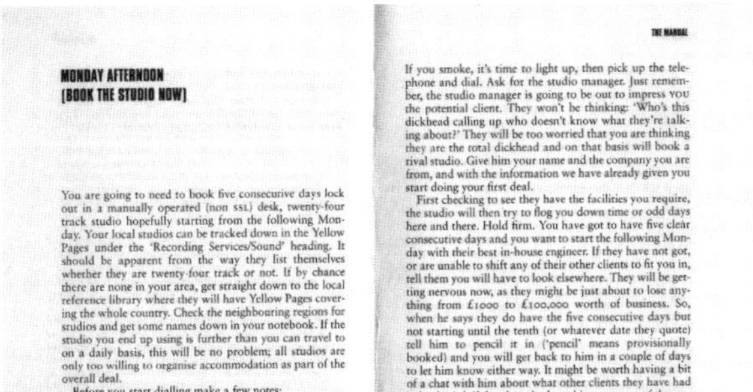
MONDAY AFTERNOON
(BOOK THE STUDIO NOW)

You are going to need to book five consecutive days lock out in a manually operated (non SSL) desk, twenty-four track studio hopefully starting from the following Monday. Your local studios can be tracked down in the Yellow Pages under the 'Recording Services/Sound' heading. It should be apparent from the way they list themselves whether they are twenty-four track or not. If by chance there are none in your area, get straight down to the local reference library where they will have Yellow Pages covering the whole country. Check the neighbouring regions for studios and get some names down in your notebook. If the studio you end up using is further than you can travel to on a daily basis, this will be no problem; all studios are only too willing to organise accommodation as part of the overall deal.

Before you start dialling make a few notes:

1. Pay no more than £40 per hour (exclusive of VAT) for the basic rates.
2. Ensure it includes fees for the best available engineer.
3. Be aware that you will also be charged for the tape you use and extra gear that is hired in specially for your session. Remember to get the rates for these.

32

THE MANUAL

If you smoke, it's time to light up, then pick up the telephone and dial. Ask for the studio manager. Just remember, the studio manager is going to be out to impress YOU the potential client. They won't be thinking: 'Who's this dickhead calling up who doesn't know what they're talking about?' They will be too worried that you are thinking they are the total dickhead and on that basis will book a rival studio. Give him your name and the company you are from, and with the information we have already given you start doing your first deal.

First checking to see they have the facilities you require, the studio will then try to flog you down time or odd days here and there. Hold firm. You have got to have five clear consecutive days and you want to start the following Monday with their best in-house engineer. If they have not got, or are unable to shift any of their other clients to fit you in, tell them you will have to look elsewhere. They will be getting nervous now, as they might be just about to lose anything from £1000 to £100,000 worth of business. So, when he says they do have the five consecutive days but not starting until the tenth (or whatever date they quote) tell him to pencil it in ('pencil' means provisionally booked) and you will get back to him in a couple of days to let him know either way. It might be worth having a bit of a chat with him about what other clients they have had in lately. Ask if they have had any hits come out of the studio, that sort of thing. This helps you build up a bit of a vibe where the studio's at. Then call the next studio on your list and repeat the process.

Once you have got through your list of studios in your local(ish) area, go and put the kettle on, take a leak and make yourself a cup of tea (coffee if you have to), as the

33

13

Un ami m'a raconté récemment comment c'était il y a quelques années – il avait bien plus de vingt ans – quand il s'est vraiment rendu compte que les deux guerres mondiales avaient eu lieu en couleur, comme si le monde avait été en noir et blanc avant la télé couleur. Nous entrons maintenant dans la partie noir et blanc, ou en niveaux de gris, comme si on avançait dans les années 30. J'ai eu du mal à réduire cette partie pour qu'elle soit égale à celle en couleur comme l'ont dicté les limitations de ce livre. C'est important aussi: le travail ici est inventif de façon économique, tirant un effet maximum avec des moyens mini, transformant des limitations en avantages, et la première de ces limitations est normalement l'impression avec une seule couleur. C'est ce qui se passe ici aussi, bien sûr: le 16 CMYK / 16 BW préscrit est utilisé pour structurer la présentation, nous obligeant à réfléchir sur le fonctionnement du début et de la fin, ce point de croisement, ou la symétrie sous-entendue au travail. (J'aime l'idée que la présentation est réversible).

13
Jimmy Cauty & Bill Drummond, THE MANUAL (HOW TO HAVE A NUMBER ONE THE EASY WAY), Londres, 1988

"Le coût a une influence tellement directe sur le graphisme, mais on en parle rarement lorsqu'on le décrit ou le critique. Bien qu'au premier coup d'oeil, *The Manual* n'a pas beaucoup de rapport à *Never Mind the Bollocks*, graphiquement, ils ont cette espèce d'esthétique des débuts en commun – l'archétype du premier album – rugueux, basique, probablement imparfait en terme de techniques, mais avec cette authenticité irréfutable d'une année d'idées affûtées, comprimées. Cauty et Drummond tra-

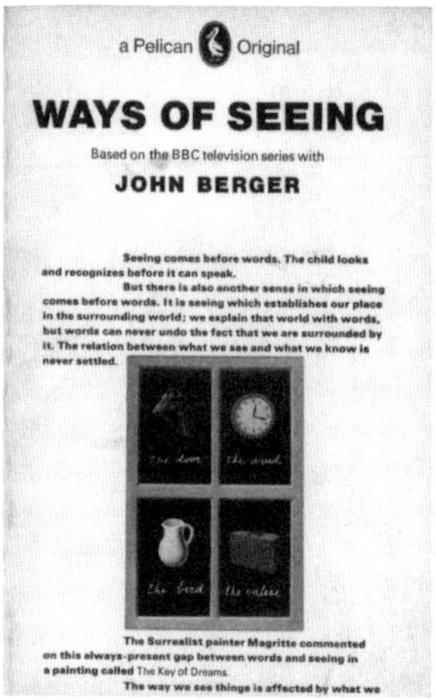

a Pelican Original

WAYS OF SEEING

Based on the BBC television series with

JOHN BERGER

Seeing comes before words. The child looks and recognizes before it can speak.

But there is also another sense in which seeing comes before words. It is seeing which establishes our place in the surrounding world; we explain that world with words, but words can never undo the fact that we are surrounded by it. The relation between what we see and what we know is never settled.

The Surrealist painter Magritte commented on this always-present gap between words and seeing in a painting called The Key of Dreams.

The way we see things is affected by what we

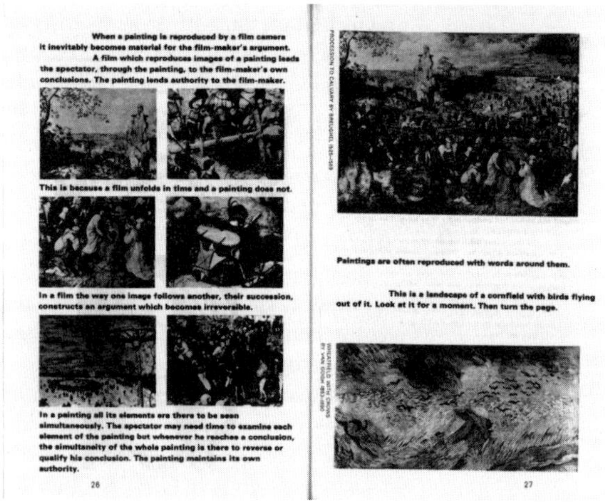

When a painting is reproduced by a film camera it inevitably becomes material for the film-maker's argument.

A film which reproduces images of a painting leads the spectator, through the painting, to the film-maker's own conclusions. The painting lends authority to the film-maker.

This is because a film unfolds in time and a painting does not.

In a film the way one image follows another, their succession, constructs an argument which becomes irreversible.

In a painting all its elements are there to be seen simultaneously. The spectator may need time to examine each element of the painting but whenever he reaches a conclusion, the simultaneity of the whole painting is there to reverse or qualify his conclusion. The painting maintains its own authority.

26

PROCESSION TO CALVARY BY BRUEGHEL 1525–1569

Paintings are often reproduced with words around them.

This is a landscape of a cornfield with birds flying out of it. Look at it for a moment. Then turn the page.

27

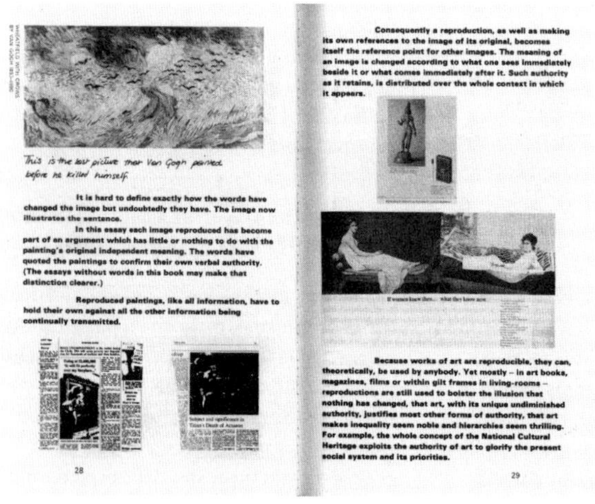

This is the last picture that Van Gogh painted before he killed himself.

It is hard to define exactly how the words have changed the image but undoubtedly they have. The image now illustrates the sentence.

In this essay each image reproduced has become part of an argument which has little or nothing to do with the painting's original independent meaning. The words have quoted the paintings to confirm their own verbal authority. (The essays without words in this book may make that distinction clearer.)

Reproduced paintings, like all information, have to hold their own against all the other information being continually transmitted.

28

Consequently a reproduction, as well as making its own references to the image of its original, becomes itself the reference point for other images. The meaning of an image is changed according to what one sees immediately beside it or what comes immediately after it. Such authority as it retains, is distributed over the whole context in which it appears.

Because works of art are reproducible, they can, theoretically, be used by anybody. Yet mostly – in art books, magazines, films or within gilt frames in living-rooms – reproductions are still used to bolster the illusion that nothing has changed, that art, with its unique undiminished authority, justifies most other forms of authority, that art makes inequality seem noble and hierarchies seem thrilling. For example, the whole concept of the National Cultural Heritage exploits the authority of art to glorify the present social system and its priorities.

29

14

then continued to resurge with increasingly obscure and eccentric projects on the fringes of art, music and literature. In the middle of all this they wrote and published this self-explanatory DIY book, and all I really want to point to here is the importance of their decision (or non-decision) to bypass graphic design. This is about as unmolested as an idea gets, lacking even the minimal refinement of the average novel – just poorly typeset by a friend. In this case the lack of refinement only emphasizes the text, the intent and the insistence. It says the words are important rather than how they are dressed. And even so, here are those same condensed grotesque *Bollocks/BLAST* capitals on the cover, as if they can't help filtering through to herald more obnoxious activity.

14
John Berger, WAYS OF SEEING, London, BBC/Penguin, 1977, designed by Richard Hollis

"*Ways of Seeing* was made by a team of five (including designer Richard Hollis) with more or less overlapping roles. It demonstrates a childlike state of working, rejecting conventions and preconceptions to set out from zero. Such innocence is mirrored in Berger's opening line, 'The child looks and

vaillaient en tant que KLF au début des années 1990, ont fait une série de tubes, ont notoirement brûlé 1 million de £, ont annoncé qu'ils se retiraient de la vie publique, et puis continuaient à resurgir avec des projets aussi obscurs qu'excentriques en marge de l'art, la musique, la littérature. Au milieu de tout cela ils ont écrit et publié ce livre de bricolage qui se passe d'explication, et tout ce que je veux montrer c'est l'importance de leur décision (ou non-décision) de contourner toute notion de graphisme. Une idée ne peut guère être moins maltraitée, n'ayant même pas le raffinement d'un roman moyen – juste mal mis en page par un ami. Dans ce cas, le manque de raffinement ne fait que renforcer le texte, l'intention. Il dit que ce sont les mots qui sont importants plutôt que comment ils sont habillés. Et tout de même on a toujours ces mêmes capitales grotesques *Bollocks/ BLAST* sur la couverture, prônant encore plus d'agitation publique.

14
John Berger, WAYS OF SEEING, Londres, BBC/Penguin, 1977, conçu par Richard Hollis

"*Ways of Seeing* a été fait par une équipe de cinq participants avec des rôles qui se chevauchaient plus ou moins, dont le graphiste recognizes before it can speak', and his team's subsequent articulation of this idea is consistently engaging precisely because so extraordinarily obvious. The book's hypothesis begins on the cover where it immediately embodies its opening statement that seeing comes before words: you *see* the idea of the text starting on the cover before you *read* the words: you *see* Magritte's image before you *read* the explanation, and this easy synchronicity of form and content is maintained throughout. The text is set in bold Univers so that text and image are visually equal, and this principle is followed through to details such as the captions being set at ninety degrees up the sides of images to discourage the speed-reading of illustrations. *Ways of Seeing* was originally a BBC TV programme, conceived as an antithesis to the existing treatment of fine art on television (more or less Sister Wendy), relating art to pornography, advertising, biography, children; basically, to the everyday, methodically deconstructing and demystifying. For the book, Berger's team filters the transience of TV through the stasis of the printed page, and the result is an emphatically animated book. In the bottom right hand corner of one spread, for example, a detail of a Van Gogh landscape is captioned, 'This is a landscape of a cornfield with birds flying out of it. Look at it for a moment. Then turn the page.' The image is then repeated at the top of the following spread, with the text altered and handwritten: 'This is the last picture that Van Gogh painted before he killed himself'.

15
B.S. Johnson, ALBERT ANGELO, London, 1964 (republished as part of OMNIBUS: ALBERT ANGELO, HOUSE MOTHER NORMAL and TRAWL, London, Picador, 2004)

"These are pages from what the British avant-garde writer B.S. Johnson considered his debut, even though it was actually his second published novel. Throughout this largely plotless character study of a would-be architect working as a supply teacher in a series of difficult London schools, Johnson writes each new scene in a different style of language (and as such it might reasonably be considered a practical application of Queneau's *Exercises in Style*, or even a pop version of Joyce's *Ulysses*). Johnson's formal experiments were rarely gratuitous, drawn directly from the particular demands of his subject matter. In fact he resented the label 'experimental', arguing that any experiment by definition remained in his notebooks,

Richard Hollis. Cela montre un état presque infantile de travail, en rejetant des conventions et des idées préconçues afin de commencer à zéro. Une innocence aussi consciente est annoncée dans le texte d'ouverture de Berger: 'l'enfant regarde et reconnaît avant qu'il ne sache parler', et l'articulation de cette idée par l'équipe est rigoureusement engageant, car elle est tellement inhabituellement évidente. L'hypothèse du livre commence à la couverture où elle incarne immédiatement le principe de base, que le regard précède les mots: vous *voyez* une idée du texte qui commence sur la couverture avant de *lire* les mots: vous *voyez* l'image de Magritte avant de *lire* l'explication, cette synchronisation très simple de la forme et du contenu est maintenue à travers tout le livre. Le texte est mis en Univers gras, de façon à ce que le texte est les images soient équilibrés, et cette insistance est poursuivie jusqu'à des détails comme les légendes, qui sont mis à 90° le long des bords des images pour décourager une lecture rapide des images. *Ways of Seeing* était une émission télé au départ, conçue comme une antithèse aux traitement habituel des beaux arts à la télé (généralement une nonne était devant un tableau religieux, expliquant son histoire, sa composition et représentation). Au lieu de cela, Berger faisait un rapport entre l'art et la pornographie, la publicité, des biographies, des enfants - en fait, au quotidien, en le déconstruisant et le démystifiant systématiquement. Le livre reprend les qualités éphémères de la télé, les filtrent à travers les qualités statiques de la page imprimée, et le résultat est un livre résolument animé. Dans le coins en bas à droite d'une page, par exemple, figure un détail d'un paysage de Van Gogh, avec le texte manuscrit: 'Ceci est un paysage d'un champs de maïs avec des oiseaux qui en sortent. Regardez-le un instant. Et tournez la page' et l'image est répétée en haut de la page suivante, seul le texte ayant changé: 'Ceci est le dernier tableau de Van Gogh avant sa mort, avant qu'il ne se suicide'.

15
B.S. Johnson, ALBERT ANGELO, Londres, 1964 (réédité en tant que partie de OMNIBUS: ALBERT ANGELO, HOUSE MOTHER NORMAL and TRAWL, Londres, Picador, 2004)

"Ce sont des pages de ce que l'écrivain avant-gardiste britannique B.S. Johnson considérait comme ses débuts, bien que ce soit en fait son deuxième roman publié. Tout au long de cette étude sans intrigue du caractère d'un homme qui voudrait être architecte mais qui travaille en tant qu'enseignant remplaçant and that whatever made it into published works were rather his best solutions to the particular problems thrown up by the subject matter, which might succeed or fail on their own terms, but could no longer be considered experiment or research. Albert Angelo – both character and book – is a chaos of rhetoric towards capturing the fragmented nature of life and personality. For example, Albert begins one day in a single column of interior-monologue narration, then as the first class begins the column bifurcates, with the classroom action and dialogue continuing in the left column, and Albert's simultaneous italicised thoughts in the right. This exterior/interior device continues for the remainder of the class, whether tracking Albert's self-doubt during teaching, or his daydreaming about a girl while the class silently works on an assignment. From the reader's point of view this doublethought is surprisingly accessible, with the distribution and speed of corresponding action and thought paced in a convincing approximation of realtime. At a later point in the book a hole is cut through two pages to reveal a future event. Johnson uses this device to prematurely announce a death, effectively collapsing time while typically pointing to the conceit of fiction.

As Johnson's biographer Jonathan Coe points out: 'the best way to think about B.S. Johnson's novels is to conceive of them not as experiments, but as "literary heresies" – a heresy being 'any opinion or doctrine at variance with the official or orthodox position'.

82 *Albert Angelo*

some places it is almost white, in others it is all shades of grey, green, a kind of blue, pink, deep red, brown and black. There's a particularly lovely grey-blue one which comes from Penmaenmawr in North Wales, which is . . .

Irrelevant.

Another place you can often see granite in all sorts of different colours is in cemeteries, where, because it is . . .

——Ooh!
——Eerh!
——You bin wandrin' round any cemeteries lately?
——My dad just 'ad wood.
——'E's right orf it.

Ignore. Louder.

. . . because granite is such a very hard stone I suppose people think their names cut in it will last that much longer.

Bloody stupid remark. Must go over and see Zulf and his fearful cemetery this week.

But granite is not the only igneous rock, though it is the most commonly used one . . . .

Definite evidence for that remark? None. Never mind.

that I didn't feel shitscared all the time, but that I accepted it and would have fought, I think, if occasion had arisen. Pro who had been rolled came back past us, on own. Terry

mortal wound above his right eye (the blade penetrating to a depth of two inches) from which he died instantly Christopher Marlowe, Poet, February 1564 to May 1593

15

dans une série d'écoles difficiles à Londres, Johnson écrit chaque nouvelle scène dans un style de langage différent, une application pratique des *Exercices de Style* de Queneau (un exercice dans l'exercice de style). Les expériences formelles de Johnson étaient rarement gratuites, toujours basées sur des exigences particulières des sujets. En fait, il rejetait l'étiquette '*expérimental*', en disant que les expériments restent dans ses cahiers; ce qui en faisait des œuvres publiées, c'était les meilleures solutions à ses problèmes particuliers, qui ont peut-être réussi ou échoué elles-mêmes, mais qui ne pouvaient plus être considérées comme des expériments ou de la recherche. Alberto Angelo – le personnage et le livre – est un chaos à multiples facettes de la rhétorique pour la capture du chaos à multiples facettes de la vie. Albert commence une journée dans une colonne unique d'une narration de monologue intérieure, et puis quand le premier cours commence, la colonne bifurque, avec l'action de la salle de classe et le dialogue qui continue dans la colonne de gauche, et les pensées simultanées d'Albert en italiques à droite. Ce mécanisme extérieur/intérieur continue pour le restant du cours, à travers des périodes où Albert enseigne et se demande si ses connaissances sont précises, ou en train de rêver pendant que la classe se taît en faisant le devoir pendant quelques instants. Du point de vue du lecteur, toutes ces double-pensées sont étonnamment accessibles, avec la distribution et la vitesse de l'action correspondante et la pensée au rythme du temps réel et totalement convaincant. Un peu plus tard dans l'histoire, il y a un trou coupé sur deux pages pour révéler un événement à venir. Johnson utilise

16
Richard Hamilton, HOW A GREAT DAILY ORGAN IS TURNED OUT (from the ULYSSES series), 1988–90

"This is one piece of work from an ongoing series based on James Joyce's *Ulysses* that Richard Hamilton has worked on intermittently over the past forty years. Of the many finished pieces and studies, this one both typifies and encapsulates the rest. It demonstrates the same duality that this talk attempts: the overall composite describes the same nature as its component parts. Hamilton was also interested in translating from one form to another, in this case written to graphic language. he compounded the challenge by using the twentieth century's masterpiece of literary rhetoric as source material. (Each chapter of *Ulysses* is famously written in a different style, with a web of embedded symbols and correspondences to Homer's *Odyssey*.) Hamilton's self-appointed task was to represent each chapter by an appropriately-corresponding choice of image and graphic technique, towards capturing the spirit of Joyce's work, as Themerson did with Schwitters. The piece here represents the 'Aeolus' chapter, set midway thorough the book in a newspaper office. *Ulysses*' main character Leopold Bloom is an advertising canvasser, and spends this chapter at work, where the regular narrative is punctuated by random headlines. To mirror this particular location and situation, Hamilton takes a number of trial etching plates made for other chapters – each already loaded with their own unique styles and stories – and combines them within the rough frame of a newspaper page, as and when they can fit alongside each other. As with a newspaper, the result is one overall form containing a number of others, each telling their own

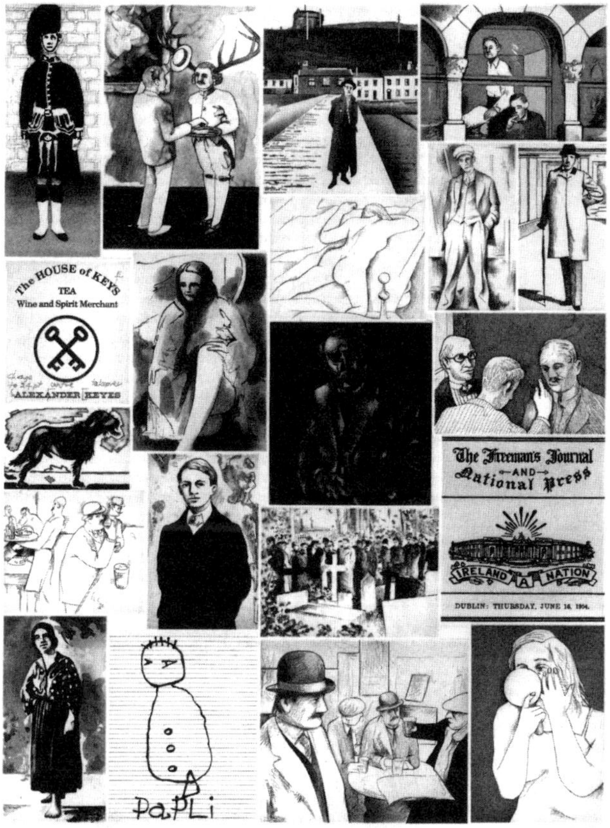

16

ce mécanisme pour annoncer une mort, en repliant effectivement le temps tout en soulignant la vanité de la fiction. Comme le biographe de Johnson, Jonathan Coe l'a fait remarquer: 'la meilleure façon d'aborder les romans de B.S. Johnson est de ne pas les concevoir comme des expériments, mais comme des "hérésies littéraires"; une hérésie étant 'toute opinion ou doctrine qui diverge de la position officielle ou orthodoxe.'

16
Richard Hamilton, HOW A GREAT DAILY ORGAN IS TURNED OUT, de la série Ulysses, 1988–90

"Ceci est une œuvre d'une série continue basée sur *Ulysses* de James Joyce, sur laquelle Richard Hamilton travaille depuis quarante ans de façon intermittente. De toutes les œuvres et études terminées, celle-ci est typique et englobe le reste. Elle montre la même dualité que cette présentation, comment un composite global décrit la même nature que ses composants. Hamilton s'intéressait aussi à la traduction d'une forme à une autre, dans ce cas de la langue écrite à la langue graphique. Il a composé cette complexité en travaillant avec le chef d'œuvre de style littéraire et de rhétorique du vingtième siècle. Il est connu que chaque chapitre d'*Ulysses* est écrit dans un style différent, avec une toile de fond de symboles et associations à *l'Odyssée* de Homer. La tâche que Hamilton s'est posée était de représenter chaque chapitre par un choix approprié et correspondant d'images et de technique graphique, pour capter l'esprit de l'œuvre de Joyce, comme Themerson l'a fait pour Schwitters. L'œuvre ici représente le chapitre connu sous le nom de Aeolus, au milieu du livre et qui se déroule au bureau du journal.

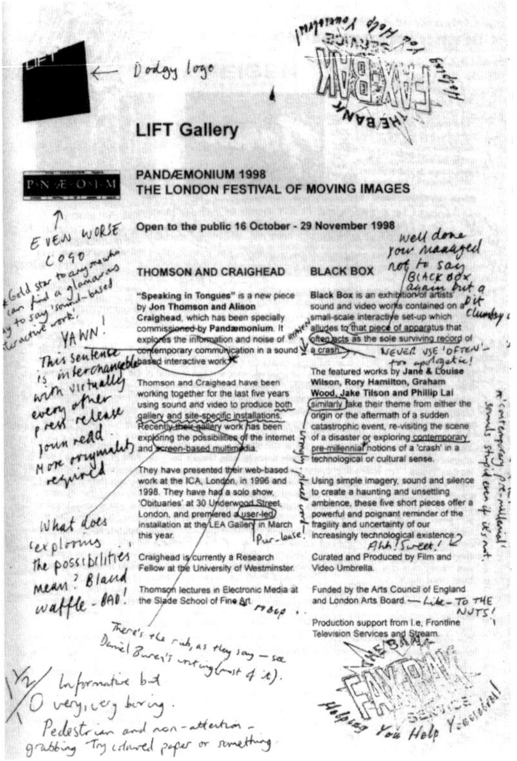

LIFT Gallery

PANDÆMONIUM 1998
THE LONDON FESTIVAL OF MOVING IMAGES

Open to the public 16 October - 29 November 1998

THOMSON AND CRAIGHEAD

"Speaking in Tongues" is a new piece by Jon Thomson and Alison Craighead, which has been specially commissioned by Pandæmonium. It explores the information and noise of contemporary communication in a sound based interactive work.

Thomson and Craighead have been working together for the last five years using sound and video to produce both gallery and site-specific installations. Recently their gallery work has been exploring the possibilities of the internet and screen-based multimedia.

They have presented their web-based work at the ICA, London, in 1996 and 1998. They have had a solo show, 'Obituaries' at 30 Underwood Street, London, and premiered a user-led installation at the LEA Gallery in March this year.

Craighead is currently a Research Fellow at the University of Westminster.

Thomson lectures in Electronic Media at the Slade School of Fine Art.

BLACK BOX

Black Box is an exhibition of artists' sound and video works contained on a small-scale interactive set-up which alludes to that piece of apparatus that often acts as the sole surviving record of a crash.

The featured works by Jane & Louise Wilson, Rory Hamilton, Graham Wood, Jake Tilson and Phillip Lai similarly take their theme from either the origin or the aftermath of a sudden catastrophic event, re-visiting the scene of a disaster or exploring contemporary pre-millennial notions of a 'crash' in a technological or cultural sense.

Using simple imagery, sound and silence to create a haunting and unsettling ambience, these five short pieces offer a powerful and poignant reminder of the fragility and uncertainty of our increasingly technological existence.

Curated and Produced by Film and Video Umbrella.

Funded by the Arts Council of England and London Arts Board.

Production support from I.e. Frontline Television Services and Stream.

Dodgy logo
EVEN WORSE LOGO
YAWN!
This sentence is interchangeable with virtually every other press release you read. More originality required
What does exploring the possibilities mean? Bland waffle - BAD!
Well done you managed not to say BLACK BOX again but a bit clumsy
NEVER USE 'OFTEN' - too apologetic!
Ahh! Sweet!
LIKE - TO THE NUTS!
1/2 / 10 Informative but very, very boring. Pedestrian and non-attention-grabbing. Try coloured paper or something.
THE BANK FAX BAK SERVICE Helping You Help Yourselves!

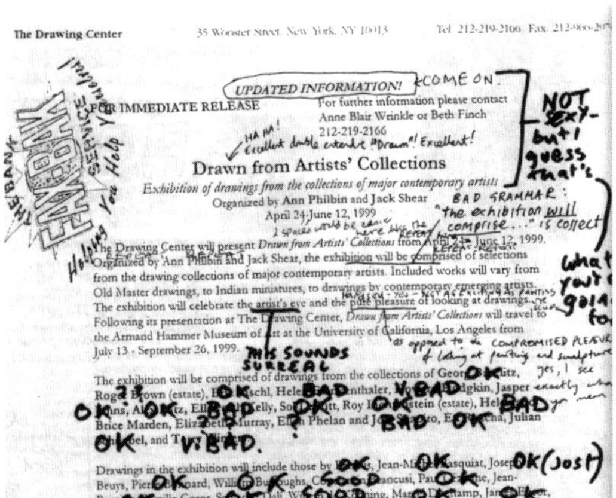

The Drawing Center 35 Wooster Street, New York, NY 10013

UPDATED INFORMATION! COME ON

FOR IMMEDIATE RELEASE

For further information please contact Anne Blair Wrinkle or Beth Finch 212-219-2166

Drawn from Artists' Collections

Exhibition of drawings from the collections of major contemporary artists

Organized by Ann Philbin and Jack Shear

April 24-June 12, 1999

The Drawing Center will present *Drawn from Artists' Collections* from April 24 - June 12, 1999. Organized by Ann Philbin and Jack Shear, the exhibition will be comprised of selections from the drawing collections of major contemporary artists. Included works will vary from Old Master drawings, to Indian miniatures, to drawings by contemporary emerging artists. The exhibition will celebrate the artist's eye and the pure pleasure of looking at drawings. Following its presentation at The Drawing Center, *Drawn from Artists' Collections* will travel to the Armand Hammer Museum of Art at the University of California, Los Angeles from July 13 - September 26, 1999.

Exhibition Catalogue

The exhibition will be accompanied by a catalogue with an essay by Robert Storr, Curator of Painting and Sculpture, The Museum of Modern Art, New York. Published in a hard-cover edition, the catalogue will have 128 pages and 79 color illustrations. Price: $35.

NOT SEXY - but I guess that's ...
BAD GRAMMAR: "the exhibition will comprise..." is correct
THIS SOUNDS SURREAL
IN LIST TWICE
THE BANK FAX BAK SERVICE Helping You Help Yourselves!

17

story, whether a sketch for the typography of a pub sign, a hallucinogenic portrait, or a child's drawing of his father following Joyce's exact – childlike – description: 'a large globular head with five hairs erect, two eyes in profile, the trunk full front with three large buttons, one triangular foot.'

17
Bank, FAX BAK, faxed press releases, 1998

"These are two out of more than a hundred examples from a project by the now defunct London artist group Bank. One week towards the end of 1998 they asked all the London galleries to fax their latest press releases to Bank's studio, then set about rabidly correcting the grammar and spelling, offering candid comment on the gallery exhibition and artists, awarding a mark out of 10 (rarely higher than a 2) and rubber-stamping the slogan 'Helping You Help Yourselves!' before faxing back to the source. Such gallery propaganda is typically written by some intern to a template of institutional pretension, and as usual Bank were naming and shaming a superfluous and even sinister art world mechanic with a combination of pitbull humour and alarming acuity. Once again, the form of the work effortlessly

Le personnage principal d'Ulysses, Leopold Bloom, est vendeur d'espace publicitaire, et passe ce chapitre au travail, où la narration normale est ponctuée de titres arbitraires. Pour refléter ce lieu et cette situation en particulier, Hamilton prend un certain nombre de plaques de gravure utilisées pour d'autres chapitres – chacune déjà chargée de son propre style et histoire – et les mélange à un cadre brut d'une page de journal, quand c'est possible, les unes à côté des autres. Comme un journal, le résultat est une forme globale comprenant un certain nombre d'autres, chacune racontant sa propre histoire, que ce soit une esquisse pour une typographie, un panneau de café, un portrait hallucinogène, ou le dessin d'enfant de son père – infantile – d'après la description exacte de Joyce: 'une grande tête globulaire avec cinq cheveux érigés, 2 yeux en profil, le tronc de face avec trois grands boutons, un pied triangulaire.'

17
Bank, FAX BAK, communiqués de presse faxés, 1998

"Voici deux exemples d'une collection de plus de 100 d'un projet du feu groupe d'artistes londonien Bank. Vers la fin de 1998 ils ont demandé à toutes les galeries londoniennes de leur faxer leur dernier (literally without effort) mirrors the attitude: the staid, uptight gallery PR scrawled all over with righteous black felt-tip, equal parts schoolteacher and adolescent. There are two footnotes: when Bank presented the faxes at a show, framed on the gallery wall, the prevailing irony of the late-1990s London art scene resulted in galleries buying back their own faxes. But when they repeated the show half a year later in the USA with New York gallery faxes, the response was overwhelmingly hostile, an international mis-translation of humour accidentally documented on a collection of middle-of-the-night transatlantic phone messages to Bank's studio.

18
Alasdair Gray, 1982, JANINE, London, Cape, 1984

"I'm showing a few pages of the Scottish writer Alisdair Gray's second novel to emphasize how he manipulates the form of the book in line with his particular idiosyncrasies – a kind of honed isolation and hallucinatory depression – in a way that a third-party designer never could. There are two examples here, one subtle and one extreme. The former is the inclusion of ever-changing running heads (or sides) from page to page, which distill the story into a series of clipped phrases or single words. The latter is a specific sequence in which the story's protagonist swallows a jar of sleeping pills with suicidal intent, but fails, instead plagued by a collection of simultaneous voices, including that of God. The typography is suitably haywire, but still tightly packed within the frame of the page, emphasizing the narrator's mental claustophobia.

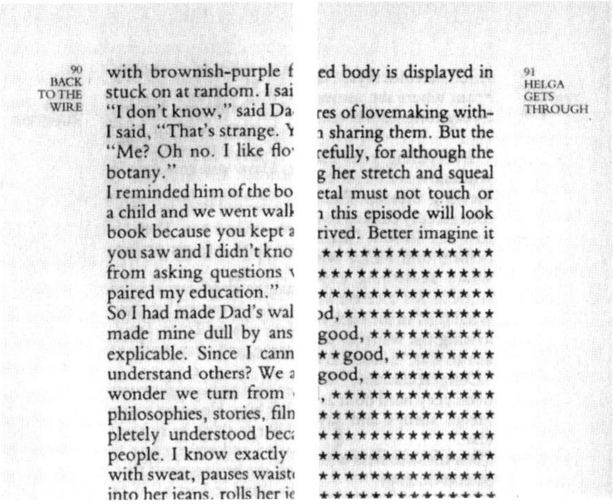
90 BACK TO THE WIRE

with brownish-purple f
stuck on at random. I sai
"I don't know," said Da
I said, "That's strange. Y
"Me? Oh no. I like flo
botany."
I reminded him of the bo
a child and we went walk
book because you kept a
you saw and I didn't kno
from asking questions
paired my education."
So I had made Dad's wal
made mine dull by ans
explicable. Since I cann
understand others? We a
wonder we turn from
philosophies, stories, filn
pletely understood bec
people. I know exactly
with sweat, pauses waist
into her jeans, rolls her je

91 HELGA GETS THROUGH

ed body is displayed in
res of lovemaking with-
n sharing them. But the
refully, for although the
g her stretch and squeal
etal must not touch or
n this episode will look
rived. Better imagine it
****
****
****
od, ************
good, **********
good, ******
good, **********
, *************
****
****
****
****
****

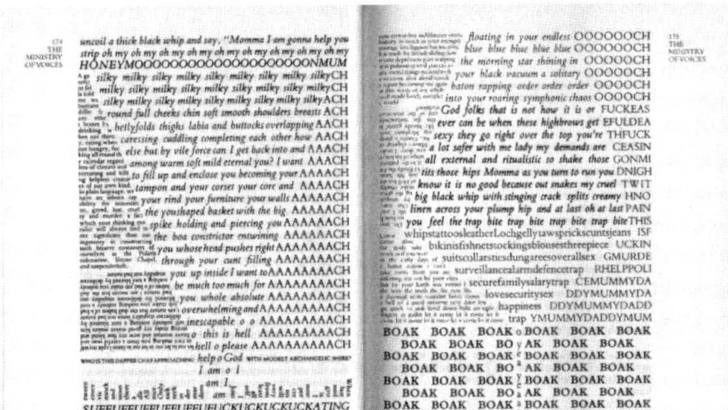
174 THE MINISTRY OF VOICES

175 THE MINISTRY OF VOICES

18

communiqué au studio de Bank, et se sont mis à corriger la grammaire et l'orthographe, commenter le expositions et artistes actuels et à venir sans contrainte, donnant une note sur 10 (rarement plus de 2) et les tamponner '*on vous aide à vous aider vous-même*' avant de les refaxer à la source. De telle propagande de galeries est typiquement écrit par un interne selon un modèle d'une prétention institutionnelle et comme d'habitude,

Bank couvrait de honte un mécanisme superflu du monde de l'art avec l'humour d'un pit bull, uniquement tempéré par une intelligence alarmante. Une fois de plus, la forme du travail reflétait sans effort – littéralement – l'attitude: les RP coincés et guindés des galeries griffonnaient partout les justifications au feutre noir. Et, c'est un peu plus qu'une simple note de fin, lorsque Bank a présenté les fax dans une exposition, encadrés au mur de la galerie, l'ironie de la scène artistique à Londres à la fin des années 1999 a poussé la plupart des galeries à racheter leur propre travail. Mais lorsqu'ils ont refait l'exposition six mois plus tard à New York, avec des fax des galeries new yorkais, la réponse fut extraordinairement hostile, comme en témoigne l'enregistrement d'une collection de messages sur le répondeur de Bank, une bonne indication du trou noir international de la traduction.

18
Alasdair Gray, 1982, JANINE, Londres, Cape, 1984

"Je montre quelques pages du deuxième roman de l'écrivain écossais Alisdair Gray pour souligner comment il manipule le forme du livre en phase avec sa particularité, une sorte d'isolation aiguisée dans une

19

Arthur Wainwright, PENNINE WAY COMPANION, 1968

"From the late 1940s on, Arthur Wainwright developed a complete personal graphic vocabulary in his renowned series of English walking guides, remarkable not only for their concise on-site articulation of information through direct experience, but also for the fact that they were completely handwritten. Wainwright's graphic language covered every aspect of the book, with the style of his handwriting changing according to the relative formality of the variouskinds of texts (from formal introductions, through the detailed information of the walks themselves, to informal personal reflections and post-walk notes) in the same way his drawings articulate different physical textures (from trees, through mountain ranges, to stone houses). Every aspect of the complex design seems truly weathered and refined through the slow logic of meditative hiking; the result is naturally practical as well as beautiful. My favourite of the series of twelve completed in his lifetime is the *Pennine Way Companion*, in which Wainwright's personal logic counters that of conventional Western reading by beginning on the last page and moving laterally to the front of the book, from right to left and bottom to top. An introductory note explains how the south-to-north nature of this particular walk makes more sense when read 'up the page', paragraph to diagram to paragraph, following the common direction of the route, itself dictated by another unique logic: British weather.

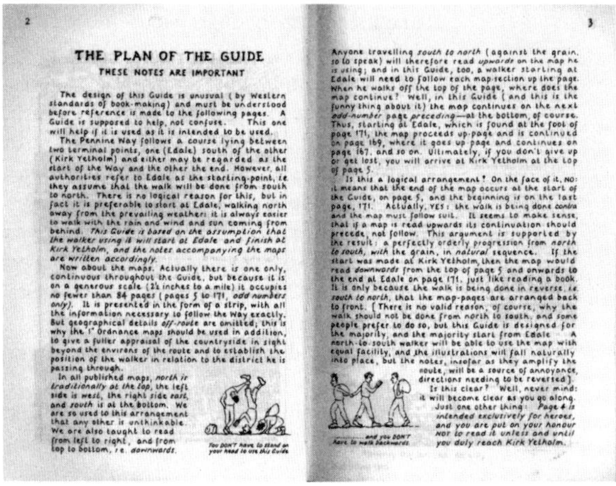

2

THE PLAN OF THE GUIDE

THESE NOTES ARE IMPORTANT

The design of this Guide is unusual (by Western standards of book-making) and must be understood before reference is made to the following pages. A Guide is supposed to help, not confuse. This one will help if it is used as it is intended to be used.

The Pennine Way follows a course lying between two terminal points, one (Edale) south of the other (Kirk Yetholm) and either may be regarded as the start of the Way and the other the end. However, all authorities refer to Edale as the starting-point, i.e. they assume that the walk will be done from south to north. There is no logical reason for this, but in fact it is preferable to start at Edale, walking north away from the prevailing weather: it is always easier to walk with the rain and wind and sun coming from behind. *This Guide is based on the assumption that the walker using it will start at Edale and finish at Kirk Yetholm, and the notes accompanying the maps are written accordingly.*

Now about the maps. Actually there is one only, continuous throughout the Guide, but because it is on a generous scale (2½ inches to a mile) it occupies no fewer than 84 pages (pages 5 to 171, *odd numbers only*). It is presented in the form of a strip, with all the information necessary to follow the Way exactly. But geographical details *off-route* are omitted; this is why the 1" Ordnance maps should be used in addition, to give a fuller appraisal of the countryside in sight beyond the environs of the route and to establish the position of the walker in relation to the district he is passing through.

In all published maps, *north is traditionally at the top*, the left side is *west*, the right side *east*, and *south* is at the bottom. We are so used to this arrangement that any other is unthinkable. We are also taught to read from left to right, and from top to bottom, i.e. *downwards*.

You DON'T have to stand on your head to use this Guide

3

Anyone travelling *south to north* (against the grain, so to speak) will therefore read *upwards* on the map he is using; and in this Guide, too, a walker starting at Edale will need to follow each map-section up the page. When he walks off the top of the page, where does the map continue? Well, in this Guide (and this is the funny thing about it) the map continues on the next *odd-number* page *preceding*—at the bottom, of course. Thus, starting at Edale, which is found at the foot of page 171, the map proceeds up-page and is continued on page 169, where it goes up-page and continues on page 167, and so on. Ultimately, if you don't give up or get lost, you will arrive at Kirk Yetholm at the top of page 5.

Is this a logical arrangement? On the face of it, NO: it means that the end of the map occurs at the start of the Guide, on page 5, and the beginning is on the last page, 171. Actually, YES: the walk is being done *contra* and the map must follow suit. It seems to make sense, that if a map is read upwards its continuation should precede, not follow. This argument is supported by the result: a perfectly orderly progression from *north to south, with* the grain, in *natural* sequence. If the start was made at Kirk Yetholm, then the map would read *downwards* from the top of page 5 and onwards to the end at Edale on page 171, just like reading a book. It is only because the walk is being done in reverse, *i.e. south to north*, that the map-pages are arranged back to front. [There is no valid reason, of course, why the walk should not be done from north to south, and some people prefer to do so, but this Guide is designed for the majority, and the majority start from Edale. A north-to-south walker will be able to use the map with equal facility, and the illustrations will fall naturally into place, but the notes, insofar as they amplify the route, will be a source of annoyance, directions needing to be reversed.]

Is this clear? Well, never mind: it will become clear as you go along.

Just one other thing: *Page 4 is intended exclusively for heroes, and you are put on your honour NOT to read it unless and until you duly reach Kirk Yetholm.*

............and you DON'T have to walk backwards

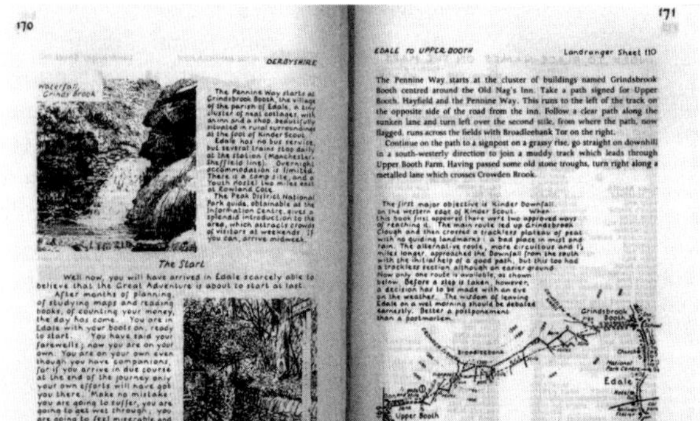

170

DERBYSHIRE

Waterfall, Grinds Brook

The Pennine Way starts at Grindsbrook Booth, the village of the parish of Edale, a tiny cluster of neat cottages with an inn and a shop, beautifully situated in rural surroundings at the foot of Kinder Scout.

Edale has no bus service, but several trains stop daily at the station (Manchester–Sheffield line). Overnight accommodation is limited. There is a camp site, and a Youth Hostel two miles east at Rowland Cote.

The Peak District National Park guide, obtainable at the Information Centre, gives a splendid introduction to the area, which attracts crowds of visitors at weekends. If you can, arrive midweek.

The Start

Well now, you will have arrived in Edale scarcely able to believe that the Great Adventure is about to start at last.

After months of planning, of studying maps and reading books, of counting your money, the day has come. You are in Edale with your boots on, ready to start. You have said your farewells; now you are on your own. You are on your own even though you have companions, for if you arrive in due course at the end of the journey only your own efforts will have got you there. Make no mistake: you are going to suffer, you are going to get wet through, you are going to feel miserable and wish you had never heard of the Pennine Way. But there will be days of bright sunshine too, and moments of fun; many interesting experiences and a vision of beauty in desolate places will be your reward.

If you start, don't give up, or you will be giving up at difficulties all your life.

Entrance to footbridge, Grinds Brook

Right then, let's get going. You have checked your rucksack and made sure you haven't forgotten anything vital. Kirk Yetholm, we are on our way. Be seeing you soon.

171

EDALE TO UPPER BOOTH Landranger Sheet 110

The Pennine Way starts at the cluster of buildings named Grindsbrook Booth centred around the Old Nag's Inn. Take a path signed for Upper Booth, Hayfield and the Pennine Way. This runs to the left of the track on the opposite side of the road from the inn. Follow a clear path along the sunken lane and turn left over the second stile, from where the path, now flagged, runs across the fields with Broadleebank Tor on the right.

Continue on the path to a signpost on a grassy rise, go straight on downhill in a south-westerly direction to join a muddy track which leads through Upper Booth Farm. Having passed some old stone troughs, turn right along a metalled lane which crosses Crowden Brook.

The *first* major objective is Kinder Downfall on the western edge of Kinder Scout. When this book first appeared there were two approved ways of reaching it. The main route led up Grindsbrook Clough and then crossed a trackless plateau of peat with no guiding landmarks: a bad place in mist and rain. The alternative route, more circuitous and 1½ miles longer, approached the Downfall from the south with the initial help of a good path, but this too had a trackless section although on easier ground. Now only one route is available, as shown below. Before a step is taken, however, a decision has to be made with an eye on the weather. The wisdom of leaving Edale on a wet morning should be debated earnestly. Better a postponement than a postmortem.

Come out of that tuckshop! .... Ready now? *Let's go!*

Page revised 1994.
The two drawings on the facing page depict features which are on the original route up Grindsbrook Clough from which the Pennine Way has now been diverted.

19

dépression presque hallucinatoire qu'un graphiste extérieur ne pourrait jamais transmettre. Il y a ici deux exemples, un qui est subtil et l'autre extrême. Le premier est une inclusion de têtes qui changent continuant d'une page à l'autre, ce qui distille l'histoire en une série de phrases coupées ou mots isolés. Le deuxième est une séquence où le protagoniste avale un pot de somnifères avec l'intention de se suicider, mais il se loupe et au lieu, il entend cette myriade de voix simultanées, y compris celle de Dieu. La typographie est passablement détraquée, mais reste dans le cadre de la page ce qui accentue la claustrophobie.

19

Arthur Wainwright, PENNINE WAY COMPANION, 1968

"A partir de la fin des années 1940, Wainwright a développé un vocabulaire graphique personnel complet à travers une série de guides de randonnée anglais. Ceux-ci étaient déjà remarquables par leur articulation concise sur site de l'information par l'expérience de première main; ils étaient également écrit totalement à la main. Le langage graphique de Wainwright couvrait tous les aspects du livre, l'écriture qui change selon les différents types de texte (allant d'introductions formelles à la clarté de l'information sur les randonnées elles-mêmes, à des pensées personnelles informelles et des notes après les randonnées) de même que ses dessins illustraient des différentes textures (arbres, chaînes de montagne, maisons en pierre) et chaque détail d'une conception complexe donnait l'impressions d'être forgé par la logique lente d'une randonnée méditative. Et donc, de la série de douze qu'il a fait durant sa vie, je préfère le *Pennine Way*

20
Mike Nelson, A FORGOTTEN KINGDOM, London, ICA, 2001

"This book was produced in lieu of a regular catalogue for a solo show at London's ICA. The photograph on the cover shows a detail from a typical Nelson installation, all heavy gothic-mythic atmosphere constructed from the collection and juxtaposition of found objects and furniture, with manipulated light. The book's corresponding translation from 3D to 2D is a collection of excerpts from a number of established authors, such as H.P. Lovecraft, Jules Verne and Albert Camus, whose work is rooted in the same mood and colour. Generally, whole chapters are lifted from existing novels, but Nelson and his editor Will Bradley follow this idea through to the borrowed title page (*The Plague*), contents, preface and index. Like the installations, every detail is vital, cut-and-pasted from somewhere else to form a new work. And again, of great significance, or great design: it cost only £5 at the ICA bookshop, with the added benefit of exposing the superficiality and unnecessary expense of the surrounding heavyweights, generally more bricks than books.

Companion, où la logique personnelle de Wainwright contre celle de la lecture occidentale conventionnelle en commençant par la dernière page. Dans une note d'introduction, il explique comment la nature sud-nord de cette promenade est plus logique quand on lit à l'envers 'vers le haut de la page' paragraphe à figure à paragraphe, selon la direction de la route, qui est elle-même dictée par une autre logique singulière: la météo anglais.

20
Mike Nelson, A FORGOTTEN KINGDOM, London, ICA, 2001

"Ce livre a été produit à la place d'un catalogue normal pour une exposition personnelle au ICA de Londres. La photo de la couverture montre un détail d'une installation typique de Nelson, dans une ambiance gothique-mythique lourd, basé sur la collection et juxtaposition d'objets trouvés, du mobilier et la lumière. La traduction correspondante dans le livre, du 3D à 2D est une collection d'extraits d'autres auteurs reconnus comme H.P. Lovecraft, Jules Verne et Albert Camus, dont le travail est enraciné dans les mêmes ambiances et couleurs.
En général, des chapitres entiers sont extraits de romans existants, mais Nelson et son

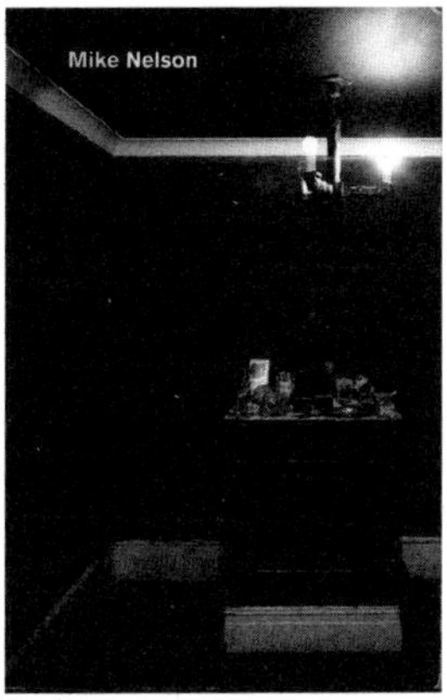

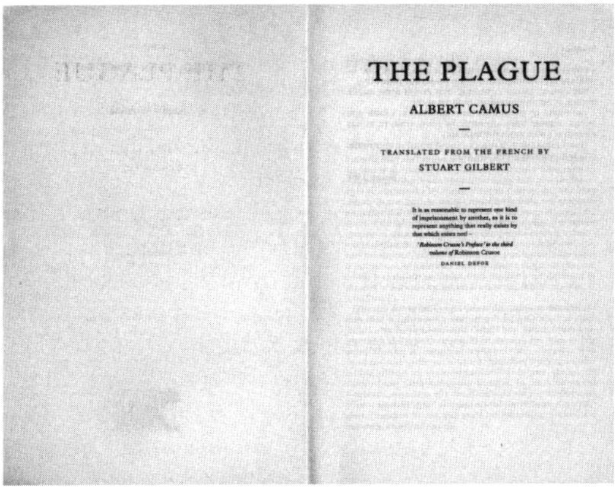
THE PLAGUE

ALBERT CAMUS

TRANSLATED FROM THE FRENCH BY
STUART GILBERT

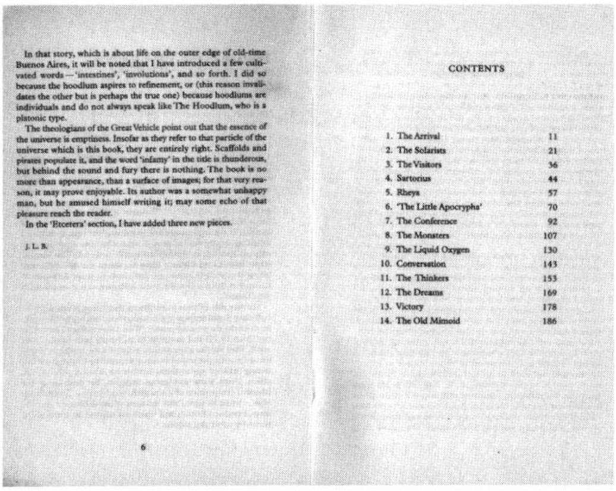
CONTENTS

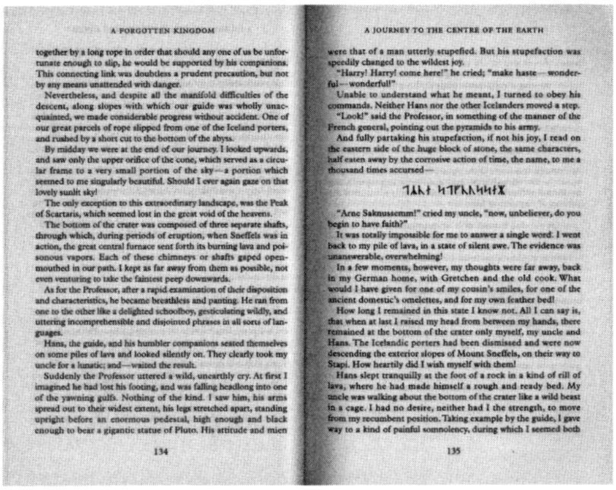
A FORGOTTEN KINGDOM

A JOURNEY TO THE CENTRE OF THE EARTH

134 135

21
Mevis & van Deursen, Corporate wall designs, Vienna, 2000

"These are two views of a project Mevis and van Deursen made for a Hong Kong-based telecom company who asked them to propose a project to fill 14 empty walls of a circular space in their new Vienna office. I was working at M&vD's studio in Amsterdam's Chinatown around the time they were trying to come up with an idea over a couple of months. Like most studios, one wall was permanently covered in found ephemera of

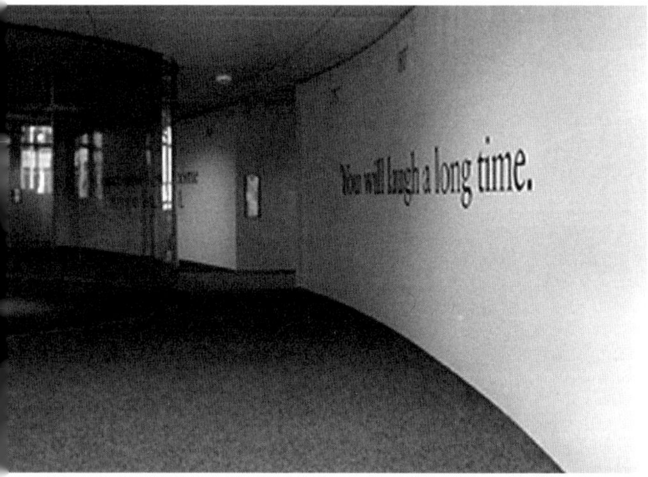

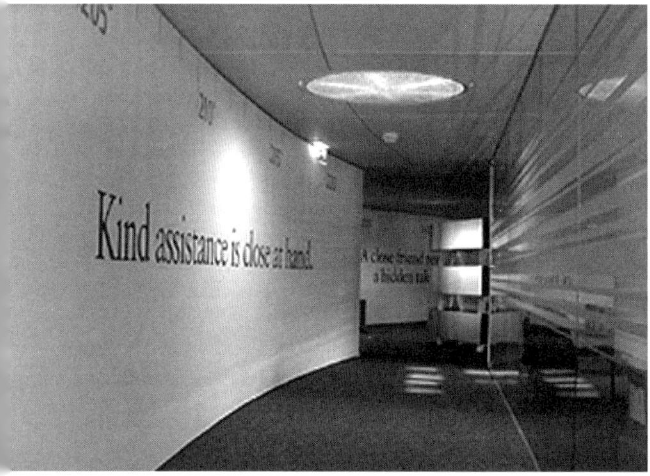

21

éditeur Will Bradley vont poursuivre ce principe jusqu'à la première page (La Peste), la table des matières, la préface et l'index. Comme dans les installations, tous les détails sont importants, coupés-collés d'ailleurs pour former une nouvelle œuvre. Et encore, d'une grande importance, d'un grand graphisme: cela ne coûte que £5 au magasin de ICA avec l'avantage qu'il montre la superficialité et les dépenses inutiles des poids lourds environnants.

random inspiration (newspaper cuttings, photos, postcards) slowly being assimilated into daily work; but on another surface a tiny slip of paper stuck had been hanging around waiting to be remembered for months. On the eve of the deadline of the Vienna job, still nothing had been decided. Linda van Deursen was staring blankly at this slip of paper when an idea took shape: it had come out of a local fortune cookie, and read: 'Kind assistance is close at hand'. She went out, bought a box of cookies, and soon had 14 fortunes, later rendered on the Vienna walls in precise proportion and set in the same centred Times New Roman.

22
Marshall McLuhan & Quentin Fiore, THE MEDIUM IS THE MASSAGE, New York, Bantam, 1967

"Quentin Fiore might well be the first graphic designer to be pictured on the back of someone else's book, as honorary blurb. For years I'd talked about this as being a great example of how graphic design should be made – as author and designer working in tandem, with equal, implicit trust, like Berger's team on *Ways of Seeing*. Of course, I found out later that actually McLuhan had nothing to do with the making of this book.

21
Mevis & van Deursen, corporate wall designs, Vienne, 2000

"Ce sont deux photos d'un projet Mevis et van Deursen a réalisé pour une entreprise de télécom basée à Hong Kong qui leur a demandé de proposer un projet pour remplir 14 murs vides d'un atrium circulaire dans leurs nouveaux locaux de Vienne. A ce moment je travaillais au studio de M&vD quand ils essayaient de trouver une idée sur quelques mois. Comme la plupart des studios, ils avaient un espace mural plein d'inspiration trouvée (coupures de presse, photos, cartes postales et d'autres objets éphémères) qui n'attendait qu'à être assimilée dans des œuvres, mais sur un autre mur, il y avait un tout petit bout de papier collé au milieu d'un étendu de blanc, qui était là depuis des mois. La veille de l'échéance pour le travail à Vienne, rien n'avait encore été décidé, et Linda van Deursen portait un regard vide sur ce bout de papier lorsque l'idée lumineuse est arrivée. Leur studio se trouve au milieu du quartier chinois d'Amsterdam, et le bout de papier venait d'un beignet chinois et disait: '*De l'aide bienveillante est proche*'. Elle est sortie, a acheté une boîte de beignets et avait bientôt 14 devises, plus tard elle les a rendu sur les

The text was just compiled from other texts by an independent editor and handed over to Fiore, who never even so much as consulted the author. (Similarly, upon speaking to Richard Hollis I found out Berger's team were apparently as childish and bitchy as any community locked in a room with some glue and a deadline.) It's easy to overlook the subtitle here – *an inventory of effects* – but it's worth rereading, not only as a description of McLuhan's casual prophecies, but also of Fiore's toolbox of graphic and typographic tricks, pushing the potential of then contemporary photosetting to its limits, with reversed pages, zooms, sequencing, line drawings, blown-up halftones, cartoons, etc. etc. This is the American cousin of *Ways of Seeing*, articulating the zeitgeist by example, turning the potentially dull subject of media analysis into entertaining pop philosophy without talking down to the reader. *Massage* is also strongly marked by the influence of TV, in terms of both the speed and style of presentation of their bits of information. One of Fiore's most inventive gestures was this sequence of abstract details on the right hand pages, clarified in a full-frame thumbnail overleaf, each used to trigger one of McLuhan's introductory tangents.

murs à Vienne en proportion en utilisant le même Times New Roman centré.

22
Marshall McLuhan & Quentin Fiore, THE MEDIUM IS THE MESSAGE, New York, Bantam, 1967

"Quentin Fiore pourrait bien être le premier graphiste en photo sur le dos d'un livre de quelqu'un d'autre, dans les accréditations. Pendant des années j'en ai parlé comme un exemple superbe de comment le graphisme devait fonctionner – l'auteur et le graphiste travaillant en binôme, avec une confiance égale, implicite, comme l'équipe de Berger avec *Ways of Seeing*. Bien sûr, j'ai appris plus tard que McLuhan n'avait rien a voir avec la production de ce livre. Le texte a juste été compilé à partir d'autres textes par un éditeur indépendant et donné à Fiore, qui n'avait jamais consulté l'auteur non plus. (De la même manière, en parlant à Richard Hollis, j'ai appris que l'équipe de Berger était apparemment aussi infantile et vache que toute communauté enfermée dans une salle avec un peu de colle et une échéance.) C'est facile d'ignorer le sous-titre ici – *un inventaire d'effets*, mais c'est une superbe description non seulement des prophéties détendues de McLuhan, mais aussi de la

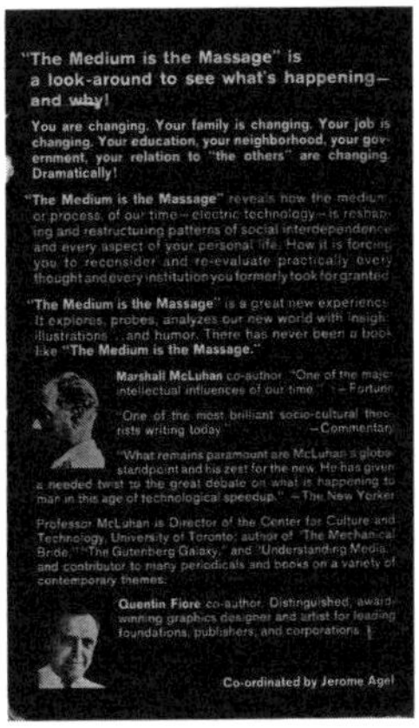

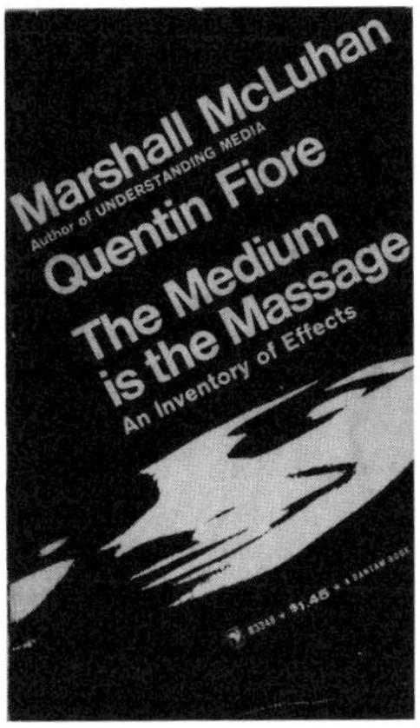

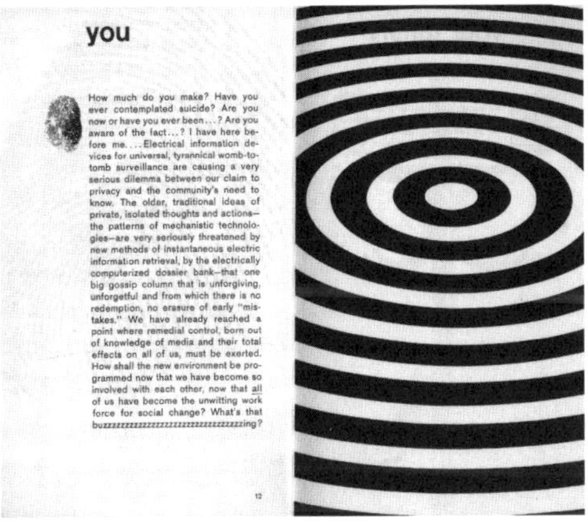

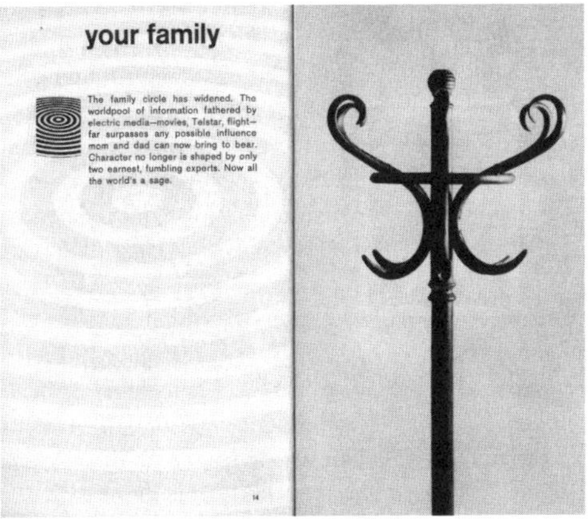

22

23
Frances Stark, COLLECTED WRITING: 1993–2003, London, Book Works, 2003

"I'm only showing the cover, for a change, of this compilation of short, intimate texts. It should be just about clear from this scan that the white is smudged and slightly dirty, even though my copy is only a few months old. White covers, especially uncoated ones, are anathema to most publishing houses, being paricularly susceptible to rubbing and staining. In this case the author insisted on uncoated white for precisely this reason; to allow the the book to become visibly worn by use, embracing and amplifying the reality of the object. In effect, the user – the reader – completes the design. The idea was in slight homage to the Joy Division album *Still*, whose absorbent card gathered a similar filthy dignity in a record collection over a couple of decades. And so we're back to the lens of the late 1970s again.

24
J.D. Salinger, FRANNY AND ZOOEY, original publication: Boston, Little, Brown, 1961

"But to end, I want to span the whole second half of the twentieth century with a few more covers, leading me to the proposition that in the time period roughly covered by this talk, the American author J.D. Salinger made one of the greatest graphic design decisions – as opposed to *a piece of graphic design*. That distinction is important, as everything I'm promoting here is from the perspective of considering design a verb rather than a noun, *to* design rather than *a* design; an open, cerebral process rather than a fixed, physical object. All the images depict objects, of course, but they are being offered as the iceberg-tips of thought processes. In the 1950s Salinger had a clause put in his publishers' contracts that insisted only the text of the title of the book and his name

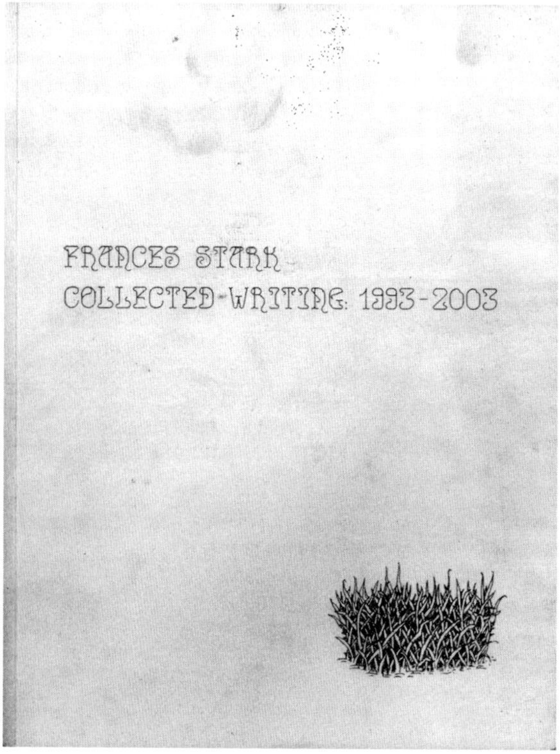

23

boîte d'outils d'astuces graphiques et typographiques de Fiore, repoussant ainsi les limites de la composition photo de l'époque: des pages renversées, des zooms, des séquences animées, des photos, des lignes, des demi-tons, des bandes dessinées etc. C'est le frère américain des *Ways of Seeing*, à la fois traitant du Zeitgeist, transformant un sujet potentiellement ennuyeux sur l'analyse des médias en une philosophie divertissante pop, sans mépris pour le lecteur. Comme je l'ai dit avant, les deux livres sont fortement influencés par la télé, en termes de la vitesse et du style de la présentation des bribes d'information. Un des gestes des plus inventifs de Fiore était cette séquence d'introduction de détails abstraits sur les pages de droite, clarifiés par un verso plein cadre, chacun pour déclencher une des tangentes de McLuhan.

23
Frances Stark, COLLECTED WRITING: 1993–2003, Londres, Book Works, 2003

"Pour changer, je ne montre que la couverture de cette compilation de petits textes intimes. On devrait pouvoir voir sur le scan que le blanc est taché et un peu sale, même si le livre n'a que quelques mois. Facile à tacher et à frotter, ces couvertures blanches, surtout celles sans revêtement, sont la hantise des maisons d'édition, mais dans ce cas, l'auteur a insisté pour faire une telle couverture et précisément pour cette raison. Pour que le livre puisse visiblement s'user, comprendre et amplifier la réalité de l'objet, pour que l'utilisateur, – le lecteur - complète la création. L'idée était un peu en hommage à l'album de Joy Division dont la carte absorbante ramassait la dignité bien sale sur des décennies dans une collection de disques. Et nous voilà de retour à l'objectif de la fin des années 70.

were to appear on any future editions of his work, and absolutely no images. This hard-line was particularly prompted by an early fatal experience with a publisher who covered a collection of short stories, then titled *For Esmé – with Love and Squalour* (after one of them) with a dramatic illustrated portrait of a seductive blonde. Salinger's outrage is understandable: his Esmé is a precocious young girl of seven, and the story depicts a chance encounter and redemptive conversation with a soldier on the verge of a nervous breakdown. Nevertheless, it's instructive to see how various publishers and nationalities have dealt with Salinger's legal one-liner over the past half-decade of reprints and new editions. I saw a recent Estonian edition with a portrait of Salinger himself. It was one of his last press shots, so already about 35 years out of date, which, given his self-imposed public exile and hatred for literary biography, must be an even worse crime than Esmé's prostitution. But there have been plenty of handsome Salingers passing through bookshops since his withdrawal. The Penguin publishing history alone maps a neat shift in ideas as well as the prominent graphic style of each decade. An early 1964 paperback edition follows the then-standard cover form developed by Jan Tschichold and upheld by Hans Schmoller, where the golden section was used as a basis for calculating the proportions of roughly top third for the penguin, publisher and price, then the title, then the author, and the lower two thirds for image. To comply with Salinger's demand, the 'image' was actually an image of the title transferred from an earlier American Bantam Books edition with charming drunken calligraphy. A subsequent edition in the cool, chrome early eighties does away with the image altogether, leaving the residue of mini-

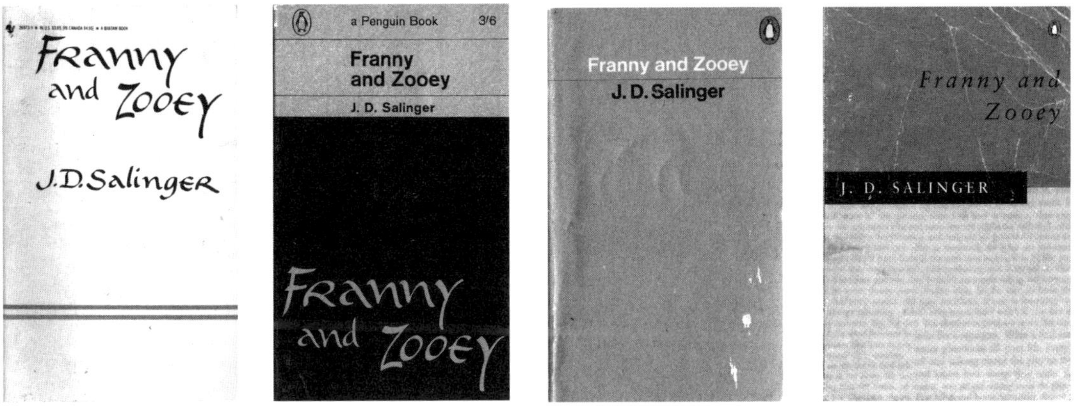

24

24
J.D. Salinger, FRANNY AND ZOOEY, publication originale: Boston, Little, Brown, 1961

"Mais vers la fin, nous pouvons couvrir toute la deuxième moitié du 20ème siècle avec encore quelques couvertures, ce qui me fait dire que pendant la période couverte par cette présentation, l'auteur américain J.D. Salinger a pris une des plus grandes décisions de l'art graphique – par opposition à '*une œuvre d'art graphique*'. Cette distinction est importante, comme tout ce que j'encourage ici est dans une perspective où on considère design comme un verbe plutôt qu'un nom, *faire* du design plutôt qu'*un* design; un processus ouvert, cérébral plutôt qu'un objet fixe, physique. Toutes les images ici montrent des objets bien sûr, mais elles sont montrées en étant les parties visibles de l'iceberg du processus de pensée. A la fin des années 1950, Salinger a fait mettre une clause dans les contrats de ses éditeurs insistant que seul le texte du titre du livre et son nom devaient figurer sur toute édition à venir de son travail, et pas d'images du tout. Cette ligne très dure a été provoquée par une expérience fatale au début de sa carrière avec un éditeur, qui avait couvert une collection de nouvelles, et ensuite l'a intitulée '*Pour Esmé – avec Amour et Misère*' (après une des nouvelles) illustré de façon dramatique par un portrait une blonde séduisante. L'indignation de Salinger est compréhensible, comme son Esmé est une petite fille de sept ans, assez précoce, et l'histoire décrit une rencontre fortuite et une conversation rédemptrice avec un soldat au bord d'une dépression nerveuse. Néanmoins, c'est instructif de voir comment différents éditeurs et nationalités se sont sorti avec le mot légal de Salinger sur ces dernières cinquante années de rééditions et de nouvelles éditions. J'ai vu une édition estonienne récente avec un portrait de Salinger lui-même. C'était une de ses

malist-neutral International Style, or maybe the seed of Terence Conran with its flat silver and arched-eyebrow 'object quality'.
Then in the late 1990s, Penguin astutely pushed another series of covers through the loophole by using *a photograph of some text* – a nice exercise in lateral thinking, though the idea is better than the staid result.
My easy favourite, though, is the modest Little, Brown series, still being published: black type on white, happily centred as pure and sure as Salinger's prose, refusing bourgeois space between capitals but admitting a coy corner streak of rainbow rising from dexter to sinister, printed on cheap uncoated card, welcoming smudges from clutching hands and dog-ears from the jacket pockets of angry young men, all bound around cheap, light-as-air pulp paper allowing them to be sent to friends on the other side of the world at minimum cost. *This* is a graphic design perfectly in tune with the (zen buddhist) spirit of its author and subject matter. For the most part I salute and wholeheartedly endorse Salinger's case against graphic design – as form generally fucking function and getting away with it – but the collection of work offered here proposes a few hardy witnesses for its defence."

dernières photos de presse, donc déjà vieille de 35 ans, ce qui, étant donné son exil auto-imposé et sa haine de la biographie littéraire, doit être un crime encore plus grave que la prostitution d'Esmé. Mais depuis sa retraite, il y eu plein de jeunes Salinger très beaux qui sont passés par les librairies. L'histoire éditorial de Penguin à elle seule trace un déplacement très net dans les idées ainsi que le style graphique proéminent de chaque décennie. Une édition de poche de 1964 suit la couverture standard de l'époque développée par Jan Tschichold et maintenue par Hans Schmoller, où la partie dorée était utilisée comme base pour le calcul des proportions d'environ un tiers pour le pingouin, l'éditeur et le prix, ensuite le titre, et l'auteur, en enfin les deux tiers du bas pour l'image. Pour se plier à la demande de Salinger, 'l'image' était en fait une image du titre transféré d'une édition américaine précédente avec une calligraphie charmante, bancale, éditée par Bantam Books. Une édition ultérieure dans les années cool et chromées des 1980, élimine l'image tout court, laissant un résidu d'un style minimaliste-neutre international, ou peut-être même la graine de Terence Conran avec ses plages d'argent et le sourcil courbé 'qualité de l'objet'. Et puis, à la fin des années 90, Penguin a ironiquement fait passer une série de couvertures par une faille dans le contrat en utilisant une image photo de texte – un bon exercice de pensée latérale, bien que l'idée soit meilleure que le résultat assez guindé. Mais mon préféré, est la petite série modeste, sans prétention de Little, Brown (qui est encore publiée): des lettres noires sur du blanc, heureusement centrées aussi pures et sures que le contenu, refusant même cet espace bourgeois entre les capitales, mais admettant un trait d'arc en ciel faussement discret qui s'étend de droite à gauche, imprimé sur un carton sans finition, qui accueille des taches des mains qui le tiennent et les coins abimés des poches de veste de jeunes hommes en colère, le tout relié autour d'un papier on ne peut plus léger et cheap pour qu'on puisse les envoyer à des amis à l'autre bout du monde pour pas grande chose.
C'est un graphisme parfaitement en phase avec l'esprit (zen bouddhiste) de son auteur et sujet. Pour une grande partie, je salue et défends de plein cœur le cas de Salinger contre le graphisme, – puisque quand la forme encule la fonction, elle se fait rarement prendre – mais la collection de travail présentée ici, propose quelques témoins intrépides pour sa défense."

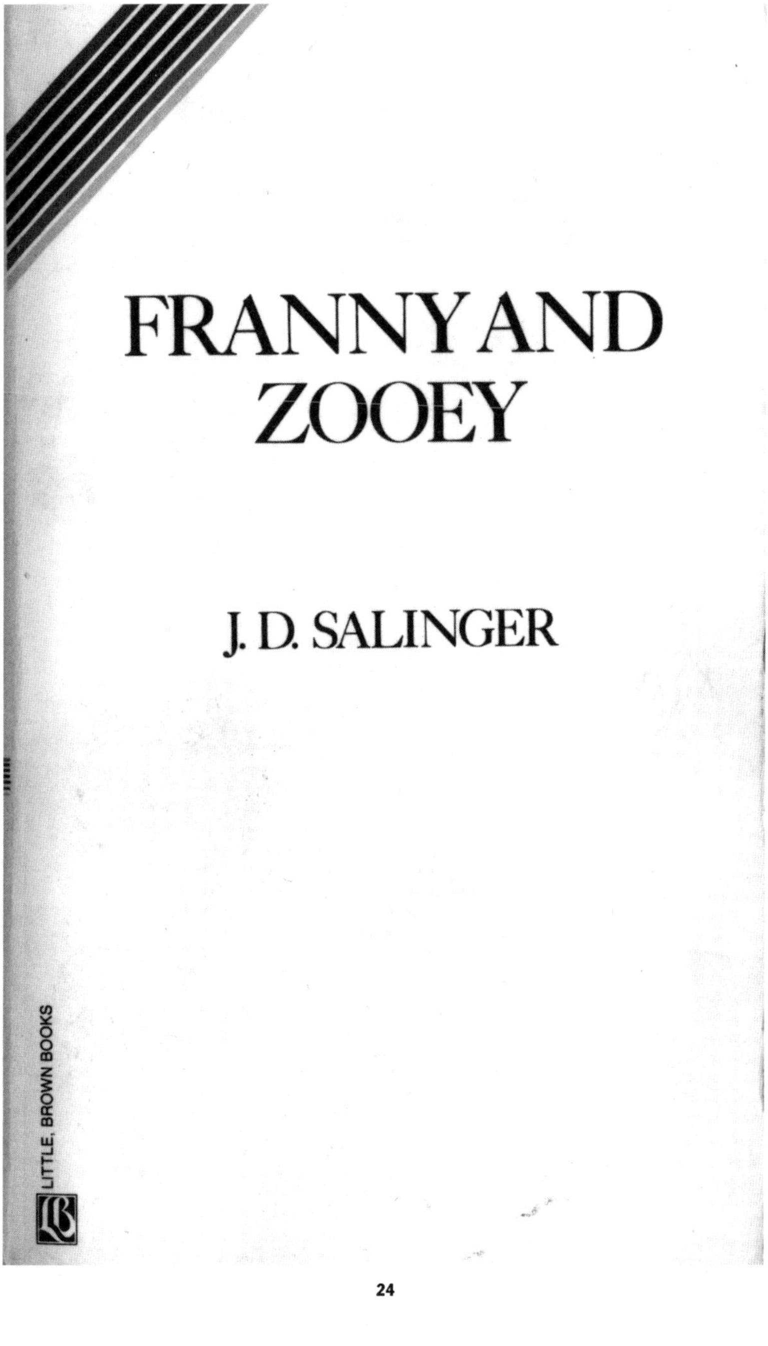
FRANNY AND
ZOOEY
J. D. SALINGER
LITTLE, BROWN BOOKS

PEU IMPORTE LES CONNERIES (d'aprés Jamie Reid) [NEVER MIND THE BOLLOCKS (after Jamie Reid)]

pp. 209–240, Dutch Resource, Chaumont, France, 2005

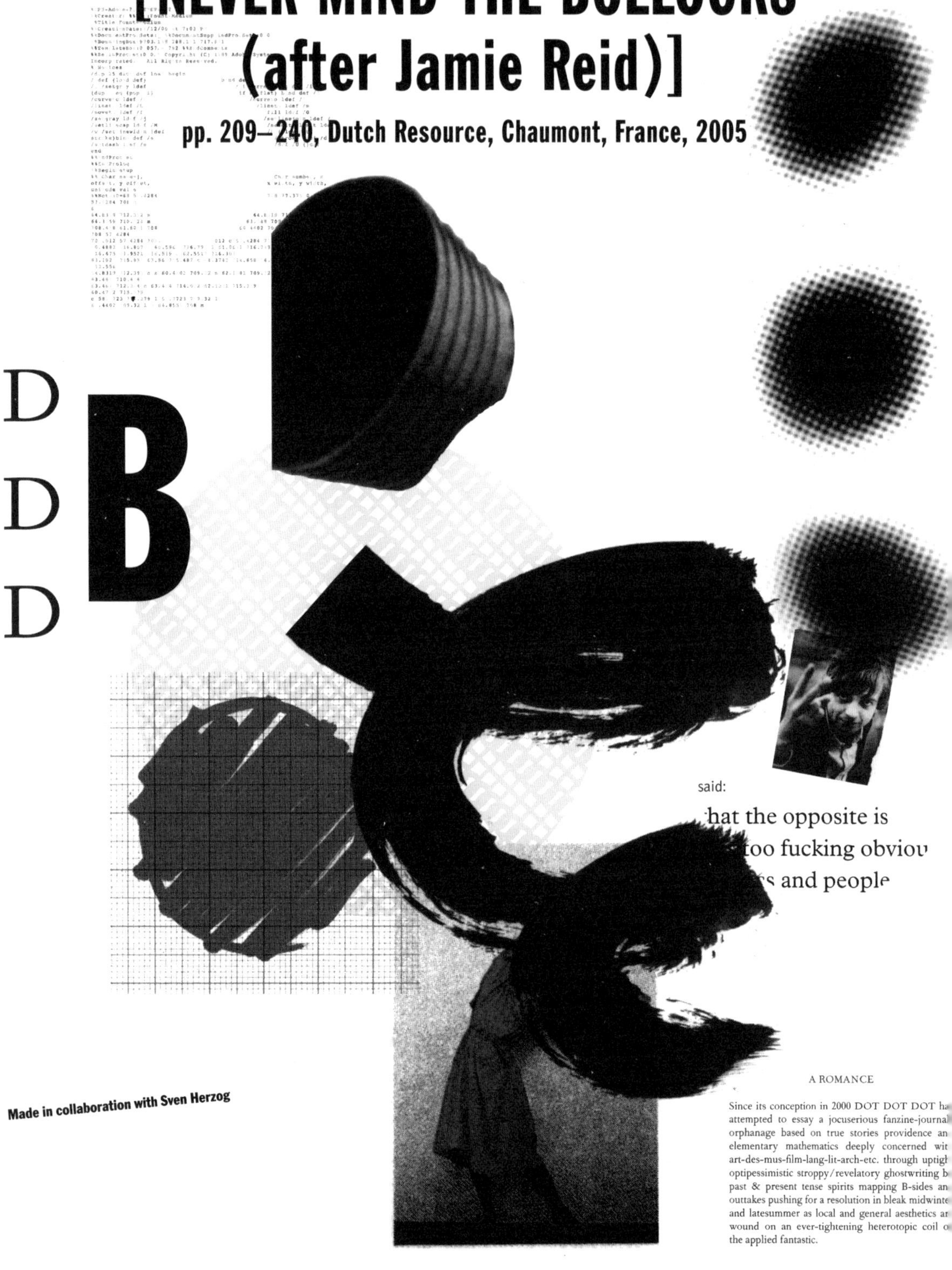

Made in collaboration with Sven Herzog

A ROMANCE

Since its conception in 2000 DOT DOT DOT ha attempted to essay a jocuserious fanzine-journal orphanage based on true stories providence an elementary mathematics deeply concerned wit art-des-mus-film-lang-lit-arch-etc. through uptigh optipessimistic stroppy/revelatory ghostwriting b past & present tense spirits mapping B-sides an outtakes pushing for a resolution in bleak midwinte and latesummer as local and general aesthetics ar wound on an ever-tightening heterotopic coil o the applied fantastic.